bracket—

architecture, e[
digital culture

ᴇᴅ ᴊ +ᴄ APPLIED RESEARCH +DESIGN PUBLISHING

almanac 4

bracket

4   Call to Action
Mason White and Neeraj Bhatia

6   REACTION
8   People Problems:
Empowering Forms of Assembly
Mason White

16   Design Activism:
Towards Agonistic Pluralism
Kees Lokman

24   #action
Mimi Zeiger

28   A Collective Living Room
Matthew Mazzotta

30   Whatever Happened to Action?
Christopher Austin Roach

36   (No) Stop Marconi
Nahyun Hwang and David Eugin Moon

46   Oh baby let's get political!
A Rant
Foreign Architects Switzerland (FAS)

50   COUNTERACTION
52   Reflections on Action
Belinda Tato and Jose Luis Vallejo

58   The Private Space of Collective
Resistance
Lindsay Harkema

68   The Space of the Commons:
Dheisheh Refugee Camp
Alison Hugill and Dan Dorocic

76   The "As If" Society
Azadeh Zaferani

86   Staging Publics: The Renewal
of Place de la République
TVK Architectes Urbanistes

92   Acting from the Outside
Markus Miessen

96   Insitu
uAbureau

100   INTERACTION
102   Commonalities in Architecture
Yoshiharu Tsukamoto

110   Mayhem and Source Code
Albert Pope

118   The Image of the Square:
Redefining Citizenship by Design
Samaa Elimam

124   Dialogic Spaces: Cities without
Architecture
Claudia Mainardi

132   Exit Spaces: From Koreshan Cults
to Wireless Mesh Networks
Tobias Revell

138   Shared Grammars, Individual Desires
Gabriel Duarte

146   Within Generic Archetypes and
Cross-Subsidies: Productive Housing
in Guatemala and Central America
Posconflicto Laboratory

158   FACTION
160   Precarity and Power
Neeraj Bhatia

168   Housing Resistant Forms-of-Life:
Housing Projects and Social Movements
in Tehran, 1941– 53
Hamed Khosravi

178   Cultivate Collective: Housing for a
Contemporary Subject in China
De Peter Yi

190   Spaces of Conflict
Lori A. Brown

198   Delirious Actions: Gender Tactics
in Public Space
Serafina Amoroso

206   Hellinikon and the Question of
the Large Urban Void
Aristodimos Komninos

214   Borderlands: An Exploitation of
the U.S. Political Geography
Cesar Lopez

222   INACTION
224   Production/Reproduction:
How to Live Together
Pier Vittorio Aureli and Martino Tattara (Dogma)

236   Post-Squat NL: Reprogrammable City
David Eugin Moon

244   Take Me, I'm Yours:
Reclaiming Free Space in the City
Jill Desimini

250   What a Body Can Do: The Political as
Generator of a Common Spatiality
Lucía Jalón Oyarzun

256   Mobile Loitering: Public Infrastructure
for a Highly Gendered Urban Context
Mariam Kamara

260   Contested Energies
Ersela Kripa and Stephen Mueller

268   The Empty City: Building a Nomadic
Industrial Complex
Martin Sztyk

272   RETROACTION
274   A Letter to Architects
Vishaan Chakrabarti

278   What is a Tomb for?
Steven Chodoriwsky

284   Cultivating Resilience
Karen Lewis

292   Creating a Nation's Memory
Jin Young Song

298   Off the Wall
Parker Sutton and Katherine Jenkins

304   Open Museum for Peace
Rafi Segal and David Salazar

310   Elastic Commemoration
Guy Königstein

316   Editorial Board
318   On Sharing—Almanac 5
320   Credits

takes action

CALL TO ACTION

Mason White and Neeraj Bhatia

Hannah Arendt's 1958 treatise *The Human Condition* cites "action" as one of the three tenants, along with labor and work, of the *vita active* (active life). Action, she writes, is a necessary catalyst for "the human condition of plurality,"[1] which is an expression of both the common public and distinct individuals. This reading of action requires unique and free individuals to act toward a collective project and is therefore simultaneously bottom-up and top-down. In the almost sixty years since Arendt's claims, the public realm in which action materializes—what Arendt refers to as "the space of appearance"—and the means by which action is expressed, has dramatically transformed. Spatial practice's role in anticipating, planning, resisting, deflecting, or absorbing action has been broadly challenged by shifts in notions of ownership, social practices, forms of communication, and roles of government. How and where to act today is increasingly uncertain, as it requires different techniques and arrangements that reflect the distinct spatial tendencies of particular factions and their associated values. This is to say, we *appear* in a multitude of ways today—spatially and non-spatially—and therefore the forms that our actions take also need to be re-examined.

The rise of several divisive leaders within contemporary politics, has once again brought action to the foreground. As a new generation assembles to have their voices heard, they are grappling to find effective platforms for action. For instance, the political paralysis many feel in the United States is part of a longer trend that Noam Chomsky has referred to as the "democratic deficit."[2] Chomsky's deficit manifests when an open society no longer feels that they have the ability to change the systems around them. The feeling of helplessness—the opposite of action—poses a direct threat to participatory politics. Therefore, action is a key indicator on the health and durability of democracy. The most recent yearning to act, and subsequent dilemma on how to act, produced a hybrid of traditional forms of action, such as protests and marches, with contemporary tools, such as social media and GPS. As Albert Pope provokes in his piece, if the street was the "hardware" for action for a previous generation, is it still an effective site for protest today? Despite differing views on the impact of such protests, we can't deny the power of the aerial images that document the gathering of thousands of voices, from Cairo to Hong Kong to New York. When compared to the gathering of constituents in virtual space, however, these protests are modest aggregations—yet, their powerful imagery, which reveal the spatial dimensions and scale of collectivity, make us consider the formal and enduring role of Arendt's space of appearance. And, if we understand conflict as native to human assembly, then as Markus Miessen suggests, spatial planning becomes the management of these (spatial) conflicts. Space thereby can be viewed as a political medium that implicates spatial design as a critical factor within this debate. However, the sites and forms of action are not as predetermined today, since we communicate and gather through more complex and often mediated channels. This reveals a wide array of new forms of action that *Bracket [Takes Action]* seeks to assemble. At the core of this issue is a deeper debate of where and how design agency resides within political sociology.

The notion of action simultaneously evokes a conversation on what we collectively value as well as what we are acting for. If action, as Arendt posits, emerges from distinct individuals working in concert, then we are reminded of the power of the individual within the collective. This is particularly important to consider at a moment when the systems from the top—Governments and corporations —appear more distant to the distinct voices on the ground. At the same time, within an increasingly pluralistic society, what we collectively value is increasingly unclear, which presents a primary challenge on acting. *Bracket [Takes Action]* arrives at a critical point in history where the who, what, where, and how of action need to be re-conceptualized to better relate to who we are, how we live, and how we communicate today. The role of design and the agency of the designer are at stake in facilitating or stifling action.

This collection is structured into six sub-themes: ReAction, CounterAction, InterAction, FAction, InAction, and RetroAction. These themes reveal the diversity of issues, methods, and, most importantly, relevancy of the topic to designers and design-thinkers. *ReAction* consists of bold statements and projects that are reactionary in nature. This refers to reconceptualizing everyday elements of life—such as the suburban home or speculative office tower—to the challenging negotiation within agonistic pluralism. What can design do when it is entitled to simply react? *CounterAction* offers unique and alternative sites for action at various scales. These include playful surfaces, hidden kitchens, refugee camps, and the new demands of the civic square. How can the overlooked sites of appearance in our contemporary commons promote alternative forms of action? *InterAction* consists of projects and articles that consider how participatory interactions can occur, how new stakeholders are introduced, and how the relationships between people and their environment impact politics. What is the spatial agency of the individual in relation to the pluralistic collective? *FActions* are situated within a particular constituency and interrogate how these groups act internally as well as interface with other groups. These projects and articles foreground the commonality of the subject as a way to consider specific forms of action. In what way is the formation and emergence of sub-collectives informed and empowered by design? *InActions* are ways of acting by not-acting. From squatting and loitering to waiting lands, in particular contexts, inaction has proven to be an effective way to sidestep, undermine, or identify loopholes within a system. How might design engage socio-political change with the least means necessary? Finally, *RetroActions* are projects and texts that center on the contemporary role of memory, memorials, and commemoration on our understanding of valuing and giving place to history. How do forms of action participate in the registration of memory and foster a sense of historical recollection?

The intent of the fourth almanac of Bracket is to unpack the issue of action in design. The projects and texts herein oscillate between historic examinations and speculative worlds. For *Bracket [Takes Action]*, we have invited Pier Vittorio Aureli, Vishaan Chakrabarti, Adam Greenfield, Belinda Tato, and Yoshiharu Tsukamoto as editorial board members to help frame the possibilities for action today. The scope of projects and texts selected by the editorial board elucidate the expanded role of design to take more agency over systems—political, economic, and ecological among them—to better reflect the contemproary condition of the space(s) of appearance(s). Our contention here is that a democracy in deficit cannot be repaired without a deeper investigation in how today's actions can be designed, accommodated for, and encouraged. Equally, this is a call to action—it is time for design to take action and greater accountability for its actions in contemporary socio-political spheres. *Bracket 4 [Takes Action]* provokes spatial practice's potential to incite and respond to action today.

Notes
1   Hannah Arendt, *The Human Condition* (Chicago: University of Chicago Press, 1958), 7.
2   For more on the encroaching "democratic deficit" in the United States, see Noam Chomsky's *Failed States: The Abuse of Power and the Assault on Democracy* (Metropolitan Books, 2006).

RE

ReAction consists of bold statements
and projects that are reactionary in
nature. This refers to reconceptualizing
everyday elements of life—such
as the suburban home or speculative
office tower—to the challenging
negotiation within agonistic pluralism.
What can design do when it is entitled
to simply react?

AC
TION

PEOPLE PROBLEMS: EMPOWERING FORMS OF ASSEMBLY

Mason White

"Architecture is too important to be left to architects."[1]
—Giancarlo De Carlo

"It is impossible to represent architecture without representing the human."[2]
—MOS

Introduction

Architecture has a people problem. And by people, I am referring to what is implied when architects cite users, occupants, participants, clients, or what is often oversimplified as "the public."[3] People are an inevitably unpredictable element in any project, and its representation, that alludes to both scale and, more importantly, use. People perform as actors, if only extras, in the spatial theater of architecture. However, many architects consider people, and their actions, to mount a form of resistance to architecture. Arguably, the history of modern architecture is also the history of the struggle for architects to accept people's "misuse" of architecture. This history has led to a contemporary schism between the passive, obedient figures depicted in architectural representation (primarily in images and photographs) and the active, expressive figures that comprise contemporary society. This debate unfolds in the complex portrayal of people, or lack thereof, in the representation of architecture. There are direct correlations between architectural representation and the reflection of society through the means of inclusion or exclusion of people and their forms of assembly in both images and photographs of architecture.

Today, people are often portrayed as docile and obedient background figures in the representation of architecture, implying accepted behaviors in the completed project. Yet, more often than not, people are an active and disobedient figure disrupting the expected use of a space. This is not necessarily to suggest that people can be predicted or controlled in the design, but to reveal the bias of people serving simply as "entourage," which is symptomatic of architecture's current people problem. In particular, the humanist agenda of Team 10 in the 1950s and 1960s recall the dramatic disciplinary shift toward a more profound and complex understanding of people and their active role as spatial practitioners. However, successive waves of formal and technological biases in architecture since then have suppressed and reduced the influence of people—as users and occupants—on design, inciting the current people problem in architecture.

Beyond accommodating human needs and program-specific expectations, architects are challenged by how people assemble in unexpected ways in response to a space. But, we might ask if a non-architect can be trusted to know what they need or want spatially? Although, what expertise do architects necessarily possess that make them exclusively knowledgeable about

Giancarlo De Carlo,
University College at
Urbino, Italy, 1962–82.
UNIVERSITÀ IUAV DI VENEZIA,
ARCHIVIO PROGETTI, FONDO
GIANCARLO DE CARLO, COLLEGI-
UNIVERSITARI A URBINO, PHOTO
CESARE COLOMBO, S.D. (C. 1970).

takes action   People Problems

Giancarlo De Carlo,
Colonia Marina Enel,
Riccione, Italy, 1963.
UNIVERSITÀ IUAV DI VENEZIA.
ARCHIVIO PROGETTI, FONDO
GIANCARLO DE CARLO, COLONIA
SIP A RICCIONE, PHOTO ITALO
ZANNIER, (1963).

human behavior in response to spaces? People's forms of assembly in space have assumed even greater complexity since Team 10's heady 1960s, through increased ubiquity of digital tools, shifts in models of democracy, and new forms of action by splintering cultural groups. These pressures and shifts are not always present in the conceptualization of a work, nor in its presentation (drawn or photographed). However, architects ignore forms of assembly at the risk of the project because these forms embody larger ideals and the will of society. This essay will chart a thread from 1960s humanist architecture through to contemporary political theory of dissensus and agonism, to offer a renewed understanding of how people can be empowered through architecture.

De Carlo's Forms of Assembly

An architect that embodies a profound acceptance of the unpredictability of people is mid-century modern Italian architect Giancarlo De Carlo, also a critical founding member of Team 10. He is best known for his masterwork Urbino University campus, realized between 1962 and 1982, which demonstrates his commitment to an architecture that responds to social and lived experience. In particular, the commissioned photographs by Cesare Colombo, shot in 1968 soon after Urbino's Collegio del Colle student residences opening, reveal the depth of De Carlo's interest in an architecture accepting of unpredictable forms

of assembly. One of these photographs is taken towards the student residences from one of the many concrete stair-walkways that criss-cross campus-wide and down. There is nothing special about the view to the building in the photograph. In fact, the cropping is unflattering, the lighting is too high contrast, and the camera's downward angle gives an awkward orientation and framing. However, what is significant about it is the presence of people and their prominence. As if caught off-guard, 14 people occupy the stair-walkway. They stand on its landings, on its treads, looking back at the camera, looking forward at the residences and beyond, talking to each other, leaning against the railing, and even one has wandered off into the site. In an instant, each person becomes an empowered independent actor in the spatial theatre of De Carlo's Urbino. How we assemble generates what kind of society emerges in response to it. De Carlo's architecture, its representation, and its empowerment of people are synonymous.

Architectural photography often communicates space and scale, but the potential to simultaneously convey or suggest forms of assembly, particularly disobedient ones, is overlooked. Colombo's photographs communicate the spaces and architecture of Urbino, but also the looseness with how they might be occupied. The use of loose space, not necessarily open space, is essential to the project's empowerment. Loose space can be thought of as space that implies

Giancarlo De Carlo,
Colonia Marina Enel,
Riccione, Italy, 1963.
UNIVERSITÀ IUAV DI VENEZIA,
ARCHIVIO PROGETTI, FONDO
GIANCARLO DE CARLO, COLONIA
SIP A RICCIONE, PHOTO ITALO
ZANNIER, (1963).

a use without being bound by it. People are more than entourage supporting the project; their active presence simultaneously completes and reappropriates the work. People informally gathered in the space, and therefore the buildings and its site accept and induce the notion of will, recalling Arendt's "free action."[4] Without people in the photograph, and even with people posed and composed, it would not give the same impression of the project. The work and its documentation embody De Carlo's position that the architecture and its users must "dissolve in a condition of creative and decisional equivalence where each – with a different specific impact – is the architect, and every architectural event – regardless of who conceives it and carries it out – is considered architecture."[5] De Carlo sees the relationship between the work and its users as collaborative, rather than antagonistic, toward a formation of the social. As many have noted, the Urbino project is architecturally significant for how it drapes over the hill and how the network of walkways connect the distributed campus on the site. Photographs of the project without people would certainly convey the static functional role of this network and the spaces it creates, but the populated photograph carries with it a scenario of the project's social argument. De Carlo employs loose space to invite the inhabitants and users to complete the work by revealing forms of assembly within it, even inviting misuse of it.

Another project by De Carlo catalyzing forms of assembly is the more modest Colonia Marina Enel in Riccione, Italy. Completed in 1963, the "holiday camp" was part of a wave of children-oriented environments at the time that was meant to provide healthy alternative temporary accommodations to the industrializing spaces of the city—which was believed to incubate poor health. The u-shaped project (in plan) was sited by the coast to offer access to clean air and water, framing a central sandy courtyard. Photographs taken soon after Enel's opening convey De Carlo's acceptance of inhabitants, of all ages, to participate in the completion of the project. In the series by photographer Italo Zannier, people—children, especially—assemble in the courtyard, around the arcades, or at the building's beach frontage. In one official project photograph, children are tightly gathered in the sandy court-yard around an instructor without acknowledging either the photographer or De Carlo's crenulated four-story complex. They are in a world of their own facilitated by Enel's siting, massing, and inventive circulation. The photography presents a project that operates as a catalyst for informal assembly and other forms of occupation. With the same provocation and power, another photograph by Zannier tracks back away from the complex toward the beach. In fact, it takes its vantage point from about shoulder-height in the water, with the symmetrical façade of Enel in the background taking up only a small portion of the frame.

The architecture is secondary to the action and inhabitation of its society, yet still remains the catalyst for that action. In an unexpected reversal of priorities, people (society) are foregrounded while architecture remains in the background. For De Carlo's Enel, the architecture and its landscape become the catalyst for forms of assembly and the kind of society it seeks to perpetuate. The architecture, in turn, is completed by people's action, and the forms of assembly it fosters.

Reinforcing the deep commitment to the contributing role of people in architecture, De Carlo remarks in a 1987 interview that a building "is only the outline of a potential; it is only made relevant by the group of people it is intended for."[6] He further reflects that the difficulty of giving form to a project is parallel to the difficulty of giving form to an organization, or society. The implication is that both formal and social organizational ambitions should be conceived of as mutually dependent. The embrace of forms of assembly in these two works is apt when considering De Carlo's role—along with Aldo van Eyck, Peter and Alison Smithson, and others—in Team 10.[7] Their critique of CIAM functionalism toward a "renewed dialogue with the user" spawned a humanist outlook in architecture that accepted, and even invited, the unpredictable element of human action in design.[8] Unlike their CIAM predecessors, Team 10 saw the public not as a mass but rather as a group of diverse individuals. In particular, Team 10's prioritizing of people and assembly, such as Van Eyck's "By-Us-For-Us" principle of social relationships, the Smithsons' niches and "streets in the sky," or De Carlo's generous use of corridors and walkways in housing. With spaces providing a loose framework (not just open space) for various forms of assembly, people could activate and push back against allocated spaces as an expression of society. While the term "forms of assembly" is being used abstractly, it also has literal manifestations; people gather in intimate pairings, group clusters, or as expressive crowds. De Carlo and his contemporaries sought an architecture that was participatory, in process, but also in occupation. This approach acknowledged that people will adapt spaces, transform their functions, and might ultimately make their own mark on it. This shift suggested that design must include the unpredictable impact of peoples' use and even misuse of the spaces. Given the cultural and political climate of the time, participation and inclusion were radical and risky design approaches for the architect to introduce. Does the cultural and political climate of today not suggest similar disciplinary challenges encountered in the 1960s? And might this historical narrative offer a rationale to address architecture's contemporary people problem?

Scale Figures

Architecture's troubled relationship with the role and presence of people within representations of or completed projects is quite different today.

People are often believed to misbehave, obscure, or even spoil the intentions of architecture and design. How people occupy, inhabit, and ultimately use the spaces made available to them produces a critique of the space. To avoid this, architects employ the scale figure—characters inhabiting a space in an innocuous way primarily to convey scale or enhance the reading of the space. Modernity brought architects' current usage of "scalies" to bear. For example, modernists Corbusier, Aalto, Kahn, and Bo Bardi, as well as contemporaries Siza, Holl, and Sejima, all have their scale figures of choice.[9] These figures serve as both scale reference and, in many cases, an author's signature. However, several counter-examples of this signature tendency can be found in the work of Interboro Partners (USA) and Raumlabor (Germany), in which the representation of figures actively participate in expressing forms of assembly and notions of society. In parallel to the signature figures devised by some architects, figures are frequently populated in imagery as a persuasive, yet subconscious, marketing tool. A 2015 exhibition at UC Berkeley, "Designing People," presented drawings and photographs from the Environmental Design Archives with a curatorial focus on how scale figures are used to "sell a design to the client" by showing "happy, busy, satisfied people to illustrate how the design will be successful."[10] Both uses of figures, signature and marketing, further reinforce the sense of distrust of people, because while they provide a character to humanize the space, they do very little to suggest forms of assembly or a larger reading of society. Scalies have primarily become either a signature or marketing tool, rather than an expression of a society made possible by its host architecture.

An unscientific survey of photographs and imagery today reveals projects and proposals both with and without people. Those that are uninhabited display the most overt distrust of people because architecture is never without the ephemerality of people and their possessions, so there is little logic in illustrating or documenting spaces without people. Those that are inhabited present a glimmer of society's response to the project. However, more often than not, the distrust of users/inhabitants has led to the antiseptic and sterile portrayal of people—and, therefore, society—in contemporary architectural imagery. Consider, for example, today's common practice of "staging" a space with architect-approved furniture and possessions. Similarly, people are arranged and placed within a photograph or rendered imagery in an over-choreographed manner. Instead, the appearance of people in a work should be an extension of the work itself —a social scenario of its use. The ongoing antagonistic fissure between designer/design and user/space creates misunderstandings and misuse, which architects often see as a threat to, rather than a testing of, their intent.

In architectural representation, the curation of entourage has sometimes reinforced racist,

Scale figures available from www.skalgubbar.se.

Scale figures available from www.nonscandinavia.com.

People in Commons: Dissensus and Agonism

What has become of the humanist project in architecture, and the wider acknowledgement of peoples' role, since the provocations of Team 10? De Carlo—as well as Van Eyck—influenced architecture's social engagement for a generation. Though much of this interest faded since then, recent concern for the status of the public realm and, more specifically, "the commons" as a relevant spatial product, renews contemporary approaches to humanism. In distinction to public space, the commons is primarily interested in what is shared among a group. Interest in the commons can be seen to simultaneously be a belief in forms of assembly, and the societies they connote, to complete architecture. How people permeate and occupy the commons is contingent on the potential of the space, while they simultaneously test the limits of it. Contemporary practices such as Atelier Bow-Wow (Japan), Lacaton and Vassal (France), or Secchi Viganò (Italy), Ecosistema Urbano (Spain), among others, integrate the commons and forms of assembly in a range of strategies promoting loose space. We would find in many of their works, and in their representation, a celebration of individuality, a recognition of social collectives, and an awareness of "free action."

A young 21st century was witness to a wave of profound revolutionary demonstrations, which I will only make a cursory reflection on. The most significant protests were galvanized around the Arab Spring movement initiated in Tunisia in December 2010. The movement gathered momentum in Bahrain, Algeria, Kuwait, Sudan, and others well into 2012. The Egyptian revolution unfolded in Tahrir Square in 2011. The Umbrella Revolution in the streets of Hong Kong during 2014. The Arab Revolution was about authoritarianism, the North American Occupy movement was about inequality and economics. In fact, the Occupy Wall Street movement began with a call from the Canadian media outlet Adbusters that "America needs its own Tahrir," an interesting conflation of a movement and a specific space.[12] In the case of Occupy Wall Street, the encampment at Zuccotti Park illustrates the complex manner in which a privately owned public space became territorialized. Food, water, and waste management quickly became issues to the almost 200 people who chose to sleep in Zuccotti. While this scale and motivation for assembly are radically different than De Carlo's more intimate intent, they suggest the ongoing need for loose space and offer an inevitable spatial factor in societal expression. In all these instances, people became factions testing the capacity of a space—a street, a park, a public space, or even a private space. These tests are an expression of society unfolding in space, against the backdrop of architecture (and infrastructure). These are not scale figures, these are citizens acting out through forms of assembly. Forms of assembly, even at this magnitude, do not always imply a consensus among its collective. Just as with the occupants in

sexist, and colonial tendencies.[11] And in photography, people are blurred, obscured, erased, or passed by in a photo-shoot. In addition to the manipulation of people, spaces are sterilized to remove the unpredictable clutter of the users' life. The elaborate arrangements, staging, and choreography of the architectural photo-shoot reveals this distrust. In their most rudimentary role, people and possessions are used for scale reference. The legacy of this can be found in the contemporary practice of digital libraries of scale figures from which design projects are then populated. Files and folders are organized by scale, detail, activity, climate, body orientation, and other factors. A drawing or rendering can be efficiently populated from these files with any combination of characters to enhance the image. Beyond scale, people and their possessions show how a represented space is used, as well as what kind of society it implies. People give action to space; they activate architecture. But sometimes, and maybe more often than not, people are absent or disempowered in the images and photographs of architecture.

Occupy Wall Street at Zuccotti Park, New York City, September 17, 2011.
PHOTO BY DAVID SHANKBONE / CREATIVE COMMONS.

De Carlo's Urbino project, individuals maintain individuality even within a group.

Here it is useful to consider philosopher Jacques Rancière's notion of dissensus, as a counter-position to consensus, and the rise of its usage since the 1960s of De Carlo and Team 10. Rancière uses consensus to refer to "what is proper," while dissensus empowers the improper as action against authority.[13] Extrapolating here, we might find conceptual lineage in the sequence of consensus-proper-use and dissensus-improper-misuse. If dissensus is considered "a gap in the sensible self" rather than a confrontation between interests or opinions, it pits the recognition of individuality against the recognition of the crowd.[14] The assembly of many individuals in (public) space reveals simultaneously acts of consensus and dissensus. Architecture, however, privileges consensus as the expected action within its spaces. To consider dissensus would entail new and novels means of portrayal of people in spaces, and in most cases would suggest a loosening of the architects control on the staging of representation. Although, the intention is not to suggest that architects design exclusively for the binary dissensus-misuse, but simply that we should de-privilege the binary consensus-use. Broadening this observation, political theorist Chantal Mouffe agrees that there has been "too much emphasis on consensus," and identifies a "struggle among adversaries," or agonism, as a productive mode.[15] Agonism offers a parallel understanding of the oscillation between use-misuse and proper-improper. To situate this within spatial design disciplines reveals the expectation for people to perform in a proper manner and with clarity of use. However, agonistics recognizes that misuse-improper is just as common and is in fact more conducive to the formation of contemporary society.

People come in various forms of assembly within and around architecture. There is the individual; the granular unit measured as an occupant or user. There are the collections of individuals that aggregate to form groups, collectives, and crowds. And each of these can attain qualities in just tweaking their nomenclature, such as an audience, a throng, or a mob. How these groups and crowds permeate space and what actions they assume becomes an indicator of the reception of that space to unexpected uses. Equally it becomes a register to the tolerance or acceptance by the architect for users to complete, participate, or re-imagine a work. The capacity of space is the testing ground for actions and autonomy by societal groupings. A representation of a public space or large park rarely shows a crowd or mob or protest within it. Although that may not be a common usage of it, the primary reason is that it might be considered a liability to the design scheme, and those that might support it. However, architecture represented as empty or generic, in photograph or image, has no society to claim it. It literally has no people, no audience, and no users. The ability for spaces to coerce forms of assembly can be subtle with the inclusion of minor obstacles, level changes, and the articulation of edges. These are all evident in De Carlo's Urbino and Riccione projects. Space can be witnessed first-hand or experienced through photographs (built) and images (unbuilt). How people are represented, if there are any at all, is complicit with the capacity of that space to house or react to individuals and collectives.

Returning to the claim of architecture's current people problem, a way forward might lie in several parallel approaches. Most elucidating would be to reclaim a contemporary form of humanism in architecture, one more tied to free action. This would acknowledge the increased influence of forms of assembly on design, and it would broaden the trust of users-inhabitants to complete a work. De Carlo's argument that architecture is "too important to be left to architects" offers a still prescient rallying cry for the inclusion of others before and after design.[16] The implication for the discipline today might suggest that dissensus and agonism are the new normal, and people act as contributing designers to a work, rather than only occupants. Architecture must confront its people problem to contribute to societies formation. This argument began with a criticism of representation but extends to larger implications of architecture's role within the formation of society. How architecture is represented, its images (drawn and photographed), are a direct reflection of the capacity for it to accommodate forms of assembly and the societies they carry. Architecture both reflects and participates in the transformation of society.

Notes

1 Giancarlo De Carlo, "Architecture's Public," in *Architecture and Participation*, ed. by Peter Blundell Jones, Doina Petrescu, and Jeremy Till (Abingdon: Spon Press, 2007), 13.
2 Michael Meredith and Hilary Sample, "Architects Draw People," in *An Unfinished Encyclopedia of Scale Figures without Architecture*, ed. by MOS Architects (2016), ii.
3 I have chosen to use the term people over human so as not to confuse with the increasing interest of posthuman in the design disciplines. Also, the term people implies more of the intended social and political dilemmas explored in this text over the biological implications in using human.
4 Hannah Arendt invokes "free action" in reference to the writing of Hans Jonas in her second volume, "Willing," of *The Life of the Mind* (New York: Harcourt, Inc., 1971), 32.
5 De Carlo, "Architecture's Public," 13.
6 Roemer Van Toorn and Ole Bouman, "Architecture is too Important to Leave to the Architects: Interview with Giancarlo De Carlo," in *The Invisible in Architecture*, ed. by Van Toorn and Bouman (London: Academy Editions, 1994), 382.
7 An expanded version of this text might include the representation (through photographs) and design intent of Aldo van Eyck's numerous

playground designs throughout 1947-78 all across the Netherlands. Equally, it might include the use of figures in the collaged drawings of Peter and Alison Smithson's 1953 competition proposal for Golden Lane Estate. Both of these architects, like De Carlo, produced work that deeply considered people in the design process and in the allocation of space and use.
8 Van Toorn and Bouman, *The Invisible in Architecture*, 382.
9 MOS Architects edited a massive, yet incomplete, collection of scale figure representation by modern and contemporary architects. Produced for the Istanbul Triennale in 2016, *An Unfinished Encyclopedia of Scale Figures without Architecture* (2016) collects over 1,500 scale figures removed from their original drawings and alphabetized by architect. The collection promotes both the signatory aspect of scale figures, but also powerfully conveys each architect's subconscious value of people as representations of society.
10 Exhibition description of "Designing People," curated by Waverly Lowell and Chris Marino, Environmental Design Library, University of California, Berkeley, from February 11 – May 19, 2015.
11 As architects and practices collect and produce their own digital scale-figure libraries, it was inevitable that

some would appear online. The website Skalgubbar (http://skalgubbar.se/), developed by Swedish architect Teodor Javanaud Emden, is one early adopter of online sharing of figure libraries. He only includes figures that he knows. In reaction to the immense popularity of using figures from Skalgubbar, the website Nonscandinavia (http://www.nonscandinavia.com/), developed by students from Columbia University, emerged to offer a counterpoint of scale figures. Nonscandinavia simultaneously criticized the former, with the statement that "renderings should project a future that values diversity and acceptance of all people." (http://www.nonscandinavia.com/about/ accessed August 12, 2017.)
12 A June 9, 2011 tweet from Adbusters twitter account wrote: "America needs its own Tahrir acampada. Imagine 20,000 people taking over Wall Street indefinitely." (https://twitter.com/adbusters/status/78989903232376832?lang=en accessed August 13, 2017)
13 Jacques Rancière, *Dissensus: On Politics and Aesthetics*, trans. by Steven Corcoran (London: Continuum, 2010), 46.
14 Ibid., 46.
15 Chantal Mouffe, *Agonistics: Thinking the World Politically* (New York: Verso, 2013), 7.
16 De Carlo, "Architecture's Public," 13.

DESIGN ACTIVISM: TOWARDS AGONISTIC PLURALISM

Kees Lokman

Designers have long been occupied with what types of objects can be created technically, structurally, aesthetically, and more recently, environmentally. But with the challenges of ongoing population growth, water and food shortages, climate change, pending energy crises, and economic uncertainty, to name a few, there is a need to expand the scope and responsibilities of design practices. The recent emergence of more critical formulations of design, such as design activism, design for social innovation, public interest design, and design for democracy as well as the founding of organizations such as Architecture for Humanity (1999), Designers without Borders (2001) and Design that Matters (2003) all support this trend. These practices no longer simply approach design as a tool to produce an object but rather as a process for radical change. Still, most conventional design practices and professional design schools do not explicitly engage the political dimension of design discourse. And for those who do, there are varying degrees to which their attitudes and approaches actually enable participants to constitute political agency in order to transform and subvert socio-cultural and spatial-temporal conditions.

This essay begins with a brief literature review to discuss current notions of design activism. I will draw on the notion of agonistic pluralism to further explain the possibilities for more politically and publically engaged modes of design practice. Finally, I will highlight a number of contemporary design projects to illustrate how design can be a vehicle for contesting dominant social and political conditions. As such, this essay aims to explore how critical design approaches can help engage individuals and social groups in the co-production of political agency and new forms of public space by allowing certain differences to develop in dialogue with others.

The Role of Activism in Design

In his article "Design Activism...for Whom?," Randy Hester eloquently states that "every act of city making, landscape architecture, environmental planning, and architecture is a creative act, a direct action to achieve an end, the very definition of activism."[1] However, Hester also emphasizes that not every designer consciously uses activism, or the agency of design, to challenge and confront entrenched socio-political powers. Hester makes a distinction between five types of designers—the blissfully naïve, the savvy naïve, servants, contextualists, and catalysts—of which, he argues, only the catalysts fully commit to operating outside the realm of "polite politics." Most other designers and conventional spatial practices tend to follow the normative political agendas of their clients without acknowledging or confronting the political, social, or environmental consequences of their actions.[2]

Greenpeace protest
on the Houses of
Parliament, 11:00am
on October 12, 2009.
PHOTO: NICK WEBB, CREATIVE
COMMONS LICENSE

For Hester, this is partially attributed to the fact that most professional design curriculums instill the idea that design and politics are separate from each other. Instead, he calls for the development of curricula and courses that introduce students to politics and ethics in order to provide them with the necessary methods and skillsets to deal with competing worldviews in the face of power. Similarly, design historian Kenneth Frampton has argued that "at this juncture one can hardly emphasize enough how the substance of political process needs to be articulated within the field [of design], both pedagogically and otherwise, not only in relation to the big politics of large-scale environmental policy, to be argued for agonistically in the public realm, but also in the small politics of psycho-social well-being and sustainability as these factors may be incorporated at a micro-scale into environmental design."[3]

Drawing from Hester and Frampton, questions emerge as to how designers might establish and articulate more critical agendas towards pressing social and environmental issues. In the following paragraphs, I will discuss a number of recent frameworks of design activism. Here, design is understood as a tool and process that not only aspires to publicize social-political and environmental issues, but also aims to raise questions concerning the conditions of these issues in order to reconcile differences and generate alternative solutions.

Framing Design Activism

Ann Thorpe is among a group of authors, including Bryan Bell and Alastair Fuad-Luke, whose recent work has focused on shaping a conceptual framework for design activism. She argues that it is critical to formulate how activism, as defined within design culture, is different from characterizations of the term in political science and sociology.[4] Whereas conventional forms of activism in sociology and political science often refer to "protest" or "resistance," design activism should focus on how design processes and its outcomes can affect people's perceptions and emotions. Thorpe also underlines that design activism should not be confused as simply raising awareness for pressing societal issues without aiming to change people's behaviors. Accordingly, design activism should, in addition to revealing social and environmental issues, frame viable alternatives to change public opinion and put pressure on those in positions of authority.[5]

Along these lines, Fuad-Luke, author of *Design Activism: Beautiful Strangeness for a Sustainable World* (2009), explores the notion of disruption as one of the traits and necessary outcomes of design activism: "Forms of activism are also an attempt to disrupt existing paradigms of shared meaning, values and purpose to replace them with new ones."[6] In this sense, rather than being simply resistant to current paradigms, design has the capacity to generate alternatives and introduce transformational ideas to help shape a changing society. Moreover, Fuad-Luke introduces the term "beautiful strangeness" to underline the central role of aesthetics and visualization in design disciplines. Design activism must be used as a counter-narrative to replace the "current version" of beauty—which is largely in service of consumerism—with "a beauty that is not quite familiar, tinged with newness, ambiguity and intrigue, which appeals to our innate sense of curiosity."[7] In this perspective, aesthetics can be understood as a mechanism to directly affect people's senses, perceptions, and emotions in relation to notions of in/exclusion, authority, and power.[8] In order to promote radical change, designers have to resist commercially driven design tendencies that result in greenwash projects—a term defined by the *Oxford English Dictionary* as "disinformation disseminated by an organization so as to present an environmentally responsible public image." Instead, the aim is to encourage self-conscious resistance against conventional ideologies to generate social and change-oriented practices.

Unfortunately, while Fuad-Luke's book offers an impressive set of approaches and techniques illustrating how designers can engage citizens and social groups in tackling social and environmental issues, it is often unclear how these methods are directly tied to design activism. This is reinforced by his general definition of design activism as "design thinking, imagination, and practice applied knowingly or unknowingly to create a counter-narrative aimed at generating and balancing positive social, institutional, environmental, and/or economic change."[9] Fuad-Luke seems to suggest that unintended positive design outcomes (unknowingly) can somehow be labeled as design activism. As such, he puts emphasis on the effects of design over its intent while both are equally important, especially in the context of design activism. In addition, the role of design activism is not necessarily to generate balanced change but to give rise to new social formations and shape counter-public spaces in order to disrupt existing systems of power and authority.

Towards Agonistic Pluralism

Participatory design is perhaps the most popular approach in addressing social question in design. Here, participation is often framed as a democratic vehicle to achieve consensus and agreements among a diverse set of interests, aspirations, and ideas. However, in recent decades there has been a growing body of literature discussing some of the problematics related to participation in the context of consensus-oriented democracies.[10]

Belgian political philosopher Chantal Mouffe, in particular, has argued that rather than aiming for consensus and conflict resolution, democracy should be based on facilitating and enabling dynamic disputes and struggles amongst groups and individuals with competing values, ethics,

and beliefs.[11] Within this framework, consensus should be seen as a "temporary result of provisional hierarchy" but should not result in the "stabilization of a particular set of social relations norms and courses of action."[12] Mouffe's agonistic model of democracy seeks "a vibrant clash of democratic political positions."[13] It emphasizes permanent conflict and creates spaces of contest that do not specifically aim for reconciliation and unified expression.

This framework offers possibilities for and expanded notion of design activism. The direct goal is not to violently overturn institutional power, but rather to use design approaches and methods to subvert and reconfigure dominant social/political orders. Design, as a form of resistance, becomes a vehicle to mobilize and empower marginalized social and political voices. Especially by revealing and visualizing "that which is repressed and destroyed by the consensus of post-political democracy," design can play a critical role in the production and destabilization of social and spatial relations.[14]

Contestation Through Design

From publications, (temporarily) installations, and community mobilization to information sharing using web and open source platforms, there are various formats, mechanisms, and strategies for designers to become potential agents for radical social and environmental change. Following Mouffe, design practices should strive to act or perform agonistically in order to create spaces of contestation that directly confront or reveal power relations. In the following paragraphs, I will highlight a number of contemporary design/research projects that include agonistic approaches to question and change normalized practices, systems, or authorities.

A first example is the *iSee Project* by the Institute for Applied Autonomy (IAA). The project questions authority and increased surveillance of public space. Today, our public behavior is documented on thousands of video cameras scattered across the urban fabric in order to limit potential (terrorism-related) crime—often without much public or legislative oversight.

Paths of east surveillance.
IMAGE: COURTESY OF THE INSTITUTE OF APPLIED AUTONOMY

->
Installation view of
"Vacant NL" in Dutch
Pavilion at the
2010 Venice Biennale
in Architecture.
PHOTO: ANDERS LANZEN,
CREATIVE COMMONS LICENSE

Within this context, the IAA created a web-based application that maps the locations of closed-circuit television (CCTV) surveillance cameras in cities like New York and Amsterdam. Primarily envisioned as a discursive tool to provoke conversation, the iSee website acts as an inverse surveillance system and allows users to find alternative routes that avoid CCTV cameras. As argued by IAA: "Theoretically, it allows people to play a more active role in choosing when and how they are recorded by CCTV cameras by providing a means for them to avoid surveillance cams if they want."[15] The project empowers citizens to respond and act to a previously unknown condition. Instead of passive onlookers, iSee allows citizens to become active participants in shaping new spatial-temporal relationships. As such, the project illustrates a type of design activism in which citizens themselves have the opportunity to change their behavior and react against current surveillance practices. It provides a two-way model of communicative action in which there is a free translation between the website and its users to engage in reconfiguring existing social/political order.

Another example is *Vacant NL: Where Architecture Meets Ideas*, a project by Rietveld-Architecture-Art-Affordances (RAAAF) for the 2010 Venice Biennale in Architecture. Instead of celebrating architects and their physical objects, which typically happens at the Venice Biennale, the project challenges designers to become directly involved in contesting pressing social and political questions.[16] As a direct response to the 2009 European housing bubble and credit crisis, the project visualized the more than 10,000 existing vacant government-owned buildings in the Netherlands. More than simply a powerful visual statement, the vast display of miniature houses not only exposes the Dutch government for a lack of flexibility and innovation in relation to re-appropriation of their vacant buildings, it also provides opportunities and mechanisms for citizens to utilize vacant and temporarily unoccupied buildings. And even though the content of *Vacant NL* provides a "kind of inquiry into the political condition," the immediate agonistic potential of the project lies within its direct critique of the dominant architectural design practices and discourses.[17] RAAAF explicitly uses the Venice Biennale—perhaps the most notable international platform for art and architecture—to critique dominant practices and discourses in architectural design disciplines. *Vacant NL* destabilizes the notion of the architect as the sole author-designer of physical objects. Instead, the project promotes the idea of design as a productive agency of public discourse in order to stimulate open dialogue, visual communication, and collective action. *Vacant NL* promotes architecture as a public process: a social and political space in which new relationships can be shaped and conflicts are played out. Here, the installation as well as surrounding events and performances are used as vehicles to engage participants and reveal the possibilities for action, appropriation, and (re)use of public space.

The last, and perhaps most potent, example of the type of design activism I am trying to promote is *Het Blauwe Huis* (The Blue House), which confronts the ways in which contemporary urban planning practices often fail to recognize the importance of public spaces for spontaneous social interaction and open-ended activities. In 2005, artist Jeanne van Heeswijk bought a cobalt-blue-colored detached single-family house in IJburg—a newly built suburb of the city of Amsterdam—and transformed it into a space for community programming, artistic production, and cultural activities. Over the period of four years, *Het Blauwe Huis* involved thousands of participants, including local residents, artists, designers, and politicians. The project provided temporary physical spaces for various resident-run public functions and activities that were not provided by the designers of IJburg: for example, a café, a children's library, an affordable restaurant, and a flower shop. In addition, it allowed outside participants, such as artist Hervé Paraponaris—who re-scaffolded the outside of the house to expand programming opportunities for local performances, events, and exhibitions—to engage in the production of alternative public spaces. Inspired by Van Gogh's *Yellow House* in Arles, France and Frida Kahlo's Casa Azul in Coyoacán, South Mexico—both hubs for creativity and social exchange—van Heeswijk envisioned *Het Blauwe Huis* as "a space of reflection that builds on the notion of community as a temporary construct, founded on multiple desires, possibilities, intentions, promises, necessities, expectations, and confrontations."[18] While curated by van Heeswijk to enable the discursive and material production of art, the active engagement and co-production of contested space by participants over the duration of the project allowed for lasting transformations of urban processes on a neighborhood scale.[19] In this sense, *Het Blauwe Huis* can be understood as a form of design activism that operates in between architecture and public art, something that Francesco Careri describes as civic art.[20] It provides a platform for the continuous process of "participant-driven, social- and community-responsive interventions."[21] The four-year timetable allowed for the emergence of a complex set of interactions and self-organization. It also created feedback loops between those involved in the project and city planners to discuss future projects and possibilities. Taken together, *Het Blauwe Huis* offers a model based on active dialogue between diverse individuals and modes of participation for assimilating new forms of knowledge about the socio-cultural aspects of our built environment. The construction of this type of social framework allows for a multitude of social practices, civic possibilities, and shared lived experiences to emerge in order to activate new domains for interactions for communities in the making.[22]

Het Blauwe Huis acts
as an incubator
for critical community
engagement and
co-production of public
space by artists
and other participants.
PHOTO: CASPER RILA

Conclusion

The multiplicity of contemporary social, environmental, and economic challenges, demands that designers and design education become more explicitly engaged in the political realm. This starts by re-engaging the political realm, something that has been lacking in architectural discourse since the 1960s and 1970s.[23] There is also no one right approach to our predicaments but it is critical that designers have to be more deliberate in figuring out how and where design can leverage power in contesting current paradigms. This means reaching out to broader social movements and disciplinary fields to discover where design can assist or fill in gaps where existing modes of activism are lacking.

The projects I have highlighted provide different examples of how the "unseen was rendered visible and the un-said discursive."[24] These examples by no means provide a comprehensive overview of what methods and modes of design activism are currently being deployed. Instead, they outline different sets of relationships between the site/context of the intervention and the participation and co-production of intended audiences. Still many questions remain. For example, to what extent is work that addresses political themes political? Can work address political themes but not be activist? How can we reconcile the differences in design intent as well as goals and outcomes? In particular, research and testing needs to be done to prevent one-way models of design activism that don't result in a clash of opinions among a diverse group of stakeholders. As such, I hope this article—as a small contribution to an emerging approach to design—will spur future debate and studies in search of more political, disruptive, and interdisciplinary forms of design activism.

Kees Lokman is a principal of Parallax Landscape and an assistant professor of Landscape Architecture at the University of British Columbia. His research focuses on the intersections of geography, economy, ecology, and infrastructure.

Acknowledgements
I am thankful to both Jesse Vogler and Mason White for their comments and suggestions on drafts of this paper.

Notes
1   Randolph T. Hester, "Design Activism…For Whom?" *Frameworks* 1 (Berkeley: College of Environmental Design, University of California, Berkeley, 2005): 8-15.
2   Hester, 8-15.
3   Kenneth Frampton, "The Work of Architecture in the Age of Commodification," *Harvard Design Magazine*, n°. 23 (Fall/Winter 2005): 5.
4   Ann Thorpe, "Defining Design as Activism," Unpublished article submitted to *Journal of Architectural Education* (2011), http://designactivism.net/wp-content/uploads/2011/05/Thorpe-definingdesignactivism.pdf
5   Thorpe, 5.
6   Alastair Fuad-Luke, *Design Activism: Beautiful Strangeness for a Sustainable World* (London & New York: Routledge, 2009), 10.
7   Fuad-Luke, 188.
8   See Jacques Rancière, *The Politics of Aesthetics* (London: Continuum, 2004); Jacques Rancière, *Dissensus: On Politics and Aesthetics* (London & New York: Continuum, 2010); Thomas Markussen, "The Disruptive Aesthetics of Design Activism: Enacting Design Between Art and Politics," *Design Issues*, vol. 29, n°. 1 (Winter 2013): 38-50.

9   Fuad-Luke, 27.
10   For example, see Mahmoud Keshavarz and Ramia Mazé, "Design and Dissensus: Framing and Staging Participation in Design Research," *Design Philosophy Papers*, vol. 11, iss. 1 (2013); Chantal Mouffe, *The Democratic Paradox* (London: Verso, 2000); Carl DiSalvo, "Design, Democracy and Agonistic Pluralism," presented at the *Design Research Society Conference*, Montreal, (July 7-9, 2010); Erling Björgvinsson, Pelle Ehn, Anders-Per Hillgren, "Participatory Design and Democratizing Innovation," *Proceedings of Participatory Design Conference*, Sydney, Australia, (December 2010).
11   Chantal Mouffe, *The Democratic Paradox* (London: Verso, 2000).
12   Keshavarza and Mazé, 10.
13   Mouffe, "Democratic Politics and Agonistic Pluralism," 10.
14   Chantal Mouffe, "Art and Democracy: Art as an Agnostic Intervention in Public Space," in *Art as a public issue: how art and its institutions reinvent the public dimension*, (Amsterdam, NL: Open, 2008), 6.
15   Erich W. Schienke and IAA, "On the Outside Looking Out: an Interview with the Institute for Applied Autonomy (IAA)," *Surveillance & Society* 1(1) (2002): 102-119.
16   Erik Rietveld and Ronald Rietveld, "Vacant NL, where architecture meets ideas. Curatorial Statement for the Venice Biennale 2010," http://www.raaaf.nl/downloads/Curatorial%20statement%20by%20Rietveld%20Landscape.pdf
17   Carl DiSalvo, "Design, Democracy and Agonistic Pluralism," paper presented at the *Design Research Society Conference*, Montreal (July 7-9, 2010).
18   Paul O'Neil, "The Blue House" in *Locating the Producers: Durational Approaches to Public Art* (Amsterdam: Valiz, 2011).
19   For example, the project played an essential role in convincing city planners of the necessity to establish a more permanent cultural center in IJburg. See Paul O'Neil, "The Blue House" in Locating the Producers: Durational Approaches to Public Art (Amsterdam: Valiz, 2011).
20   Francesco Careri and Lorenzo Romito, "Stalker and the Big Game of Campo Boario," in *Architecture and Participation*, ed. Peter Blundell Jones, Doina Petrescu, and Jeremy Till (Abingdon: Spon Press, 2007), 249-256.
21   O'Neil, 42.
22   O'Neil, 19-69.
23   This period included a wide-range of groups and architectural discourses with outspoken social-political agendas, including the situationists, structuralists, metabolists, environmentalists and socio-technical utopian thinkers.
24   Keshavarza and Mazé, 22.

#ACTION

Mimi Zeiger

Can a tote bag emblazoned with a hashtag spark change? Over the course of the 2014 Venice Biennale in Architecture vernissage, one of the unspoken fundamentals of the Rem Koolhaas-curated exposition, as with any trade show, was the swag bag: the free cotton or nylon tote offered as a token of solidarity between viewer and exhibitor. Of the hundreds of bags carried on the beleaguered shoulders of Giardini visitors, from national pavilion to national pavilion, one stood out—a plain muslin tote bag with the words #STAYRADICAL printed in black ink. #STAYRADICAL. Conjunctive and imperative, the tote was handed out on behalf of the three-part conversation series, "Towards a New Avant-Garde" curated by the group Superscript and aligned with the "Monditalia" installation "Radical Pedagogies," which brought together contemporary architects and thinkers to discuss Italian architectural impulses of the 1960s and 1970s.

"Radical Pedagogies" is a collaborative project of six authors: Beatriz Colomina, Britt Eversole, Ignacio Galan, Evangelos Kotsioris, Anna-Maria Meister, and Federica Vannucchi, with a host of affiliates and contributors drawn from the circle around the PhD program at Princeton University's School of Architecture. An academic research project manifesting across platforms —exhibitions, online and print publishing, and events—It's subtitle employs terms keyed into an activist trajectory: action, reaction, inter-action. "Radical Pedagogies" chronicles shifting educational models and charts the postwar flow of ideas between sites and individuals: Archizoom and Superstudio in Florence, Autogobierno at UNAM in Mexico City, or Metabolist mentor Kenzo Tange's "Tange Laboratory" at the University of Tokyo. Or as described on the project's website, "...a new kind of cartographic network of the contested spaces of pedagogical transformation: spaces of ACTION (the radical questioning and reformulation of the discipline), REACTION (the pedagogical and political friction created by the urgency of these reformulations) and INTERACTION (the constant fluctuation of this information by the movement of ideas and people)."[1] The case studies mapped on the "Radical Pedagogies" website underscore a changing global condition leading into and extending from 1968. Each illustrated case study is a snapshot of activist architecture held nimbly in time.

Historicizing radical practice fixes radicalism in the rear-view mirror, while the Twitter-friendly tag #STAYRADICAL suggests that the act of staying radical is a progressive action. The phrase, however clever, elicits two uncomfortable queries: Is a Biennale the place for radical, activist, and/or contrarian views? And, given the pervasive desire for and absorption of all things alternative and disruptive, is it even possible for architecture to get radical?

On the occasion of the 2012 Venice Biennale in Architecture, activists protested outside the Russian Pavilion during the Golden Lion award

General view of "Radical Pedagogies" at the Corderie of the 2014 Venice Biennale in Architecture.
PHOTO: MIGUEL DE GUZMAN

ceremony as the Russian team received a special mention for their efforts. Then, a group of women dressed in Pussy Riot-like ensembles—brightly colored dress paired with clashing balaclava—held up a hastily made banner in support for the jailed musicians. It read: "FREEDOM for PUSSY RIOT, and for all activists! #OCCUPYBIENNALE." Their chants of protests and demands rose up against the polite speeches under the awards tent, a performance amply photographed by nearby Giardini visitors and news crews.

And so action is sublimated into spectacle. Indeed, both retro and contemporary political actions are dependent on the media for the amplification and broadcast of messaging across traditional outlets and social web platforms (if we can even separate the two). In the context of the Biennale, however, the artificial public established by the Venetian setting denatures acts of protest. Any disruption must counter and exceed the somewhat jaundiced eyes of the audience: architects, curators, academics, and media gathered from around the world to laud its own. Action flames and fizzles without a reactive site, leaving a hollow act of acting out, a mimicking of known protest forms and compositions.

Should we mourn this conversion of architectural actions into reenactments of radical acts of yore? No. The grieving period already happened. The mirrors of radicalism were draped in black as radicalism moved from a political to formalist stance. "Radical Pedagogies" includes the 37th Biennale di Venezia (1976) as a case study, citing the debate around the exhibition *Europa-America: Centro storico-suburbio* (Europe-America: Historical Center-Suburb) sites of pedagogical shift. The show, according to the "Radical Pedagogies" text, "focused on the dialectical pairings between Europe and America, urban centers and peripheries, theory and practice, providing the grounds for experimentation by way of architectural speculation, theoretical pronouncement and representational strategies."[2] More important than the dialectic between Europe and America, the show marked a general divide and pitched Team X

practitioners, including affiliates such as Aldo van Eyck, Giancarlo De Carlo, and Alison and Peter Smithson against a younger generation including Manfredo Tafuri, Aldo Rossi, Peter Eisenman, and Robert Stern.[3] According to case study author Léa-Catherine Szacka, the debate itself, entitled "Quale Movimento Moderno" and chaired by Joseph Rykwert, is critical in leading to a formal speculative agenda. (A juicy part in the case study text points to a moment within the debate when Van Eyck, on stage, and Tafuri, in the audience, squared off, with van Eyck personally attacking the theorist arguing "…he is trying to persuade architects on something that does not exist.")[4]

Still, the romance of political action remains a strong rhetorical device across the discipline. For example, in Austrian architect Wolf Prix's essay "Exile On Ringstrasse; Excitations on Main Street," first published in the 2007 exhibition catalog *Coop Himmelb(l)au: Beyond the Blue*, Jeff Kipnis proposes a chronicle of the birth of the firm—a phoenix-like rising from the actions of 1968:

"January 1968: Hollein's explosive manifesto 'Alles ist Architekur' appears in Bau. March '68: the group Utopie organizes the seminal inflatables exhibition, 'Structures Gonflables,' that draws a surreal but compelling equation between inflatable architecture and radical situationist-inspired political action. March 1968: Coop Himmelb(l)au is born from an inflatable uterus, The Cloud, amid the trauma. Vietnam War—the Tet offensive, My Lai massacre, General Nguyen Ngoc Loan shoots a Viet Cong prisoner in the head on the front page of every newspaper in the world. Worldwide antiwar demonstrations. U.S. civil rights riots. May. Red Army Faction. Martin Luther King Jr. and Bobby Kennedy assassinated, Andy Warhol shot…. The 'concept album' kills the 45 rpm single."[5]

The tensions produced by this shift from action to form, from the immediacy of the single 45 hit to the artistic indulgences of the concept album also reveal themselves within the radical architecture movement in Italy. In 1972, Emilio Ambasz curated the exhibition "Italy: The New Domestic Landscape" at the Museum of Modern Art in New York. Ambasz collected and commissioned works for the show from Superstudio, Ettore Sottsass, Gaetano Pesce, 9999, Archizoom, and others. The "Radical Pedagogies" refers to the exhibition as a catalytic case study that "shifted the center of the discussion from production and technique to symbols and social critique, as was encapsulated in the key-words with which Ambasz chose to define contemporary design: 'landscape,' 'environment,' 'media,' 'counter-design,' and 'politics.'"[6] It is a note by Ambasz in the influential exhibition's catalog, however, that best illuminates skepticism of the efficacy of design as tool of action. The architect-curator included a text by designer Enzo Mari, who by 1972 had distanced himself from the designed

object, positioning himself as a critic of contemporary society. The note, signed "E. A." accompanies Mari's untitled manifesto.

"Knowing Mr. Mari's position, the Museum extended him a formal invitation not to design an environment. He consented and produced the following essay, in which he attempts to reconcile the fact that, although he is the designer of many beautiful objects, including a number presented in this exhibition, he nevertheless does not believe that the task of designing object, as physical articles to be executed and sold, has any significance today. He proposes, instead, that the only valid sphere of action for the designer is that of communications and that the only honorable strategy open to him is that of renewing language—the alphabet included."[7]

Returning to the #STAYRADICAL conversations, a tweet by Anna Marie Meister, Princeton PhD candidate and a member of the "Radical Pedagogies" research group, sums up the tension between present-day action and wistful reenactment: "@tweetissima: #stayradical @superscriptco asks if we still need manifestos. Would say: they have to emerge from urgency, not nostalgic longing."

Since 2006, the Dark Side Club organization has staked out oppositional ground at the periphery of the Venice Biennale in Architecture. This year an international group of influential male architects—François Roche, Peter Noever, Patrik Schumacher, Winy Maas, et al—gathered at *Ristorante ai do Forni* for a salon-like discussion of "Future Fundamentals of Architecture." Their concerns as architecture's gatekeepers and provocateurs were largely disciplinary and part of a long-time struggle over the political and aesthetic legacy of the avant-garde. In a post on his own website, Marx-ish Roche was one of the first to fire a critical shot over the biennale's bow, accusing Koolhaas of turning the radical into the marketable and peddling "fake activism."

Yet, as radical discourses simmered over prosecco and streamed online, architects Yolande Daniels and Manuel Shvartzberg—representatives of New York-based advocacy organization The Architecture Lobby—took up protest positions at the entrance of the Giardini. The Architecture Lobby, founded in late 2013, advocates on behalf of architectural workers and argues for recognition of real value—fair compensation, not simply cultural kudos—for labor within the discipline, profession, and among the general public. Megaphones in hand, the pair read off the group's manifesto:

We are precarious workers; these are our demands!
1. Enforce labor laws that prohibit unpaid internships, unpaid overtime; refuse unpaid competitions.
2. Reject fees based on percentage of construction or hourly fees and instead calculate value based on the money we save our clients or gain them.
3. Stop peddling a product—buildings—and focus on the unique value architects help realize through spatial services.
4. Enforce wage transparency across the discipline.
5. Establish a union for architects, designers, academics and interns in architecture and design.
6. Demystify the architect as solo creative genius; no honors for architects who don't acknowledge their staff.

Manuel Shvartzberg and Yolande Daniels reading the manifesto of The Architecture Lobby at the protest.
IMAGE: COURTESY OF THE ARCHITECTURE LOBBY

7. Licensure upon completion of degree.
8. Change professional architecture organizations to advocate for the living conditions of architects.
9. Support research about professional labor rights in architecture.
10. Implement democratic alternatives to the free market system of development.[8]

The 2014 Venice Architecture Biennale lends itself to critique regarding labor. Not only does the event embody the combined labors (often underpaid efforts of love) of architects, curators, researchers, writers, interns, and students, it unprecedentedly brings performers into the mix. There are dancers in the Arsenale, actors and archivists in the Swiss pavilion, and Shvartzberg is one of the six teams of practicing designers acting as partners at "OfficeUS" in the US pavilion.

When asked if the group ran the risk of being absorbed into the political theatre undercurrent of the exhibition, Shvartzberg acknowledged that the lobby was leveraging the spectacle and the massive gathering of architects. "The idea is that these ideas need to be talked about now as rigorously and as critically as possible," says Shvartzberg with urgency. "This needs to happen. It's more permanent and difficult to change infrastructure, otherwise it is superficial."[9]

In June 2014, Brendan Cormier—curator, writer, urban designer, and then managing editor of *Volume* magazine—took to Twitter to call for a unionization of cultural workers within and around architecture. The painfully low pay offered by The Power Plant, a major art gallery in Toronto with corporate sponsorship, for a coveted curatorial fellowship sparked his protest. He bristles as he notes that suppressed wages are the outcome of two parallel trends: cultural institutions losing funding and the popular rise of curating, with university churning out young graduates gunning for entrance into the field.

"How much unpaid and underpaid jobs are we willing to take on as cultural practitioners in order to gain experience and prestige, before we start saying no," Cormier writes in an email. "And where is the institutional protection to stop exploitation? We won't solve some of these larger systemic problems by simply dropping out of the system or radicalizing, by doing another pop-up shop or appropriation of a vacant lot. We'll solve these problems by a full on confrontation with the mechanisms in the system."

Cormier represents a growing anger within groups of architecture, art, and culture workers who face the precarity of low pay and insecure employment in a marketplace that consumes and celebrates creative production, but rarely rewards it. But it should be noted that, following Chantal Mouffe's categorization of the political as antagonism, successful action is contingent on leaving behind an individualist approach and expectations of any one fix. "To take account of 'the political' as the ever present possibility of antagonism requires coming to terms with the lack of a final ground and acknowledging the dimension of undecidability which pervades every order," she writes.[10] "It requires in other words recognizing the hegemonic nature of every kind of social order and the fact that every society is the product of a series of practices attempting to establish order in a context of contingency."[11]

In 2008, a group of artists founded WAGE (Working Artists and the Greater Economy), a New York-based activist group committed to protecting artist fees and developing a sustainable model for contracting between nonprofit art institutions and artists. Among the international coalition's efforts is an opt-in certification process for institutions that adhere to best labor practices. WAGE certified organization conform to set standards of artist compensation. Their online fee calculator breaks out the details based on the operating expenses of the organization: solo shows, panel discussions, commissioned text for publication. The floor fees are modest: $1,000 for a solo show, $100 for a panel discussion, 25 cents/word for a text. What's important is that the labor is valued as part of the production of art, not as a "labor of love" or CV builder.

WAGE isn't nostalgic for past radicalism. The group confronts economic conditions head on and its concerns put pressure on contemporary systems to evolve. It's time for architecture institutions to be held to similar standards. Rather than reminiscing about what lies under the cobblestones, architects and architectural cultural producers need to make their own demands. There's work to be done.

Mimi Zeiger is a Los Angeles-based journalist and critic. She is the west coast editor of the *Architects Newspaper* and has covered art, architecture, urbanism and design for a number of publications including *The New York Times*, *Domus, Dezeen*, and *Architect*. She teaches in the Media Design Practices MFA program at Art Center College of Design and is co-president of the Los Angeles Forum for Architecture and Urban Design.

Notes
1 *Radical Pedagogies*, http://radical-pedagogies.com.
2 Léa-Catherine Szacka, Radical Pedagogies website, "Vittorio Gregotti, Franco Raggi, Peter Eisenman, Robert A.M. Stern 37th Biennale di Venezia," http://radical-pedagogies.com/search-cases/v02-biennale-venezia/.
3 Léa-Catherine Szacka, *Display & Debate: An Oral History of the 1976 Europa/America Show at the Venice Biennale, RIBA Research Trust Award 2011–2013*, Final Report, http://www.architecture.com/Files/RIBA ProfessionalServices/Education/Funding/RIBASummarySzacka.pdf.
4 Szacka, "Vittorio Gregotti, Franco Raggi, Peter Eisenman, Robert A.M. Stern 37th Biennale di Venezia."
5 Jeffery Kipnis, *A Question of Qualities: Essays in Architecture* (Cambridge, MA: The MIT Press, 2013), 36.
6 Luca Molinari, "Emilio Ambasz: The new domestic landscape exhibition at MoMA," *Radical Pedagogies*, http://radical-pedagogies.com/search-cases/a01-new-domestic-landscape-exhibition-moma/.
7 Emilio Ambasz, *Italy: The New Domestic Landscape* (New York: Museum of Modern Art, 1972), 264.
8 *The Architecture Lobby*, "Venice Committee," http://www.architecture-lobby.org/venice-committee/.
9 Brendan Cormier, interview by author, June 2014.
10 Chantal Mouffe, *On the Political* (New York: Routledge, 2007), 17.
11 Ibid., 17.

A COLLECTIVE LIVING ROOM

Matthew Mazzotta

In 2011, I was invited by the Coleman Center for the Arts, a local arts organization, to begin a project with the town of York, Alabama—one of the poorest towns in the United States. Over the last few years, I have worked with the people of York to develop the town's only civic space that is open to all members of the community. Recently, we had the inauguration of *Open House*—a transforming theater built from a blighted property in York's downtown. Retaining the shape of a house, the project can physically transform into a one-hundred-seat open-air theater for the community.

On my first visit to York, I initiated a dialogue with the community by asking them to bring something from their living room to the meeting. This was intended to help envision how the community could recreate a living room outdoors, in the middle of the street, as a way to provoke new possibilities for civic space. From this conversation, we developed a project that repurposes the materials of an abandoned house and its land, to construct a transforming structure sited on the footprint of the old house.

I believe public space is always political. Understanding the power of the built environment to shape our relationships and experiences, we can see that when the only spaces a community has to meet each other are the transitional spaces of the streetscape or commercial institutions, only certain types of dialogues can be fostered. When considering the project in York and gauging the possibility of change from it, I believe that if people can sit together they can dream together. *Open House* is about generating an opportunity for people to come together and view their situation from a new perspective, supported by the time and space to exchange perspectives. At its core, the project is about dissolving social hierarchies inherent in so much of our contemporary world and allowing people—who might not feel comfortable at meetings and official events, or only being able to have short conversations in the checkout line—to be together and exchange ideas, which eventually resonate throughout the social fabric.

Matthew Mazzotta is an artist that creates community-specific public artworks. Matthew received an undergraduate degree from the School of the Art Institute of Chicago and a Masters of Science in Visual studies from the Massachusetts Institute of Technology.

Top:
On a typical day when it is not being used as a community event space, *Open House* is folded back into the shape of a house and the land is used as a public park.
PHOTO: COURTESY OF NATHAN PURATH

Middle left:
A day before an *Open House* event, workers from the city open the physical structure and transform the 'house' into an open-air theater for one hundred residents. Opening the house the day before the event helps to alert the surrounding community of an upcoming event.
PHOTO: COURTESY OF NATHAN PURATH

Middle right and bottom left:
It takes four people an hour and a half to open up and transform *Open House* from a 'house' to an open-air theater. City employees open the ten arms of the structure that unfold twice to transform the seventeen-foot wide 'house' into a fifty-five foot wide theatre.
PHOTO: COURTESY OF NATHAN PURATH

Bottom right:
After the sun goes down, the surrounding community comes to enjoy the movies, music, and shows programed by the Coleman Center for the Arts, a local arts organization that has been in York for the last thirty years.
PHOTO: COURTESY OF NATHAN PURATH

WHATEVER HAPPENED TO ACTION?

Christopher Austin Roach

More than six years after the global financial collapse, architecture is still waking up from a hangover. As we continue to grasp for effective ways to bring our disciplinary knowledge to bear on the challenges of global urbanization, social justice, and climate change, architects remain caught in the limited field of possibilities delineated by earlier academic and professional discourses. Even if we have passed through the "semantic nightmare"[1] of postmodernism, played out the self-referential indulgences of autonomous architecture, and awakened from the decade-long fever dream of "post-critical" production, we still seem to find ourselves without a normative framework for what can be done with architecture, and in particular, what architecture can do for the city.[2]

A whole host of architects and urban theorists have offered a response to this paradoxical state by positing various forms of direct action as alternatives to these perceived ideological dead-ends of theory and practice. Not coincidentally, the energy and interest devoted to these explorations blossomed exponentially around the time of the 2008 recession, coalescing into a de facto grassroots movement that received widespread attention in both popular culture through the internet and social media, as well as within the more traditional academic forums of lectures, exhibitions, and publications. With such a prolific outpouring of energy and work it would seem impossible to address the entire spectrum of

thinking and writing that has developed in this vein. Yet, in 2008, there was a milestone exhibition, event, and publication that codified the discourse around action and that today can be read as a transect of the various writers and actors plying the field at that time. Mirko Zardini and Giovanna Borasi's *Actions: What You Can Do with the City,* was published by the Canadian Centre for Architecture as a catalog for its eponymous 2008 exhibition, and presented a cross section of the alternative spatial practices that had emerged from the groundswell of so-called "guerrilla urbanism."[3] Curators Borasi and Zardini framed these practices within an argument for action itself—as an ideological position uniquely available to both architects and ordinary citizens. By documenting a selection of these actions in the exhibition and catalog, and by having a host of critics reflect on their implications in a series of essays, the editors aimed to capture the imaginative power of this renewed populist discourse and stake out new territory for design practices in the city. In this way, *Actions* is symptomatic of the various texts and positions that have been fielded within the discourse to date, and a critique of this text gives us an opportunity to elucidate these positions and unpack the possibilities and pitfalls that they have come to represent, as a way of re-appraising "action" and interrogating its relevance today.

Zardini sets our critical expectations high in his opening essay through an erudite summary of the geopolitical conditions of contemporary architectural practice, which leads to a compelling argument for why we should reexamine the idea of social practice now. According to Zardini, we have passed into an "urban age" not only because the majority of humans live in cities but also because the entire world is effectively organized by urbanism, and therefore, "the only possibility of action now lies within the urban world."[4] Zardini argues that the functionalist twentieth century paradigms of urbanism have ultimately resulted in a city optimized for capitalism, while the post-Fordist economy has transformed the modern city from the center of production to the center of consumption. The result of this shift, according to Zardini, is the fragmentation of the public into identity-based communities based on consumption patterns, paralleled by an increasing marginalization of "defective consumers" (those unable to participate legally in consumer society because of their economic or political status). The fragmented and fortified urban territory is littered with massive amounts of waste generated by capitalist accumulation.

Zardini suggests that the first step in reversing this decline is to change our perceptions of consumerism and to challenge conventional notions of progress and development. In parallel, he argues that we must confront the deteriorating social fabric of cities, which has produced a loss of meaningful citizenship and a resulting passivity in the populace. Zardini insists that the search for such a "post-development" model for the city requires not only a radical reconsideration of the growth-oriented mode of urbanization, but also a profound recognition of limits, including the limitations of rationalist planning itself. He recalls how Team X offered a counterpoint to the rational-functionalist urbanism of C.I.A.M by attempting to connect architectural ideals to "everyday life," thereby enabling citizens to participate in the design of the city. He proposes that while "participation" is no panacea, it is a means by which this search for a new model can begin from the ground up—where the "microbe-like, singular, and plural practices"

which emerge from individual actions can combine to form a more complete picture of this new paradigm.[5] Zardini argues that previously untapped sources of imagination and opportunity are emerging from individual everyday activist practices resurfacing after their post-1970s hibernation.

Actions documented how the recent increase in urban activism and its multivalent expression through guerilla gardening, urban agriculture, pop-up parks, and other acts of reclaiming public space (including the Occupy movement) represented localized popular responses to the dismantling of the welfare state and a frustration with the inability of urban professionals in public and private sectors to adequately address pressing issues of everyday urban life such as access to local food and public spaces. For instance, activist and amateur horticulturalist Richard Reynolds argues for the spontaneous greening of neglected public spaces by ordinary citizens for the purposes of seeking food and pleasure as a necessary response to tightening municipal budgets, corrupt contractors, and the slow moving hand of bureaucracy. Reynolds characterizes these illicit gardens, or "guerrilla gardens," installed by clandestine crews of amateur horticulturalists in the dark of the London night, as typical of what he considers a tactical response to the lack of green space in the modern metropolis.[6] Similarly, Spanish architect Santiago Cirugeda's *Recetas Urbanas* ("Urban Recipes") operate under the assumption that the activist architect must shift to work within the interstices and gaps left by market-driven urban development. Like recreational versions of guerrilla gardens, his temporary parks, parasitic structures, and other public installations use vacant lots, recycled materials, or repurposed public works equipment to provide amenities in the undeveloped blind spots of the city.[7]

These actions, among many others documented in the book, celebrate the potential of everyday life activities (walking, gardening, playing, recycling) to open up new avenues for imagining alternatives to the dominant social and spatial order. While clearly drawing on a legacy of urban theorists and activists whose roots can be traced back to the *dérives* and *détournements* that the Situationist International was promoting more than fifty years ago, the editors have nonetheless put their finger on the pulse of a "DIY zeitgeist" that has proliferated in urban culture, culminating in its potential apotheosis at the 2012 Venice Architecture Biennale. Perhaps more importantly, according to Zardini, they have attempted to recover a connection between design-practice and the objective conditions of urban life that had been previously (though incompletely) explored by groups such as Team X and Archigram. This locates the central agenda of *Actions* squarely in the realm of architecture, and provokes the inevitable question: how can these activities lead to new forms of material practice in architecture?

This is a question that the mini-movement coalescing around guerilla urbanism has so far

View of the 2008 exhibition, *Actions: What You Can Do With the City*.
PHOTO: COURTESY OF THE CANADIAN CENTRE FOR ARCHITECTURE

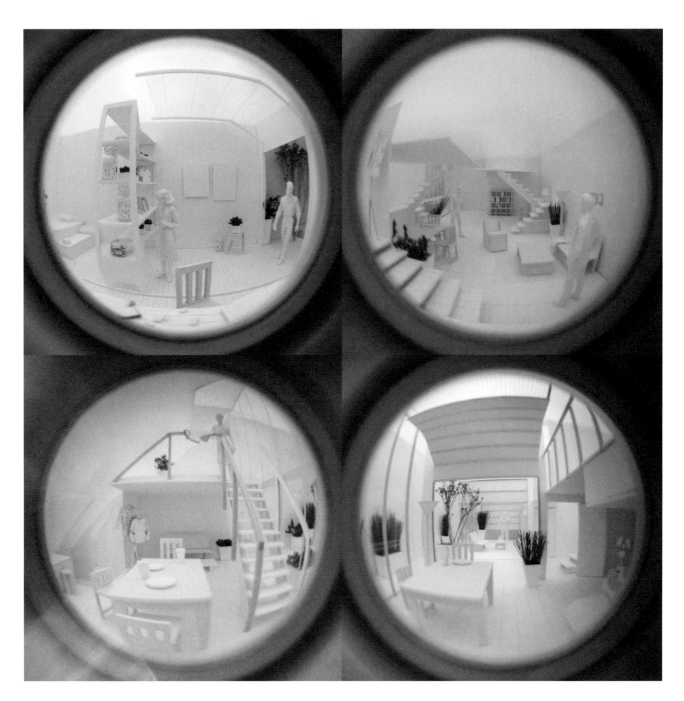

Urbanism from Within,
a research project on
domestic space carried
out at The California
College of the Arts and
led by Neeraj Bhatia
and Christopher Roach.
IMAGE: COURTESY OF THE URBAN
WORKS AGENCY/CCA

failed to adequately address—the vivid examples of crowd-sourced urbanism are too often taken at face value as being inherently good and not critically assessed for their potential to address the enormity and seriousness of urban challenges. Like the proponents of Everyday Urbanism, its prophets focus on finding alternative meanings and interpretations of the city, and avoid any deep responsibility for how the shaping of physical space can engage the forces of urbanization at an adequate scale.[8] How can this everyday urbanism, operating in the fine grain of the public realm, ever add up to more than the sum of its parts and truly improve the urban condition globally?

In "City 2.0," Borasi explains the editors' rationale for why we should focus on these every-day actions now: They are important both as tools for reinterpreting the city in ways accessible to everyone, and as practices that are "invisible" to planning authorities. She claims that it is precisely because they are outside the typical framework of planning that these actors have the power to "radically rethink the urban experience."[9] Borasi has faith that more forms of practice can be "teased out" of these actions, inspiring "a new modus operandi, promoting a *productive* critical attitude" among designers who seek to act in and on the built environment.[10] As Borasi states, "all our research tends to demonstrate that it is possible to find potential actions, actors, and instruments with this intentional energy to help devise new arrangements and to see beyond simply feeding into the systems already set in place."[11]

Actions appeared at an opportune time, as the 2008 financial meltdown instigated an existential crisis in global superstructures. What emerged from that moment, through a combination of optimism and extreme hardship, was a renewed belief in the power of small-scale local actions, and architects and planners have turned to these alternative practices a potential source of creativity and agency. *Actions*' catalog format has made it an accessible primer on such individual practices, but this, like the subject it documents, is also its weakness: It offers up a banquet of actions and options that are each individually stimulating or inspiring, but that collectively suggest no solid overall reformist programs. While the short essay format is easily digestible and allows for a multitude of voices, the contents rarely venture beyond description. Even Borasi's essay, which comes closest to offering a definitive statement, concludes in a kind of anti-manifesto:

> What all these ideas offer is a parallel system. They make no claim to represent a new world that could arrogantly replace the one now in our cities. [They] do not constitute a unison response but offer *everybody* a system of possible alternatives.[12]

While all this potential is quite enticing, it relies on a Habermasian faith in the ability of activities in the "lifeworld" to recode the city and resist the "system,"[13] yet it is never clear how these changes in meaning of the everyday allow the development of a new framework for the emerging issues of the city as well as design practices. However, if there is indeed a beach underneath these cobblestones, perhaps it is to be found in the book's essays on urban agriculture and guerilla gardening. It is here that we can see how an activity that has grown out of the cracks and spaces left in the city after the retreat of the public sphere, has been positively co-opted by city governments and other "public space professionals" (architects, planners, maintenance personnel). Just as New York's illegal community gardens from the 1970s have been legitimized and turned into public-private adjuncts to the city's official parks,[14] so have the contemporary opportunistic gardeners profiled in *Actions* begun to shift the scale of their appropriation of open space.

A key component of this shift has been reconsidering the role of urban green space as one of production rather than solely of recreation or beautification. Debra Solomon and Hans Ibelings turn our attention to food production in "The Edible City," contrasting the small-scale and fragmentary gardening practices prevalent in European and North American cities with the more significant role that urban agriculture plays in cities of developing nations. They fervently advocate for architects and planners to implement urban agriculture at a large scale as both a way to provide sustainable food security and as an agent of urban transformation, arguing that a more substantial and well-designed form of gardening could replace the predominantly ornamental green spaces of our cities.

It is in this leveraging of what begin as individual practices into scalable strategies for larger-scaled transformation where the real potential of "action" opens up new possibilities for urban trans-formation. However, like a community garden, *Actions* relies more on participation than on vision, and makes room for a plurality of contributions, from the mildly provocative to the pragmatically useful and entertaining. It is in the articles on urban agriculture that the scalar leap from gardening to the reorganization of the urban territory around food infrastructure is most easily made, and it is also where the book makes a subtle but important shift into the realm of design.

This reconceptualization of the city's open space as a productive infrastructure is radicalized in Andre Viljoen and Katrin Bohn's essay "Everything is Continuous." Their concept of a Continuous Productive Urban Landscape (CPUL) originates from a recovered awareness of the historical tie between food and the city[15] and attempts to channel environmental awareness and the growing enthusiasm for urban agriculture into a coherent urban design strategy. In the CPUL, the urban landscape's productivity is predicated on a recon-ception of the city's open spaces as a matrix that operates on the order of infrastructure, and it is here that the tie between small-scale action and real transformation at the urban scale seems the most promising. As well, this is where the book's examples begin to pivot from action to design.

This part-to-whole thinking is critical for beginning to address the larger urban territory as a totality that is unknowable in its entirety, and it is this attempt to access the whole through a structural understanding of the part that is the ambition of Yoshiharu Tsukamoto and Momoyo Kaijima's work as Atelier Bow-Wow. "A View From Tokyo" (reprinted from a 2000 interview in 10+1 magazine) outlines their interest in developing an approach to a metropolis as immense as Tokyo. According to the authors, Tokyo's structure is neither geometric nor topographic, but is characterized by repetition and relationships among similar parts, and thus the focus of their practice resides in changing the relationships among these parts in a way that effects the whole urban mass. Deploying hybridized typologies that highlight the nature of this part-to-whole relationship through the effects of their naive and uncanny juxtapositions, creates a fundamentally different approach to making urbanism legible than that of the previous generation of Japanese architects, such as the megastructures of Kenzo Tange, which relied on the organization of material at the scale of infrastructure. The desire is to put the total quantity of urban material to use by changing the relationships among existing elements. The focus on changing relationships rather than objects, they liken to "urban recycling," where "it is preferable to bring a new state into being without removing or adding anything."[16] The "typological recycling" of Atelier Bow-Wow is the most clearly architectural "action" in the book, as both the analytical documentation of underused spaces, idiosyncratic forms, and programmatic mash-ups, as well as their redeployment in Bow-Wow's own work, which concretizes the unrelenting logic of urban development at the scale of the individual and gives them a tangible scale of action. In this way, urban recycling not only allows the individual to act on the totality through the cascading effect of relational systems, but also addresses the massive amount of waste generated by a mode of urbanism predicated on the overproduction of objects. Here, we can see how applying this more expansive concept of recycling to the production of the larger built environment allows both designers and ordinary citizens to intervene in these cycles of resource and waste management and their human consequences. As Tsukamoto and Kaijima suggest, recycling is a concept that is easily understood by everyone, and applying it to the built environment allows and encourages the participation of ordinary citizens. And, as opposed to more "resistant" forms of action, this user-generated activity can only benefit when it is encouraged and supported by public policy. Furthermore, by operating under the rubric of recycling, designers can approach the city both as a user and a maker, allowing a different city to come into view where new possibilities can

Parkour is a style of movement through the city invented by the Frenchmen David Belle and Sébastien Foucan in the late 1980s and now practiced worldwide.
PHOTO: COURTESY OF RACHEL GRANOFSKY

emerge. As the authors say, "the pleasure of design lies in releasing everyday objects from their conventional framework."[17]

A more recent exploration of this type of micro-urban recycling occurred in San Francisco, in a research project initiated by the Urban Works Agency at California College of the Arts. Entitled "Urbanism From Within," this collaboration with the city's Planning Department and San Francisco Planning and Urban Research (SPUR) resulted in an exhibition and catalog that explored the "secondary unit" as a similar kind of urban recycling operation that has been occurring in San Francisco for at least the last thirty years. San Francisco's acute housing crisis has instigated programs for the legalization and creation of secondary (in-law) units embedded within or located upon existing residential properties. Currently, the city estimates that over 50,000 illegal secondary units exist within the city limits; hidden in garages, attics, rear yards or underutilized spaces of homes. The city's Planning Department recently enacted a pilot program and subsequent legislation to legalize existing secondary units and incentivize construction of new ones. As a result, what was once a marginal and almost completely invisible housing type may become an essential part of the puzzle to address the current housing shortage.

Urbanism From Within shows how this legitimization of secondary units within the interior of the domestic fabric will require micro-transformations to the architecture of the city—small artifacts and interventions that can mediate between the domestic world of the interior and the external urban environment. Yet, as the domestic fabric continues to be both limited and re-organized by capital, its interior can be rapidly and continually parsed to find new efficiencies and social arrangements. Focusing on the unique typology of the secondary unit and its interaction with the larger systems of a city enabled the Urban Works Agency to make a deeper investigation into how a diffused form of individual interiors creates new connections, power structures, forms of sharing, cross-pollenization of public and private realms, and formal architectural mutations. This close reading of the secondary unit not only interrogates the feedback mechanisms between the individual pixel of domestic space and the collective framework of the city, it implicates the interior in an investigation of how urbanism can be reformatted from within.[18] Thus, Urbanism From Within is not a utopian project, but interrogates how secondary units and their diffused form of density can create a bottom-up strategy for addressing the housing crisis, creating a new world not from the whole cloth, but from what is already at hand.

Yet, it is this expansion of the imagination outside conventional frameworks that we need most in the first years of the "urban age." There are times that call for utopian thinking, when incrementalism, "muddling through," and change from within simply won't cut it. These times reveal the weakness of pluralism: its individualized solutions produce a fragmented and segregated built environment. Alternatively, even if utopia is not workable or even desirable, imagining it allows us to directly engage in the conceptualization of radical otherness. Fritz Haeg captures the struggle with this choice in "Architecture After the Front Lawn," his manifesto for the transformation of urban space one lawn at a time. Haeg succinctly lays out the paradoxical choice we face:

> Between the utopian fantasy of starting over and the impossibility of continuing in the direction that we are headed, there lies a middle ground in which we come to terms with the urban decisions that have already been made and repurpose aspects of our existing built environment in strategic ways.[19]

Zardini and Borasi imply an answer to this paradox in the book's subtitle "What You Can Do with the City," suggesting the inevitability of the city as an artifact, and the belief that "you" (the ordinary citizen) have both the power of a user as well as an agent of change. For the design professions, the answer has become even more urgent, for if the various adjectives that have recently preceded urbanism (new, landscape, everyday, ecological, infrastructural, generic etc.) have yet to provide a clear framework for action, what exactly are we to "do" with the city? While the actions that the book details offer some compelling suggestions, it is not clear that they provide us with a tangible set of strategies within the material practice of architecture. Even if these individual actions don't address the scale and complexities of design practice in the urban age, they give us plenty to "do" while we think about it. And yet, perhaps all of this doing is overrated. If we're all out acting and not thinking, drawing, and planning, haven't we potentially lost touch with what it means to be architects and urban designers? Perhaps what differentiates our particular form of agency from the protestor or politician is that the act of design is by necessity both distanced from its subject through abstraction and representation, and pro-active in its organization and shaping of material processes, rather than reactive to the diffuse and fragmentary forces shaping the city. "What if we simply declare that there *is* no crisis,"[20] and it is rather this constant tension between the need to make, and the impossibility of designing without first developing a framework for engaging with the material forces of the city, that makes architecture the medium that can, and must, answer Zardini's call to connect the tactical to the strategic? Then, more than ever, designing is all we have, or need, to do.

Christopher A. Roach is a San Francisco-based architect, urbanist, and educator, and principal of Studio VARA. He holds a Bachelor of Architecture with Honors from the University of Texas at Austin, and a Master of Architecture in Urban Design with distinction from the Harvard Graduate School of Design. He is currently an adjunct professor of architecture at California College of the Arts, and co-director of CCA's Urban Works Agency.

Notes
1   Rem Koolhaas, quoted in Stan Allen, *Points and Lines: Diagrams and Projects for the City* (New York: Princeton Architectural Press, 1999).
2   George Baird, "'Criticality' and Its Discontents" in *Harvard Design Magazine* 21, Fall 2004/Winter 2005, 16–21. See also Wes Jones, "Big Forking Dilemma" in *Harvard Design Magazine* 32, Spring/Summer 2010, 8–17.
3   Various manifestations of this guerrilla urbanism, also known as "tactical urbanism," "insurgent urbanism," or various other monikers, have proliferated in the years since Margaret Crawford's *Everyday Urbanism* first marked out this popular domain. See John Chase, Margaret Crawford, and John Kaliski, *Everyday Urbanism* (New York: Monacelli Press, 1999). For more recent examples see publications such as Jeffrey Hou, *Insurgent Public Space* (New York: Routledge, 2010), and Florian Haydn and Robert Temel, *Temporary Urban Spaces* (Basel: Birkhäuser, 2006), as well as in the *New York Times Magazine*'s architecture issue, *Guerrilla Gardening* (June 8, 2008), and numerous blogs such as Santiago Cirugeda's "Recetas Urbanas" (http://www.recetasurbanas.net/).
4   Giovanna Borasi & Mirko Zardini, eds. *Actions: What You Can Do with the City* (Montreal: Canadian Centre for Architecture, and Amsterdam: Sun Publishers, 2008), 12.
5   Ibid., 14.
6   Ibid., 83.
7   Ibid., 123.
8   Michael Speaks, "Every Day Is Not Enough" in Douglas Kelbaugh, *Everyday Urbanism: Margaret Crawford vs. Michael Speaks* (Ann Arbor: The University of Michigan A. Alfred Taubman College of Architecture + Urban Planning, 2005).
9   Giovanna Borasi & Mirko Zardini, eds. *Actions: What You Can Do with the City* (Montreal: Canadian Centre for Architecture, and Amsterdam: Sun Publishers, 2008), 21.
10   Ibid., 23.
11   Ibid., 23.
12   Ibid., 24.
13   Jürgen Habermas, *The Theory of Communicative Action*, translated by Thomas McCarthy (Cambridge: Polity, 1984–87).
14   For instance, Bette Midler's New York Restoration Project owns and operates over 100 community parks and gardens that were sold off by the City of New York in 1999; http://www.nyrp.org/.
15   For an excellent account of this history and its implications in the modern city, see Carolyn Steel's *Hungry City*, (London: Vintage, 2009).
16   Giovanna Borasi & Mirko Zardini, eds. *Actions: What You Can Do with the City* (Montreal: Canadian Centre for Architecture, and Amsterdam: Sun Publishers, 2008), 127.
17   Ibid., 126.
18   Neeraj Bhatia and Christopher Roach, "Urbanism from Within" in *Urbanism From Within: A typological Survey*, Neeraj Bhatia, ed., (San Francisco: The San Francisco Planning Department, 2015), 2–5.
19   Ibid., 90.
20   Rem Koolhaas, "Whatever Happened to Urbanism?" in *S,M,L,XL* (New York: The Monacelli Press, 1995).

(NO) STOP MARCONI

Nahyun Hwang and David Eugin Moon

How do we acknowledge the significance of underutilized spaces and their unchallenged reproduction? *(No) Stop Marconi* is a research and speculative design project that explores the spatial and political potentials in the re-appropriation of these spaces and their infra-structures. Not only can these spaces serve as the cogent sites of alternative actions, they also offer an effective framework for new forms of spatial production, which may instigate the reestablishment of the civic in the urban.

After Speculation, Empty Density

Obsolescence and vacancy are widespread spatial demonstrations of shortsighted and volatile global economic and political processes. Specifically, the empty office tower is a particularly identifiable type in Holland due to the nation's long sustained real estate policy that supported speculative and high-risk investments by large capital. Construction of office towers was encouraged during the pre-bubble boom, and their vacancy and emptiness were exacerbated and highlighted in the context of decline and stagnation following 2008. The ninety-three meter tall Europoint Towers, or Marconi Towers, by Skidmore, Owings & Merrill (1971–1975) in Marconiplein at the fringe of Rotterdam, may become entirely vacant within the next few years. The last occupant and its own developer, the City of Rotterdam, is slated to relocate to De Rotterdam by OMA, the largest building ever to be erected in the history of the Netherlands. The Europoint Towers are emblematic, and yet represent only a fraction of an increasing number of usable but vacant office towers in Europe and beyond. In Holland alone, 6.74 million square meters of unoccupied workspace exists in high-rise towers as of 2011.[1]

Dense Vacuum, a "New" Tabula Rasa

Monuments to the persistent desire to expand and accumulate, the case of Europoint and similar towers, only seem to highlight the irreversible demise of over-speculation. This gross complacency within political and economic processes has yielded readily available, tightly packed, and ubiquitously distributed spaces of empty urban towers. These

Excerpts from poster, Marconi the Idea(l)s: Selected documents from the Europoints' past and present. The empty spaces in the Marconi and similar towers are the foreclosed homes of the post-bubble, post-2008 European economy. IMAGES: COURTESY OF EZRA STOLLER/ESTO (LEUVEHAVEN WORLD TRADE CENTER PROPOSAL MODEL), CITY OF ROTTERDAM ARCHIVE (DRAWINGS AND OTHER GRAPHIC DOCUMENTS OF EUROPOINT TOWERS AND THE ADJACENT AREA), AND WIKIMEDIA COMMONS (PHOTOGRAPH OF DE ROTTERDAM UNDER CON-STRUCTION). ALL OTHERS COURTESY OF AUTHOR

–>
Te huur ("to let") is one of the most ubiquitous street signs found all over the Netherlands, translated as "for rent," ambiguously indicating both development and decline, availability and inaccessibility. Depicting the moment when the municipality vacates the Marconi Towers, *Marconi Te Huur* also suggests the Towers' alternative future when new residents are moving in to reoccupy their slates.

De Rotterdam, the New Home
to the Municipality of Rotterdam,
under construction, 2012

Europoint Towers seen from Kiefhoek
Workers' Housing, 2010

J.J.P. Oud, Workers' Housing in
adjacent Tusschendyken, Rotterdam,
The Netherlands, 1918–1921

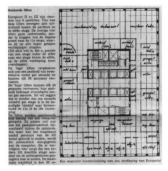

Europoint Technisch Bekeken—Possible
office layout, 1973

"Extra Europoint"

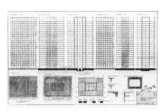

Skidmore, Owings and Merrill, Europoint
Towers, Sections, Plans, 1969

Typical Vacant Office Space, Rotterdam,
The Netherlands, 2007

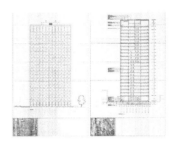

Skidmore, Owings and Merrill, Europoint
Towers & Sections, 1969

Skidmore, Owings and Merrill, Europoint
Towers, Site Plan, 1969

Vacant Europoint Towers Interior, 2010

Europoint Towers with "Googly Eyes"
Anti-Crime Initiative, 2010

View over adjacent housing blocks from
Europoint Towers, 2010

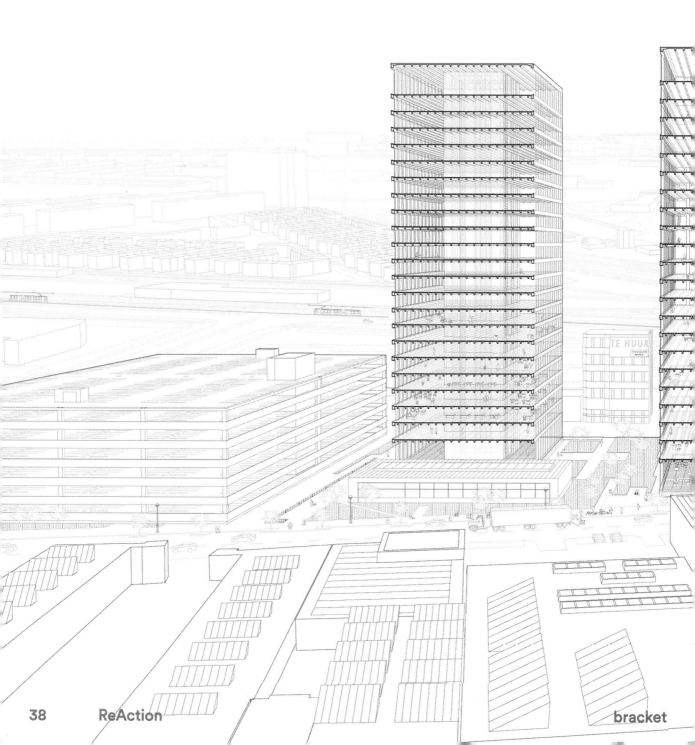

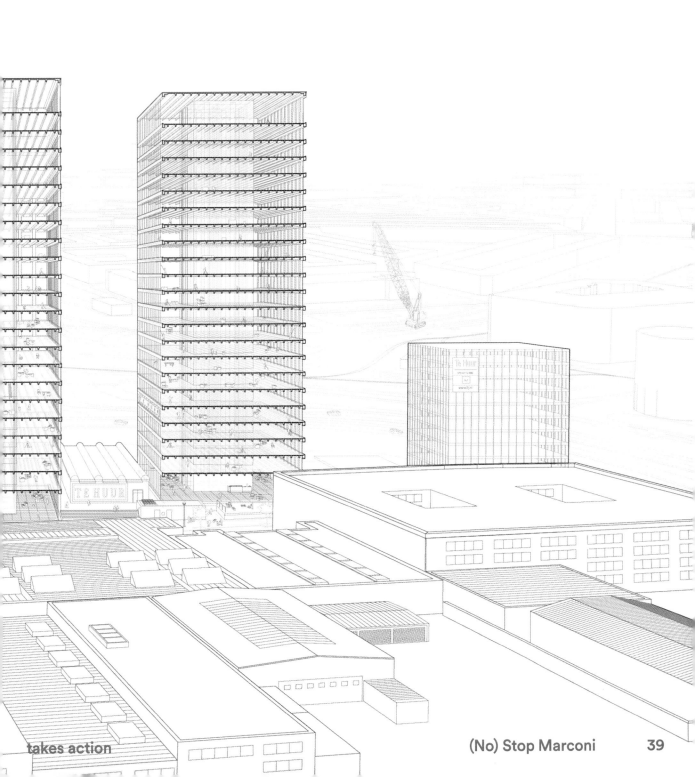

Folded Bridge

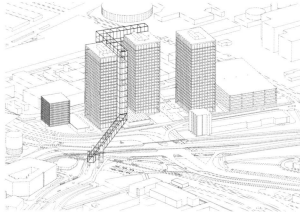

A folded bridge crosses the multiple intersections and lands of infrastructure dividing the towers and port area from the city nearby. As the folded bridge spans across the roofs of the towers, it cuts into the top level of each tower, creating an abrupt adjacency to the typical open office plans.

Externalized Core

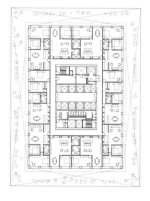

The relationship of the core, slate, and shell are re-imagined yet reminiscent, relegating the corridor to the facade and extending both the public and private realm. The externalized core is transformative for the facade, interior, as well as the landscape, extending into the site with ramps and stairs.

Instant City

Prefabricated low-cost housing units are mass produced off-site, at a precise size matching window openings of the existing Europoint Towers. The units are lifted and positioned via a construction crane. Once installed, the aggregation of units converts the vacant office 'slates' into low-cost housing.

Duplex + Raised Yard

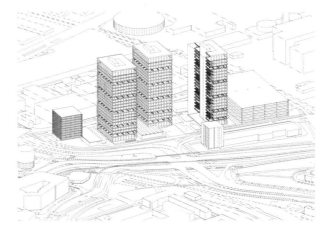

Every fifth floor is transformed into an outdoor lawn shared by the two-level duplex units above and below. Every resident is given a private plot, providing a suburban yard desirable to young professionals, students, and families who want to stay within Rotterdam.

Horizontal Connector

The verticality of the three tallest Europoint towers is disrupted by an abrupt horizontal connecting plane. Several of the mid-rise levels are "blown out" to create new landscapes. The addition of an urban mezzanine is circulation, monument, and occupiable public space.

Post-Squat Core

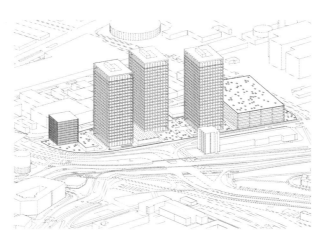

During the conversion from vacant office to affordable housing, excess elevators and other unused spaces in the core are transformed into a communal space. The space is designed for a predefined and curated range of activities but also allows for unexpected conditions beyond the traditional dichotomy of multi-use and prescriptive program.

Densifier + Public Square

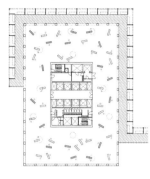

The towers are a band of diverse and intensified urban programs. As the band touches and connects the towers, the hyperactive and condensed commercial and semi-public programs in the wrapping band activates the programs of the tower. A large slab, a new public square, hovers over the impenetrable tangle of roads creating a new forum.

Scuptify

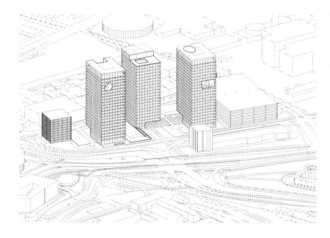

The existing massing and impenetrability of the towers is challenged through a series of subtractions. Each subtraction allows for the addition of public amenities as well as visual signification of public occupation.

Econi

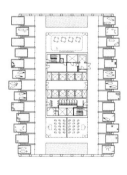

Behind the towers are large container-like post-industrial facilities. Subject to a related masterplan, the Marconi towers are converted to a space for eco-tech programs. Each floor is redistributed into zones for education, research, and consumption of the "green."

spaces could be the unintended yet effective grounds for the new city—where the renewed legibility of the public can gather within the generic structure of the towers, the spatial currency of the market. Neatly stacked in the form of a dense urban vacuum, each new floor, or "slate," is an underexplored tabula rasa of our time, which remembers and challenges its own origin and provokes the possibilities of newly defined productivities of the city and its space. Having become irrelevant to its own creator, the market, the liberated "slates" may be the sites for reinvigorated collectivity.

Nine Schemes

Engaging the extraordinary history of enduring speculation and the famously uncertain futures of the Europoint Towers, *(No) Stop Marconi* questions the readily accepted processes and mechanisms in the making and transformation of cities. Demonstrating dynamic programmatic possibilities of the existing space beyond rigid preconceptions, the proposals instigate the typological identification of the vertical voids and their networks as sites for a new civic realm. These suggest a more productive definition of development and improvement in the context of contemporary cities. Exploring the endless programmatic potentials in the vacant tower's density and verticality, the project articulates nine proposals of the "new" Marconi that examine prototypes for the new slates, reshaping the dense yet distributed urban vacuum. For example, among the nine schemes, *the duplex, folded bridge*, and *horizontal connector* proposals explore the possibilities of new spaces for inhabitation, exchange, and interaction, respectively. In *the duplex*, every fifth floor of the towers is transformed into an outdoor lawn shared by the two-level duplex units above and below. The existing windows are removed and replaced with a transparent guardrail. Every resident is given a private plot, a fenced yard within a shared outdoor space, which is integrated with the circulation of the existing towers. The *folded bridge* crosses multiple intersections and lanes of infrastructure that divide the towers and old port area from the transportation hubs and the city nearby. The bridge begins as a pedestrian walkway, providing a public route to the towers, and then ascends and terminates into an observation deck, visitor center, cafe, and market. The *horizontal connector* uses a plane between the mid-rise levels of the separated towers to create new landscapes, in addition to an urban mezzanine that is both circulation and a monumental occupiable public space.

If deployed throughout the empty towers in the city, the strategies laid out in *(No) Stop Marconi* could afford the intensified nodes of the public realm with the forms and framework of participation. This transforms the seeming predicament of decline and disuse into a civic opportunity—the re-making of the city from the excesses of the market. By highlighting the possibilities of the new collectivity latent in the existing city, the project confronts the conventional spatial practice and

Exploring the endless programmatic and architectural potentials of vacant towers, the multiple proposals of the "new" Marconi artic-ulate the multitudinous scenarios of renewed collectivity afforded by the novel sites of the "new" slates.

urban policies that tend to value architecture and the city as static artifacts or mere commodity. The circumstances explored in *(No) Stop Marconi*, although rooted in local politics and the post-bubble economy, also acknowledge that large shifts and dramatically changing conditions often create a mismatch between speculative development and actual needs. Within this mismatch, inventive spatial practice can create possibilities for new appropriations.

Nahyun Hwang is a partner at N H D M and teaches at Columbia University's Graduate School of Architecture, Planning, and Preservation. N H D M is a New York-based design and research collaborative, founded in 2010.

David Eugin Moon is a partner at N H D M and teaches at Cornell University Architecture Art and Planning. N H D M is a New York-based design and research collaborative, founded in 2010.

Notes
1   R.L Bak and NVM Data & Research, "State of Affairs Netherlands Office Market 2011," *NVM Business*, (March 2015), https://www.nvm.nl/~/media/NVMWebsite/Downloads/English/Market/State of Affairs Netherlands Office Market 2014.pdf.

OH BABY LET'S GET POLITICAL! A RANT

Foreign Architects Switzerland (FAS)

On Architectural Activism

Within the current reframing of neo-liberalism, architects have witnessed the fading importance of their role—sidelined by technology, normative construction methods, or informal construction. While usually prompt to vocally express grievances, it seems surprising that so few architects have provided proactive answers to the crisis of the profession.[1] Activism, as a form of intentional effort that brings about innovation and social or political change through architectural and urban actions, appears to be a path less followed by those of us stuck in the putrid cesspit of daily commercial work. We contend that activism should be a mode of operation to be reactivated by contemporary architects.

Michel de Certeau's distinction between strategies and tactics illuminates two possible choices that are related to forms of activism. To be part of a strategy, is to be in a place where one can "capitalize on its advantages, prepare its expansions, and secure independence with respect to circumstances."[2] To rely on tactics involves the means "in which the weak are seeking to turn the tables on the strong."[3] For designers and planners, activism typically occurs in two forms based on de Certeau's reading. It is either a political or social action taken as a reaction to direct crisis with support of an administrative body (state, governments, municipalities, etc.) and produces change as part of a strategy. Alternatively, it entails being part of the crisis

and acting tactically with collective groups, civil societies, and individuals. The latter is a path that few planners and design professionals have chosen.

A Brief Overview of Activism

There are historical examples in the former Soviet Union of architectural practices that merged with political activism. Dissident architects were operating both publicly (the Czech architects of the SIAL group) or in secrecy (Imre Makovec in Hungary, Maks Velo in Albania).[4] Other inspiring cases of architecture and urban activism, such as the political commentary of Ant Farm and Superstudio embedded in the 1960s and 1970s architecture counterculture, while impacting the genealogy of activism have become invalid for our current time.[5] Still, these practices, even if primarily relying on architectural representations tools (drawing, collages, etc.) and utopias as projects, also undertook more classical forms of dissent in their time—communal living, sit-ins, art works, happenings—that endure as powerful acts.

Departing from the agitprop political work of the 1970s and examining current practices, few can be identified with audacious forms of architectural and urban activism, and even fewer can claim the righteousness that Keller Easterling insists activism demands.[6] Skimming through the literature that indexes recent architectural and design activism, one comes across the

Cover of FAS, Issue 01, which acted against the minaret ban.

projects listed by Bryan Bell and Katie Wakeford in *Expanding Architecture: Design as Activism*, which classify the design and implementation processes of urban projects of social interest and public impact, wherein design professionals are working alongside the community.[7] Similarly, albeit expanded to non-architect and design practices, the database established by Nishat Awan, Tatjana Schneider, and Jeremy Till in *Spatial Agency: Other ways of doing architecture* compiles several projects where design undertakes social and public action towards change.[8] However, if the authors call for more ethics in design, they also consider architecture not to be the prerogative of architects. Furthermore, they advocate for less architecture and more social agency, a position that undermines the very activity of the discipline. This is not far from Regina Bittner and Andres Lepik's position in *Moderators of Change* as they evaluate a few recent examples of design strategies as social activism, while calling for a wider form of architectural commitment that goes beyond the sole act of building.[9] Conversely, in the Verb series titled "Crisis," architecture and design are forces of change predominantly motivated by architects and planner themselves, operating strategically within the discipline.[10] If spatial justice, or social, political, and theoretical engagements appear as the main motivations of the listed schemes, one should note the temporary aspect of resistance and dissidence to established

forms of practice. While some practitioners have expressed a sustained commitment to activism and social engagement such as Lucien Knoll, Patrick Bouchain, Atelier d'Architecture Autogérée, Teddy Cruz, and OH.A, among others, there exists a series of practices that have gained recognition and moved away from their activism roots, as in the case of Coop Himmelb(l)au, Urban Think Tank, Didier Faustino, and Raumlabor, and Vastu-Shilpa consultants. This shift away from activism exposes the difficulty of maintaining a sustained engagement to activism in the profession.

To convey the very message that incites architects towards architectural activism is challenging as the modes of action are dictated by the very conditions one fights against. In *"L'insurrection qui vient"* (The coming insurrection), a small anonymous book calling for self-organisation and revolution, the first task is to find oneself and what drives one's rebellion, and then to find others, driven by the same sentiment.[11] In an online note from 2009 entitled "Architecture and Resistance," Lebbeus Woods shares a similar sentiment "To say that you are resisting something means that you have to spend a lot of time and energy saying what that something is, in order for your resistance to make sense."[12] Accordingly, we recognize that this brief overview of tested forms of activism is of limited value for the architect confronted with, or embedded within, unacceptable political or social situations.

Cover of FAS, Issue 03, which acted through love.

Cover of FAS, Issue 04, which called for a union of architects.

The Political Architect

Foreign Architects Switzerland (FAS) is a collective of Swiss-based architects, founded through collective reaction to the general political apathy and neutrality of the profession within Switzerland, on the occasion of the minaret ban in 2009. We align ourselves with Jean Nouvel's statement, the "Architect's responsibilities begin with their silence and their disengagement."[13] Originating by taking up arms in protest against the restriction of the constructed environment, as well as against the xenophobic sign this vote represented, the collective developed into objecting the common indifference of architects and planners towards appalling political situations, real-estate pressures, and the general trend of conservatism. Against this building constraint ("The building of minarets is forbidden"), we are attempting to fight over a general disillusionment throughout the local architecture community over its ability—or interest—to be agents of change. Without support from existing professional organizations (The Swiss Society of Engineers and Architects, The Federation of Swiss Architects, etc.), we needed to craft the tools of action. Using the very tools of architecture and hoping for the ego of architects to play along, a counter-competition was launched to design a mosque in a prominent location in Zurich. Hoping to raise awareness among the profession, the call addressed many topics that agitated FAS, as politically aware architects and urbanists. The relevance of such activism has only been reconfirmed by the territorial and spatial implications of the recent referendum in February 2014 that is restricting immigration by re-establishing quotas. Initiated by extreme-right parties of Switzerland, this vote was pushed through with arguments related to "personal space" and "density-stress." Here again, exists a moment for architects to resist, rebel, and take action.[14] Woods's checklist for resistance states: "Resist the idea that architecture can save the world" but also "Resist the idea that architecture is an investment" and "Resist all claims on your autonomy."[15] Woods highlights some of the paradoxes architects are confronted with, if we are to accept responsibility in addressing contemporary political problems. FAS considers itself the opposite of the notorious letter of Patrick Schumacher[16] on the duty of political non-interference. Instead, we feel that architects should mobilize and dissent whenever necessary. We believe that architects are responsible for the form of the city—that it is up to us to organize social relationships—and that architects are capable of constructive, creative, and engaged dialogue, if we dare to speak up.

Foreign Architects Switzerland (FAS) is a collective of Swiss-based architects founded in reaction to the political apathy and neutrality of the profession on the occasion of the minaret ban, voted in 2009. FAS is also a publication dedicated to filling the gaps of theoretical and political dialogue in the Swiss architectural community.

Notes

1 Design blogs and architectural magazines are overflowing with endless acrimonious opinion pages, readers comments, etc. (Dezeen, Archdaily, Frame, designboom, etc.)
2 Michel de Certeau. *The Practice of Every Day Life*, (California: University of California Press, 1984).
3 Ibid.
4 Ines Weizman (ed.), *Ahra Annual International Conference*, (London: London Metropolitan University, 2012).
5 Felicity D. Scott, *Architecture or Techno-Utopia : Politics after Modernism* (Cambridge, MA: MIT Press, 2007)
6 Keller Easterling, "Lecture: Logistical Urbanism. Recent Urban Research," in *Urban Mutations on the Edge*, ed. Deane Simpson, Architecture Department (Chair of Architecture and Design, Prof. Dr. Marc M. Angélil: Swiss Institute of Technology, Zurich, 2008).
7 Bryan Bell and Katie Wakeford, *Expanding Architecture: Design as Activism* (New York: Metropolis Books, 2008).
8 Nishat Awan, Tatjana Schneider, and Jeremy Till, *Spatial Agency: Other Ways of Doing Architecture* (New York: Routledge, 2011).
9 Regina Bittner and Andres Lepik, *Moderators of Change : Architektur, Die Hilft* (Ostfildern: Hatje Cantz, 2011).
10 Mario Ballesteros, Verb Crisis (Barcelona; New York: Actar, 2008).
11 J. De Bloois, "Comitè Invisible: L'insurrection Qui Vient, Paris: La Fabrique, 2007," *Hist. Mater. Historical Materialism* 22, no. 1 (2014).
12 Lebbeus Woods, *Architecture and Resistance: Resistance Checklist*, https://lebbeuswoods.wordpress.com/2009/05/09/architecture-and-resistance/, May 9, 2009.
13 Jean Nouvel and others, *L'urgence Permanente- the Permanent Emergency* (Marseille: Galerie Navarra, 2001).
14 David Harvey, *Rebel Cities: From the Right to the City to the Urban Revolution* (New York: Verso, 2012).
15 Lebbeus Woods, *Architecture and Resistance: Resistance Checklist*, (May 9, 2009), https://lebbeuswoods.wordpress.com/2009/05/09/architecture-and-resistance/,
16 "I also doubt that architecture could be a site of radical political activism. I believe that architecture is a sui generis discipline (discourse and practice) with its own, unique societal responsibility and competency. As such it should be sharply demarcated against other competencies like art, science/engineering and politics" Patrick Schumacher, "Schumacher Slams British Architectural Education," *Architectural Review* (January 31, 2012), http://www.architectural-review.com/view/overview/ar-exclusive-schumacher-slams-british-architectural-education/8625659.article.

COU
N
TER

CounterAction offers unique and alternative sites for action at various scales. These include playful surfaces, hidden kitchens, refugee camps, and the new demands of the civic square. How can the overlooked sites of appearance in our contemporary commons promote alternative forms of action?

ACTI
ON

REFLECTIONS ON ACTION

Belinda Tato and Jose Luis Vallejo

In the context of the current digital revolution, contemporary sociopolitical dynamics demand reflection on the way architects teach, learn, and design. Spaces and instruments for teaching, places and distance of communication, as well as methods and hierarchies have all been brought into question. Beyond learning, there is an ongoing paradigmatic shift that involves almost every aspect of culture and society. The way society addresses and manages processes, products, and knowledge is evolving —aided by new technological possibilities and critical meta-reflections. It spans from competition to collaboration and cooperation; from centralization to peer-to-peer; from pyramidal structures to grassroots, horizontal networks; from professional secrecy to transparency; from closed research-and-development to crowdsourcing; from intellectual property restrictions to copyleft and open-source initiatives; from closed designs or services to open roadmaps that embrace perpetual beta testing.

Regardless of this complex shift in contemporary culture, design education too often focuses on the end result. It proceeds as if disconnected from both other disciplines and the real world, and disinterested in the constraints and challenges that exist beyond the classroom. Both of these could, in fact, enrich and inform the project to produce more meaningful results. As educators, we continuously strive to deploy the most appropriate teaching methods, bringing the tools to respond to the fast-paced and ever-changing rhythm of society into the classroom.

The networked urbanism approach adopts a framework of experiential education, which promotes learning through direct action on the ground, as well as reflection in a continuous feedback loop. With this approach, designers are actively posing questions, assuming responsibilities, exerting curiosities, as well as investigating, experimenting, and constructing meaning. From this, there is the potential to become more intellectually, emotionally, and socially engaged in the design process. This involvement can produce a learning process that is authentic and real. However, working in practice often leads to outcomes that cannot be predicted or controlled, meaning designers have to take risks during the process, which may lead to frustrations or uncertainty. In this design approach, network building, communication, and dialogue become essential elements.

We have, therefore, developed a networked urbanism toolbox, which is a set of guidelines that can be applied throughout the design process. It is meant to assist and guide designers in developing the skills necessary for this new reality and for the expanded role that will be expected of them. A networked urbanism design-thinking methodology reflects on the actions central to the search for solutions and their implementation beyond the generation of ideas.

Cuenca Red, Ecosistema Urbano, Cuenca, Ecuador (2015). Improvement and reactivation of public spaces in Cuenca's Historical Centre, showing the pilot project Febres Cordero School.

1. EXPLORE:

Reality offers an inspiring environment to identify design possibilities. Ordinary life processes provide an incredibly rich and fertile field for experimentation, while at the same time offering the potential to make a genuine difference in society. Designers can, and should, reach toward utopian ideals even with one foot firmly on the ground.

2. RESEARCH:

Become an expert on the topic. The research process is open-ended. It is natural for the line of inquiry to evolve, taking on a life of its own and leading in unforeseen directions.

3. NETWORK:

Create a network—from citizens to experts; explore connections at both the official and grassroots level. Today's complex reality requires not just a multidisciplinary approach, but also a transdisciplinary one, and the definition of new instruments, models, and protocols that occur when professions do not work separately. In the early stages of a project, designers are encouraged to establish relationships with a variety of experts and stakeholders. They are asked to build networks of advisors and supporters from academia, the public and private sectors, and potential community members. The progress of a project depends on their ability to elicit the support and cooperation of people who often have different agendas. Subsequently, an internally-generated idea becomes a collaborative effort, which instrumentalizes its development.

4. SHARE:

Confront and experience ideas outside your own sphere; feedback is a treasure. It is extremely important to listen and engage with people in dialogue throughout the creative process. Incorporating feedback vastly enriches how to analyze an issue, which by extension, ensures that solutions are more relevant and viable.

5. BE OPEN:

Start with a detailed plan, but be prepared to revise it in response to new developments. There is an increasing public awareness of the implications of design, allowing designers to acquire new inputs, incorporate feedback mid-process, and make adjustments before the creative process is complete. Designers should be flexible in their approach to a challenge and how they arrive at solutions. The process is often not a linear path, but a dendritic one that follows an unpredictable course. It is valuable for a designer's development to become comfortable with open-endedness and uncertainty.

Reaching out and absorbing reality introduces serendipity into the process, which can increase the possibilities for meaningful connections.

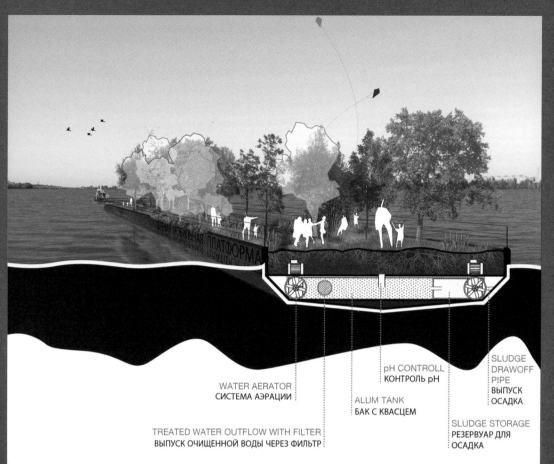

Voronezh Sea
revitalization,
Ecosistema Urbano,
Voronezh, Russia
(2014). Ecological
reconfiguration
and water-quality
improvement of
the reservoir.

->
Plan CHA, Ecosistema
Urbano, Asunción,
Paraguay (2014).
Masterplan of the
historic downtown of
Asunción discussed
during a participatory
meeting with citizens.

Dreamhamar, Ecosistema
Urbano, Hamar, Norway
(2011). Public event
during the participatory
process for collectively
reimagining the
Stortorget Square.

pH CONTROLL
КОНТРОЛЬ pH

SLUDGE
DRAWOFF
PIPE
ВЫПУСК
ОСАДКА

WATER AERATOR
СИСТЕМА АЭРАЦИИ

ALUM TANK
БАК С КВАСЦЕМ

SLUDGE STORAGE
РЕЗЕРВУАР ДЛЯ
ОСАДКА

TREATED WATER OUTFLOW WITH FILTER
ВЫПУСК ОЧИЩЕННОЙ ВОДЫ ЧЕРЕЗ ФИЛЬТР

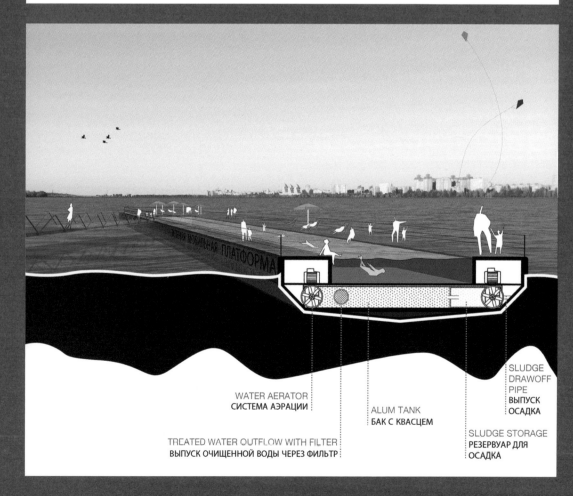

SLUDGE
DRAWOFF
PIPE
ВЫПУСК
ОСАДКА

WATER AERATOR
СИСТЕМА АЭРАЦИИ

ALUM TANK
БАК С КВАСЦЕМ

SLUDGE STORAGE
РЕЗЕРВУАР ДЛЯ
ОСАДКА

TREATED WATER OUTFLOW WITH FILTER
ВЫПУСК ОЧИЩЕННОЙ ВОДЫ ЧЕРЕЗ ФИЛЬТР

Reflections on Action

 **UBICACIONES**

MENSAJES

PALABRAS CLAVE

IMÁGENES

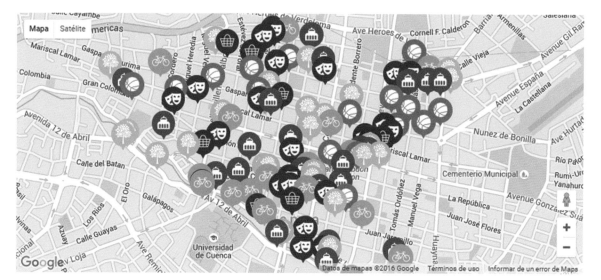

 REINICIAR   ACTIVIDAD   CULTURA   ECONOMÍA   M. NATURAL   MOVILIDAD   PATRIMONIO

6. THINK BIG:

Design a strategic overall vision by focusing on a small-scale design that has potential at a larger scale. The best way to address a major societal challenge is to begin with a manageable pilot project, while still envisioning a larger strategy. Big changes often happen incrementally.

7. START SMALL:

Any approach can be the starting point; it will grow as the project develops. Designers are encouraged to begin the process as quickly as possible without concern that there is only one way. The important thing is not where to start, but simply to start. In keeping with the flexibility inherent in networked design, it is natural for things to change as the process unfolds, so there really is no single, correct way to begin.

8. ACT NOW:

Prototype and implement a small but significant part of the design at actual scale. It is important to put initiatives in motion. Action should come first, followed by reflection, in an ongoing feedback loop. Prototyping an aspect of the design is a critical step so that eventually it can be scaled up. The horizon is often blurry, but can only be reached by moving toward it.

9. COMMUNICATE:

Take your initiative to a broader audience. By using today's digital technologies and the networks that they have created, designers are able to extend the reach and impact of their proposals. In addition, they need to find the most powerful and appropriate way to spread the word about their initiative. At this point, unexpected and exciting connections usually develop that propel the project much farther. Acquiring and applying skills in outreach and social networking are not typical aspects of a design school education, but are increasingly relevant for designers today.

10. MOVE BEYOND:

How can ideas be developed and pushed forward? As designers see their proposals finding traction in the real world, they may be motivated to carry them forward. They need to have the confidence to know that they can implement their ideas, and a willingness to push past their own preconceived limitations.

Local_in, Ecosistema Urbano (2010). Online mapping tool, mobile version for Distrito Central and screenshot of Cuenca Red version.

Centro Histórico
Abierto, Participatory
Process for the
transformation of
Distrito Central, Wall
of Dreams, Installation
at MIN Museum,
Ecosistema Urbano,
Distrito Central,
Honduras.

The goal of a networked urbanism approach
is to encourage designers to contribute
their knowledge and creativity with an open
mind to the spaces they live in and the
communities they are a part of. The aim is also
to empower them to be creative problem
solvers, builders of effective networks, and
therefore, builders of smarter urban communities.
Simultaneously and throughout the process,
designers naturally grow as entrepreneurs.
The term "entreprene-urbanist" might be a way
to characterize designers who are innovating
in the urban context and developing ideas that
immediately improve and impact urban life.

Let's get into action!

Belinda Tato is a founding director at the Madrid-based
ecosistema urbano. She currently teaches in the core program
at Harvard University Graduate School of Design.

Jose Luis Vallejo is a founding director at the Madrid-based
ecosistema urbano. He currently teaches at Columbia University
Graduate School of Architecture, Planning and Preservation.

THE PRIVATE SPACE OF COLLECTIVE RESISTANCE

Lindsay Harkema

Public action originates in private space—a whispered fury, a persistent desire, an idea shared behind closed doors, a rebellious act committed with few, or perhaps no, witnesses. Collective action then takes a public stage—Hannah Arendt would call this a political act[1]—a demonstration, a movement, a revolution. The root of these acts are in the individual ideas and hidden social exchanges which preceded them. Without its private roots, there is no public action.

An act of protest is a rejection of a perceived and unwanted future. Throughout history, forms of protest have been significant agents of social and political change—from underground countercultural movements, to the most public, and publicized, mass demonstrations. The most significant of these movements affect societal progress and leave physical traces on the city. For instance, centuries after its operation, one can still follow the secret route of safe houses and passages that made up the Underground Railroad in the prerevolutionary American South. Similarly, Christiania, the makeshift anarchist enclave on the site of former army barracks in Copenhagen, Denmark has functioned as a self-governed commune for decades.

What is a space of protest? Our first thought is typically of a mass demonstration in a public square such as Tiananmen, Tahrir, Independence, Bolotnaya. Our impulse is to equate the power of an action with the mass of its demonstration, or its influence with its publicness. We tend to think of the highly broadcasted image of surging crowds rallying against a political entity—shouting, insults, rage, tear gas, blood. What is less obvious is the importance of a deeper, private critique, shared through rational conversation and mutual hope. This hidden countercultural undercurrent of opposition has a broader, and in certain cases, more significant impact on society and its progress than the public outburst. Private forms of protest inhabit the backstage of our physical environment and shapes new ideas about how it should be formed.

Russia's modern history of protest is a testament to underground opposition—from the secret societies, which fostered opposition to the Tsar, to dissident kitchen conversations in the Soviet Union, to underground art and literary movements that occupied private residences in avoidance of state censorship. The Russian Avant-Garde was born at the height of the nation's revolutionary fervor, when a future communal utopia seemed attainable if only society could transform quickly enough. Lenin and the Bolshevik Army had overthrown the Tsarist regime, paving the way for a new communist government in the name of the people. Through radical experimentation, artists, poets, and architects strived to foresee and realize the formal language of this utopia. As the newly established Soviet state was rethinking the future of society, the Avant-Garde was reinventing the everyday. By transforming daily life, society would also transform from individuals

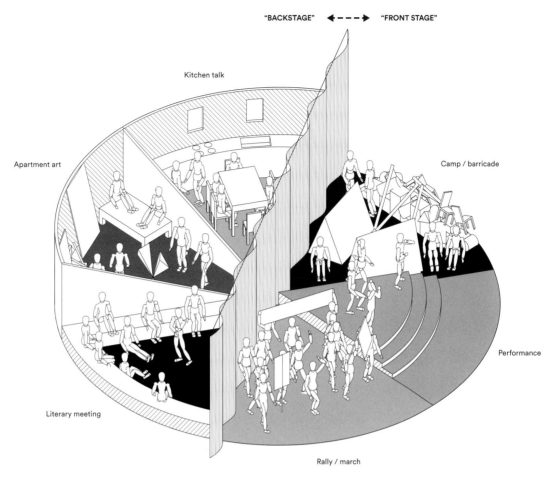

"BACKSTAGE" ◀ - - - ▶ "FRONT STAGE"

Kitchen talk

Apartment art

Camp / barricade

Performance

Literary meeting

Rally / march

into communal, social beings. These ideas took the form of the bold geometries and novel typologies of Constructivist architecture during the 1920s and 1930s. Government funded building projects prioritized social institutions and spaces of production, minimizing private life in favor of communal activity. The majority were residential, factory, and community buildings: new ideas and new spaces for the new life of the new man.[2]

Russia's tumultuous social history reveals a difficult relationship with the past and future. Throughout the nineteenth and twentieth centuries, the ambition of the nation alternated between an idealization of the future and of the past. Often the perspective of the government has not aligned with the views of citizens, leading at times to significant political turmoil, and inspiring a creative oppositional social discourse. Ideologically charged groups and movements produced some of the most significant innovations in art, architecture, literature, and science, of the twentieth century. Further, counter-cultural motivations were an incredible stimulus and inspiration for critical innovation that shaped the nation's social, cultural, and physical heritage.

Early nineteenth century ideas of revolution, which ultimately led to the October Revolution of 1917, were the product of a deep, private rebellion that spread underground throughout working class communities. Oppositional ideas, disseminated through written texts, called

for protests against the widespread oppression under the Tsar. The government's attempt to limit this activity by imposing strict censorship laws only strengthened its underground existence. Secret assemblies met in private residences and universities, operated cells within factories, and even set up printing presses in secluded locations far from the city.[3] They published essays, circulated pamphlets and newsletters, and composed manifestos, which strengthened their collective opposition and eventually gained enough strength to emerge in public. Through the underground circulation of ideas, these individual acts aggregated into a collective movement. When a small group of revolutionaries met to write a statement or print a rebel newspaper, they acted in representation of a larger dispersed population with shared goals. Somewhere in another secret place, there were others doing the same things. And sometime in the future, it would become a larger public action.

The Moscow uprising of 1905 erupted somewhat spontaneously out of this common spirit of protest that had been flourishing in the underground. A product of shared private sentiment, it emerged organically, "the initiative came from below—from the workers themselves."[4] Organized in factories, it exploded into a public revolt in the Presnya district of Moscow, where rebels clashed with authorities for days and constructed barricades in the streets. Up until its outburst, the growing insurgence had occupied

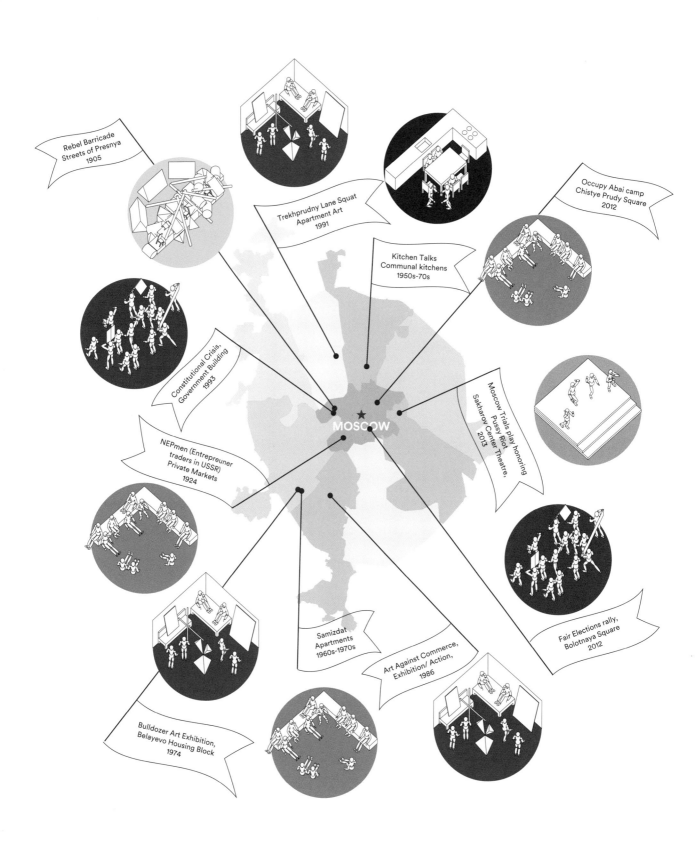

Rebel Barricade
Streets of Presnya
1905

Trekhprudny Lane Squat
Apartment Art
1991

Occupy Abai camp
Chistye Prudy Square
2012

Kitchen Talks
Communal kitchens
1950s-70s

Constitutional Crisis,
Government Building
1993

Moscow Trials play honoring
Pussy Riot,
Sakharov Center Theatre,
2013

NEPmen (Entrepreuner
traders in USSR)
Private Markets
1924

MOSCOW

Samizdat
Apartments
1960s-1970s

Art Against Commerce,
Exhibition/ Action,
1986

Fair Elections rally,
Bolotnaya Square
2012

Bulldozer Art Exhibition,
Belayevo Housing Block
1974

almost exclusively private spaces in avoidance of the Tsar's surveillance of the public realm. In the following years, many factions continued to assemble in opposition to the imperial regime, leading up to the 1917 October Revolution and the establishment of a socialist state later known as the Soviet Union. Underground movements like these secret societies represented early forms of counterculture—the rejection of mainstream societal norms. From artistic movements to political factions, countercultural communities would continue to be platforms for social experimentation and critique throughout the following century.

After the revolution, an extensive propaganda initiative was instituted by the new Soviet state. From political ideology to cultural experimentation, the ambition was to display communal life as the enlightened future utopia. Born from earlier countercultural artistic movements, such as Futurism and Dadaism, the Russian Avant-Garde emerged out of the ideological outburst of the early twentieth century, at the moment when the aggressive pursuit of the future was fully being embraced by the state. In the new Soviet republic, a young generation of designers was commissioned to design the graphic propaganda, called *agitprop*, and build structures that would demonstrate the emancipation of the workers' state. They embraced the industrial language of modernism, demonstrating technological advancement through angular, cantilevered forms, exposed structural joints, and the contrast of heavy, solid walls with transparent, glass volumes. Constructivism encompassed art and architecture, realized and unbuilt—from the abstract geometries of Kazimir Malevich's paintings to Vladimir Tatlin's spiraling design for a Monument to the Third International to the cylindrical glass stairwell of Ilya Golosov's Zuev Workers' Club. Each was conceived with a social agenda as the physical embodiment of progress. Throughout the 1920s and 1930s, architecture became the means of transformation towards a future collectivized society.

These ambitions were reflected in new building typologies that accommodated and facilitated socialist life. The state distributed building commissions to young, innovative architects who had previously been marginalized in the pre-revolutionary academia. In 1920, the Vkhutemas school was established in Moscow as the state art and technical university under an official decree for excellent technical training and innovation. Charged with the spirit of the revolution, a new generation of designers imagined architecture as a means to create the new socialist life, as stated:

> They took every aspect of traditional architecture and tried to change it. For example, historical architecture until the beginning of the 20th century was according to gravity, and it showed this sense of gravity. Avant-Garde architects experimented with the ideas of architecture against gravitation.[5]

Iakov Chernikhov's bold graphic drawing, entitled *Architectural Fantasy*, depicts a hammer and cycle-shaped building that appears to be in motion, departing from the ground and rising upward by structural innovation. For the Constructivists, architectural design was a means of spatial imagination and invention for the redesign of society.

New building typologies emerged as spaces for the daily life of the future society. Thought of as social activators, these buildings for the everyday were designed around an idealized collective life, enabled by the building itself. Communal houses were intended to minimize private life and promote collective domestic life, with minimal apartment spaces and shared service facilities. Ivan Nikolaev's block-like massing of the Communal House of the Textile Institute distributed the daily activities of residents in a sequence from studying, exercising, and socializing, to sanitizing and sleeping. The sleeping quarters, a disproportionately long corridor of tiny cabins, was only accessed through the sanitary zone, thereby keeping residents in the shared social spaces for the entirety of their waking hours.

Workers' clubs were built as places for social interaction and cultural production after working hours, as stated by El Lissitzky, "The important thing about a club is that the mass of the members must be directly involved. They themselves must find in it the maximum self expression… The ultimate role of the club is to liberate men from the oppression of the State."[6] Konstantin Melnikov's Rusakov Workers' Club, with an array of three floating auditorium volumes protruding from its façade, was designed to accommodate large cultural and political performances. Each auditorium space could be closed off and used for simultaneous smaller gatherings, all funneling attendees out through the building's central communal lobby. Citizens were intended to visit these social clubs for physical, cultural, and mental exercise, as part of the constant pursuit of personal improvement.

Private space was diminished as shared social facilities prevailed—the spatial pursuit of a more utopian communal society. In the 1920s and 1930s, Moscow was a laboratory of Constructivist architectural experimentation. Hundreds of buildings were designed and built to be social condensers for the betterment of the community. This avant-garde architectural boom was short-lived, however, as it came to an end almost as abruptly as it began. Today, many of the surviving buildings of this era stand as shells of a former utopia; several are dilapidated, caught in a web of legal battles and ownership disputes, while others are facing demolition.

The end of Constructivism was signaled in 1932 by the Palace of the Soviets design competition for the prominent riverbank site in central Moscow, where the reconstructed Cathedral of Christ the Savior stands today. The competition marked a shift in the architectural interests of the State. Ambitious avant-garde proposals were rejected in preference of monumental, neoclassical designs representing power and stability. From this point on, Soviet architecture was transformed from the innovative community-scale buildings of the Constructivist era into a demonstration of power and excess: the decadence of the present rather than the pursuit of the future, a representation of deeper ideological shifts. The chosen design for the Palace, selected by a jury led by Joseph Stalin, was a massive neoclassical tower culminating in a giant statue of Lenin. The decision enraged members of the avant-garde around the world. Sigfried Gideon, secretary general of the *Congrès International d'Architecture Moderne* (CIAM), declared the decision "a direct insult to the spirit of Revolution ...a tragic betrayal."[7] After this moment, Moscow's visionary Constructivist buildings faded into the background, mirroring the decay of the avant-garde's pursuit of communal progress.

In his book, *Architecture in the Age of Stalin*, Vladimir Paperny describes the period of the avant-garde as "Culture One" and the era of the Soviet Empire as "Culture Two": "Culture One and Culture Two exist in opposition: One reaches for the future and [...] the other transforms the future into eternity while turning its gaze back on the past." The avant-garde acted in pursuit of the future while the Empire slowed progress to stagnation, "the future postponed indefinitely."[8] This was reflected in the shift in architectural design from the human scale of the Constructivist movement based on modernism and experimentation to the massive neoclassical tradition of the Soviet Imperial Style.

In the early 1930s, the Central Committee of the Communist Party declared the elimination of all artistic and literary groups, which were to be replaced by official state organizations.[9] From this point on, art, architecture, literature, music, and theatre had to conform to official standards, which restricted progressive innovation. The revolutionary experimentation and radicalism of the early Soviet era was replaced by an ideology of power and control; the state aesthetic shifted from the spirited avant-garde to monumental, neoclassical, Soviet Realism. By imposing sweeping restrictions against intellectualism, innovation, and imagination, the state rejected the future it had been building since the Revolution, turning backwards to past ideas and historical symbols of control. The Soviet Union would gain world power not by ingenuity but by stability and productive dominance—forming an invincible machine.

The Soviet regime also rejected certain aspects of Russia's unique history. The state anti-religious campaign prohibited religious activity, tore down religious buildings, and destroyed important artifacts. Traditions, mythologies, and folklores of the past were lost as the state enacted a widespread rewriting of history. The built environment was a visible victim to this; more than seven thousand historical buildings were demolished between 1917 and 1953.[10] In 1954, the General Secretary of the Communist Party of the Soviet Union, Nikita Khrushchev, gave a speech, which once again redefined the architectural agenda of the nation. Focusing on building up rather than tearing down, he called for more efficient construction methods, industrial production, and the "elimination of superfluity" in building design.[11] With this statement, Khrushchev deployed a state building standard that left no room for innovation or experimentation. Buildings would be produced as systematically as possible, with minimal new design. From this point on, Russian cities constructed uniform housing blocks in the singular language of massive concrete slab buildings located at the urban periphery. Now fully deactivated and separated from social life, the architecture of the everyday fell silent in monotonous succession.

The state-mandated public demonstrations, which protested conditions of the world outside the Soviet Union, were an integral part of maintaining the state ideology during the Soviet era. After the revolution, Communist ideology was forcefully spread by State propaganda. The public realm became a controlled platform for demonstrations of state loyalty. May 1, or the Day of International Solidarity of the Working Class, was celebrated with compulsory parades glorifying the Soviet Union. Flags and banners displayed provocative text and imagery to inspire enthusiasm and a collectivized spirit.

Public space, the space of state manipulation and control, was active with demonstrations of criticism towards the outside—the other that was not the Soviet Union. Therefore, any disfavor of the state was a risk to express in public. Amid strong state propaganda and increasing restrictions against artistic experimentation, forms of private opposition and counterculture emerged underground. Shared residential spaces, the original spaces of socialist life, became hotbeds of political discussion and critique. Underground art communities avoided State censorship by exhibiting their work in apartments and even

in nature, outside the surveillance of the city. As free expression was made obsolete in public, dissent was fostered behind closed doors. As posited by Lynne Viola, "The private sphere was in many cases strengthened as a result of the swelling and oppressive encroachments of the public sphere. The kitchen table became a back stage social space for successive generations of the intelligentsia."[12] Informal discussions in shared residential spaces, or kitchen conversations, were a common outlet for citizens to express their opinions and share their opposition. Like the underground activities of earlier revolutionaries, these private discussions happened amid a collective awareness of shared sentiment. Kitchen conversations were the means of expressing outrage at the government's oppression and affirming communality in their secret opposition.

New artistic forms of dissent thrived behind closed doors. Samizdat, the practice of hand-making and distributing literature that was banned by the State, emerged in rebellion against government censorship in the 1960s. Underground art movements emerged in protest of the state mandate against art forms other than Soviet Realism. A group of conceptual artists began to self-organize exhibitions and events around their work in the private sphere. Moscow Conceptualism, as the movement came to be known, rejected the official doctrine but was not inherently political. Rather, "The Moscow

Conceptualists looked for spaces of exception— it was about installing inside society [...] not to fight against the censorship, but to avoid the space where censorship was a problem."[13] *Collective Actions*, a performance art group, took their work far outside the city, often to the country or woods, as an attempt to fully escape the city and its control. In 1974, artists staged an exhibition of their work on the grounds of the Belyaevo residential district, which was physically bulldozed when discovered by the state authorities.

The countercultures of kitchen conversations, samizdat, and underground art in the Soviet Union were highly significant in that they expressed the dissent that was felt by many but was difficult to be shared or cultivated under the government's extreme control. Avoiding the state-controlled public realm, they inhabited the spaces of communal domestic life that had been originally conceived by the Constructivists as spaces for social progress. Once a state-supported means of architectural experimentation, the shared spaces of communal housing and social clubs became places where alternative ideas could be exchanged in avoidance of the government. These forms of counterculture demonstrated a current of grassroots protest, which reflected not only an oppositional ideology, but also a space of exception for a progressive discourse, despite the harsh political context. Architecture was the enabler of private revolt.

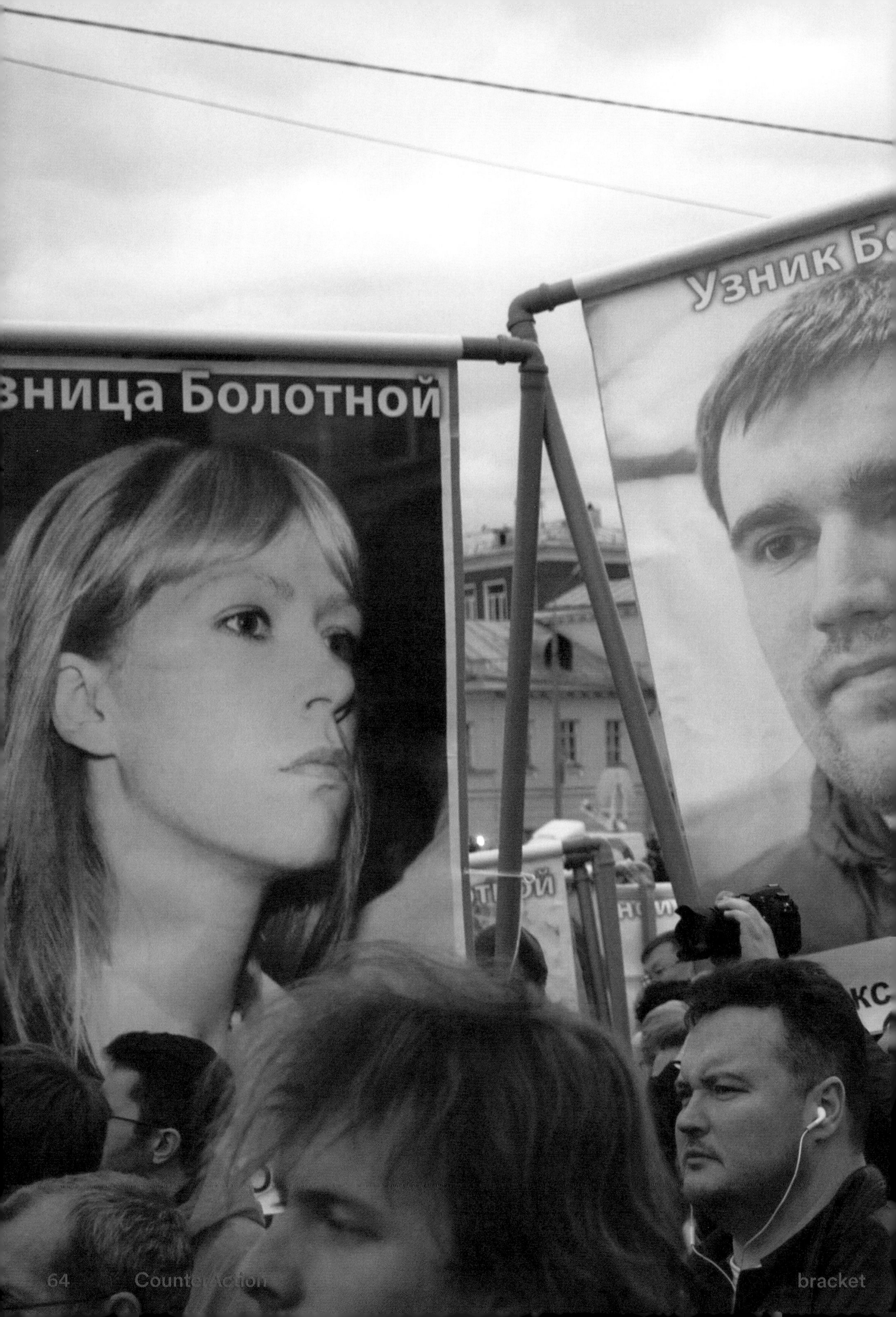
зница Болотной
Узник Бо

Узник Болотной
КОМИТЕТ 6 МАЯ
АСКАРОВ
КОМИТЕТ 6 МАЯ
колай КАВК
Узник

After the Soviet Union's break up in 1991, Moscow's marginalized artistic community, suddenly liberated in public, shifted their opposition towards institutions. Despite their newly granted appearance in the public realm, artists maintained their underground presence with actions such as squatting illegally and continuing to hold exhibitions in private apartments. During this time, the newly elected Mayor Luzhov initiated a period of reconstruction in Moscow. Pre-revolutionary architectural icons that had been destroyed during the Soviet Union were rebuilt in attempt to revive an earlier Russia[14], while the constructivist monuments continued to decay. The city's urban fabric could be read as the physical evidence of a superficial healing of the past, while simultaneously lacking a vision for the future.

In 2012, Moscow witnessed the largest public demonstrations since the end of the Soviet Union, when citizens gathered in public space to protest against the government's manipulation of the presidential election. Despite the impressiveness of these events, the most significant resulting political changes were a series of new restrictions against public expression, signaling a decline in personal freedom. What was and was not allowed in public became increasingly ambiguous. The Pussy Riot incarcerations after their "punk prayer" performance in the Christ the Savior Cathedral in February 2012 and the prosecution of participants in the May 6 anti-government rally in Bolotnaya Square, further revealed the decline of effective public action. Oppositional leaders were again silenced in public and confined to house arrest[15] and a crackdown on independent and non-governmental organizations has led to the exodus of many nonprofit and international agencies in Russia.[16] Presently, citizens are once again less actively taking ownership of public space. Since the wave of public protests of 2012, the attendance at opposition events has been declining. What does weak public activity imply about the private realm? It reveals that the essential backstage social spaces that have historically enabled counter-culture and productive dissent have grown silent.

Alexei Levinson, head of research at the independent social polling agency at the Levada Center, believes that there is a growing level of private dissent in the population. In 2013, Levinson speculated that the declining number of protesters revealed a shift in the general mindset of citizens.[17] According to 2012 public opinion surveys, the majority believes that open criticism of authority is good, and most support the opposition movement. However, only a minority supports the mass protest movement and even fewer believe it has a sound objective.[18] The belief that a form of opposition is necessary is growing, but public protests are not considered to be an effective means of expression. The recent protest movement is mostly reactionary, not visionary. Today, political rallies take place to demonstrate opposition to things that have already occurred. Despite growing frustration with the current

situation, there is little imagination for an alternative future or creative interrogation of the problematic reality.

Moscow's history of protest has shown that social action can manifest in two spheres—the front-stage and backstage spaces of the city. The most influential ideological shifts are fueled by the underground countercultures that critically engage with ideas about alternative futures. The Constructivist architects of the 1920s and 1930s shaped buildings for everyday life around a vision of social collaboration. Later, in the Soviet Union, those communal spaces fulfilled this desire as backstage spaces of protest— where dissident conversations and activities were enabled by their privacy.

The decay of Moscow's Constructivist architecture is a mirror of a fading notion that the built environment can be active in shaping the private lives, thoughts, and dialogues of its occupants. Buildings such as the Melnikov House, Shukhov Tower, and Narkomfin Building face uncertain futures threatened by dilapidation, ownership disputes, and a lack of governmental action for their preservation.[19] Not unlike other

Moisei Ginzburg's Narkomfin building was designed to promote the socialist life of the residents through shared facilities and flexible apartments. The design later influenced modernist housing projects such as Le Corbusier's Unite d'Habitation.
PHOTO: COURTESY OF NATALIA MELIKOVA (2014)

Despite its current state of disrepair, a community of illegal residents has been living in Narkomfin in recent years, re-activating its communal living function.
PHOTO: COURTESY OF LUCIANO SPINELLI & NATALIA MELIKOVA (2014)

megacities across the globe, Moscow continues to expand and develop its residential fabric at a mass scale through generic towers in sleeping districts outside the city. Sometimes the massive housing towers precede social and physical infrastructure, such as schools and sidewalks, needed to accommodate residents' lives. Communal actions such as informal markets and neighborhood organizations are grassroots undertakings, unconsidered in the design of the buildings and neighborhoods that house them.

Regardless of political agenda, the idea that the architecture of everyday life can enable social progress and reflect ambition of future revolution is a powerful one. As stated by Reinier de Graaf, "Community is a product of protesting against society, a form of bonding through a rejection of a mainstream thing."[20] That this critical discourse of a larger society is channeled through private social spaces highlights the significance of their design and potential. The community building scale is the spatial equivalent of rational conversation and productive collaboration, between a private thought and the public outburst of anger. Moscow's lingering network of decaying Constructivist buildings stand as a dispersed monument to a past vision of the future and the rich potential of architecture as social activator. Whether the ambitions of the avant-garde will be relevant to the future city remains to be seen. If so, hopefully it will be charged not by state mandated decree but by the ambitions and actions of the designers and citizens themselves.

Lindsay Harkema is a New York-based designer who splits her time between professional architectural practice, teaching, and research-based design projects of her own. She holds a Masters of Architecture from Rice University and completed a research fellowship at the Strelka Institute for Media, Architecture and Design in Moscow.

Notes

This project was developed as part of a larger body of research by the "Foresight in Hindsight" studio led by Reinier de Graaf and Laura Baird at the Strelka Institute for Media, Architecture and Design in 2013. Special thanks to Natalia Melikova of The Constructivist Project for the use of her photographs and collages of avant-garde buildings today. The Constructivist Project is dedicated to promoting Russian avant-garde art and architecture and the preservation of constructivist monuments.

1   Hannah Arendt, "The Public and the Private Realm," *The Human Condition* (Chicago: University of Chicago Press, 1958).
2   Jean-Louis Cohen, "Architecture and Revolution in Russia," in *The Future of Architecture*, Since 1889 (London: Phaidon Press Limited, 2012), 161-175.
3   Avrahm Yarmolinsky, *Road to Revolution: A Century of Russian Radicalism* (New York: The Macmillan Company, 1956), http://ditext.com/yarmolinsky/yarframe.html.
4   Alan Woods, *Bolshevism: the Road to Revolution* (London: Wellred Books, 1999), www.marxist.com/bolshevism-old/index.html.
5   Marina Khrustaleva, discussion

on the avant-garde at Strelka Institute, Moscow, April 29, 2013.
6   El Lissitzky, "Russia: An architecture for world revolution" (1929), referenced in "Soviet workers' clubs in the 1920s," The Charnel House, June 1, 2014. Also online at: http://thecharnelhouse.org/2014/06/01/soviets-workers-clubs-in-the-1920s/.
7   Oliver Wainwright, "Top 10 Unbuilt towers: Palace of the Soviets by Boris Iofan," BD Online (Sep 26, 2011), http://www.bdonline.co.uk/top-10-unbuilt-towers-palace-of-the-soviets-by-boris-iofan/5025152.article.
8   Vladimir Paperny, *Architecture in the Age of Stalin* (Boston: Cambridge University Press, 2002).
9   James von Geldern, "1934: Writers' Congress," *Seventeen Moments in Soviet History*, http://soviethistory.macalester.edu/index.
10   Edmund Harris, "Ecclesiastical Architecture," *Moscow Heritage at Crisis Point II* (2009), 35-47.
11   Nikita Khruschev, "Industrialised Building Speech" (1954), in *Volume*, (March 1, 2009), http://volumeproject.org/2009/03/industrialised-building-speech-1954/.
12   Lynne Viola, *Contending with Stalinism: Soviet Power and Popular Resistance in the 1930s* (Ithaca: Cornell University Press, 2002), 40.

13   Boris Groys, discussion about Moscow Conceptualism, Ameron Hotel Abion, Berlin. March 21, 2013.
14   Dasha Paramonova, *Luzhkov Era* (Moscow: Strelka Institute, 2011), 23-25.
15   Andrew Roth and Ellen Barry, "Russian Protest Leader Put Under House Arrest," *New York Times* Feb 9, 2009), www.nytimes.com/2013/02/10/world/europe/russian-protest-leader-put-under-house-arrest.html?_r=0.
16   Daniel Treisman, "Why the Kremlin Hates the Levada Center," *The Moscow Times*, May 24, 2013, www.themoscowtimes.com/opinion/article/why-the-kremlin-hates-levada-center/480433.html.
17   Alexei Levinson, "City Built and City Virtual: What is Moscow?" Strelka Institute, Moscow, (March 5, 2013).
18   The Levada Center, *Annual Public Opinion Survey*, Moscow, 2012.
19   Robert Mull and Xenia Adjoubei, "Ruins of Utopia," *The Architectural Review*, March 29, 2013, www.architectural-review.com/essays/ruins-of-utopia/8644716.article.
20   Reinier de Graaf, "Architecture and Community," Strelka Talks Series, May 16, 2013. Video online at: http://vimeo.com/64876602.

THE SPACE OF THE COMMONS: DHEISHEH REFUGEE CAMP

Alison Hugill and Dan Dorocic

Hannah Arendt's essay "Labor, Work, Action," published in 1958 as part of *The Human Condition*, produces a definition of action and public space that is connected to a politically democratic tradition, stemming from Greek antiquity. Arendt's treatise proposes that the actions of individuals—their capacity to begin ever anew within a plurality of beings—is what distinguishes them and reveals the meaning of each human life. Great words and deeds form a part of every person's individual (thus implicitly social) narrative. Arendt's depreciation of labor, both productive and reproductive, allows her to privilege action as the main pillar of the human condition, by accepting the "oldest, pre-philosophical hierarchy" of labor-work-action, before Marx and Nietzsche performed what she calls their "theoretical reversals."[1]

From a materialist perspective, it is clear that capitalist social relations are deeply entwined with each layer of Arendt's "human condition." While they may manifest most transparently in the realm of labor, they are inextricable from individual pursuits in terms of action, and permeate modern notions of both public and private space. In reality, the so-called "public realm"—the space of appearance for Arendt—is not free or independent from state or economic imperatives. On the contrary, the public realm is saturated with these concerns. Rather than returning to the reductionist and exclusive Greek model of politics, wherein the wealthy and educated represent those who cannot speak, we suggest an expanded political understanding based on the idea of the commons, primarily understood via Italian autonomist-Marxists Silvia Federici and Antonio Negri.

This essay examines the fraught nature of public space in the Palestinian context, with particular focus on its role in the Dheisheh refugee camp near Bethlehem in the West Bank. Public space and participatory initiatives are observed to understand their relevance and potential in this context. The Arendtian notion of man as "political animal," vis-a-vis Aristotle, is problematic here. Instead, many refugees living in camps are seeking to actively build common spaces that exist independent of institutional or governmental bodies, individual economic pursuits, or the apparatus of occupation. In particular, a research group within the organization Campus in Camps, an educational and

West Bank Refugee Camps and Area Division.

The 19 Refugee Camps in the West Bank

A size comparson of the 19 Camps in the West Bank

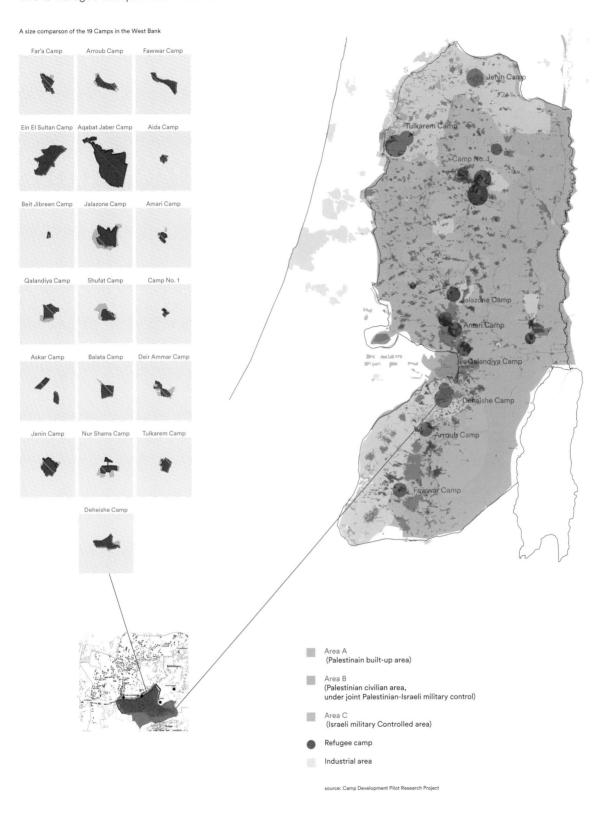

Far'a Camp

Arroub Camp

Fawwar Camp

Ein El Sultan Camp

Aqabat Jaber Camp

Aida Camp

Beit Jibreen Camp

Jalazone Camp

Amari Camp

Qalandiya Camp

Shufat Camp

Camp No. 1

Askar Camp

Balata Camp

Deir Ammar Camp

Jenin Camp

Nur Shams Camp

Tulkarem Camp

Deheishe Camp

Jenin Camp

Tulkarem Camp

Camp No. 1

Jalazone Camp

Amari Camp

Qalandiya Camp

Deheishe Camp

Arroub Camp

Fawwar Camp

Area A
(Palestinain built-up area)

Area B
(Palestinian civilian area,
under joint Palestinian-Israeli military control)

Area C
(Israeli military Controlled area)

Refugee camp

Industrial area

source: Camp Development Pilot Research Project

project-oriented program developed out of the Camp Improvement Program, is interrogating the "unbuilt" spaces in Dheisheh.[2] Participants isolated several sites within Dheisheh that have the potential to be transformed for collective use. Following the work of the Decolonizing Architecture Art Residency (DAAR) and Campus in Camps, we position the public realm and action within the theoretical and political framework of the commons and dissensus, against traditional understandings of Arendt's "space of appearance."

Public Space vs. the Commons

In her essay "Feminism and the Politics of the Commons," Silvia Federici writes: "the idea of the common/s [...] has offered a logical and historical alternative to both State and Private Property, the State and the Market, enabling us to reject the fiction that they are mutually exclusive and exhaustive of our political possibilities."[3] In opposition to Arendt's definition, Federici's commons refutes the overused dichotomy of space divided between public (political/social) and private (domestic). The commons is positioned against statist models of revolution that seek a new state formation to challenge capitalism. Rather, the commons designates the shared resources, or "the wealth of the material world,"[4] and social production that might be harnessed against privatizing impulses and in the service of an alternative political framework.

This theory is particularly useful for bottom-up, participatory design initiatives in the Dheisheh refugee camp. Refugee camps in the West Bank are governed and maintained by a number of sovereign entities, including the United Nations Relief and Works Agency (UNRWA), and host authorities such as the Palestinian Authority (PA) and Israeli forces. Since the space in the camp is not the property of individual inhabitants or a communal whole, and the living situation is considered to be temporary, many difficulties arise in terms of overall planning as well as camp improvements.[5] There is widespread concern that improvements in the camp environment will undermine the Palestinian right of return. Making the space more livable and taking care of it implies a certain valorization that many inhabitants feel impedes the political project of returning to their homeland. Therefore, within the Dheisheh refugee camp, the term public space does not apply in a typical urban way, as posited by DAAR:

> Decolonization today is about taking public squares—which, notably, have mostly been traffic roundabouts. In effect, these roundabouts have been turned into a form of symbolic public ground. But in Arab cities, the term 'public' is associated with the state and its repressive mechanisms; that is to say, the 'public' was never owned by the people. It was these places throughout the region that became the vortex of new common forums of political action.[6]

Many refugees living in Dheisheh are seeking to actively build common spaces that exist independent of institutional or governmental agendas, individualist pursuits, or the apparatus of occupation. Participants researching the unbuilt space of Dheisheh have isolated several sites that have the potential to be transformed for collective use. The goal of Campus in Camps is to make improvements within the common space of the camp without seeking to normalize their refugee status or undermine their political demands for return.

Spatial Initiatives in the Refugee Camp

The multi-disciplinary participants of Campus in Camps developed a collective dictionary in which they define key terms. The booklet defines the commons as "everything in life used by the whole community for free."[7] Importantly, the commons cannot include capitalist practices, which undermines it through the pursuit of profit. The dictionary mentions that the commons is always in flux and can apply to specific sites within the camp at times, and at others (such as a raid by Israeli soldiers) it can expand to the entirety of the camp. Public space, therefore, is no longer relegated to traditional fixed meeting points such as public squares or the equivalents of the Greek agora. Even domestic spaces can be part of the commons in a particular situation. This potential expansion of the commons disturbs the duality of private and public space implied in Arendt's formulation, and imagines a form of collective living that eschews this binary. If, in this context, public spaces are not imposed from the outside as in conventional public squares or forums, then where are they to be found?

The main square has typically been considered the site for political action—the primary site of protest and conflict. However, the public square today is a site often under the control of large corporate or political entities. The everyday conflict of slogans and advertisements continues while staged political events are covered by the media. Although these events create a narrative of political transformation in our memories, they bring little change to everyday reality. After the eruption of spectacles, the return to normality is quick. By considering public space as expansive and malleable, rather than as exceptional, the idea of designated protest areas or approved times that are sanctioned within a mainstream political discourse can be abandoned.

Dheisheh refugee camp, and other small camps and neighborhoods, has the potential to resist these powerful actors and serve as the site of production of political action. The potential of the camp comes from the precarious status of the community living within it, in relation to the wider political and economic context. The Campus in Camps initiative emphasizes mental decolonization as crucial to their thinking, which reimagines the definition of public space in terms of the notion of the commons. Historically in Dheisheh, as elsewhere in the Arab world, common space was found at the mosque or the in-between space of streets and covered enclaves. These spaces, although often public,

DENSITY (people/km²)

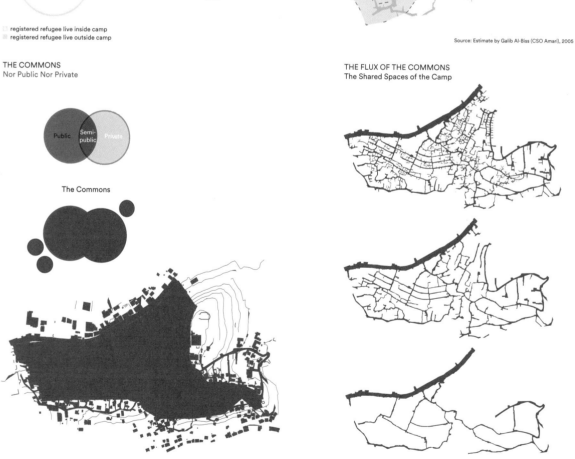

NORWAY (13 people)   ISRAEL (364 people)   DHEISHEH (38 000 people)

UN COMPOUND

OUTMIGRATION

Out-migration of refugees
with camp code

SHOPS

☐ registered refugee live inside camp
▨ registered refugee live outside camp

Source: Estimate by Galib Al-Biss (CSO Amari), 2005

THE COMMONS
Nor Public Nor Private

Public Semi-public Private

The Commons

THE FLUX OF THE COMMONS
The Shared Spaces of the Camp

The commons of the
Dheisheh camp, and the
flux of the commons.

weren't always common. The main squares in Palestine, although legally public, are rigorously controlled by a number of hegemonic forces, including many religious groups.

One architectural initiative run through Campus in Camps considers spatial agency in the Three Shelter site of Dheisheh. The site is named for the three different concrete UNWRA shelters developed in the 1950s, '70s, and '90s. Starting in the mid-1950s, each displaced family received a nine square meter shelter, and each group of fifteen families shared one bathroom. Today, the three UNRWA shelters still occupy the middle of the camp as a manifestation of an era that the camp endured.[8] During the initial phase of the project in collaboration with the "unbuilt" group from Campus in Camps, we considered how to stage events that activate the site as a common space. A debate surrounds the Three Shelter site, polarized between those who wish to memorialize it as commemorative of Palestinian expulsion and the difficult early stages of the refugee camp and those who seek to transform it for future use.

The proposed conversion project in Dheisheh is not intended to produce a singular public square, but works on the scale of small urban actions to re-appropriate spaces in the camp. For example, a tilted platform is proposed in the Three Shelter site, highlighting it as an archeological story-telling device for refugees to explain the history of the camp to younger generations and international visitors. The platform does not touch the ground, in response to the contested nature of the site and the uneasiness towards solidifying new built projects or improvements in Dheisheh.

Other areas in the camp are being transformed as well. The walls throughout the camp are used in a similar fashion, to tell different stories about the everyday struggles of the refugees through painted murals. The pedestrian bridge across Hebron Road, linking Dheisheh camp to Doha refugee city, is being re-oriented as a Saturday flea market and exhibition space. Elsewhere, there is an initiative by a group of women in Fawwar Refugee Camp near Hebron to take over the main square, a site where women don't often feel comfortable and are rarely seen. The actions by the group include handicrafts, cooking, and storytelling as ways of occupying the square. The intention is to encourage women to feel comfortable performing these actions in a public context at any time.

The temporary nature of these design proposals are a necessary outcome of certain factors that make permanent architecture in the area difficult to implement: concerns about normalization and the ever volatile political situation. Many proposed spatial initiatives act as a counter-tectonic to the heavier, more monumental architecture displayed by the Palestinian Authority and the illegal Israeli settlements.

Performance of the State

After sixty-five years, Dheisheh and other refugee camps in the area are increasingly urbanizing and, with normalization of the camps, property and everyday life become increasingly privatized. The Palestinian Authority operates as though the region is in a post-colonial situation, despite the signs of persistent Israeli occupation. The PA have constructed elaborate headquarters throughout the region and concern themselves with the aesthetics, accessories, and performance of a nation state (uniform, flag, etc.) while the people they represent remain—in the global context—virtually stateless. The state of emergency that was originally common in the occupied territories is now largely covered over by these accoutrements of Western, "free" societies.[9]

Some members of the Palestinian elite are building new suburban developments that seem to spring out of the desert—such as the planned city of Rawabi, which closely resembles an Israeli settlement—and putting up prisons, police compounds, and shopping malls, which all use the built language of the Israeli occupier. This post-colonial Palestinian dream is happening within the still occupied territory of the West Bank. Thus, the project within Dheisheh is not one of improving the camp in the manner of the UNWRA projects of the past, but of creating a model of spatial agency that initiates an alternative use of common space as a forum for discussing and preserving the complex nature of Palestinian identity. This is not to insist on a discourse of victimhood but to expose the still very real mechanisms of control at work in Palestinian society.

Dissensus and the Commons

The idea of the commons employed in this text is not built on a communal shared identity. The concept of dissensus—introduced by Jacques Ranciere and employed by Claire Bishop in her recent critique of participatory art practices, *Artificial Hells*—is helpful for this understanding of action and its relation to the commons. Ranciere observes that there is a politics because the commons is inherently divided. Whereas in her essay "The Public and the Private Realm," Arendt begins with the Aristotelian premise that man as a "speaking animal" is at the core of politics, Ranciere proposes that there is already a divide, from the beginning, within this so-called common capacity to speak (in public):

> Aristotle tells us that slaves understand language but don't *possess* it. This is what dissensus means. There is politics because speaking is not the same as speaking, because there is not even an agreement on what a sense means. Political dissensus is not a discussion between speaking people who would confront their interests and values. It is a conflict about who speaks and who does not speak, about what has to be heard as the voice of pain and what has to be heard as an argument on justice. And this is also what 'class war' means: not the conflict between groups which have opposite economic interests, but the conflict about what an 'interest' is, the struggle between those who set themselves as able to manage social interests and those who are supposed to be only able to reproduce their life.[10]

Those who work primarily in the realm of reproductive labor, disparaged in Arendt's account, are therefore excluded from the traditional definition of politics. The commons is, rather, thought of as a space of dissensus, where political space is reimagined from the perspective of those whose interests are systematically oppressed. In the context of Dheisheh and other refugee camps in Palestine, there is the potential for a more expansive definition of politics and the commons, as well as the correlative concepts of action and public space. The bottom-up spatial initiatives enacted by participants of Campus in Camps are seeking to develop a lived experience of the commons against traditional, liberal, and neoliberal understandings of the political space of appearance.

Alison Hugill has a MA in Contemporary Art Theory from Goldsmiths College, University of London. Her research focuses on Marxist-feminist politics and aesthetic theories of community, communication, and communism. Alison is an editor, writer, and curator based in Berlin.

Dan Dorocic has a Master in Architecture from Bergen Arkitekthøgskole and is co-founder of architecture collective ON/OFF. Dan worked on a number of participatory and community-led building and design workshops in Germany, Palestine, Belgium, and Italy.

Notes

1 Hannah Arendt, "Labor, Work, Action," in *The Portable Hannah Arendt*, ed. Peter Baehr (New York: Penguin Books, 2000), 170.
2 Aysar Alsaify, Isshaq Albarbary, Qussay Abu Aker, and Ahmad Laham (Campus in Camps participants), "The Unbuilt," (June 2013), http://www.campusincamps.ps/projects/09-the-unbuilt/ accessed June 2, 2014.
3 Silvia Federici, "Feminism and the Politics of the Commons," in *The Commoner: A Web Journal for Other Values*, www.commoner.org.

4 Michael Hardt and Antonio Negri, *Commonwealth* (Cambridge, MA: Harvard University Press, 2009), viii.
5 Philipp Misselwitz and Sari Hanafi, "Testing a New Paradigm: UNWRA's Camp Improvement Programme," *Refugee Survey Quarterly*, vol. 28, nos 2 & 3. UNHRC, (2010).
6 Sandi Hilal, Alessandro Petti, and Eyal Weizman, Architecture After Revolution (Berlin: Sternberg Press, 2013), 33.
7 Nedaa Hamouz, Nabà Al-Assi, Mohammed Abu-Alia, Murad Odeh, Isshaq Al-Barbary, BraveNewAlps (Campus in Camps participants) "Common I:

Collective Dictionary," http://www.campusincamps.ps/projects/common-1/.
8 Ahmad Laham, Aysar Alaify, Isshaq Albarbary, Qussay Abu Aker (Campus in Camps participants), "The Unbuilt," (June 2013), http://www.campusincamps.ps/projects/09-the-unbuilt/.
9 Yazid Anani, "Schizophrenia, The Urban Experience and Temporal Art Intervention," Lecture, Campus in Camps (February 22, 2014).
10 Jacques Ranciere, "The Thinking of Dissensus: Politics and Aesthetics," in *Reading Ranciere*, ed. Paul Bowman and Richard Stamp (London: Continuum, 2011), 2

THE "AS IF" SOCIETY

Azadeh Zaferani

The country is an 'as if' society. People live as if they were free, as if they were in the West, as if they had the right to an opinion, or a private life. And they don't do too badly at it. I have now visited all three of the states that make up the so-called axis of evil. Rough as their regime can certainly be, the citizens of Iran live on a different planet from the wretched, frightened serfs of Saddam Hussein and Kim Jong II.[1]

City-Islands

In 1977, characterized by an extreme spatial contrast between an enclave of dense urban fabric and the vast emptiness caused by wartime destruction, the city of West Berlin was contemplating its future at a time of urban crisis and depopulation. Soon it was understood that the city center could no longer be addressed by restoration and that a new model was needed as a response to its shrinking population. In the midst of these events, the German architect, O.M. Ungers, together with Rem Koolhaas, Peter Riemann, Hans Kollhoff, and Arthur Ovaska, proposed to radically treat the existing condition of the city as a projective model for Berlin's shrinking future. The manifesto, entitled "Berlin: A Green Archipelago", demonstrated a process of demolition and infill through which enclaves were sculpted, defined, and converted into archeological sites liberated from the anonymity of the city and transformed into an "islands." The empty spaces between the island sites were then to be filled in by a forest over time. Instead of healing the wounds of the war, Ungers intensified the differences among the islands through definition and distance, preserving Berlin for its future.[2]

Two years after Unger's vision, John Hejduk unveiled a project as part of Prinz-Albrecht-Palais competition for design of a memorial park on an old Gestapo site in Berlin. This project was named "Victims." The site was an enclosed plot with two layers of tall hedges, between which a tram circulated. Not unlike the double-tiered Berlin wall with limited checkpoints, the site for Victims was entered through a controlled entry point by way of a bus stop from which the visitors proceeded over a drawbridge and through a gatehouse. Within the hedges, a grid of young evergreens colonized the site that was to reach full maturity over the course of the first thirty-year cycle. Over the second thirty-year cycle, Hejduk offered the citizens of Berlin the opportunity to insert any number of his sixty-seven anthropomorphic structures, or Victims, into the site as well as the opportunity to decide upon the time sequence of their construction and their relationship with one another. The Victims maintained their autonomy while simultaneously implying a loosely held together network.

Hejduk's Victims tested the transferability of the islands-within-an-island model found in Unger's Berlin manifesto to an architectural scale. While Ungers provided stability in an unstable

Development of Tehran from Qajar to Pahlavi dynasty. From top to bottom: Tehran 1841 (Berezin map); Tehran 1857 (Krziz map); Tehran 1890 (Abd-ol-Ghafar map); Tehran 1937.
MAPS: COURTESY OF TEHRAN GEOGRAPHIC INFORMATION CENTER

Tehran, 1841

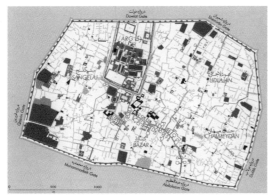

Tehran, 1857

Tehran, 1890

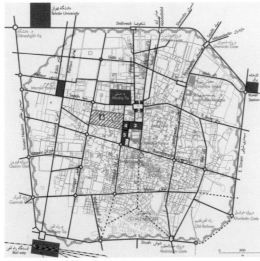

Tehran, 1937

condition by treating the city as a museum of islands, Hejduk injected instability into a stable and quarantined city in which structures oscillated between the role of contemplation and participation, within a walled island. While different in origin, in both islands, the hard boundaries around the sites form new universes and allow for the smaller islands within to be removed from any sense of scale or reference. The logic of this mixture, in which new forms of connectivity emerge within hardened boundaries, is the precursor to many conditions we see in cities today.

Today, it's not hard to imagine a city within which similar conditions apply; a city that is shrinking due to sudden changes in migration. In some of these cases, borders solidify, not from rigid and physical walls, but from the introduction of sanctions and embargos. This yields ports unable to receive goods, planes incapable of flying out, and a city in isolation from the globe. Built areas stand still, yet open spaces are converted into dollars, as densities are sold off to make up for the financial loss of an in debt government. The public realm loses identity, leaving the victims of our city in search of alternatives for their public presence. One way or another, in many parts of the world and under many totalitarian regimes, this is part of people's everyday life. Among many other cities such as Pyongyang, Riyadh, Caracas, or Beijing, Tehran emerges as a powerful example of a contemporary city-island condition.

Tehran

Since 1800s, Tehran has grown from a small town with population of 50,000 to one of the largest cities in the world with over fifteen million inhabitants in 2015. Iran's integration with the global economy has happened through commodification of agriculture and the establishment of the oil industry, making it a bridge between the country and the rest of the world. Discovery of oil in Iran happened when the fiscal and financial affairs of the country was dominated by two Russian and British banks.[3] In 1928, and under their influence, the first National bank of Iran was inaugurated, with a right to issue currency. With the advent of credit notes, loans and high rate of returns on investment, banks started to motivate the private sector's interest in housing developments. Under the name of modernization and in favor of the capitalist system, the built environment of the city should have walked away from the scene, transforming itself to a system that benefits economic agendas. This is how the one- or two-story, inward-looking, courtyard buildings lost the ground in favor of a higher, extroverted form of construction. The change in building form has been largely associated with the change in the street system. These new types of buildings were products of land subdivision, rationalization, and standardization of the size and shape of land parcels, which was consistent with the orthogonal blocks and streets. This transformation of the built

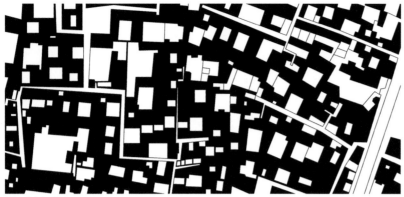

Urban Fabric, 1850s

Religious Rituals (Ashura), 1850s

Urban Fabric, 1890s

Zograscopes, 1900s

Urban Fabric, 1930s

Moulin Rouge Cinema, 1960s

Evolution of street
system and their related
concepts of public
entertainment.
MAPS: GENERATED BY
ALI MADANIPOUR,
AUTHOR OF *TEHRAN: THE
MAKING OF A METROPOLIS*

form caused a transformation in social structure of the city as well. By taking away the courtyard from the built environment, the balance between public and private life was distorted.

Prior to the post-capitalist transformation of the city, there existed a hierarchy among courtyards, varying from private courts within houses to bigger semi-public courts in the neighborhood and larger public courts associated with religious buildings and city plazas. The history of revolution in Tehran shows how these courts would form a system where the contest between government and revolutionaries transpired.

The civic moves have always been with the support or betrayal of merchants in the Bazaar, Tehran's business district. While the new imposed street layouts encouraged infill development of courtyards, the new land-use regulations and block definitions weakened the strong commercial core from which modern Tehran was born.[4] Due to political motivation of the state to dismantle the Bazaari merchants' perceived monopoly over economic activities and space, new land-use patterns demanded the dispersal of commercial activities out of the central zone and into the newly laid out street networks. Consequentially, these newly made commercial nodes should have represented a new definition of commerce. This is how many new commercial concepts such as shopping malls and department stores as well as entertainment programs, such as cinemas, were created to replace the abandoned public courts by new concepts of social gatherings. Eventually, the modernization of the city gave birth to these enclaves of commercialization and the very first city-island conditions started to appear. According to Reza Talachian, a film historian, before the advent of cinema in Iran, entertainment was a luxury afforded by only a small, well-to-do segment of the population while the great majority of the people had no money to spare. Religious theatres, public gatherings, and mingling in alleyways of the Bazaar were common ways of socializing for the poor. Early filmmaking in Iran was often supported by the royalty of the time who were only interested in the entertainment value of the medium. "Most of films of this period are newsreels of activities, such as various royal and religious ceremonies, which were mostly screened in the royal palace. One could see these newsreels at the homes of dignitaries during weddings, circumcision celebrations, and birth ceremonies."[5] Consequently, public gatherings started to migrate from open courts to interior spaces with the help of modern technologies.

In the West, cinema complemented the existing popular forms of entertainment such as theaters, traveling musical shows, and various stage productions. But in Iran, cinema virtually replaced most forms of mass entertainment for various political, economic, and cultural reasons. When cinema came to Iran it was a diversion for the well-to-do for about ten years or so before it turned into a mass entertainment medium. Since 1905, when the first movie theater opened in Tehran, the Iranian government made a point of keeping ticket prices low so that all segments of the population might have access to this source of recreation. Of course, the government's new approach to the concept of "recreation" had an interwoven relationship with initial western modernist's ideas behind city planning. When Naser Edin Shah returned from his second trip to Europe, he ordered an avenue to be built in the middle of Khalesi Garden which was connected to Ala Al-Doleh (Ferdowsi) street from the west and to the Royal Filkhaneh from the east. By the King's order, benches were installed on both sides of the avenue to resemble the Champs-Élysées Avenue in Paris. The avenue was solely built for the desire of having an avenue. After the First World War, Lalehzar—with a tramway running along it—became the ideal place for foreigners and modernized residents of Tehran to be entertained. This Avenue became the first entertainment spine. Initially, only the most famous theatres and cabarets lined it, but eventually numerous cinemas arrived, converting this spine to a prominent site for a modern mass entertainment.[6] This trend migrated to most of the major squares in the city center. In the late 1960s and early 70s, many of these squares were surrounded by cinemas, transferring the function of old courtyards and squares of the city from a central node to a perimeter block, leaving the inner court a dead social node. While there was no social interaction within the square, due to vehicular traffic, the social function of the square had shifted to the built isolated islands around it. The importance behind these formal nodes of social interactions was rooted in planning strategies of the second Pahlavi dynasty.[7]

First Pahlavis carried on Naser Edin Shah's vision of Parisian Boulevards. However, during second Pahlavis, there was a twist in city planning strategies. Under Shah's land reform revolution, the White Revolution of 1963, Iranian government asked the American firm Victor Gruen Associates, who developed the concept of the shopping mall as a community facility, to draw up a comprehensive master plan for the city of Tehran together with the Iranian master architect Abdolaziz Farmanfarmaian. Gruen was just one of hundreds of private firms that swarmed to Iran in the wake of the American Government's deep engagement with the second Pahlavi regime. Gruen's plan formed the framework for the satellite towns, apartment complexes, office buildings, parks, palaces, highways, road systems, and other facilities built in and around Tehran between the mid 1960s and the Islamic Revolution of 1979.[8] Gruen's plan for Tehran can be described as a diagram of the metropolis stretched out over the city of Tehran and pulled in a western direction along the foothills of the Alborz Mountains, thereby forming something between a central city and a linear one. Yes, it was composed of ten cities; yes, the green landscape would separate the cities from each other and create the backdrop for an extensive network of flowing highways;

Typical private
courtyard.
PHOTO: COURTESY OF
MANSOUR SANE FROM
"IN MEMORY OF SHIRAZ"

Typical public
courtyard.
PHOTO: COURTESY OF
MANSOUR SANE FROM
"IN MEMORY OF SHIRAZ"

and yes, the cities would be subdivided into towns, which would be built up of communities, and made out of neighborhoods. The diagram was not only adapted to the geology of the city, but also to its socio-economic structure. However, as Vanstiphout describes it in "The Saddest City in the World," the plan had obstacles in its way:

> The Tehran Comprehensive Plan by Gruen and Farmanfarmaian had functioned for more than ten years; it had provided a structure that guided decision making processes for smaller building projects through out the city... After the Islamic revolution the plan was treated as a detestable legacy of the worldly regime of the Shah. At the same time it was the only plan they had. After the revolution an attempt was made to make a new plan; this plan was rejected by the city. One of the reasons was that the government provided no financial resources to implement this plan. The city then made the choice to go on with the old plan and to generate their own income ... The TCP plan provided them with a reliable source of income because it made such precise statements about which kind of building densities were allowed at which locations. The city could then sell of these densities to individuals and companies who wanted to maximize the usage of their plots but found themselves stopped by the still officially valid plan ... The strategy of the municipality was quite brilliant in a nihilist sort of way: hanging to a plan that they do not believe in, in order to collect money by selling off the excess densities, was much more manageable, than creating a new plan, that they would have to believe in, support, implement and pay for. It seems that sometimes a bad plan is more useful than a good one.[9]

Deviation from Gruen's proposed master plan and its comprehensive urban studies was not the only outcome of the Islamic Revolution of Iran. Under the imposed Islamic regulations, the status of Tehran's public realm entered a new round of debates. Tehran's multipurpose enclaves, from shopping malls and department stores to cinemas and cabarets, were considered western interventions and were doomed to demolition and abandonment. On one hand, the traditional presence of the public realm was stolen from the city, and on the other hand, the modern substitute of it was forbidden for use. Under the given circumstances, what would be the possibility of an absolute public realm for civilians of such society? Returning to Christopher Hitchens' impressions, this has led to the possible reading of Tehran as an "as if" society.

Public Realm
Today, the public realm is typically identified in relation to the presence of power. This domination has been realized through arrangements of space, making it a fundamental element in the exercise of power; an act that Michel Foucault

has referred to as the spatial arrangement of surveillance.[10] Foucault uses Jeremy Bentham's panopticon as a metaphor for what he saw as central to the way deviant individuals were disciplined. Under the pressure of being observed, the observed disciplines himself.[11] Even though this surveilled environment can form docile subjects, it is also capable of laying the ground for contests against power. According to sociologist Michel de Certeau, strategies create and control specifically marked places by putting them under the control of the powerful state. In the case of totalitarian societies, strategies reveal themselves under a centralized government as internal political orientations, expanding the government's authority across the country into various spheres of life. This is a practice of power that has had different players yet mutual goals in all ruling regimes. Tactics, however, are oppositions that appear in situations that are not completely under control. In other words, tactics create spaces. Those who use tactics are always waiting for the proper opportunity to perform. And with such moments, resistance is born, enabling the resistant to challenge the rigid organization of the place in order to create a space of defiance. The oppressed cannot escape the scene of oppression; instead, he/she can manipulate it. These tactics don't need to be political actions, they could be tricks or distortions, threatening the repressive order at an individual level. De Certeau refers to these distortions as the "everyday life" of individuals.[12] In short, people create alternative spaces for their social interactions and engagements. The "as if" society serves as the foundation for such tactics. It is a society where the missing courtyard converts into a basement where musicians perform concerts, breweries produce beer, couples get married, and the youth go clubbing, even though these acts are against the law of the state. In such a society, the decentralized commercial zone would not enhance the authority of the state; instead, it would turn to a sexualized space where people have the rare opportunity of "presenting" themselves to the other sex. It transforms itself into malls where shopping is not just a background activity to prepare them for a performance, but rather the main act. They dress up and go to these spaces to be seen. On the other hand, there exists the complementary act of watching and being *flâneur*; the being that Keith Tester refers to as "a secret spectator of the spectacle of the spaces and places of the city."[13] In Tehran, this is the act that replaces sorrows of a gender-segregated society with a sense of life and liberation. In the "as if" society, coffee shops and public transport systems become new types of public spaces, where gender segregation has no place. Resisting banal politics and away from the prying eyes of the moral police, the ski slopes of Mount Alborz become the haven for youth.[14] Women enjoy the freedom of replacing their headscarves and robes with ski caps and jackets. While restaurants offer non-alcoholic beverages, parties go on in surrounding rental villas serving alcoholic

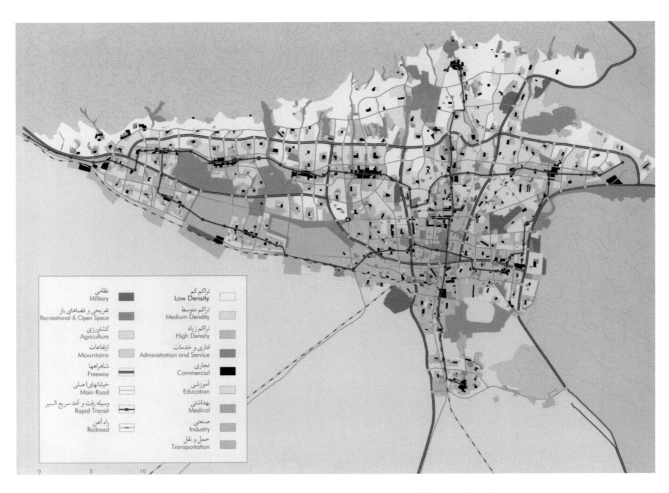

Legend:
نظامی Military
تفریحی و فضاهای باز Recreational & Open Space
کشاورزی Agriculture
ارتفاعات Mountains
شاهراهها Freeway
خیابانهای اصلی Main Road
وسیله رفت و آمد سریع السیر Rapid Transit
راه آهن Railroad
تراکم کم Low Density
تراکم متوسط Medium Dendity
تراکم زیاد High Density
اداری و خدمات Administration and Service
تجاری Commercial
آموزشی Education
بهداشتی Medical
صنعتی Industry
حمل و نقل Transportation

First master plan of
Tehran, 1968. All
commercial nodes are
highlighted in black.
MAP: COURTESY OF TEHRAN
GEOGRAPHIC INFORMATION
CENTER

drinks and mingling sexes. In short, people live "as if" these heterotopias are for real. Heterotopias of deviation; Spaces hosting individuals whose behavior is deviant in relation to the state. Heterotopias, as Michel Foucault introduces them, are similar to counter-sites. These counter-sites are effectively utopias in which the real site, all the other real sites that can be found within a culture, are simultaneously represented, contested, and inverted.[15] In conclusion, just as Slavenka Drakulić observed the Communist Eastern European societies in 1987, politics in Iran is not an abstract concept rather it is a powerful force having its hand in any possible everyday activity of individuals. In a society where politics intervenes in everyday life, every daily action becomes a political act by nature. In such a society, as Foucault claims, spaces of defiance or heterotopias of deviation are like boats. The boat is a floating space that exists by itself and is closed in on itself and at the same time is given over to the infinity of the sea in search of a place to reside in. This is how the boat becomes the island and the sea becomes the city within our city-island condition. In civilizations without boats, dreams dry up, espionage takes the place of adventure, and the police take the place of pirates. It is under the influence of these everyday life resistances that civic movements such as the Arab Spring of Egypt or the Green Movement of Iran revitalize the forgotten influence of individuals in the formation of an absolute public realm.

Waking of the City-Island Capital
Today, over thirty-five years since the Islamic Revolution, Iran and the Western countries are negotiating new possible channels of communication and trade. As Iran is rejoining the global market, new axiomatic urban strategies have taken place in the country. Under the influence of neighboring countries such as U.A.E and Turkey, the urban development of the city is refreshing Western inventions of early Modernism. Tehran is, once again, bombarded by a new wave of shopping mall developments, creating controlled environments of social interactions. On the contrary, as commerce is finding its place back in our divorced market, civic activities are departing from the scene. Libraries, publishing houses, galleries, museums, cafes, independent cinemas, and many communal acts are in a major state of turmoil. This sudden interest or disinterest is generating a shift in the economy and politics of the country. As always, any imposed strategy demands civilian's tactics. Change today occurs as a series of film-like jump-cuts, with effects appearing from out of view and without any sense of how the changes occurred. As with Gilles Deleuze's definition of "oceanic islands," cities are filled with fragmented urbanisms that can be only understood in retrospect, when historical narratives help piece together the disparate events.[16] Rejigging of such existing behaviors, encouraging an accumulation of interventions as a means of catalyzing change, and demanding a renewed

Toopkhane Sq, Late 1800

Toopkhane Sq, Early 1900

Toopkhane Sq, 1920

Toopkhane Sq, 1940

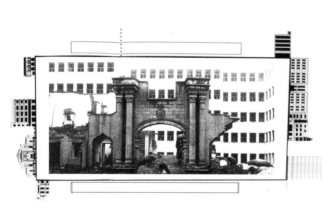

Toopkhane Sq, 1960

Toopkhane Sq, 1980

Transformation of
Toopkhaneh Square from
1880 to 1980.

IMAGES AND DRAWINGS:
COURTESY OF MINISTRY OF
HOUSING AND URBAN
DEVELOPMENT, URBAN PLANNING
AND ARCHITECTURE VICE
DIRECTORATE, FARROKH
MOHAMMADZADEH MEHR AND
ALI KHADEM'S ARCHIVE

connection to the local political economy, seems to be a new way toward a meaningful realization of an urban archipelago. At a time of unstable economic horizons, the grand gestures of a modernist tradition fail to address specific conditions, yet, similarly, "everyday urbanism" rejects the top-down flow of capital and all-too-readily abandons the role of design in shaping cities and stimulating their recovery.[17] As a result, there seems to be a desire to fill in the city's weak spots not with unique projects but with systemic transformations that are neither top-down nor bottom-up and instead negotiate a middle-ground through a direct interaction between architecture and the economic as well as political sphere.[18]

While derived from Ungers' initial idea of an urban archipelago, Hejduk extended the concept as a system that can translate itself to an experiencing economy in the physical world. In the same world, the urbanist of the future is an urban designer-cum-imaginer, melding usage and experience through a Machiavellian approach to given resources. If historical buildings were the starting point for Ungers, for our future urbanists commerce and commercial built forms shall be a substitute. In his book, *Possibilities of an Absolute Architecture*, Pier Vittorio Aureli refers to Carl Schmitt's definition of an enemy to be the recognition of one's opposite that is instrumental to avoiding self-deception. For him, the figure of a friend is always in the background. "A friend, by virtue of his benevolence, can only confirm our situation of self-deception," writes Aureli; "The enemy, on the other hand, estranges us from our familiar self-perception and gives us back the sharp contour of our own position."[19]

In our contemporary definition, an enemy resembles a violent and non-civic way of being. However, if we look at it from an economical point of view, such violence adds no profit to the cycle. To make it profitable, such violence should change into competition. As a result, those who find themselves facing the existing order of the civil society, lose their sense of recognition when it comes to identifying the counterpart— the enemy. The competition turns into an endless struggle without any acknowledgement of the enemy. It is through realization of such economic camouflage that opportunity arises.[20]

Therefore, as mentioned previously, an opportune context within which a true suppressed public realm and its associated cultural and entertaining programs can be rescued is the shopping mall. Placing this newborn concept in its forgotten and historical context is the key to access collective memory and collective reaction. Lalehzar and its network of abandoned cinemas is one of those weak spots of the city that is crying out loud for a renewed connection to the emerging local political economy of the city. Rejiggering and revitalizing this strong yet flickering archipelago of historical buildings could be a possible direction towards another heterotopia of defiance, where each cinema converts into a component of a mall while preserving its historical presence and loose network of connections; a heterotopia that constantly converts its commercial identity into a civic act, borrowing instructions from everyday tactics of civilians. These tactics can enable a spatial transformation from a supermarket to a gallery, a playground to a bookshop, a food court to a library, parking to a theatre, a commercial office to an exhibition area, a shop to a music store, etc. These objectified tactics, the constant transformation of interior objects, and this temporality of the space and their constant transformations are what defines the key role of civilians as individual creators of the public realm—a privatized public realm that happens in an "as if" society, as if it was meant to be the most liberal space of being.

Azadeh Zaferani is a designer and researcher based in Toronto. She received her Master of Urban Design from University of Toronto and Bachelor of Architecture from American University of Sharjah. In 2015, she launched a chain of platforms on art, architecture and design under the name of Plat+Forms.

Notes
1   Christopher Hitchens, "Iran's Waiting Game," *Vanity Fair* (July 2005).
2   Mark Lee, "Two Deserted Islands," *San Rocco*, v. 1 (Winter 2011): 4-10.
3   Ali Madanipour, "The Making of a Metropolis," (Chichester: John Wiley & Sons Ltd., 1998).
4   Ibid.
5   Reza Talachian, "A Brief Critical History of Iranian Feature Film (1896–1975)," *A Survey Catalogue and Brief Critical History of Iranian Feature Film (1896–1975)*, MA dissertation, Southern Illinois University (December 1980).
6   Ibid.
7   Farrokh Mohammadzadeh Mehr, "The Toopkhaneh Square of Tehran," Tehran: Pyam Sima, 2002.

8   Wouter Vanstiphout, "The Saddest City in the World," crimsonweb.org (March 2, 2006), http://www.crimsonweb.org/spip.php?article178.
9   Ibid.
10   Michel Foucault, *Discipline and Punish: The Birth of the Prison*, trans. by Alan Sheridan (New York: Pantheon, 1975), 195-228.
11   Ibid.
12   Michel de Certeau, *The Practice of Everyday Life*, trans. Steven Rendall (Berkeley: University of California Press, 1984).
13   Keith Tester, "The Flâneur," (London and New York: Routledge, 1994), 7.
14   Shahram Khosravi, "Young and defiant in Tehran," (Philadelphia: University of Pennsylvania Press, 2008).

15   Michel Foucault, "Of Other Spaces," *Diacritics*, v. 16 (Spring 1986): 22-27.
16   Lee, 4-10.
17   Shannon Harvey, "After the City: Fast Forward Urbanism—Rethinking Architecture's Engagement with the City," *The Architects Newspaper*, (September 2011), http://www.archpaper.com/news/articles.asp?id=5452#.U_DWXmZgYVk.
18   Roger Sherman and Dana Cuff, *Fast Forward Urbanism: Rethinking Architecture's Engagement with the City*, (New York: Princeton Architectural Press, 2011).
19   Pier Vittorio Aureli, *The Possibility of an Absolute Architecture*, (Cambridge, MA: The MIT Press, 2011), 29.
20   Ibid.

STAGING PUBLICS: THE RENEWAL OF PLACE DE LA RÉPUBLIQUE

TVK Architectes Urbanistes

Increasingly, the design of buildings, the city, and the metropolis must account for how these evolving entities transform through time. Designing with time requires the production of short-term tactics and long-term strategies, which examine how the public can inhabit available spaces. What is the form of the contemporary public space that functions for today as well as tomorrow? Openness must be integrated into this space to allow for evolution while defining the public. In fact, open space enables a public to gather and act—culturally or politically—whether through protest, free speech, or collective leisure activities. The transformation to Place de la République in Paris, also referred to as "La République," was taken as an opportunity to understand how to stage publics through time. Due to its monumental size, central location, and historic association with critical social and political events, the square has always occupied a special place in the collective Parisian psyche.

Throughout the twentieth century, there have been few transformations in the public space of La République. While occupied almost daily for various sizes and types of public and political demonstrations, for the most part, the space was colonized by the automobile—functioning as a massive roundabout. The renovation of the square first considered how to expand its usage to also allow for pedestrians and bikers. This was accomplished by reorganizing the traffic circle to liberate the site for pedestrians. This enlarged public realm required an equal amount of diversity—including its uses, urban atmospheres, and scales of occupation—humanizing aspects of the monumental square. At the same time, Place de la République has always been an active place, located at the nexus of several subway and bus lines. Clear connections with the large boulevards promote transportation access for pedestrians, cyclists, and public transport, demarcating the square as a place for public gathering and infrastructural transfer. The creation of a new concourse marks the return of a calm, airy, and uncluttered space, characterized by its unusual bigness. Instead of considering the typology of the public square as a unitary, singular, and symbolic space, the renewal investigates how a public space can stage a diversity of scales, urban uses, and ultimately, publics.

Place de la République before the transformation, engulfed in a sea of automobiles.
PHOTO: COURTESY OF AIR IMAGES

Place de la République after the transformation, integrated into the surrounding fabric.
PHOTO: COURTESY OF TVK AND MYLUCKYPIXEL

—>
Axonometric of the project, showing the cohesive surface that is softly zoned into smaller atmospheres.

Staging Publics

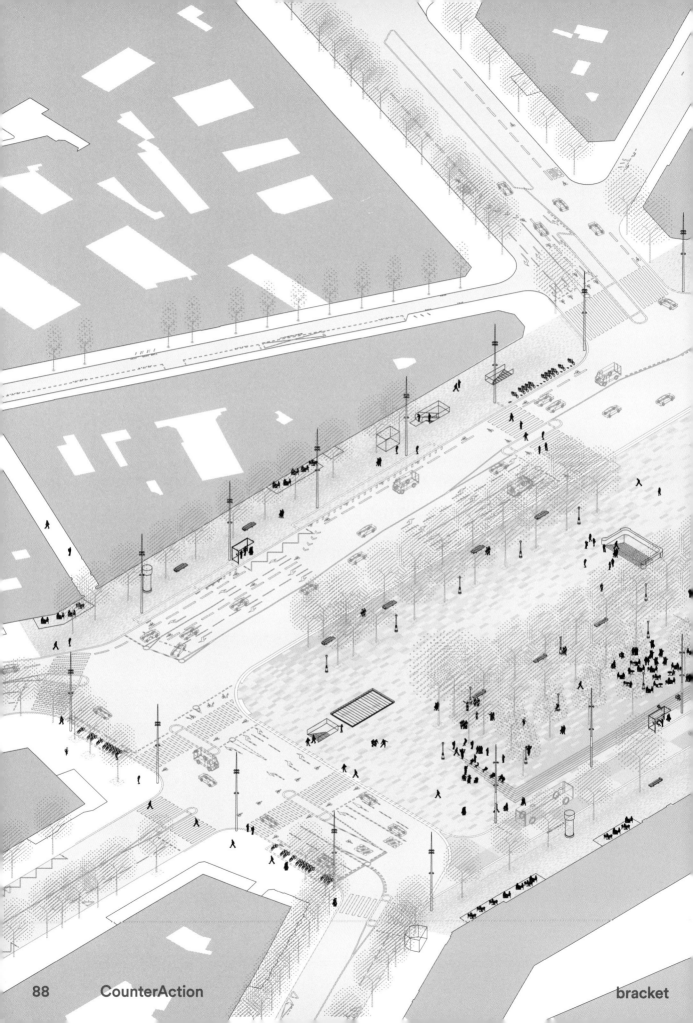

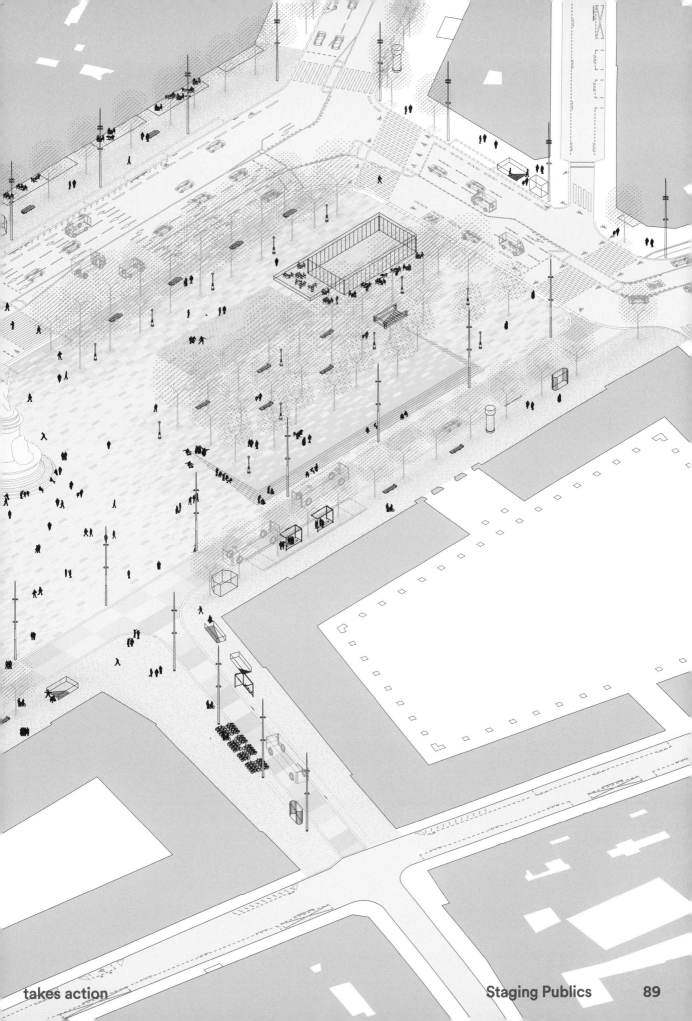

The new square functions as a large-scale landscape and urban resource, accessible and adaptable for different uses. Flexibility and unity was achieved by designing a supersurface—a radically flat surface available to be freely appropriated by the public. The continuity of the surface is negotiated by the different modes of occupation and their associated spatial organizations, from being on the terrace, below the trees, by the statue's fountain, or exiting the metro, each experience is unique yet tied into a coherent whole. In time—whether daily, seasonally, or in years to come—it is both the openness and specificity of the square's design that will allow for evolving publics to adapt, appropriate, and integrate to the square's logic.

TVK is a Paris based architecture and urban design office created by Pierre Alain Trévelo and Antoine Viger-Kohler.

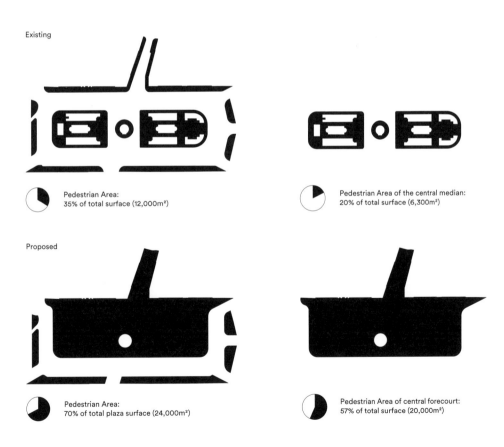

Existing

Pedestrian Area:
35% of total surface (12,000m²)

Pedestrian Area of the central median:
20% of total surface (6,300m²)

Proposed

Pedestrian Area:
70% of total plaza surface (24,000m²)

Pedestrian Area of central forecourt:
57% of total surface (20,000m²)

Area comparison
of automobile versus
pedestrian space,
before and after the
transformation.

ACTING FROM THE OUTSIDE

Markus Miessen

In his memoir *Hand to Mouth: A Chronicle of Early Failure,*[1] the American postmodern novelist Paul Auster clarified his understanding of failure by stating that, in his late twenties and early thirties he went through a period of several years when everything he touched turned to failure. As Colin MacCabe noted at a 2005 conference titled *The Value of Failure,* "Success has become one of the key terms by which people evaluate their own and others' lives."[2] When MacCabe refers to failure, he posits it as a crucial component of the development of both knowledge in the sciences and creative experimentation in the arts. He ends by asking to what degree contemporary society demands success and what happens when both public and private funding for projects in the cultural and educational sectors become increasingly success oriented. Imagine if one was to see the world through a pair of technocratic goggles for failure analysis. Supported by the comforting environments of structuralist certainty, this is actually pretty simple. One would start an analysis by determining both the mechanism and the root cause of failure in order to implement a corrective action. One could, therefore, proportionally raise the track record of "success" over time.

We often think of success as being good because it has become linked to prosperity. In MacCabe's words, "Success dominates because of its part in the global evaluation of the good life in terms of money."[3] Hence, failure has become the unthinkable—the semantic confirmation of

poverty. Looking at the current production of space, and indeed the art world, one contentedly realizes that creative production and failure come along as an inseparable couple. This, of course, may be true of almost any industry or economy, but it seems that, at least in current cultural discourse, the value of failure is being put forward as an alternative idea to success. Within such a regime of production, one might argue that the realization of "failure as the fundamental condition of surprise" is nothing new, but an interesting one to build upon. Today, the primary issue that needs to be emphasized is the fact that we have moved away, at least in creative production, from the reference model of the final product. Such a notion has fortunately been replaced by cultural laboratories in which the proto-product—in other words, the process—and its failure, is valued as knowledge production and embodies the laboratory for experimentation. If one were to understand experimentation as a vital ingredient that contributes to the cultural gravitas of spatial production, one has to coercively admit to the value of failure. Hence, the societal norm of success as the only way forward needs to be reviewed and challenged.

Considering failure and conflict from the point of view of process, the most dire situation emerges from inaction caused by a fear of failure. It is the act of production that allows us to revise, tweak, rethink, and change. Along the lines of reinventing oneself, it also opens a space

LIQUIDITY, INC., 2014,
HD VIDEO WITH SOUND, 30 MINS,
COURTESY OF THE ARTIST
AND ANDREW KREPS, NEW YORK,
INSTALLATION VIEW FROM
HITO STEYERL, RAMP AND SPATIAL
DESIGN BY STUDIO MIESSEN,
ARTISTS SPACE, NEW YORK, 2015.

In order to become an active instigator in the choreography of strategic conflicts, the uninvited outsider should be understood as neither a mediator nor a consensus-builder, but someone who ventures out of his or her milieu and immediate professional context, using a set of soft skills required elsewhere, and then applying them to found situations and problematics. What is at stake is not the suggestion of dilettantism as the cultivation of quasi-expertise, but rather a notion of the outsider as an instrumentalized means of breaking out of the tautological box of professional practice. The outsider is not necessarily a polymath or generalist—but someone who can use a general sense of abstraction in order for his or her knowledge to fuel an alternative and necessary debate, and to decouple existing and deadlocked relationships and practices in an external context.

of uncertainty that often produces unexpected knowledge and content through surprise.

If one's priority is to resist failure at all costs, the potential for surprise might not occur. This is why the results of certain investigations and inventions in many fields and disciplines have become predictable, and the outcome of a vast majority of creative and artistic output is both conventional and mediocre. To act with risk means to be incapable of preempting the outcome of an investigation. By consciously allowing a process to fail, the window of surprise will open up—the moment where conflictual involvement and non-loyal participation produce new knowledge and forms of politics.

In the 1993 six-part BBC lectures, *Representations of the Intellectual*, Edward Said introduces the public role of the intellectual as an outsider— as an amateur and disturber of the status quo. In his view, a task of the intellectual is to debunk stereotypes as well as the reductive categories that limit human thought and communication.[4] Said speaks about intellectuals as figures whose public performance can neither be predicted nor reduced into a fixed dogma or party line. He clearly distinguishes between the notion of the intellectual and that of the insider:

> Insiders promote special interests, but intellectuals should be the ones to question patriotic nationalism, corporate thinking, and a sense of class, racial or gender privilege.[5]

For Said, the ideal intellectual works as an exile, marginal figure, or amateur, and as the author of a language that tries to speak the truth to power, rather than an expert who provides objective advice for pay. This disinterested notion of what one could call the "uninvited outsider" is, in the context of this article, the most relevant of Said's writings. It puts forward the claim that universality always comes hand-in-hand with taking a risk. There are no rules. There are "no gods to be worshipped and looked to for unwavering guidance."[6] By questioning the default mode of an operation, which is clearly that of the specialist, the insider, the one with an interested agenda, he writes of intellectuals as those who always speak to an audience, and by doing so, represent themselves to themselves. This mode of practice is based on the idea that one operates according to a preconceived idea of practice, which brings with it the intellectual duty for independence from external pressures. In underlining the role of the outsider, Said exposes the need to—at times—belong to a network of social authorities in order to directly effect change. This spirit of productive and targeted opposition, rather than accommodation, is the driving force for such a practice. To understand when to be part of something and when to be outside of it; to strategically align in order to make crucial decisions, which will otherwise be made by others (most likely with a less ethically developed perspective).

Said, however, also illustrates that the role of the outsider is a lonely condition, and that it involves what Foucault calls "a relentless erudition": "There is something fundamentally unsettling about intellectuals who have neither offices to protect nor territory to consolidate and guard."[7] The uninvited outsider is someone who has a background within a particular (taught) discipline, but ventures out of his or her milieu and immediate professional context, using a set of soft skills required elsewhere, and then applying them to found situations and problematics. According to Said, this person has a specific public role in society that cannot be reduced to a faceless professional. It is precisely the fact that one is operating without professional boundaries that one can start to articulate concerns, views, and attitudes that go beyond the benefit of the individual or particularities. On the one hand, there is a benefit to professional boundaries, such as expertise and specific knowledge. On the other hand, it could be argued that specific sets of outside knowledge can most productively apply to situations precisely when they are not based on disinterested principles. This can particularly emerge when driven by "symbolic personages marked by their unyielding distance to practical concerns,"[8] driven by a consciousness that is skeptical and engaged, and devoted to moral judgment:

> The independent artist and intellectual are among the few remaining personalities equipped to resist and to fight the stereotyping and consequent death of genuinely living things. Fresh perception now involves the capacity to continually unmask and to smash the stereotypes of vision and intellect with which modern communications swamp us.[9]

The intellectual should be understood as neither a mediator nor a consensus-builder, but "someone whose being is staked on a critical sense, a sense of being unwilling to accept easy formulas, or ready-made clichés, or the smooth, ever-so-accommodating confirmations of what the powerful or conventional have to say, and what they do. Not just passively unwillingly, but actively willing to say so in public."[10]

In this context, it is necessary to raise a simple but crucial question: What language does one speak and whom is one addressing? From which position does one talk? There is no truth, only specific situations. There are responses to situations. How one talks or reacts should be modeled from these situations. Therefore, it is also a question of scale. It may be the case that a specific situation might lead to potential readings of larger bodies and relationships. Once the specifics are dealt with, its larger ramifications are usually easily understood. In terms of communicating a message, it is essential to break away from one's milieu. Otherwise, one willingly reduces his or her audience to the current disciplinary crowd of one's background: to produce new publics and

audiences that would not convene without one's practice. In the context of the uninvited outsider, exile can also be understood as a metaphorical condition. As the saying goes: one cannot be a prophet in one's own country. This also applies to one's professional background.

Such exile can be understood as a nomadic practice, not one that is necessarily driven by territorial shifts, but one that sets a course that is never fully adjusted, "always feeling outside the chatty, familiar world inhabited by natives."[11] According to Said, exile—as dissatisfaction—can become not only a style of thought, but also a new, if temporary, habitation. Said further makes a claim for a kind of amateurism, an "activity that is fueled by care and affection rather than by profit and selfish, narrow specialization."[12] As a result, today's intellectual ought to be an amateur, "someone who considers that to be a thinking and concerned member of a society one is entitled to raise moral issues at the heart of even the most technical and professionalized activity."[13] Instead of simply doing what is expected, one can inquire about reasons and protocols of actions. Practitioners in exile are individuals who represent not the consensus of the external practice, but express doubts about it on rational, moral, and political grounds. Questioning long-established agreements and consent, these outsiders can represent and work toward a cause, which might otherwise be difficult for those entangled in the force fields, power relations, and politics of the context that the pariah enters. What is important to realize at this point is that Said deliberately emphasizes the need to be in some form of contact and relationship with the audience in order to affect change:

> The issue is whether that audience is there to be satisfied, and hence a client to be kept happy, or whether it is there to be challenged, and hence stirred into outright opposition or mobilized into greater democratic participation in the society. But in either case, there is no getting around the intellectual's relationship to them.[14]

What is at stake is not the suggestion of dilettantism as the cultivation of quasi-expertise, but rather a notion of the outsider as an instrumentalized means of breaking out of the tautological box of professional practice. The outsider is not necessarily a polymath or generalist—the Renaissance image and description of the architect[15]—but someone who can use a general sense of abstraction in order for his or her knowledge to fuel an alternative and necessary debate, and to decouple existing and deadlocked relationships and practices in an external context. In order to become an active instigator in the choreography of strategic conflicts, one can appropriate the potential of weak ties. An understanding of surplus value through otherness is essentially antithetic to the notion of Gnostic knowledge. This is to say, the idea that the specialist is "good" and trustworthy, and that only specialist knowledge should be accepted in field of practice. It further entails that the status quo is accepted by not engaging with it if one is not an expert. The outsider does not accept this. Venturing out of both the boundaries of expertise and discipline is crucial to remain curious of the specialized knowledges of others. Moreover, it is important that, once in exile, one builds up what architect Teddy Cruz calls a "critical proximity,"[16] a space in which the role of the outsider is to tactically enter an institution or other construct to understand, shuffle, and mobilize its resources and organizational logic.

What then emerges is a discipline without profession; a discipline without a set of prescriptions or known knowledges, but a framework of criticality; a discipline from the outside, a parasitic and impartial form of consulting. Knowledge and the production of knowledge is not fueled by accumulation, but editing and sampling. Or as Jorge Davila argues about Foucault's analytics of power: to cut is to start something new— knowledge itself is a cut, a moment of rupture, a moment of exception driven by the moment of decision.[17] But just as with participation, "critique" can also become a form and force of normalization. Critique can be normalized and absorbed just as rebellion is being subsumed. For critical spatial practice to remain productive and unforeseen, the situation in which criticality turns into yet another modality of commodification must be avoided.

Markus Miessen is an architect and writer, who received his PhD from the Centre for Research Architecture at Goldsmiths College. The initiator of the "Participation" tetralogy, his work revolves around questions of critical spatial practice, institution building, and spatial politics. Miessen is the author of *The Nightmare of Participation* (2011) and *Crossbenching: Toward a Participation as Critical Spatial Practice* (2016), both published by Sternberg Press.

Notes

1   Paul Auster, *Hand to Mouth: A Chronicle of Early Failure* (New York: Henry Holt, 1997).
2   *The Value of Failure*, conference at Tate Modern's Starr Auditorium, June 2005.
3   Ibid.
4   Edward Said, *Representations of the Intellectual (The 1993 Reith Lectures)* (New York: Random House, 1996), xi.
5   Ibid., xiii.
6   Ibid., xiv.
7   Ibid., xviii.
8   Ibid., 7.
9   C. Wright Mills, *Power, Politics, and People: The Collected Essays of C. Wright Mills*, ed. Irving Louis Horowitz, (New York: Ballantine, 1963), 299.
10   Edward Said, *Representations of the Intellectual*, op. cit., 23.
11   Ibid., 53.
12   Ibid., 82.
13   Ibid.
14   Ibid., 83.
15   See also Andrew Saint, *The Image of the Architect* (New Haven/London: Yale University Press, 1983).
16   See also interview with Teddy Cruz by Sevin Yildiz, "With Teddy Cruz on 'Power' and 'Powerlessness,'" on *Archinect*, http://archinect.com/features/article.php?id=93919_0_23_0_M.
17   See Jorge Dávila, "Foucault's Interpretive Analytics of Power," *Systemic Practice and Action Research*, vol. 6, no. 4 (August 1993).

INSITU

uAbureau

INSITU is an initiative that was founded in 2011 to implement projects that investigate the informal development of cities, its non-consolidated urban spaces, and auto-construction processes. The primary objective of the initiative is to explore how the ecological and social environments of the city can be merged to create new and unforeseen landscapes.

INSITU is directed to students and young professionals from urban, art, architecture, design, and construction fields to work in conjunction with their own local communities to design and build a series of small-scale public interventions. In the summers of 2012 and 2013, INSITU was structured as a design-build workshop focused in the barrio of Manantiales in Medellín, Colombia. In the fall of 2013, INSITU was approached by a consortium of public administrative bodies, headed by Ruta N and Universidad Nacional de Colombia (UNAL), to develop a city-wide project for the inaugural Medellin Innovation Festival. The project, entitled "INSITU: Comuna Innova" (or, "Innovative Neighborhoods"), was conceived as a social and participatory project to develop community driven strategies that incubate social and technological innovation.

The metropolitan area of Medellín consists of sixteen *comunas* (districts) and five *corregimientos* (greater urban areas). The project was comprised of twenty-one public installations that consolidated urban spaces that were once unoccupied into places for all. The concept and siting of each intervention was assessed, and then collaboratively designed and built between external stakeholders and local communities over the period of seven weeks. INSITU addressed the design of the city from within and between the psycho-geographical limits of its neighborhoods, activating local communities and the public spaces they inhabit.

The rapidly urbanized city produces one type of material naturally: waste. In developing and developed countries alike, waste is improperly disposed of, and migrates from and between non-consolidated urban spaces. INSITU has developed an on-site production process in which specifically designed industrial machines are installed to process and transform construction waste or solid demolition debris into a hybrid cement aggregate. It is an innovative form of urban conservation, reducing the carbon footprint of transportable material by utilizing construction waste while preserving the memory of a demolished structure or public

Before: Playground. Barrio Manantiales.
PHOTO: COURTESY OF JAMES BRAZIL

Preparing a playground surface by forming the earth with a laser-cut cardboard waffle structure. Barrio Manantiales.
PHOTO: COURTESY OF JAMES BRAZIL

space. We are working with communities to identify potential spaces and introduce material strategies in the social production of place, often creating micro-economies of waste collection in the process. The administration of design-build interventions in public spaces through participatory processes relies on a compressed timeframe. Successful completion builds INSITU's most important asset, trust from external stakeholders and the community. Our approach to the design and fabrication process is subsequently highly malleable, allowing us to move quickly between prototyping and design development phases. We use advanced computational tools and digital fabrication techniques to manage the projects and prioritize speed of deployment, ease of replication, and durability.

The design guidelines for the assembly and installation of the public space are conceived of to allow for maximum participation by the community. Highly responsive systems of fabrication, production, and installation facilitate an exchange between rapid prototyping and participatory design. In the production phase of the project we transform, in the case of "INSITU: Comuna Innova," every available place of fabrication in the city, into a temporary productive space. In the future we aim to build custom on-site digital fabrication machines in the local community centers, schools, and businesses, which are activated by the production of adjacent public spaces they share.

Each INSITU project involves collaboration, community interaction, and learning about the city, including its local processes and its citizens. Projects are varied in scale and type, ranging from playgrounds, skate parks, and community kitchens to an array of urban furniture designs and forms of urban agriculture. INSITU projects are being developed in partnership with various universities, city municipalities and local communities in Australia, El Salvador, Colombia, Peru, Spain, Venezuela, and Turkey.

uAbureau, founded in 2010 by James Brazil and Nicholas Waissbluth, is an international collaborative design studio based out of Spain, Canada, and Colombia. uAbureau is comprised of a dynamic team of urbanists, architects, designers, artists and constructors working at various scales within industry and academic realms, to promote and showcase public and participatory design-build projects.

Project Credits
James Brazil, Fabio Lopez, Rafael Machado, Nicholas Waissbluth

INTE
R

InterAction consists of projects and articles that consider how participatory interactions can occur, how new stakeholders are introduced, and how the relationships between people and their environment impact politics. What is the spatial agency of the individual in relation to the pluralistic collective?

ACTI
ON

COMMONALITIES IN ARCHITECTURE

Yoshiharu Tsukamoto

Recently, people in Japan have expressed how the nation has become affluent and yet people remain unsure of their happiness. This seems to be a sign that they are anxious from being unable to discern where they stand within a society and environment that has rapidly modernized. Architecture has been instrumental in this process of modernization, so we should hold it accountable.

It is undeniable that the postwar reconstruction of cities and the development of Japan's territory were fueled by growth in the construction industry. Since 1950, the state and regional governments —the public—advanced the upgrading of social infrastructure at unprecedented scales with new technologies under the banner of protecting the assets and lives of the people. Rivers and roads were treated as quantifiable things and measured in terms of water or traffic volume, with steel and concrete constructions built to control them. As a result, rivers were less likely to flood, but were also more difficult to access, while roads were reduced primarily to a means of transportation. Meanwhile, government policies encouraged the private ownership of property and houses. Regulatory measures to make houses fireproof and earthquake-resistant motivated homeowners— individuals—to tear down old houses that did not conform to this standard. The construction of houses led to the consumption of electrical appliances and furniture, as well as tableware and beddings, with the economic impact of this extending society-wide. This was how the industrialization of environmental management and house-building fueled the mass-production of safe, well-serviced neighborhoods and dwellings. In the process, the daily activities of people, a lifestyle that was previously rooted in agrarian landscapes, were transplanted into industrialized trades. Simultaneously, commercial facilities, which took up an increasingly larger share of urban space as the economy developed, grew ever more enormous in order to mobilize customers. These facilities then gave rise to spaces in which citizens, acting as customers, could use clean and safe spaces in exchange for money. In these spaces, there was the appearance that one could gain satisfaction as individuals. The behaviors involving play and pastime that had been enacted by people out in the city were then transplanted into the realm of the service industries.

The industrialization that took place propelled the miraculous growth of Japan's GDP in the late twentieth century. However, this also gave rise to unexpected by-products: people unable to come to terms with nature in the places where they lived, an inability to know what kind of houses to build, as well as confusion on how to activate public spaces. Without these things, people cannot connect with one another. They are consequently separated into individuals, yet grow dependent on the systems endorsed by the state and generated by the market. Effectively, people have been gradually deprived of the latitude and opportunities to behave autonomously at their own discretion. If considered from the standpoint of industry, with its primary interest in increasing productivity, it is more convenient that people are oblivious to this. People only need access to a wider range of choices in terms of science, engineering, economics, and design so that they can affirm their individuality. The outcome from shaping the environment and cities in this way, following the war, has resulted in the standardization of the urban landscape as witnessed in Japan today. Its disorderliness and incoherence may be "interesting," but, at best, it can only be understood as an agglomeration of individual pieces. Unfortunately, these pieces are nothing more than pieces. This is inadequate. What is lacking in this standard landscape are the architectural typologies and human behaviors that have been passed down over generations and that are shared in specific locales by transcending individual differences. This landscape is missing the lively streetscapes and exceptional urban spaces that can be formed through the recurrence of these typologies and behaviors. In order to enable these local typologies and behaviors, we must use design to transcend our generational and individual differences. People will likely develop confidence and pride if they feel that they are a member of a particular collective. Is it not because people lack such feelings that they are uncertain as to whether they are happy? What can be observed from this is that the shortcomings of architecture and urban spaces of our industrialized age are brought to the fore at moments when having a sense of sharedness is important. Certainly, it is true that much has been lost to the destruction caused by earthquakes and wars. However, these are also the vulnerabilities that have repeatedly been reinforced by remaking societal structures in their wake. These structures have the tendency to separate the collective body of the people into distinct individuals. We must be vigilant of the mode of architectural practice grounded on the individual that has been glorified within this tendency, particularly in the late twentieth century. We are suggesting that, if twentieth-century architecture placed too much emphasis on the individual and the state (public), then we must now identify a mode of architectural practice focused on the common. We propose to refer to the realms that unfold through this mode of practice as commonalities of architecture.

Commonality is not an everyday term. In Japanese, it holds the meanings of the words *kyōyūsei* (共有性: the quality of being jointly owned or shared) and *kyōdōsei* (共同性: the quality of working together or of being united). It is possible that is has been adopted in other disciplines, but the term has rarely been used in architecture. Among architects, only Louis Kahn has used the term. According to Kahn, the reason we are moved by ancient constructions is because we are connected to one another by things, or commonalities, deep within us that transcend time and place. Notions similar to this can be identified in

Jørn Utzon's 1948 manifesto "The Innermost Being of Architecture," in which the idea that the present is linked to the past by the intelligence of human beings embedded in architecture.[1] And also in what Christopher Alexander later describes in his 1979 book *The Timeless Way of Building* as the possibility of design to possess an "ageless character."[2] These are encouraging expressions that suggest that it is possible for those in the present to link with those who erected the early constructions that seemed to have risen out of the earth.

These ideas evoke a return towards an origin. However, one must be careful in returning to origins, because doing so tends to lead to a search for prototypes in a reductive manner through the disregard of time- and place-specific transformations. Our discussion on commonalities in architecture continues this line of thought. We, too, are focusing on the emergence of intelligence in architecture, but we diverge from it in how we understand human behaviors and architectural types as things that are generated "by chance" through the combination of various conditions. We are doing so because this viewpoint allows us to re-grasp the transformations that behaviors and types undergo over time as things that help us perceive changes in their boundary conditions. We cannot avoid dealing with boundary conditions if we are to create things to be shared, or commonalities. We are employing this genealogical approach in an attempt to bring the commonalities in architecture into the context of design.

What is now needed are the means for perceiving commonalities. Situations in which commonalities have been given form or have become perceptible include the condition when similar, but slightly different, buildings recur in a particular locale or along a street. Despite different owners, each building participates in shaping the town landscape or urban space with their roofs and facades, forming a collective whole that transcends private ownership. Features observed in buildings regardless of their individual differences are typologies. However, this understanding of typology is through the vantage point of the researcher. With regard to commonalities, we understand that the people living in a place share a common architecture. In other words, the fact that typologies exist signifies that people understand what type of architecture is appropriate for the particular region or community in which they live.

Another situation where people are behaving freely is in the urban plaza. However, people in this space will rarely behave in entirely unrelated ways; rather, they converge towards a certain set of behaviors. Behaviors can be seen as types also, and they can be repeated in a particular place by transcending the differences of their subjects. This enables strangers to have common ownership over the same time and place while acknowledging each other's differences without interference. A person can acquire these behaviors through repetition. They can be learned. These behaviors

Gathering around heat kept in the stone guardrail

sitting on the guardrail

showing off their customized bikes

pizza and beer

bike with speakers passing by

stone pavement warmed by the western sun

customized bike

watching the customized bikes

Dronning Louises
Bridge, Copenhagen,
Denmark, Atelier
Bow-Wow (2013).

belong to each person, but simultaneously belong to the place, and no one person can have exclusive possession of them. Conversely, it is not easy to prevent others from behaving in the same way. The behaviors are both an asset to the individuals who acquire them and a shared asset of all the people. Those who are acquainted with accepted behaviors appear refined, and there is something gentle and comforting about them. In fact, this is why they are permitted to have ownership over public spaces, if only temporarily. This privilege adds breadth to people's lives, and can encourage tolerance.

Therefore, a shared trait between architectural typologies and human behaviors is that they are perpetuated in particular regions and neighborhoods while transcending the differences of their subjects. What makes this possible is the existence of types. Considered over the long term, types change incrementally while retaining their primary attributes. Types always accompany forms and cannot exist alone as physical constructs. Types form where balances are found between various factors—whether climatic, material, lifestyle, institutional, or economic. Hence, by looking at types, we can appreciate how there are certain mutual linkages taking hold between things in which an infinite variety of combinations are possible.

Types subtly change over the years because new balances are established when any one of the numerous factors that constitute the mutual linkages change in quantity, are lost, or have new factors integrated into them. For instance, the balance maintained between a craft artist's ceramic artwork and nature is not the same as the balance maintained between mass-produced pottery and nature. In the former, the value of the artwork lies in how its form is found through a dialogue with nature (clay); in the latter case, the value of the product lies in how it is made to have no imperfections by suppressing any individual inconsistencies in the clay that is transferred to a mass production scale. If the relationship of the individual pieces to nature were to be mobilized for mass manufacturing, the degree of interaction with the elements of nature would become imperceptible among the various factors that constitute the mutual linkages associated with pottery making. The qualities of regional specificity would also diminish with it. Genea-logical studies reveal changes in mutual linkages by introducing time into the transformation of type. A genealogical examination enables the mutual linkages to be re-read as things that are dynamic, rather than static. Both architectural typologies and human behaviors are produced over and over again within mutual linkages. In this sense, they serve as indicators of the conditions of a particular place.

Architectural typologies and human behaviors can be seen as materialized forms of commonalities extending from our earlier studies of behavio-rology.[3] Our focus with behaviorology has been

Dronning Louises
Bridge, Copenhagen,
Denmark.
PHOTOGRAPH COURTESY
ATELIER BOW-WOW.

on the behaviors of natural elements (light, wind, heat, humidity, water, among others), people, and architecture (typologies) that are repeated with their own particular rhythm while transcending the differences of their subjects. We have been observing how intelligence emerges in architecture when it integrates these different behaviors into one physical entity. Our claims in behaviorology have been grounded in the practical consideration that we gave to independent problems by utilizing the insights that we gained from our observation of these behaviors. The observation of behaviors demands that we ascertain what things can and cannot be altered among the factors that shape the behaviors. For instance, we cannot alter the fact that water flows downward in accordance with gravity, but we can alter how the water flows by modifying the surface on which it travels. It is as if the attributes unable to be altered preserve their invariability by making use of those that can be altered; while the things that can be altered change by making use of the attributes that cannot be altered. The concept of commonalities is introduced in order to extract such mutual linkages or relationships that exist latently among typologies and behaviors and to make them a common resource accessed by all.

The thread of reasoning behind commonalities that leads from typologies and behaviors to mutual linkages is important because it resists the fragmentation of life, particularly in today's urban areas. However, this resistance does not fit into the conventional scheme in which there are individuals who are resisting against a state or social system oppressing them. Rather, it can be considered a resistance to the thought that the individual inherently exists. In actuality, the notion of the individual has been created interdependently with the social systems, such as the state. What has been carelessly swept away in the process is the intermediate realm of the common. There should be rich commonalities, which, like behaviors, can be acquired by individuals while also belonging to particular locales. If we look at behaviors, the individual and the common appear to merge with one another making it difficult to distinguish between them. However, this involves too much diversity to be handled within a public system, which is why it is assumed that people are individuals, or empty bodies.

Twentieth-century architecture played a significant role in reinforcing this transformation; for instance, modernist collective housing or detached housing developments. Collective housing, intended to address postwar housing shortages, was premised on delivering dwellings on a mass scale, and was enacted by superimposing the family unit onto living units—producing uniform spaces through fair, equal repetition. Within this uniformity, collective housing projects were zoned into three distinct areas: spaces for the family (individual realm), spaces used collectively by the residents (common realm), and spaces freely accessed by

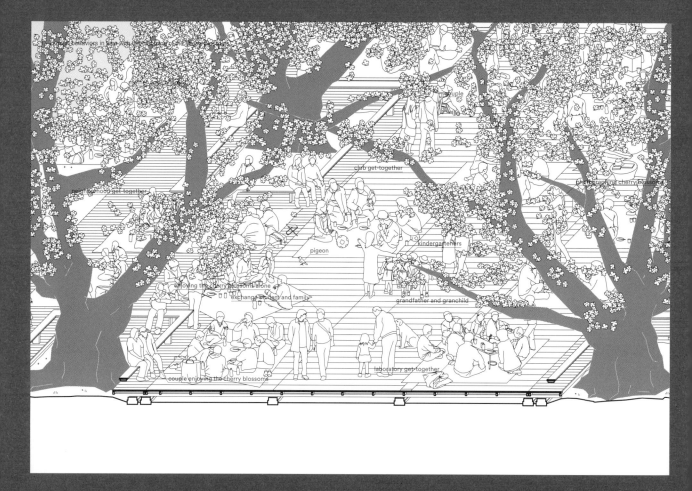

Cherry blossom viewing
at the Tokyo Institute
of Technology, Tokyo,
Japan, Atelier Bow-Wow
(2013).

Cherry blossoms,
during the Spring
bloom, at the Tokyo
Institute of Technology,
Tokyo, Japan.
PHOTOGRAPH COURTESY
ATELIER BOW-WOW.

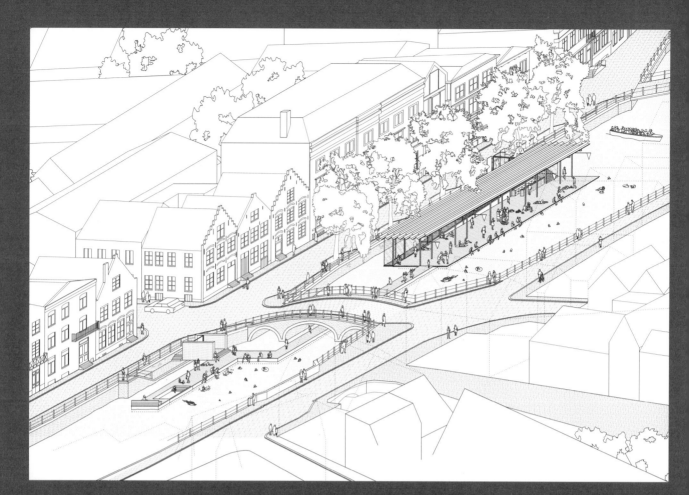

outsiders (public realm). These distinct realms for the individual, common, and public could be measured and calculated. The individual realm was typically limited to families and singles acting as residents. However, these residents were assumed to be empty, unskilled bodies unable to generate new behaviors in architecture. Housing provided common areas for connecting individuals to give meaning to the fact that they lived together. Yet, these common areas were typically nothing more than calculated floor areas set aside, merely representative of the common. Nobody knew how to use the common spaces, so they became overrun by rules written to prevent inconveniences to others—such as "No Ball Games Allowed," "No Noisy Activities Allowed," or "No Open Flames,"—ultimately becoming common nuisances that required maintenance costs but were unable to be used for anything.

Other realms that are accessible to all, such as the plazas in front of public facilities and the open areas that are created at the base of high-rise buildings in exchange for increased floor area ratios, also assume its residents as empty, unskilled bodies. Open spaces are necessary at the base of high-rise buildings for emergency evacuations of large numbers of people in a safe manner. The dimensions of such spaces should obviously correspond to the sum of quantifiable individuals. However, so-called "one-sided" public spaces with no consideration for the space of the street or their neighborhood are increasingly everywhere.

The boundary of the individual is assumed to exist as a matter of fact when decisions are made based on these vaguely defined common spaces and one-sided public spaces. This leads to the possibility that individuals might be split apart more than connecting them. As more collective housing and open spaces designed in this manner continue to be constructed, people become accustomed to the relationship between the individual and public according to the notion that the sum total of measurable individuals is equal to the whole (public).

Architectural design that integrates commonality must challenge the notion of the individual as an "empty, unskilled body." This undertaking is sure to reflect concerns about the fragmentation of modern life, misunderstandings of the mutual linkages between things that really should be giving direction to lives, and how things that used to be part of people's daily life—realm of commonalities—have been transplanted into the industrial realm. It is more effective to tie realms to everyday life, such as dwellings that are designed to be repeated, streets shaped by the repetition of such dwellings, and open spaces in which people can gather. These are the realms that will produce the rich behaviors that fall outside conventional categories and that cannot currently be observed in the spaces systematized within twentieth-century building types.

Translation by Gen Machida.

Canal Swimmer's Club, Bruges, Belgium, Atelier Bow-Wow (2015).

Opening of the Canal
Swimmer's Club,
Bruges, Belgium, Atelier
Bow-Wow (2015).
PHOTOGRAPH COURTESY OF
TRIENNALE BRUGGE.

Notes
1   Jorn Utzon, "The Innermost
Being of Architecture," (1948) in
Richard Weston Utzon: Inspiration,
Vision, Architecture (Hellerup:
Edition Blondal, 2002).
2   Christopher Alexander, The
Timeless Way of Building, (New York:
Oxford University Press, 1979).
3   Atelier Bow-Wow, Terunobu
Fujimori, et al., The Architectures
of Atelier Bow-Wow: Behaviorology
(New York: Rizzoli, 2010).

MAYHEM AND SOURCE CODE

Albert Pope

Material Evidence

When we call for collective action in the public realm today, we are often evoking a certain type of political actor—a street protestor—and a certain type of political space—the public square and the street. While recent events imply that such actors and spaces are still relevant in particular political cultures—in Cairo, Hong Kong and Kiev, for example—they seem to have a limited effect. At best, the Arab Spring reshuffled the chairs at the table; at worst, it opened the door to militant reaction. After months of protesting, Hong Kong is farther from achieving universal suffrage than it has ever been. Ukraine has not escaped Russian influence, quite the reverse. In other words, it seems that public space has failed as a significant site of power exchange. At this point, street demonstrations seem to be more about spectacle than about politics, more about theatre than about protest, more about a block party than about a "revolution." Given the radical transformation of the city over the past five decades, this should not be a surprise given that public space has not been reproduced for at least a half century.

With very few exceptions, street protests rely on an anthropomorphically-scaled urbanism of city blocks that form public plazas and public streets. Designers know that the city's public space has transformed because they know that our ability to produce such spaces has, not only changed, it has vanished. While renovations of pre-1950 urbanism have surely occurred,

in post-1950 urbanism, no city in the world has expanded in a manner that would produce a continuous anthropomorphically-scaled urban fabric. Such a remarkable shift in urban production cannot occur in isolation—it can only reflect a greater shift in economic, political, and cultural values. To say the obvious, coherent collective space is the product of coherent collective values. Absent those values, there is not a designer in the world that can produce a viable collective space. In their absence, the best any society can hope to accomplish is an occupation of the spaces it may inherit from past generations in a well-intentioned parody of a public life that is not their own. Such occupations, while public, cannot *produce* a social life if it does not exist in the first place. And there is no greater proof of its absence than in our own fifty-year refusal to create a space for public life in the cities that we build for ourselves.

Given this circumstance, we might well ask if our inherited public space has any instrumental value at all. An obvious response would be to draw a direct comparison. Shifting the argument closer to home, we can gauge the effectiveness of the Occupy Wall Street movement against the effectiveness of, say, Edward Snowden, to see that other drivers of social change have outstripped the performance of a street crowd. That one comparison may be all that is needed to suggest that the street crowd has been replaced by another, far more effective political actor—the individual behind the laptop. The Snowden affair underscores something

that we instinctively know—that keyboards and source code have long replaced street mayhem and Molotov cocktails as an effective political weapon.

Such a decline of the collective sphere and empowerment of the individual sphere precisely tracks our urban development over the past fifty years. Both the Garden City of North America and the Radiant City of Asia and Europe eliminated anthropomorphically-scaled urban fabric in favor of unprecedented advancements in individual accommodation. In other words, the city today is no longer devoted to public accommodation but is devoted almost exclusively to individual accommodation. Save the odd shopping mall or sports stadium, contemporary urban production does not create public space but instead feeds off of a pre-modern public world created by the collective ambitions of those who preceded us. In return, the individual has been liberated from the oppressive limitations of traditional urban fabric to enjoy a world of light and space and of apparent autonomy, which was unknown to its predecessors.

We do not need to be anthropologists to understand that the subjects of political action are not only defined by the urban forms which they inherit from their ancestors but are also (and more accurately) defined by the urban forms that they produce. Our unwillingness to produce a viable public realm over the past half century speaks volumes about our priorities and aspirations. Despite the endless speculation on the current state of our collective identity, the cities that we actively construct provide unassailable material evidence of exactly who we are. Needless to say, there is a correlation between the rise of a technically empowered individual—the individual behind the computer—and the unwillingness or

inability to produce a contemporary infrastructure of blocks, streets, monuments, and plazas. As always, objects and subjects align even if that alignment is ill-perceived.

The Mutation of Base Form

The shift from an empowered crowd of our past to an empowered individual of our present has largely transpired at the level of urban infrastructure. Though open street space lingers on in the imagination as the space of political action, few of us are fully aware that such space has not been reproduced for over fifty years. The anthropomorphically-scaled block and street aggregate of gridiron urbanism has long given way to the production of closed and private cul-de-sac or spine form of megalopolitan development. It is the spine, not the grid, which provides the material evidence of contemporary social identity. The shift from the open grid to the closed spine has taken place in the background of our routine awareness, yet it is no less powerful for it. The open and public corridor street—host to the street protestor—is the product of that ubiquitous staple of civil engineering: the urban grid. The space that was provided by the grid enabled a spontaneous mode of street theatre that cannot be reproduced in the isolated and scripted public events that we subscribe to today. To phrase it differently, as the empowered crowd was born of the grid, the empowered individual was born of the cul-de-sac spine.

Historically, the city's complex technical, political, and economic forces played out across the simple baseline of the urban grid-form. Beyond any specific "masterplan," the grid is what made the impossible complexities of an urban aggregation manageable. In other words, the grid was the foundational structure, or organizational DNA, of the traditional city. Today, we find ourselves at the end of a lengthy, but nonetheless, remarkable transformation of this organizational logic. As early as the 1950s, a precise graphic description of this transformation was provided in the urban project of the German-American theorist Ludwig Hilberseimer. This description was reproduced in many of his proposals in and around Chicago and can best be shown in the serial diagrams he produced for a neighborhood called Marquette Park. The diagrams show the precise evolution of an open and continuous grid-form into twelve closed and discontinuous spine-forms. Hilberseimer's diagrams make apparent the transformation of our urban base form—the organizational logic of the city—that took place over the course of the twentieth century. Owing to any number of economic, technical or political forces—the GI Bill, the mass ownership of automobiles, xenophobia, traffic engineering, consumer economy—the spine-form succeeded the grid. This shift reflects, not only a profound shift in the city's organizational logic, but also profound shift in its public demeanor. The end of the open, anthropomorphically-scaled public street reflects a dramatic (ontological) shift in the society that ceased to produce it.

2014 Hong Kong Umbrella Revolution as police attacked peaceful demonstrators with tear gas.
PHOTO: COURTESY OF THE CREATIVE COMMONS, FLICKR USER PASU AU YEUNG

–>
View from the public deck of the Sha Tin New Town Center, looking across the canal.
PHOTO: COURTESY OF MAHAN SHIRAZI

／ Notice

此處有錄影監察系統
Surveillance Recording System in use

在本大廈設置的閉路電視系統會收錄影像作保安及營業用途，
所收錄的資料將會依照個人資料(私隱)條例的規定處理。

This CCTV system installed in this building will record video images
for security and building management purposes. The recorded data
will be processed in accordance with Personal Data (Privacy) Ordinance.

NTPMSO

NTPMSO

Circuits and Terminals

Hilberseimer's depiction of the mutation of urban DNA is simple enough. What remains to be described are the characteristic differences between the old and new organizational forms. Specifically, it is important to describe how grid organizations have historically privileged collective agency and how spine organizations privilege individual agency today. Key to these descriptions is the status of points or nodes within these two networks. In this regard, the open "circuits" of the grid and closed "terminals" of the spine can be seen to establish the most fundamental of urban relationships through their respective settlement patterns. In our transition from the grid's characteristic circuits to the spine's characteristic end-points, the urban world shifts from a relatively open to a relatively closed urban system.

Following on the series of drawings that describe the mutation of the urban base form from the grid to the spine, a final overlay can be added that shows typical patterns of movement. Imagined as an actual urban experience, this movement passes down in scale from the urban freeway to the feeder, from the feeder to the collector, from the collector to the development spine, and from the development spine toward termination in a final end-point or destination. As opposed to the endless series of circuits that an open grid produces (1234 East 479th Street), this inward spiraling establishes a singular and exclusive end-point (4 Longleaf Lane). Most of us now live, not on an arbitrary grid coordinate, but at the end of an exclusive path, on an exclusive driveway, of an exclusive cul-de-sac. Less like a perambulation and more like a homing in, this pattern of movement operates in a city whose overall form is by now large and unknowable—a "sprawl." In the world organized by the spine, our delicate egos are right where we always wanted them to be, safely seated at the very origin of the spiral.

In the far-flung cul-de-sac of an American mass housing tract, the privileging of the individual subject at the expense of any form of collective identity could not be rendered more apparent than it is by this simple figure of movement. Yet its existential logic, like the spine diagram itself, extends from the horizontal dimension of the Garden City tract house into the vertical dimension of the Radiant City tower. Rotate the spine into thin air and the terminals remain terminals—privileging the isolated urban subject now exposed to the leafy mat of vegetation and the broad horizons of the natural world. While the cul-de-sac and the highrise may seem ill-matched in terms of scale, and ill-matched in terms of our rigid divide of architecture and urbanism, they align through their organizational logic. They both support exactly the same movement patterns whether that movement is in a car (cul-de-sac) or on foot (highrise). The programmatic corollary to the spine-form, both vertical and horizontal, is the explication of modern dwelling that sits at the end of the characteristic terminal points. The reorganization of the domestic program around these terminal points

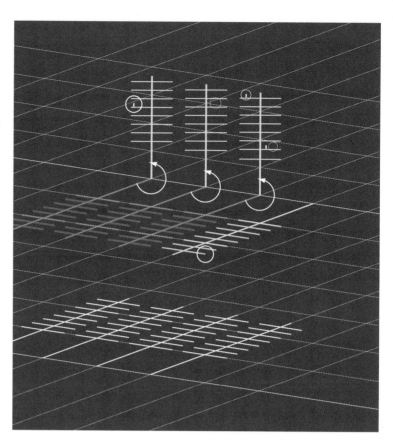

leads us to a more concise portrait of contemporary political space as inhabited by the privileged successor to the revolutionary street protestor.

The Problem of the House: Explication

The grid produces a collective agency in the form of an open and continuous public space. The spine produces individual agency, through heightened accommodation, in the form of a closed and exclusive private dwelling. This focus on the individual is achieved through the reorganization of the private dwelling. This reorganization is described in ontological terms by the German philosopher Peter Sloterdijk from his *Spheres* trilogy:

> If one had to find the quickest possible way of explaining what changes the 20th century brought for human being-in-the-world, the bulletin should read: It architecturally, aesthetically, and juridically unfolded existence as inhabitation—or, to put it simply: It made dwelling explicit. Modern building disassembled the house, the supplement to nature that makes being human possible into discrete elements, and reassigned them; it took the city, which was once at the center of a world planned in a circle around itself, and repositioned it so that it became but one position in a network of flow of streams. The analytical "revolution" that constitutes the central nervous system of modernity also infected the architectural shells of human spheres and by establishing a formal alphabet that created a new art of synthesis, a modern grammar of generating space, and a changed state of existing in an artificial milieu.[1]

The ubiquitous spine form of the cul-de-sac subdivision and the high-rise housing block indicate the shared "DNA" of Radiant and Garden City models.

Under a new "analytical revolution" that he refers to as explication, Sloterdijk argues that modernism established an entirely new urban agenda that was based, first and foremost, on the qualities of private inhabitation. Modernism redefined the individual dwelling in ontological terms as "the supplement to nature that makes being human possible." For perhaps the first time, urban existence was conceived, not as the expression of a collective enterprise—of inhabitants coming together to improve their shared existence—but as human habitation or, to put it in Heideggerian terms, "being-in-the-world." Urban existence became a problem of inhabitation focused entirely on the status of the individual. Sloterdijk suggests that modernism reduced the city to one among many positions in a "network of flow." This move from a unified "world planned in a circle around itself" into a network of targeted inhabitants—a move from hierarchy to network—gives a lucid accounting of the modern urban project's comprehensive urban effects.

If all this sounds familiar, it should. Quoting the lines from Le Corbusier's *Towards an Architecture,* "The problem of the house is a problem of the era. Social equilibrium depends on it today. The first obligation of architecture, in an era of renewal, is to bring about a revision of values, a revision of the constitutive elements of the house."[2] The connection between Le Corbusier and Sloterdijk is quite direct, making it easy to fill in the missing disciplinary pieces. With this explication of dwelling came the rise of "the unit," as the indispensable focus of urban organization. It was the unit—the private dwelling—not the street, not the monument, not the square, not any other element of collective urban existence that would become the city's new *raison d'être.* In drawing the very act of dwelling out of the background and making it explicit, private as op-posed to collective activity was privileged for the first time in urban history. This privileging is often taken for granted as mere functionalism and to some extent such a characterization is useful. To say the obvious, individuals are empowered when they do not have to live in slums. The super-dense urban fabric that tourists love so much creates embedded units that have no daylight and no air, no relation to the natural world, and reinforce no singular identity. These gross limitations put the individual on his or her back. Beyond functionalism, however, freedom from basic human want produces a quite literal form of human agency that can never be taken as granted. It is through the modernist ontological enterprise of explication (as opposed to functionalism) that we find our way from the empowered crowd on the street to the empowered individual behind the laptop. While modernism focused on the unit, the more significant impact would come from the changes this focus would impose on the city as a whole.

The Problem of the City: Foam
The recent move away from a spatially empowered crowd and toward a spatially empowered individual lines up, not only with the physical artifacts that we have produced over the past fifty years, but also with the contemporary subject positions articulated both in the human sciences and in philosophy. Following his explication of modern housing, Peter Sloterdijk's metaphor of contemporary social organization as "foam" is one of the more significant speculations on the rise of an empowered individual and its role in the formation of an unprecedented collective subject—a real alternative to the exhausted image and agency of the revolutionary street crowd.[3] What is principally at issue is how the newly empowered subjectivity described by Sloterdijk matches up with contemporary urban practices.

In a recent lecture to an architectural audience, Sloterdijk spoke quite explicitly about the relationship between the explicated urban dweller and the city that this dweller brings into existence. This relationship is described in regards to his notion of "foam" as it relates to urban density. Quoting at length, Sloterdijk argues that:

> Foam, in my opinion, is a very useful expression for what architects call density—itself a negentropic factor. Density can be expressed in psychosocial terms by a coefficient of mutual irritation. People generate atmosphere by mutually exerting pressure on one another, crowding one another. We must never forget that what we term "society" implies the phenomenon of unwelcome neighbors. Thus, density is also an expression for our excessively communicative state, and, incidentally, the dominant ideology of communication is repeatedly prompting us to expand it further. Anyone taking density seriously will, by contrast, end up praising walls. This remark is no longer compatible with classic Modernism, which established the ideal of the transparent dwelling, the ideal that inside relationships should be reflected on the outside and vice versa. Today, we are again foregrounding the way a building can isolate, although this should not be confused with its massiveness. Seen as an independent phenomenon, isolation is one form of explication of the conditions of living with neighbors. Someone should write a book in praise of isolation. That would describe a dimension of human coexistence that recognizes that people also have an infinite need for non-communication. Modernity's dictatorial traits all stem from an excessively communicative anthropology: For all too long, the dogmatic notion of an excessively communicative image of man was naively adopted. By means of the image of foam you can show that the small forms protect us against fusion with the mass and the corresponding hypersociologies. In this sense, foam theory is a polycosmology.[4]

In a single paragraph, Sloterdijk sets up a curious notion of urban density that, in relation to our current formulations, is riddled with contradiction. What he describes through the metaphor of foam is not traditional urban density of Manhattan or

View of the Caribbean Coast housing estate from the Hong Kong International Airport on Chek Lap Kok island. Note the small multi-story buildings adjacent to the estate towers.
PHOTO: COURTESY OF THE CREATIVE COMMONS, WIKIPEDIA

Hong Kong Island, nor is it the density of "classic Modernism," by which he most likely means the "Social Condenser" of Russian Constructivism. What he is after with foam is an updated version of density, which provocatively rejects the urban crowd or, in his terms, "fusing with the mass." The verb is well-chosen; Elias Canetti has taught us that the allure of a street crowd is the very prospect of shedding the existential burden of individual identity and melting into the crowd.[5] In rejecting this fusion, however, Sloterdijk does not reject the mass as the necessary prerequisite to urbanism; "foam" begins with multiplication, with mass individuation. And despite his commitment to "small forms," the rejection of the crowd should not be taken as hostility toward cities.

Acknowledging the value of density as a "negentropic factor," he implicitly abandons the entropic dissipation of the city (some call it "sprawl") that plagues both modern and contemporary urbanism alike. Rejecting dissipation, then, Sloterdijk's density is based on the provision of isolation or the "phenomenon of unwelcome neighbours." Acknowledging a "coefficient of mutual irritation," he proclaims "anyone taking density seriously will, by contrast, end up praising walls." Sloterdijk's foam is thus a kind of walled-up density that readily suggests, among other models, Le Corbusier's well-known employment of the monastic typology to project modern urban entities made up entirely of isolates. While Sloterdijk condemns our naive and thoughtless adoption of

"an excessively communicative image of man," perhaps nothing guarantees the contemporary subject's "infinite need for non-communication" than the monastic models that beats at the heart of the Radiant City. The result is an alignment of the modern project of the explicated individual dwelling and the isolated urban density or a density without propinquity that supports it.

Thus Sloterdijk uses foam to promote a multicellular "polycosmology" where urban existence becomes a problem of habitation or dwelling that is contingent upon the elevated status of the individual. Polycosmology dovetails with the modern project's critique of traditional (public) hierarchies and it's reduction of the city to isolated monad plugged into a virtual "network of flow." This reduction transitions the city from a monocentric "world planned in a circle around itself" into a polycentric network of targeted inhabitants or a model of density that replaces (metropolitan) hierarchy with (megalopolitan) network. Deprived of public hierarchies, collective action has no choice but to don nineteenth century attire and occupy the still functional scenes of its distant past. In ways that are difficult to articulate, the attire does not quite fit.

Occupy Central
"Where can u find a city with over 50K protesters, but not a single store being damaged, not a single car set fire?"
—@ocplhk

The day this sentence was written, October 1, 2014, Hong Kong was in midst of a week-long protest. The promise of "one country, two systems" made by the Chinese government at the 1997 handover was supposed to last until 2047, yet it came unraveled over the past weeks as a home-grown, pro-democracy movement has taken to the streets of Central—the colonial heart of the city. The protesters key demands are for elections free from the influence of Beijing and the resignation of its current "Chief Executive." The protests are overwhelmingly comprised of students with its key leader, Joshua Wong, being just seventeen years old. Hong Kong's Central district is an ideal venue for a street protest being among the densest places in the world. Built on top of a crooked grid that at best can be characterized as medieval, the district stands as the corporate emblem of the entire city. Crammed between a precipitous slope and the edge of Victoria Bay, Central contains all but one of the city's signature high rises that together provide a striking backdrop to the ongoing protests for universal suffrage.

Yet, for all of its global notoriety, Central is not the densest place in Hong Kong nor is it the place that many Hong Kongers actually live. Cross the harbor and pass over yet another precipitous slope and you arrive at the first of Hong Kong's New Towns called Sha Tin. The anchor of the largest of Hong Kong's eight administrative districts, Sha Tin was the pilot project in the development of the city's massive post war expansion into the zone that is officially known as the New Territories. Today the zone hosts a remarkable array of housing estates containing well over half of the Hong Kong population, and they are destined to receive the lion's share of the city's subsequent growth. Appropriately named, the New Territories are the future of Hong Kong.

In the crossing over from Central to Sha Tin, however, something remarkable happens; the city's celebrated street crowds literally vanish. In as much as the urban crowd is the public substance —if not the public soul—of Hong Kong, its sudden disappearance cannot be taken lightly, nor can it be ignored for all that it can tell us about the status of public life in the besieged city-state today. Taking the short MTR ride from Central to Sha Tin is not just a passage from the old town to the New Town, it is a passage into the existential inwardness of today's Hong Kong. In Sha Tin, of course, great numbers of people are still there—three quarters of a million at last count—but they have all been absorbed into enormous blind structures that seem like nothing more than extensions of the transit systems which connect them to the greater city. Outside, urban concrete is replaced by lush tropical plants; sidewalks morph into

pedestrian bridges and skywalks; boulevards turn into "pedestrian" promenades; parks replace plazas and monumental civic cores—once capable of dominating an entire city—are replaced by empty space. And beneath all of these remarkable displacements, the timeless metric of the pedestrian street grid is nowhere to be found. The crowds that fill the continuous street pattern in Hong Kong no longer characterize public life in Sha Tin. And when they do form, around transit stops or commercial hubs or at staged events, they have the lifespan of a mayfly—momentary and ephemeral —coming in and out of existence in minutes, providing scarcely a moment of collective self-awareness. What remains after their quick and inevitable dispersal has less to do with the physical body of the crowd and more to do with the signs and signals of its conspicuous absence. This absence is appropriate inasmuch as the true locus of Sha Tin lies in none of these places but in the thousands of cellular dwelling units that pile up in the district, endless and uncountable, like so many air pockets in a mountain of foam.

Architecture or Revolution
"The social mechanism, deeply disturbed, oscillates between improvements of historical importance and catastrophe. It is a primal instinct of every living being to ensure a shelter. The various working classes of society no longer have suitable homes, neither laborers nor intellectuals. It is a question of building that is key to the equilibrium upset today: architecture or revolution."
—Le Corbusier[6]

The pedigree of Sha Tin's New Towns housing estates is not difficult to construct. Le Corbusier via Sloterdijk has already been set up, giving rise to a whole set of interesting questions not the least of which is the role of the privileged individual in relation to the contemporary political actor—a street protestor—and his or her characteristic political space. Le Corbusier's notorious presentation of modern urbanism as an alternative to manning the barricades here runs into a future that was never anticipated—a revolution called "Occupy Central for Peace and Love," organized by twitter (@ocplhk), led by a high school student, recorded by smart phones, and documented on thousands of personal online profiles—a revolution that occurred more than fifty years ago.

Albert Pope is an architect in Houston, Texas and the Gus Sessions Wortham Professor of Architecture at Rice University. He has lectured, exhibited and written extensively on the logic of contemporary urban form and its decisive role in shaping social and environmental contexts. He is the author of *Ladders* (Princeton Architectural Press) and the founding director of Present Future, a design program and think-tank at Rice University.

Notes
1   Peter Sloterdijk, "Excerpts From Spheres 3," *Harvard Design Review 29* (Fall/Winter, 2009), 39-52 *(emphasis added)*.
2   Le Corbusier, *Towards a New Architecture*, (New York: Dover, 1986).
3   Peter Sloterdijk, *Spharen III: Schaume* (Suhrkamp, 2004).
4   Peter Sloterdijk, "Spheres Theory: Talking to Myself about the Poetics of Space," Lecture transcript in *Harvard Design Review 30* (Spring/Summer, 2009), 126-137 *(emphasis added)*.
5   Elias Canetti, *Crowds and Power*, (New York: Farrar, Straus and Giroux, 1984).
6   Le Corbusier, *Towards a New Architecture*, (New York: Dover, 1986).

THE IMAGE OF THE SQUARE: REDEFINING CITIZENSHIP BY DESIGN

Samaa Elimam

Colonel Sanders, Styrofoam blocks, toy camels, and a one-dollar bill, composed the streets and façades of a miniature Tahrir Square model constructed by one spirited protester while he occupied the space in February 2011. Acting as a mimetic device, the model was a smaller stage within an unfolding square that was experiencing a series of live transformations. Employing found objects and symbolic materials to represent the built environment, the representational square was continuously updated to capture the events that reconstituted the space. The model and its builder, conscious of their socio-political undertones, traveled through the traffic islands of Tahrir Square during the night. Engaging and interacting with different groups, the citizens created episodic moments around a tangible piece that told a new narrative of the square with every dawn. A new and accessible form of public design emerged: first as mimesis of the existing space and its events, followed by the active reinterpretation, imagination, and interrogation of spatial possibilities through the physical model. Inspired by a reactivated public realm to articulate his own reading of the environment—likely a new experience for this young citizen—such a distinct spatial practice stands for the inherent promise of using design as a tool for catalyzing public action.

Though temporary, the construction of the model incited various reactions: citizens moving pieces to invent scenarios, social and political discussions, peering photographers, and even a re-imagined mockup built across the globe.[1] The original intent embedded in the act of production, and its multiple creative reverberations, illustrates the catalytic potential of an individual citizen-driven project. Singular spatial practices such as these have the potential to create broader ramifications, as well as their associated imagery, and establish the capacity to mobilize towards a collective. Amid our contemporary rapid and connected modes of spatial production, they question routine practices and perceptions, instigating a critical reassessment of our social spaces.[2] These forms of public action—and the way we chose to document, represent, and visualize them—are critical to distinguishing a holistic legibility, the cognitive clarity of social space and one's place within it. Without them, we risk becoming suspended in a simplified mindset of pseudo-legibility—a state of false clarity that is often projected upon societies absorbed in post-revolutionary momentum. The post-revolutionary period's positivist outlook tends to highly esteem recent accomplishments as an end in themselves, rather than untangling a realistic view of impending social and political complexity. This simplified outlook privileges the utopic image of collective desire for a singular social and political objective.

Legibility and the Cognitive Image
The notion of physical legibility as a political tool of authority and statecraft often emerges as a one-dimensional interpretation of the term: states

Captured by photographer Themba Lewis, the original model was built in February 2011 by an Egyptian activist near the Sadat Metro exit in Tahrir Square, Cairo.
IMAGE COURTESY OF THEMBA LEWIS

ملابس و أدوات ضرورية

سويت شيرت أو سويتر أبو زمبوط فهو يساعد على إبعاد غازات القنابل المسيلة للدموع عن وجهك.

نظارة واقية إمكن شراؤها من أى محل حماية وجهك.

غطاء حلة يمكن إستخدامها كدرع ضد ضربات الأمن المركزى بالعصا أو الرصاص المطاطى.

كوفية لحماية فمك وانفك من الغازات المسيلة للدموع.

وردة كى نعمل اللى علينا وننضم بعضاً بمنتهى السلمية.

دوكو رش، عشان لو حدث ضرب من قبل السلطات، نرش الدوكو على زجاج الخوز والمدرعات لحجب رؤيتهم وشل حركتهم.

جوانتيات مجارة تساعد على حماية يداك من حرارة القنابل المسيلة للدموع

حذاء مريح للجرى والحركة السريعة

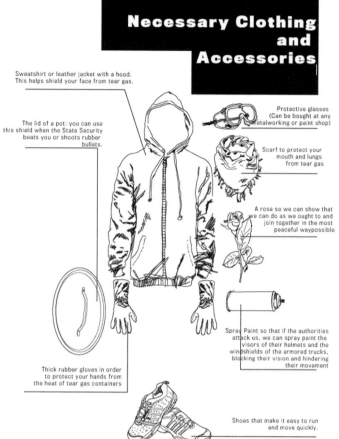

Sweatshirt or leather jacket with a hood. This helps shield your face from tear gas.

The lid of a pot: you can use this shield when the State Security beats you or shoots rubber bullets.

Protective glasses (Can be bought at any metalworking or paint shop)

Scarf to protect your mouth and lungs from tear gas

A rose so we can show that we can do as we ought to and join together in the most peaceful waypossible

Spray Paint so that if the authorities attack us, we can spray paint the visors of their helmets and the windshields of the armored trucks, blocking their vision and hindering their movement

Thick rubber gloves in order to protect your hands from the heat of tear gas containers

Shoes that make it easy to run and move quickly.

The necessary clothing and accessories diagram suggests how to use ordinary clothing and household items for protection during protests.
IMAGE COURTESY OF THE EGYPTIAN ACTIVISTS ACTION PLAN (2011)

employ legibility as an apparatus of governance, to organize and classify the otherwise complex structure and behavior of societies.[3] This view dwells on the power-driven desire for physical pattern and hierarchy, taking the legible city as a mere facilitator for the state's direct, ideal imposition of order and control onto its subjects. Recent instances of collective public action—Tahrir in Cairo, Taksim in Istanbul, Maidan in Kiev, among several others—interrogate this reading of legibility as a single-sided authoritarian device. They recall alternative dimensions of physical legibility; namely, inherent qualities of familiarity and navigability that entitle individuals to their city. It is critical then to explore a counterpoint from the citizen's perspective, one that revisits Kevin Lynch's condition of legibility as a device for cognitive image-making.

In *The Image of the City*, Lynch identifies legibility and imageability as measures of urban assessment in relation to the city's physical, and more significantly, cognitive qualities.[4] Lynch uses a bottom-up citizen-based approach that relies on extensive fieldwork, interviews, and drawings, to understand how an individual mentally maps their city. Focusing on the post-war sprawling American landscape, Lynch argues for the importance of recognizing "hidden forms" that establish familiarity and orientation amid increasing suburbanization.[5] Lynch's legibility is about the individual experience in the city and the imagery it invokes, highlighting urban elements such as the path, node, edge, landmark, and district that stand out as defining moments. These singular elements and the ability to relate them to one another is a process of selective re-composition, a sort of mental abstraction of episodic moments that compose the individual's total cognitive image. Often with shared qualities and reference points that differ from one individual to another, a citizen's ability to compose a total mental image of the urban environment allows ease of navigation and participation.

Lynch takes on a semiological reading of the image, building upon its behavioral qualities, as an instrument that conditions the way we operate in our environment.[6] He points to the behavioral influence that this can have on a citizen: to interpret surrounding information, intensify human experience, and guide action.[7] This is central to the way one operates and acts in the city: the better the capacity to read the city, the less estranged one feels from his or her surroundings. As Hashim Sarkis reveals in his essay "Disoriented," legibility is a "pacifying" quality that seeks to quell the symptoms of urban uncertainty, such as being lost or out of place. An individual's ability to create a mental map correlates with the sense of being accommodated by, and even empowered in the city. In that sense, Lynch's legibility is a pluralist project that reveres the individual abstraction of experience, that while maintaining broader commonalities, creates multiple legibilities for multiple people. Further, Lynch makes a social case for

١ - الدرع والدوكو

Shield and Spray

إثبت مكانك يامصري. صد العصاية بالدرع
وأنت تقوم بالرش في الوجه.

HOLD YOUR GROUND, EGYPTIAN!
Block the truncheon with your shield
as you're spraying them in the face.

Accompanied by encouraging statements, this spread demonstrates the use of particular items in case of a clash with authorities.
IMAGE COURTESY OF THE EGYPTIAN ACTIVISTS ACTION PLAN (2011)

legibility, its potential for "furnishing the raw material for the symbols and collective memories of group communications."[8] Deriving collective memory from individual cognition, places even greater emphasis on the empowering nature of legibility: the idea that individual clarity leads to deeper social interactions, community participation, and collective spatial practices. In that sense, Lynch's methodology recognizes the value of public entitlement to the design of the urban environment.

Individual to Collective Informality

The past three years have witnessed notable instances of collective public action that question conventional notions of state legibility and necessitate more critical readings of this concept. The focus here is on Tahrir Square, a case where the overexposure of image and the appearance of absolute homogeneity have distorted the reading of its underlying pluralist legibility. To understand the particular case of Cairo is to make a distinction between the physical nature and actual use of public space before and after 2011. Prior to 2011, the perceived space of the city conjured up images of fragmented urban moments, where streetscapes and sidewalks enabled various instances for "claiming the city" by citizens.[9] Urban spatial practices displayed a constant and conflicting oscillation between the formal and informal, particularly in dense central districts such as downtown Cairo. In an area redesigned during the mid-nineteenth century under Khedive Ismail to mimic Paris' strictly

linear Haussmann boulevards, these informal practices superimposed their own contentious and internal order.[10] A sporadic, piecemeal sense of ownership is apparent in daily urban encounters: cafés spill out into the street, kiosks encroach onto sidewalks, and niches are reserved with large unwieldy objects to be rented as parking spaces to scouting drivers. Created through the individual occupation of a clearly public space, such as a street or sidewalk, the pervasive informal order emerged as an unquestioned claim to the city, a mutually profitable relationship where informal activities fed the economy in exchange for the state's blind acceptance. Among others, these displays of informality often went unmonitored by security, rarely recognized as more than the usual fragmented and disordered character of the city.[11] These multiple small-scale informal practices challenged the notion of legibility, and the attempt of formalizing the organization of urban space.

Toward the east is Tahrir Square, a transitional urban crossroads unraveling and disentangling the traffic from the over twenty streets it serves. Before 2011, pedestrians bypassed one another to cross the streets at the roundabout's periphery, rarely interacting and certainly never thinking twice to move towards its center. Unlike a traditional public square that is more defined and enclosed in nature, such as the ancient Greek *agora* or the European *piazza*, the amorphous, unbounded area of Tahrir Square creates an exposed, outward-looking urban space.[12] The recent reorientation from the space of the street to the space of the square during the events of 2011 largely correlates with the square's multi-directional visibility, what Bruno Latour would term an "oligopticon."[13] The inconvenient position of being in the middle of the square allowed, "sturdy but extremely narrow views of a (collected) whole,"[14] a space perhaps that—being inhabited for the first time—permitted new, untold lines of sight and visual connections for its occupants. Following the events of 2011 and again in 2013, the fragmented informal day-to-day actions that challenged the streets visibly manifest at an entirely new scale. It was as though all the informal practices that composed Cairo's urban existence for decades, assembled and found their arena of expression, their one sovereign ground. Even after their political objectives were met, citizens did not leave the square. They built up momentum for occupation, an attachment to the space that became an issue of ownership—the right to the city.[15] To the international community, the images and media that circulated were the results of a coherent political narrative. To Egypt, it was the consolidation of those scattered informal actions and spatial forms of resistance, assembling to demand acknowledgement by authorities and by the world. To Egypt, it was merely a nascent step toward the self-comprehension of society's pluralities, one that had yet to dismantle the oversimplified image of the square.

Pseudo-Legibility and the Aerial Image

Image is the medium through which individuals understand and assemble the world, attaching a constructed meaning to the spatial practices they portray. Images inherently produce a "reductionist vision" of what they are meant to represent, thus the act of image-making is very political.[16] Modern aerial technology—the view from above commonly used for military purposes and historically recognized for its authoritative application—is one of the primary techniques to document civic uprising.[17] The gathering of masses in Tahrir, filling up all niches of converging open space and branching out into the Qasr al-Nil bridge towards the Nile, created a unified image—a clear, thoroughly constructed whole. The first pages of a Google Images search for the phrase "Tahrir Square" show aerial or birds-eye views of the massive uprisings.[18] These images were broadcast, publicized, shared, liked, produced, and reproduced ubiquitously because of their empowering gestalt. Though it is seductive to see a massive swirling confluence of millions of citizens, the reproduction of this image evokes a misconception of coherence and clarity at the scale of the individual. As Latour warns, despite telling the whole story, "such coherent and complete accounts may become the most blind, most local, and most partial viewpoints."[19] Implying a direct and total-izing gaze from above, a manifest spectacle of the space, this incompatible form of representation, which bypasses the underlying pluralities and finer intricacies that comprise the whole, fed a mainstream perception of the events.

Indeed the stalemate that has since ensued is proof of the complexities and multiplicities that are swallowed up by the aerial images of the square. The pluralities that have characterized the socio-political landscape for most of the country's modern history are rarely captured as the "image of the revolution." Aside from footage of clashes between differing political ideologies, there are complex socio-economic, religious, and cultural narratives that underlie civic motivations and priorities. The disembodied objectivity inherent in the aerial view, and our subsequent myopic consumption, neglects the internal dynamics at work in any pluralist society. The aerial images, and their circulation, create a condition of pseudo-legibility—an artificial clarity that blankets the intricacies of individual inter-pretations and experiences in the socio-economic arena. Rather than a genuine comprehension of the underlying socio-political pluralities, it is the appearance of transparency that makes a predisposition toward pseudo-legibility and its imagery so enticing. In the case of Cairo, pseudo-legibility then is a device to contain a type of Pandora's box, the reality of opposing political motivations, competing power-hungry parties, and profiting individual agendas.

The Agency of Design and Alternative Images

Displayed in the character of the model-builder, the individual spatial practice in Tahrir Square is an example of design manifest as a form of public action. The space was transiently redesigned to accommodate activities that were rarely part of an open public arena in the city's recent history: makeshift tents and clinics, symbolic cardboard obelisks, and performance stages. Beyond these fleeting structures, activists prepared a pamphlet, complete with drawings, diagrams, and text on "How to Protest Intelligently."[20] The pamphlet contains sketches that depict a trajectory through the typologies that compose the standard urban block, describing the street hierarchy from residen-tial streets, to major boulevards, into the square, and toward governmental buildings.[21] Another spread depicts a diagram of the "necessary cloth-ing and accessories" for protest, many of which are ordinary household items that could act as protective devices.[22] Every page graphically repre-sents a theme—assembling into a visual manual for how spatial practices could occur in the city. By way of discreet distribution throughout the neighborhoods, a subversive method of commu-nication propagated the urban fabric, collecting citizens from around the city and culminating in Tahrir Square, the final burgeoning destination.

This call to action employs the very essence of Lynch's legibility, documenting the cognitive overlay of individual citizens to distill a collective reading of urban elements and compositions in the city. Through the abstract representation of urban elements such as corner mosques and major boulevards, the activists tap into citizen's other mental maps through the recognition of relationships between the elements, recomposing several slightly different images of the city. During the early 2014 protests in Kiev, activists extracted relevant pages of the document and translated them into Ukrainian as a guide for demonstrators.[23] Parallel to the ramifications of the physical model, the act of creating and distributing the document, followed by the social and international effects, reveals a trajectory of how individual cognitive images can catalyze collective action.

Likewise, a citizen building a physical model in the square, as the space unfolds around him, is a display of public entitlement to design, one that reaffirms design's centrality in catalyzing spatial practices of resistance. Exemplifying an instinctive form of participation, the model attests to the necessity of a critical public dialogue in the reshaping of the public realm. Curating the exhibit and reimagining the model at the Graduate School of Design at Harvard University enabled yet another perception of the events unraveling in Cairo. The images that represented the piece allowed others worldwide to participate in the collective design project of the square. The act of image-making has the capacity to reveal new meanings and associations that mend the gap between conceptual and spatial realms. They reveal that, whether building a model in Tahrir Square or Harvard Square, demonstrating in Cairo or Kiev, collective associations can be formed to empower all individuals.

New Paradigm for Design, New Paradigm for Citizenship

To move past the pseudo-legibility of the images that seduced the world at the onset of 2011 and closer to the recognition and tolerance within the notion of plurality, is to transition toward a legibility that recognizes the citizen's relationship to his or her built environment, and thus, their individual role within society. Though there was a complete shift in the square's use, occupation, and perception, Tahrir Square today lingers as an artifact of the last three years, a ruin of the events. The space between cognitive legibility, one that empowers citizens to operate within a city, and spatial legibility, is where design has the opportunity to reaffirm its agency: if the square was the core of transformative events, can a new vision of social space sustain a long-term civic revitalization? The spatial practices that have reconstituted the city, often beyond the intents of designers, have been purely citizen-driven practices that demand influence in the civic design platform. This proves that a certain level of individual cognitive legibility of the built environment must exist in order for collective action to take place. The notion of legibility in design relies on the interface between the physical and cognitive: it is the extent to which the urban environment can be read, interpreted, learned, and finally, shaped by individual citizens. For citizens, legibility is to mentally identify physical elements, link their structural relationships, and find their value and meaning. Thus, in doing this, legibility empowers citizens to become actors, drivers, and to a large extent, designers, of their urban realm. Such a participatory level of discourse redefines the design process, in essence, as a public act.

Investing in the individual citizen's capacity to restructure the global design landscape creates a space of dialogue that capitalizes on the plurality of the public realm. The same way the informal practices of urban contestation gradually escalated and swelled into the space of the square, design methodology that seeks to influence spatial practice necessitates a similar trajectory. Following Lynch's collective action through individual resolve, it is critical that this sort of public momentum thrives and redefines the future form of civic participation that marks such pivotal moments in history. The right to participate in forming one's space of inhabitation is rooted in the definition of both designer and citizen. Such a projective process, sprouting from the original forms of spatial action in the square, will reveal not only a new paradigm for design, but also for citizenship. In this way, these opportunities establish a true, legible datum for what it means to inhabit the city.

Samaa Elimam is a PhD student in Architecture at the Harvard University Graduate School of Design. She previously worked as a designer at architecture firms in Cairo, Los Angeles, and San Francisco, and taught at the American University in Cairo and the Harvard's Graduate School of Design.

Notes

1 Samaa Elimam and Sara Tavakoli, *Roaming Revolution: Unfolding the Narratives of the Square*, (Cambridge, MA: Radcliffe Institute for Advanced Study, March 2012).
2 Henri Lefebvre, *The Production of Space* (Malden: Blackwell, 1991), 26-29.
3 James C. Scott, Seeing *Like a State: How Certain Schemes to Improve the Human Condition Have Failed* (New Haven: Yale University, 1998).
4 Kevin Lynch, *The Image of the City* (Cambridge: MIT Press, 1960), 2-6.
5 Ibid., 2-3.
6 Hashim Sarkis, "Disoriented: Kevin Lynch, around 1960," *A Second Modernism: MIT, Architecture, and the 'Techno-Social' Moment*, ed. Arindam Dutta, (Cambridge, MA: MIT Press, 2013).
7 Lynch, 4.
8 Ibid.
9 Salwa Ismail, *Political Life in Cairo's New Quarters: Encountering the Everyday State* (Minneapolis: University of Minnesota Press, 2006), 161-165.
10 Ibid., 162.
11 Ibid., 4-5.
12 International Making Cities Livable Council, *Tahrir Square and the Birth of Democracy?*, http://www.livablecities.org/articles/tahrir-square-and-birth-democracy.
13 Bruno Latour, *Reassembling the Social: An Introduction to Actor-Network Theory* (New York: Oxford University Press, 2005), 181-183.
14 Ibid., 181.
15 Henri LeFebvre, *Writings on Cities* (Malden: Blackwell, 1996), 147-159.
16 Ola Söderström, "How Images Assemble the Urban World," *New Geographies 4* (2011): 113-118.
17 Mark Dorrian, "The aerial view: notes for a cultural history," STRATES—*Materiaux pour la recherche en sciences sociales* 13 (2007): 105-118.
18 "Google Images," http://images.google.com (accessed February 18, 2014).
19 Bruno Latour, *Reassembling the Social: An Introduction to Actor-Network Theory* (New York: Oxford University Press, 2005), 189.
20 Egyptian Activists' Action Plan, "How to Protest Intelligently," http://info.publicintelligence.net/EgyptianRevolutionManual.pdf.
21 Ibid., 4-8.
22 Ibid., 4-8.
23 Neil Ketchley, "How social media spreads protest tactics from Ukraine to Egypt," *The Washington Post*, (February 14, 2014), http://www.washingtonpost.com/blogs/monkey-cage/wp/2014/02/14/how-social-media-spreads-protest-tactics-from-ukraine-to-egypt/.

DIALOGIC SPACES: CITIES WITHOUT ARCHITECTURE

Claudia Mainardi

The term "web-riot" refers to rebellion movements that utilize the web as a fundamental medium, and are becoming increasingly common. A web-riot is expressed using virtual media as a platform for exchanging and sharing opinions. It is a tool of political, economic, social, and cultural rights, as is the case of social networks, but it is also a tool for spatial organization during riots and is thereby used as a sounding board to maintain contact with the world in real-time. The distinguishing influence of the web-riot is linked to the rise of a new global middle class. Wherever this is being established, this social class has caused political unrest despite the difficulty of producing durable changes. The protests are no longer driven by the poor, but by young people with a high level of education and often an above average income. These are young men and women who know how to use technology and social networks to disseminate news and organize events.[1] The proliferation of smartphones, due to their low cost, has enabled easy access to an internet connection, that is not only used as mere medium to communicate but also to stimulate a collective awareness toward action or the realization of a shared social objective.

The goal of this study is the investigation of the potential offered by a web-defined spatial organization where the occupation of the space is the physical translation of a socio-political will shared on the Internet. These are bottom-up processes that use the freedom granted by the horizontality of social media in order to generate an anti-system consensus. To demonstrate this observation, three different events from 2011 are compared: Cairo and the vicissitudes of the Arab Spring, Madrid and the movements of *Indignados*, and New York and the anti-systemic Occupy Wall Street movement. The choice of these specific events stems from the fact that they are recent and yet have already been analyzed and interpreted in light of the socio-economic situation of that time. However, in spite of the opposition of the establishment, the connection between the protestors through the web continue to exercise an important role in the affairs of these contexts. In addition, although they are the product of differing issues, and produced by very different contexts, these riots share the use of virtual media as a venue for discussion and dissemination of information. The possibility of a discussion, permitted by the use of the web, determined the organization of a dissent against the system. If in Egypt the motivation was primarily political and arises from the desire to overturn the Hosni Mubarak regime, in Spain and the United States there is an opposition that is civil—with a strong political criticism in Spain and economic and openly anti-systemic in the United States.

Beyond the specifics that characterize each protest, these events share the fact that they were not solely physical riots. The constitution of a critical mass and the organization of the dissent in the squares transpired through a digital medium.

World web-riot map, October 2010 – June 2013.

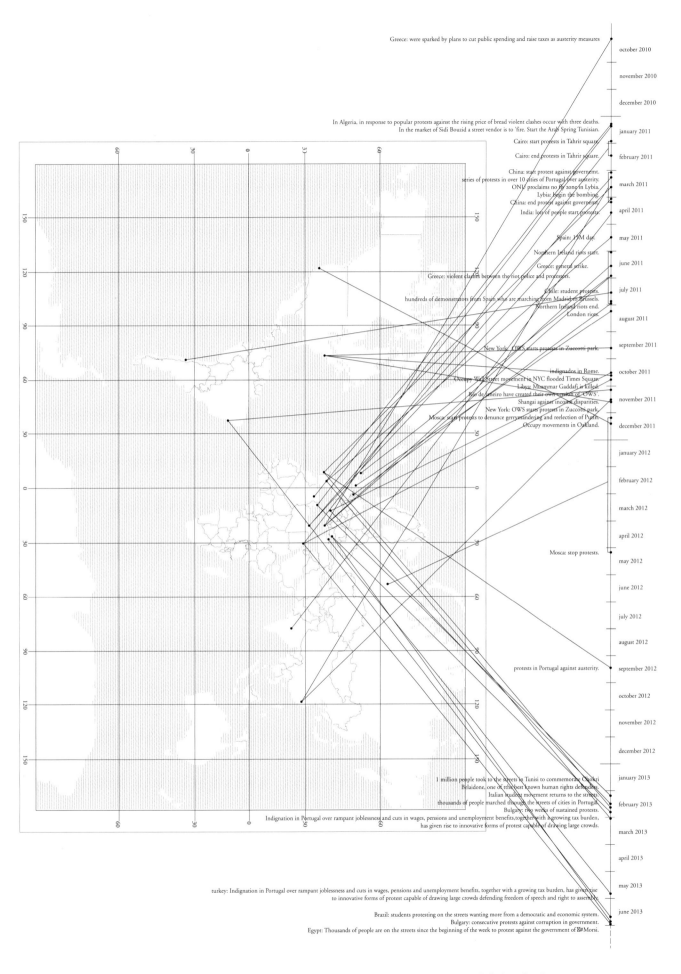

Greece: were sparked by plans to cut public spending and raise taxes as austerity measures — october 2010

november 2010

december 2010

In Algeria, in response to popular protests against the rising price of bread violent clashes occur with three deaths.
In the market of Sidi Bouzid a street vendor is to 'fire. Start the Arab Spring Tunisian. — january 2011

Cairo: start protests in Tahrir square.
Cairo: end protests in Tahrir square. — february 2011

China: start protest against governemt.
series of protests in over 10 cities of Portugal over austerity. — march 2011
ONU proclaims no fly zone in Lybia.
Lybia: begin the bombing.
China: end protest against goverement. — april 2011
India: lots of people start protests.

Spain: 15M day. — may 2011

Northern Ireland riots start.
Greece: general strike. — june 2011
Greece: violent clashes between the riot police and protestors.

Chile: student protests. — july 2011
hundreds of demonstrators from Spain who are marching from Madrid to Brussels.
Northern Ireland riots end.
London riots. — august 2011

New York: OWS starts protests in Zuccotti park. — september 2011

indignados in Rome. — october 2011
Occupy WallStreet movement in NYC flooded Times Square.
Lybia: Muammar Gaddafi is killed.
Rio de Janeiro have created their own version of 'OWS'. — november 2011
Shangai against income disparities.
New York: OWS starts protests in Zuccotti park.
Mosca: start protests to denunce gerrymandering and reelection of Putin. — december 2011
Occupy movements in Oakland.

january 2012

february 2012

march 2012

april 2012

Mosca: stop protests. — may 2012

june 2012

july 2012

august 2012

protests in Portugal against austerity. — september 2012

october 2012

november 2012

december 2012

january 2013

1 million people took to the streets in Tunisi to commemorate Chokri
Belaidone, one of tthe best known human rights defenders. — february 2013
Italian student movement returns to the streets.
thousands of people marched through the streets of cities in Portugal.
Bulgary: two weeks of sustained protests.
Indignation in Portugal over rampant joblessness and cuts in wages, pensions and unemployment benefits,together with a growing tax burden,
has given rise to innovative forms of protest capable of drawing large crowds. — march 2013

april 2013

may 2013

turkey: Indignation in Portugal over rampant joblessness and cuts in wages, pensions and unemployment benefits, together with a growing tax burden, has given rise
to innovative forms of protest capable of drawing large crowds defending freedom of speech and right to assembly.

Brazil: students protesting on the streets wanting more from a democratic and economic system. — june 2013
Bulgary: consecutive protests against corruption in government.
Egypt: Thousands of people are on the streets since the beginning of the week to protest against the government of ⊠#Morsi.

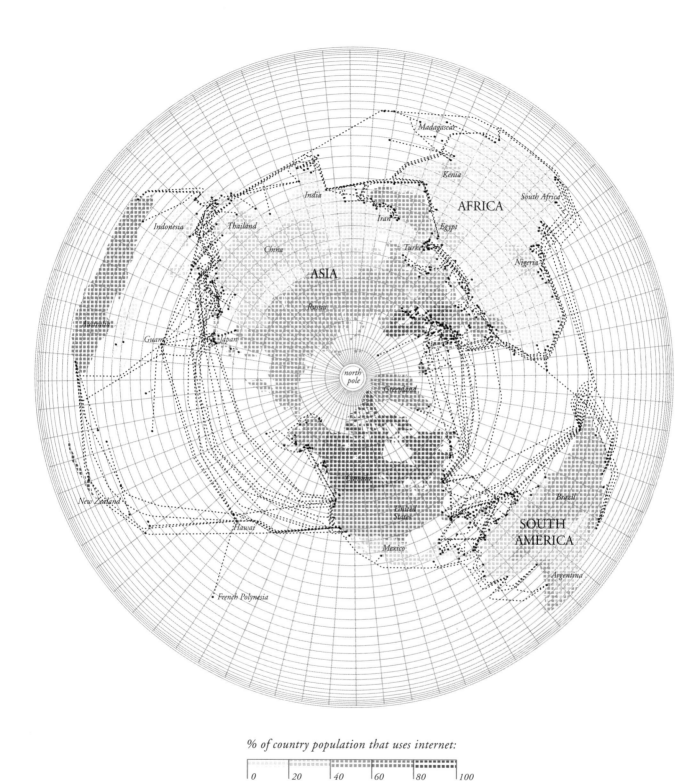

% of country population that uses internet:

| 0 | 20 | 40 | 60 | 80 | 100 |

Subsequently, the web was the principal instrument used to communicate the protest continuously and in real time. In a 2013 interview for *The Guardian*, sociologist Manuel Castells stated that:

> The combination of cyberspace and urban space characterizes this new movement. They appear and disappear but they are always present in the digital domain. For their management dynamics I define them as rhizomatic.[…] The pattern that determines the action is given by the intersection of three characters: the use of internet, the employment of urban space but also the possibility of creating a new form of democratic representation that is bottom-up. For most of them the idea is to be only at the beginning of the process where what they want is giving people the courage to think […][2]

Castells refers to Gilles Deleuze and Felix Guattari to explain that the action produced by such a context has all the features of a rhizome, which is "a non-hierarchical system that connects a somewhere with another anywhere."[3] A rhizome combines very distant concepts and phenomena, and can be found in logical or random relationships.

Cairo Riot

January 2011 saw the beginning of a series of protests and unrests that spread across the countries of the Arab League. They were produced by a socio-economic context common throughout much of the southern Mediterranean. The riots that took place shared civil resistance techniques such as strikes, demonstrations, marches, and parades as well as extreme acts such as suicide. The social networks, particularly Facebook and Twitter, played an important role in the dissemination and momentum of the Arab Spring. They fundamentally altered the way in which protestor's converse, and exchange ideas, accelerating the spread of communication that would have otherwise taken considerable time before reaching fellow protestors or the media. Therefore, citizens in countries where freedom of expression has been suppressed found immediate continuous access to social networks, which enabled the potential to unify against the system of power.[4] To understand the power exerted by the network, it is important to consider the suppression of the Internet on servers that were controlled by Egyptian State security. January 25, 2011, the day of the protest outbreak, a procedure followed that included the closure of switching nodes on the network to isolate specific areas in Egypt. In the midst of the riots, national authorities resorted to extreme measures such as the disabling of central servers and the nearly complete shutdown of the network. It was predominantly cable links, which were convenient and simple to break. Only the equipment and the government channels remained active in order to allow institutional communication among the command, the

control centers, and the troops deployed in the area. However, the dissidents managed to bypass the restrictions and disruptions to communications and data transfer using techniques common among bloggers and hackers. Another technique used satellite communication, which had wider coverage and could not be disrupted by the government. With smartphones, rioters managed to use social networks, communicate with each other, and send videos and reports of clashes in the streets around the world.

A study using GIS technology has identified the strategy that traced the paths arriving at Tahrir Square. Gathering points were often situated near mosques far from police stations and where there was a high population density to invite other inhabitants to take part in the march. The busiest roads were chosen and protestors were directed towards Tahrir Square. Small groups were then added along the march at points of convergence. The choice of Tahrir Square was not accidental. It was adequate to physically contain dense and large masses, and was one of the few areas of the city with free Wi-Fi access.

Madrid Riot

The 15M movement, also called *Indignados*, consisted of citizens—unemployed, students, activists, housewives, immigrants, among others—that have given rise to a broad mobilization of protest against the Spanish Government in the wake of the economic crisis besetting the country since 2008. It was immediately obvious that there were no leaders. Decisions were made within thematic committees, coordinated by an international commission with rotating members. Proposals, organization, and tactics were discussed in intense debates, conducted with respect. Any hint of violence was kept under control. Nonviolence was a principle accepted by all that was tested when the authorities began to use batons. The Internet has allowed people to spread the message among their own acquaintances, giving an individual vision. It was the sum of the points-of-views that strengthened the group. When the 15M took an action, it translated the power of the members assembled within the street, "stirring" the dynamics of the internet with those *de la calle*. This moment meant a first collective experiment of overlap between conditions that are part of two very different realities: *acampadas* and public assemblies on one hand and Internet discussion platforms on the other. The power was to bring them both forward in parallel. While protest marchers were organizing the squares, the Internet served an essential role to decentralize coordination and cohesion, with the interaction of individuality. It is impossible to analyze the 15M movement without considering that Internet users have built political tools using new technologies within the reach of all citizens. The interaction between the digital network and the physical road provided citizens with greater power and collective intelligence. Manuel Castells, in a June 2011 interview for *Internazionale*, posited:

Those that minimize the wiki-camps do not understand yet. The manifestations may abandon the squares, but will remain present in social networks and in the minds of those who participate. The squares are not alone anymore. This movement has found new models of organization, participation and mobilization that go beyond traditional channels, watched with suspicion by many young people. The parties and institutions will have to learn to live with this new civil society. Otherwise they will disappear while people pass away from wiki-camps in a networked democracy yet to be discovered, in a collective practice that depends on individuals.[5]

New York Riot

New York, within its fervor of crisis, constituted a peaceful protest movement to denounce the abuses of financial capitalism. A precedent for a whole generation made up mostly of non-native Americans, united with a common ideology. The origin of the Occupy Wall Street movement, or "Occupy," was initiated, in part, by Kalle Lasn and Micah White, two organizers of *Adbusters*, a Canadian magazine interested in non-profit, anti-consumerism, and anti-capitalism, which established the website occupywallstreet.org in June 2011. Mobilization began over the Internet before it materialized in a series of demonstrations in Manhattan, in Zuccotti Park from September 17 to November 17, 2011. The movement assumed Wall Street—home of the New York Stock Exchange—as a symbolic target since it is home to the New York Stock Exchange and the epicenter of world finance. Participants expressed demonstrations inspired by similar events in Egypt and of the *movimento15M*.

Occupy created a huge network of people who share the same values. During the protest, 427,000 tweets with the hashtag "Occupy Wall Street" were transmitted. One of the strongest actions carried out by a working group of Occupy was to create a micro-economy alternative to capitalism. The activities of Occupy were applied to a wide variety of issues. For example, the group Occupy University tried to rethink a University where a student could be both student and teacher. Experiments often do not come to fruition and are not durable, but they are a clear sign of turmoil and change. The exception of Occupy in the United States and in New York in particular, lies in the fact that after almost three years from the first episode, it has managed to develop a network so strong that is able to cope with the powerful institutional sphere of control.

The march of Occupy Wall Street was deliberately carried out on Broadway Street, a primary North-South road of Manhattan, and more specifically in the Financial District neighborhood. The choice of the arrival point was Zuccotti Park, a short walk from the Stock Exchange building on Wall Street. The park is large enough to accommodate over one thousand

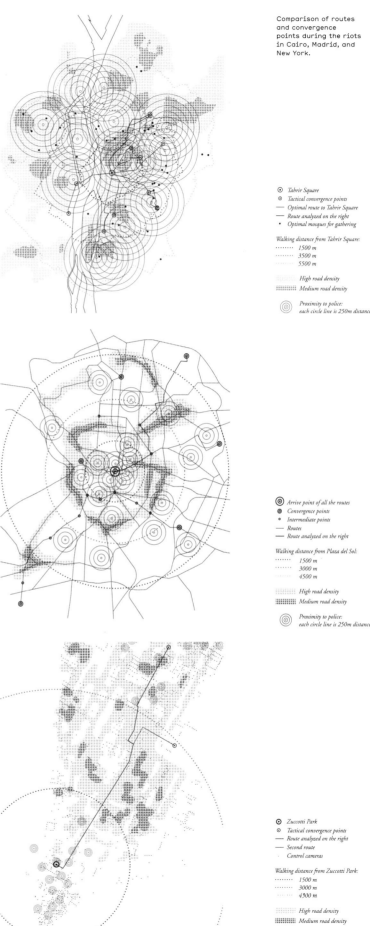

Comparison of routes and convergence points during the riots in Cairo, Madrid, and New York.

⊙ Tahrir Square
◎ Tactical convergence points
— Optimal route to Tahrir Square
— Route analyzed on the right
• Optimal mosques for gathering

Walking distance from Tahrir Square:
·········· 1500 m
········· 3500 m
······· 5500 m

High road density
Medium road density

Proximity to police:
each circle line is 250m distance

◎ Arrive point of all the routes
◎ Convergence points
○ Intermediate points
— Routes
— Route analyzed on the right

Walking distance from Plaza del Sol:
·········· 1500 m
········· 3000 m
······· 4500 m

High road density
Medium road density

Proximity to police:
each circle line is 250m distance

⊙ Zuccotti Park
◎ Tactical convergence points
— Route analyzed on the right
— Second route
· Control cameras

Walking distance from Zuccotti Park:
·········· 1500 m
········· 3000 m
······· 4500 m

High road density
Medium road density

◎ Militarized zones

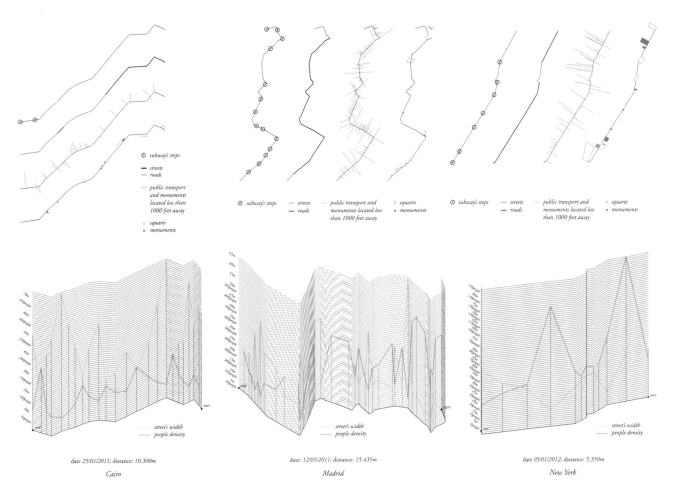

date 25/01/2011; distance: 10.300m

Cairo

date: 12/05/2011; distance: 15.435m

Madrid

date 05/01/2012; distance: 5.350m

New York

Analysis of a specific path during the riots in Cairo, Madrid, and New York.

people. Unlike the Arab Spring and *Indignados*, the march and protest was smaller in scale, in terms of people involved as well as public visibility. Unlike the other protests in which the routes to a destination were manifold, in the case of Occupy, there was only one route and it was short.

Dialogic Spaces

From the description of web-riots, we define the dialogic space as a clear example of the continuity of action due to the fact that the web becomes an "actor," as if it was a person.[6] The web is no longer just a means of communication, but an actor playing a speaking role. In this sense, communication is no longer linear but it changes from one medium to another allowing people to continue to interact, generating a continuous action as it is repeatedly reiterated.[7] Since the web creates and leaves a trace, which verbal communication doesn't, it defines a place or room at a virtual level and thus an a-geographical space.[8] Precisely because the crossed influences[9] move into an a-geographical space, they can be generated by any real point,[10] to produce an action that is able to load a degree of complexity from different contexts (social, economic, cultural). Thus, a rhizomatic space is constituted because it is made by a network and able to hold different conditions together. Actions can occur thanks to an actor-network between people and physical devices (cell phones, computers, etc.).[11] The action

determined by the fact that the web becomes an "actor" may result in real space in terms of physical action (protest, demonstration) or spatial organization (meetings, jobs, discussion). This condition determines the recognition of physical locations that give character resulting in a continuity between the real and the virtual. In this way, a space is generated that is recognized and determined by an action. This space becomes part of the process of reiteration, making its character somewhere between the virtual and the real.[12] The influences between real and virtual spaces determine the dialogic condition.

With the meaning of the dialogic condition, we want to focus on that aspect of the architecture that is not concerned with the shape of the object or the urban fabric, but rather the interpersonal dynamics that make up the social fabric. The social textile is expressed through action and communication. If the action of the protest has the character to be visible and space temporarily-concentrated, the communication is not definable if not as a space-relationship defined by the people participating through the web. The communication continues to be diffuse and weak, though weak is not necessarily negative, rather it indicates a particular process of modification and knowledge that follows natural, non-geometric logics; not concentrated processes, but reversible and auto-balancing strategies. The action is manifest, somewhat violent, and verifiable in a physical, material way.

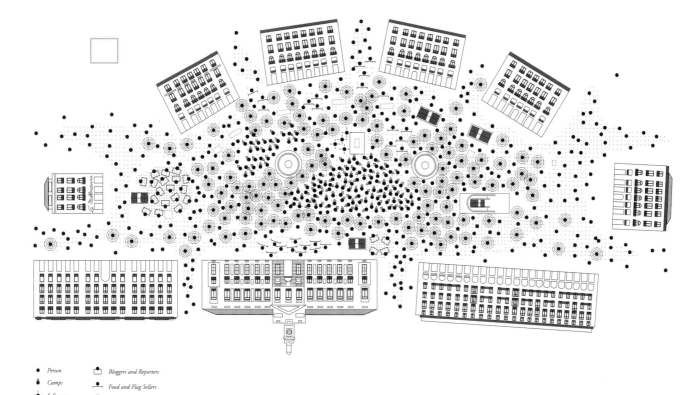

- Person
- Camps
- Infirmary

- Bloggers and Reporters
- Food and Flag Sellers
- Demonstrators

It is geo-localized, directly connected to the urban fabric in which it is realized. These factors determine the impossibility of a continuous occupation of the urban spaces weakening the effectiveness of a protest. However, these protests cannot be reduced to their physical manifestation. The state of the urban guerrilla is perpetuated through the continuation of the protest on the Internet through a process of re-organization, which alternates between street action with moments of apparent calm.

The conflicting times in which we live have produced a utopian State, whose impulse is rooted in human nature that has been reinforced by the biggest change in the previous two decades: our communication tools.[13] New technologies have allowed the construction of political instruments within the reach of all citizens. Affordability of technology has favored a horizontal use. The communication tools we have today are able to change interpersonal relationships, as a consequence to the concept of "distance," and the use of space. As philosopher Pierre Lévy has argued:

The city seems to be everywhere. Actually we don't live, work and think anymore in city spaces, but in spaces we define urban whose difference is that about urban space it can be difficult to determine the physical limits of governability. These are spaces that at the same time are unlimited and full of borders.[14]

We currently live in hybrid landscapes, which are composed of parts connected by increasingly complex communication and mobility networks. In these spaces, the urban is continuously de-located from a mix of de-territorialized physical space and intangible media space in an expanding network. In these movements, physical and mental spaces are redefined as a function of new relations of power, new social mechanisms, new ways of production, and subjectification. In an architecture of de-territorialization, human relationships produce, transform, and structure heterogeneous and interconnected spaces. These plastic spaces, which curve and deform themselves around objects that contain and organize them, arise from the interaction among people.[15] We no longer need to be in defined places to exercise communicative, productive, and organizational actions. The digital reproduction of objects, signs, messages, pictures, and voice leads to a dissolution of the territory. The network is no longer only a form of technological communication, but a truly informative and economic ecosystem.[16]

The research into web-riots has meant configuring a complex, heterogeneous account of events in which the interaction between the physical reality of the demonstrations and uprisings was influenced and coordinated by virtual phenomena. The dialogic space determined by the tension between physical and virtual spaces has been enabled through the use of the

Virtual and physical aggregation in Plaza del Sol in Madrid during 15M.

Internet during events. Dialogic space has taken on the role not only of communication, but also that of organization.

During these phenomena, the difference between constructed space, fixed in its physical form, and the space in which a public mass interacts, is apparent. The process analyzed here is intended to occupy this gap in order to determine alternative strategies able to rewrite the relationship between the constructed and social fabric. There is an attempt to find new urban geographies, whose centers are no longer determined merely by an urban structure, but rather by the immaterial components made up of the relationships that lie in the social fabric. The dialogic space condition should therefore be understood as a means to define the tension between the demands of the citizens that lay in the cyberspace, and the place where this demand translates at an urban level as organization and activism. This positive energy lessens the gap between the demands of the citizens and the physical space of the city determining new urban barycenters where cyberspace and real life combine. This produces a democratic platform that could eventually induce bottom-up processes able to orient alternative dynamics in the city.

Claudia Mainardi studied architecture at Milan Polytechnic where she met the collective Fosbury Architecture in which she is presently involved. She is currently based in Rotterdam.

Notes

1   Francis Fukuyama, "La borghesia si rubella," *Internazionale* 1008 (2013): 38-42.
2   Manuel Castells, "How modern political movements straddle urban space and cyberspace," *The Guardian*, (March 25, 2013),
3   Gilles Deleuze and Felix Guattari, *Mille piani: capitalismo e schizofrenia* (Roma: Cooper & Castelvecchi, 2003).
4   Marco Di Liddo, Andrea Falconi, Gabriele Iacovino, and Luca La Bella, "Il Ruolo dei Social Network nelle Rivolte Arabe," *Osservatorio di politica internazionale*, 40 (2011).
5   Manuel Castells, "La democrazia delle piazze spagnole," *Internazionale* (5 giugno 2011), http://www.internazionale.it/la-democrazia-delle-piazze-spagnole/.
6   Dialogy is a kind of dialogue that allows connection and interaction between the parts of which it is composed, giving rise to a process of endless construction, in contrast to dialectical dialogue where a thesis is placed against an antithesis resulting in a synthesis. According to Edgar Morin, the dialogical principle is the second of the complexity theory, which argues that it "allows us to maintain the duality within the unit; it combines two complementary and antagonistic terms. Order and disorder, for example, are enemies: the one suppresses the other, but at the same time, in certain cases, they collaborate and produce organization and complexity." Edgar Morin, *Introduzione al pensiero complesso* (Milano: Sperling & Kupfer S.p.a., 1993).
7   "Objects present themselves in only three forms: the invisible and faithful tool, the vital infrastructure, the protective screen. As tools, they faithfully transmit the social intention that runs through them, but receive nothing from and give nothing to them. As infrastructures, they are linked to one another, forming one continuous material base that will flow into the social world of representations and signs." Bruno Latour, "Una sociologia senza oggetto: Note sull'interog-gettività," http://www.bruno-latour.fr/sites/default/files/downloads/57-INTEROBJECTIVITE-IT.pdf.
8   "[...] the proxemic illusion no longer exists, and if the polis had inaugurated a political theater, with the Agora, with the forum, now there is no more than a cathode ray screen on which shadows are agitated, specters of endangered communities where kinematic motion propagates the last appearance of urbanism, the last image of an urbanism without humanity, in which touch and contact give way to the impact of television: not only 'teleconference,' which permits long-distance communication, with progress induced by the absence of displace-ment, but also 'telenegotiation,' which allows us to distance ourselves, to discuss without meeting our social partners whilst perhaps in immediate physical proximity [...]" Paul Virilio, *Lo spazio critico* (Bari: Edizioni Dedalo, Bari, 1998).
This type of practice has only ever been applied to the sphere of living subjects, thus being perceptive and observable. What we propose to do in this research is to translate this practice into a field of investigation, until now unknown, in order to try to extract a logic and an operation. Applying this practice to a virtual scope, we must reconsider and retrieve the condition that space-time is usually deleted within cybernetics. If the telematic meeting can take place anytime instantly abolishing any kind of barrier, it is therefore not in the dialogic framework where in order to meet, people must leave home, take public transport and consequently spend time. The range can surely change depending on the means of communi-cation and transport of each specific context. It can be said that at a time when there is a long distance to be covered, in a short time only an online report is possible, vice versa when the distance is limited, an off-line report can also be verified in addition to the online report.
9   "Today, with the dispersal of the city, with the reorganization of the urban at other levels (both global and cybernetic), architecture has returned, conversely, as sublimated chaos absorbed by a market that had pre-viously been characterized by confusion but which has now been rendered, via corporate-statist intervention, as simply consumerist [...] work like that of Allen and others condenses the effects of the city and captures or channels its energies and in this way architecture becomes infra-structure rather than serving as either monumental figure or infill fabric." Stan Allen, *Points + Lines: Diagrams and Projects for the City* (New York, NY: Princeton Architectural Press, 1999).
10   The virtual cannot prescind from a physical reality that allows access through interfaces or connecting devices, despite unfixed access points, which people decide to access deliberately. The condition of the virtual, and consequently the dialogical, are created only if people seek out this kind of interaction.
11   The actor-network theory is a theoretical model developed by philosopher Bruno Latour and anthro-pologist John Law to describe the development of scientific and tech-nological objects and facts. Radically departing from any essentialist tendencies of nature and society, it affirms that any scientific idea, technical product or more trivially any social fact, is produced by an intricate network of relationships in which social actors interact with humans and non-humans. In this net-work, the distribution of power and the semiotic representations of ideas or objects taken into consideration play an important role.
12   Given the two realities—one virtual and one physical—denoted by different characters, we can imagine a dialogical condition. A space that occurs only in circumstances where there is an overlap of the two condi-tions, which can be characterized as one being on-line and the other off-line, where the changes that happen on one level affect another, causing an increase in reality.
13   Ethel Baraona Pohl, "Adhocracy: From Political Choice to Formal Proposals," *DPR-Barcelona*, http://dprbcn.wordpress.com/2012/10/26/adhocracy.
14   Pierre Lévy, *L'intelligenza collet-tiva: per un'antropologia del cyber-spazio* (Milano: Feltrinelli, 1996).
15   Andrea Branzi, *Modernità debole e diffusa* (Milano: Skira, 2006).
16   Pierre Lévy, *L'intelligenza collet-tiva: per un'antropologia del cyber-spazio* (Milano: Feltrinelli, 1996).

EXIT SPACES: FROM KORESHAN CULTS TO WIRELESS MESH NETWORKS

Tobias Revell

Albert O. Hirschman's 1970 treatise *Exit, Voice and Loyalty* is a short taxonomy and analysis of possible actions an individual might take against an organization they are unhappy with. Firstly, stop buying products and/or leave the organization: exit. Secondly, express dissatisfaction in some form of protest: voice. The third option is of course loyalty, to remain intractably faithful to the organization despite one's dissatisfaction.[1] The thrust of his argument rests on the relationship between customers and businesses but, writing at a point in history fractured by political dissent, he acknowledges the space for strong parallels with the political world and the relationship between citizen and state. This essay analyzes ways in which the creation of new types of "exit spaces"—outside the realms of the existing hegemony of the state and corporate power— might provide us with imaginable alternatives with which to articulate our grievances with those structures. This would then allow the creation of an agonist politics, un-stymied by apathy and hopelessness. Examining the significance of contemporary, technologically-driven forms of exit space in seasteading, the Silk Road, and the Athens Wireless Metropolitan Network, this essay will mine these case studies as new forms of public space in the technological realm.

The Failure of "Voice"
Hirschman sees exit from an organization as the progressive next-step following the failure of voice—defined as the airing of grievances and protesting. In order to understand the interest in exit spaces it's useful to consider arguments for why voice is failing as a form of inciting change within institutions. In his essay "The Practical Utopian's Guide to the Coming Collapse," anthropologist David Graeber posits that far from being ineffective in their aim of changing the global status quo, the global protest movements of the late sixties had the significant effect of prioritizing domestic appeasement. He suggests that although they often failed in achieving their explicit objectives, they were strategically successful in creating a sense of political empowerment for the previously maligned as well as developing tactics and strategies for functional popular dissent in the framework of the United States' constitution. As a result of this success he explains that "the creation of that sense of failure, of the complete ineffectiveness of political action against the system" became a leading objective of modern government from which resulted "the imposition of an apparatus of hopelessness, designed to squelch any sense of an alternative future."[2] To this end, states and corporate organizations embarked on extensive strategies to prevent dissent on this scale in the future through acts such as carefully curated media campaigns, public relations, intelligence operations, legal and property levies on space, and the militarizing of the police. Hirschman, writing from the midst of this dissent in the late sixties prefigures this

Protestors carry
identical banners
on an all too familiar
popular march in
Washington DC 2007.
PHOTO: RAGESOSS, LICENSED
UNDER CREATIVE COMMONS
ATTRIBUTION – SHARE ALIKE

internalizing, securitizing strategy as it is used
in corporate organizations:

> [T]he short-run interest of management
> in organizations is to increase its own freedom
> of movement; management will therefore
> strain to strip the members-customers of the
> weapons which they can wield, be they exit or
> voice, and to convert, as it were, what should
> be feedback into a safety valve. Thus voice
> can become mere "blowing off steam" as it
> is emasculated by the institutionalization and
> domestication of dissent.[3]

He goes on to describe other innovative tactics
employed by organizations for suppressing dissent. For example how, during the Vietnam War
protests, the Johnson administration dealt with
government dissenters by giving them the role
of "official dissenter," a position that makes the
individual discountable and predictable. Political
theorist Chantal Mouffe, in her book *Agonistics:
Thinking the World Politically*, refers to this as
the way in which "demands which challenge the
hegemonic order are appropriated by the existing
system so as to satisfy them in a way which
neutralizes their subversive potential."[4] We could
look to the failure of the Stop the War Coalition's
2003 march—the United Kingdom's biggest ever
demonstration—to achieve its single explicit aim,
to prevent the invasion of Iraq as evidence of
this disempowerment of popular protest. I have

previously identified the modern form of popular
protest as "flatpacked protest;"[5] the protestors
organize online, carry identical banners, and protest under the watchful eye of the police within
carefully constructed legal and physical constraints.
In this, they behave as a herd, not an active polity.
As Hirschman describes, they are easily predictable
and discountable, occupying a necessary social
niche but having any real agency stripped away
through the institutionalization of protest.

The Space for "Exit"
Hirschman's term "exit," taken at its most literal,
is the actual physical departure of a dissenter from
the organization they take exception to. Exemplars
of this literal form of exit might be the American
communes, such as New Harmony, Indiana,
and Oneida, that sprung up across the territories
of the United States in the nineteenth century.
Hirschman himself notes that "exit has been
accorded an extraordinarily privileged position
in the American tradition. [...] The United States
owes its very existence and growth to millions
of decisions favoring exit over voice."[6] This is
exemplified by the number of these communes
setup by Europeans emigres looking to escape
and challenge European cultural and religious
hegemony. The American communes of the nineteenth century are endemic of how, given the
desire to form a society under an alternative set
of beliefs, the United States at the time was an
accommodating location to do it. The Koreshan

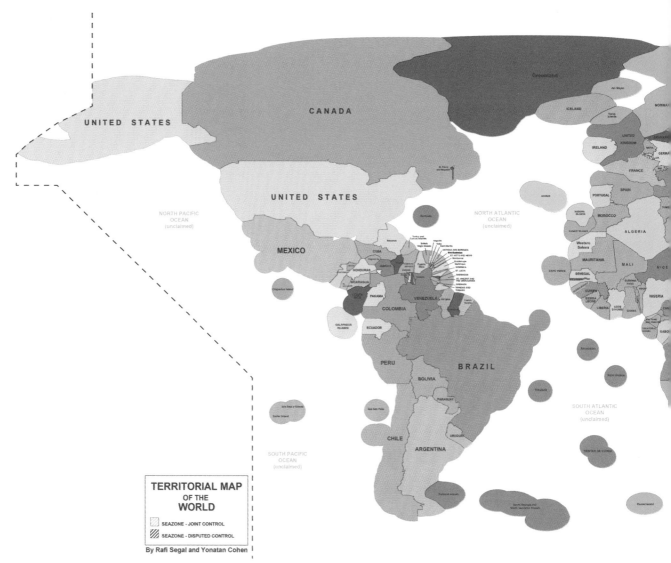

TERRITORIAL MAP
OF THE
WORLD

▨ SEAZONE - JOINT CONTROL
▧ SEAZONE - DISPUTED CONTROL

By Rafi Segal and Yonatan Cohen

Rafi Segal and Yonatan Cohen's "Territorial Map of The World" (2013) visualizes the true political territory of nation-states which seasteaders hope to escape.
IMAGE: COURTESY RAFI SEGAL

Unity movement provides a case study of the process and reasoning of these communal exits. Following altercations with the Chicago authorities, the Koreshans, led by Cyrus Teed, decided to settle in rural southern Florida in 1894. They believed that the universe existed inside a giant sphere (and tried to prove it),[7] and had a host of unhelpful social policies for a growing community, such as mandatory celibacy. Despite this, they were incredibly successful as historian Robert S. Fogarty remarks, counting almost two hundred followers at their height:

Remarkably enough the colonists succeeded in constructing and sustaining a community until Teed's death in 1908. After his death the colonists waited for him to rise from the dead and when that failed to occur the two hundred members split into warring factions.[8]

Fogarty goes on, referencing Arthur Beston to speculate as to why the Koreshans were perhaps one of the last successful and notionally accepted communes because the possibility of challenging the hegemony of the state by the early twentieth century was unimaginable:

[S]ocial patterns became so well defined over the whole area of the United States that the possibility no longer existed of affecting the character of the social order merely by planting the seeds of new institutions in the wilderness.[9]

Hirschman terms this hopeless situation a "lazy monopoly" and explains why, in 1970, exit had become a completely unfathomable tactic for the citizens of the United States and other world-leading states: "...no standard of comparison is available for the superpower which can claim, with some plausibility, that in view of its special burdens and responsibilities ordinary standards do not apply."[10] In other words, by the time Hirschman was writing in the late 1960s, there was no way for a disgruntled citizen to imagine or make an example of a better alternative to their current situation and so they sank into loyalty. Here, we find Graeber's more poetically named "apparatus of hopelessness." Exit becomes unimaginable and, importantly physically challenging when almost all hospitable land and the imagination of alternatives falls under the hegemony of the state.

Seasteading

If a line were drawn a hundred years from the Koreshans to today, the seasteading movement would be a parallel. Seasteading evolved as a movement in the late 1980s and has recently come back into vogue with Silicon Valley entrepreneurs and neo-libertarians pursuing the dream of offshore settlements in international waters, the last wholly politically neutral territory. Seasteading is usually presented from a corporate standpoint with arguments for theability to employ immigrant workers without the complexities of immigration law, the storage of data that may be illegal on-shore, or for tax-evasion and low trade levies.[11] As China Mieville, in his essay "Floating Utopias," writes:

> Their intent is to slip the surly bonds of earth not up but sideways, beyond littoral borders. It is a lunatic syllogism: "I dislike the state: The state is made of land: Therefore I dislike the land." Water is a solvent, dissolving "political" (state) power, leaving only "economics" behind.[12]

However, as Mieville alludes to, seasteading is more plausibly seen as political posturing. It's questionable as to whether any of the myriads of proposed projects, backed purely by the cult of personality built around the personal successes of its most vocal proponents, are even technically viable. The engineering complexities still to be overcome versus the actual investment in projects implies that seasteading is the "forward wedge of a political project" to gain greater leverage over the existing economic and political hegemony.[13] Seasteading also invalidates itself by openly posing as a project for an elite subset of the neo-liberal idealists, marketing itself to Burning Man hedonists and Silicon Valley billionaires, pleading ignorance to the reliance that this superculture has on the people who would construct and service their floating utopias let alone buy their products or engage with their economics.

Silk Road

The Silk Road represents a similar, if significantly more functioning, attempt at exit space as extra-statecraft. However, instead of slipping the surly bonds of earth, it subsumes itself in existing infra-structure by leveraging technological exploits. The Silk Road, often cited as the "Ebay of drugs," is a narcotics marketplace that operates using

Tor—a service that allows online users to anonymize their activity and location to prevent traffic monitoring. At its height in 2012 it was trading approximately $1.2 million a month of illegal drugs around the world by shipping products between sellers and consumers simply through domestic and international mail services.

Silk Road provides an interesting example of what might be considered an internalized exit. Unlike the Koreshans or Seasteading, Silk Road suggests no physical migration or movement in order to remove itself from the auspices of the state to pursue activities opposed to national laws or principles. The operation was largely run from San Francisco public libraries' free Wi-Fi, and Tor still relies on backbone Internet connections. It also utilized standard postal services for delivery as opposed to the nefarious courier services of the organized narcotics business.[14]

Although one would no more trust Silk Road as a political platform than one might trust Ebay as a healthcare provider, it furnishes an interesting argument for the idea of technology as a territory. Network and technological platforms have the same potential to be political spaces as town squares or floating cities. They are spaces with gatekeepers, levies, security, methods of communication, exchange protocols and travel embedded in their construction. The Silk Road is a space under a political jurisdiction (though not a particularly desirable one) whose existence is subsumed in the physicality of the state. Seasteading and the Silk Road give us two key examples of exit spaces; one which seeks to physically remove itself, and another to subsume itself. Neither is particularly desirable or sustainable, but they represent imaginable alternatives to our standard platforms and institutions of politics.

The AWMN

The Athens Wireless Metropolitan Network (AWMN) is a community-run mesh network based in and around Athens. Unlike the dominant root and branch network structure in which there are gate-keepers to access and distribution, a mesh network is a distributed peer-to-peer system where no individual node has the capabilities to control any others. As one of the architects, Vaggelis Koutroumpas described it:

> We could be considered as an alternative telco [telecommunications company] in a sense— with the important difference that this network is owned by the people and is for the people. There are no companies involved. There are no financial motivations or gains in AWMN (though many would love to capitalize on it— we constantly give a fight to keep it open and free!). It's a non-profit network. And there is no government censorship. Even if they wanted to it could be quite difficult to censor something on AWMN since we own the backbone routers and can play with routing pretty much like the internet works.[15]

The Koreshan settlement at its height, date unknown.
PHOTO: COURTESY OF THE KORESHAN STATE HISTORIC SITE

The AWMN was constructed as a community-led project in 2002 in response to poor investment in Internet connectivity by the Greek government. The network provides high-speed symmetrical broadband; symmetrical in the sense that it is an alternative to the Internet replete with its own social networks, gaming servers, media, and communications structure. In addition to providing this public infrastructure service, it also provided a backup to Internet connectivity when cell towers and Athens' tenuous broadband struggled during the austerity protests in 2010–2012 and at times when the government initiated communications shutdowns. Not only is the AWMN a functioning exit space, but it is also a largely desirable one and a format that is gaining traction as a plausible alternative to the increasingly besieged current Internet structure. Of course the success of the AWMN as opposed to other similar projects is in its locality and its situation. Hirschman himself describes how specific instances of cognitive dissonance—a disagreeable situation—might lead past voice and exit and "could lead to actions designed to change the real world when that is an alternative way (and particularly when it is the only way) of overcoming or reducing dissonance."[16] The activists and developers working on the AWMN had no desire to leave Athens to its fate and felt that their protest was unheard. Instead they took the option to construct their own exit space embedded in the infrastructure of the community they already belonged to. In this sense, the AWMN is not an exit space, but an action space, providing the construction of a real functioning imaginable alternative. How this imaginable alternative is used and how it engages with the institutions whose failures it was born from is a different matter.

Agonistic Spaces

Chantal Mouffe is one of the leading proponents of agonistic politics; a confrontation between opposing political ideals as opposed to concession or harmful antagonism. In order to do this, however, the positions of adversaries need to be established. She contends, and in agreement with Graeber and Hirschman, that with suppression of imaginable alternatives it has become impossible to exercise true dissent, "The absence of recognized alternative to the dominant hegemonic order has prevented those who have tried to resist this order from finding legitimate forms of expression."[17] She argues that in order to re-politicize people and to combat apathy there must be the construction of a "constitutive outside"—spaces or ideas occupied by a "them" and an "us." She describes this as political articulation, a clear placement of ideals and beliefs in an almost spatial sense so as to construct polities with demonstrable imaginable alternatives.[18]

What the Athens Wireless Metropolitan Network provides is a political space in which to assemble and articulate an "us." It functions as a town square for people with government grievances to assemble and organize, not just to take part in a street protest but to demonstrate the plausibility of a community-led technologically-mediated space that dually functions as a political body. The AWMN has to make decisions about its future direction, content, and principles, as a horizontally distributed network and for the last twelve years has provided a growing and exemplary instance of that kind of system. Where the Occupy movement suffered from rapid scaling and inarticulate definitions of us and them, the AWMN has built its identity as a platform and a community slowly and stably.

The Town Square in Advance of the Frontier
In spatial political terms, we could consider the Athens Wireless Metropolitan Network a town square in advance of the frontier: A new type of politically active public space that has so far avoided being dragged under the yoke of more hierarchical control and thrust into Graeber's "apparatus of hopelessness." While the AWMN is significantly dissimilar to the much more ostentatious and elitist Seasteading movement or the guiltily thrilling Silk Road, the format of

a sustainable, distributed, and community-led technological territory provides an enticing model of a future for new active public spaces. With growing cognitive dissonance activated by issues such as global surveillance, the nearing end of net neutrality, and political apathy in the developed world, opportunities for new forms of networks as platforms for political positioning and organization are becoming real possibilities for active exit spaces. Mesh networks and the technology that fuels them are rapidly becoming more available with projects like Occupy.here and Alternet, an easily buildable dark net model and a proposal for a plug-and-play mesh network node, starting to hint at consumer-grade accessibility where before they have required significant technological nous.[19]

Hirschman, even writing in the midst of the political dissent of the late 1960s was aware of the imminent failure of voice; of the institutionalization of protest and the securitization of public space in which to perform it. At the same time, the totalizing global hegemony of political institutions shaped during the Cold War saw the Koreshans and the American communes as some of the last attempts at practicing the imaginable alternative in the United States and perhaps the developed world. Now, with network technologies, used by communities in a new way, we're maybe beginning to glimpse an alternative meaning for exit. One where the physical movement of a disgruntled polity across the Earth is not necessary, when political space can be carved out from the networked society. With a more massive uptake of the technologies that enable this space-building, it's possible that we may also find real spaces in which to practice a politics of agonism, one that recognizes the viability of imaginable alternatives instead of subverting or subsuming them.

Tobias Revell is an artist and designer from London. He is a founding member of research consultancy Strange Telemetry, a designer with Superflux and a tutor and lecturer in interaction design at the London College of Communication and the Royal College of Art.

Notes
1   Albert O. Hirschman, *Exit, Voice and Loyalty; Responses to Decline in Firms, Organizations and States* (Cambridge, MA: Harvard University Press, 1970), 4.
2   David Graeber, "The Practical Utopian's Guide to the Coming Collapse" *The Baffler*, n. 22 (November 2013), http://www.thebaffler.com/past/practical_utopians_guide.
3   Hirschman, 124.
4   Chantal Mouffe, *Agonistics: Thinking the World Politically* (London: Verso, 2013), 73.
5   Tobias Revell. "Designed Conflict Territories" from tobiasrevell.com (September 2013), blog.tobiasrevell.com/2013/09/designed-conflict-territories.html.
6   Hirschman, 106.
7   The "rectilineator" was a giant ruler constructed to be perfectly straight. It would descend into the ground as it lengthened if we indeed, did live on the inside of a hollow sphere, and head away from it if we lived on the outside. Of course, it descended. "If you build it, they will come."
8   Robert S. Fogarty, "American Communes, 1865–1914," *Journal of American Studies*, v. 9: 145–162.
9   Fogarty, 145.
10   Hirschman, 117.
11   BlueSeed (found online at: https://blueseed.co/) exists almost expressly for this aim.
12   China Mieville, "Floating Utopias," *In These Times* (September 2007), http://inthesetimes.com/article/3328/floating_utopias.
13   Philip E. Steinberg, et al., "Atlas Swam: Freedom, Capital, and Floating Sovereignties in the Seasteading Vision," *Antipode*, v. 44, n. 4 (2012), 1532–1550.
14   Nate Anderson and Chris Farivar, "How the feds took down Dread Pirate Roberts," *Ars Technica* (October 2013), http://arstechnica.com/tech-policy/2013/10/how-the-feds-took-down-the-dread-pirate-roberts/.
15   Koutroumpas, Vaggelis, email to author (July 14, 2014).
16   Hirschman, 94.
17   Mouffe, 19.
18   Mouffe, 5.
19   Occupy.here: http://occuphere.org and the Alternet: http://www.sarahtgold.co.uk/the-alternet.

SHARED GRAMMARS, INDIVIDUAL DESIRES

Gabriel Duarte

Canto de Itaipu is a traditional fishermen community in Niterói, a satellite city to Rio de Janeiro. Mostly occupied by informal housing, it is currently "graded" as a coastal slum (*favela*, in Portuguese) by the State Government of Rio de Janeiro. Located in an environmentally and politically sensitive area, the neighborhood has been subject to imprecise planning regulations, illegal occupations, and had to endure severe economic hardships. Several of the economic issues are due to conflicts between its traditional fishing techniques and nearby oil-related logistics, which are blamed for having caused major reductions in the availability of fish. Chosen to be the first region for a new urban regeneration program, specifically targeted at fishing communities and created by the Rio de Janeiro State Department of Economical Development, Canto de Itaipu has become the testing ground for an alternative mode of participatory planning.[1]

Having taken part in numerous other participatory projects in the past, particularly dealing with slum regeneration, it was clear for the partners at CAMPO that—despite obvious good intentions—processes solely based on consultation were not achieving long-lasting results. Specifically, in Brazil, the status quo of participatory planning still relies on an outdated structure of problem-identifying and solving, which is aimed at building consensus. This idea focuses almost exclusively on a continuous cycle of consultation and correction of plans and briefs in order to achieve a balanced state among all stakeholders, such as the community and government.[2] However, the idea of consensus building has proved to be flawed in most cases, the exception being when all stakeholders are able to adequately calibrate their channels of communication.[3] This process unfairly places planners and designers in the role of problem-solvers, creating expectations that cannot be fulfilled within the lifespan of a project and within the established participatory frameworks. The strategies being employed rely on outdated modes of consultation, such as the development of diagnostic surveys and interviews to anticipate potential areas of intervention/concern based on supposedly scientifically correct data collection.[4] These predictive approaches have been used since the first slum upgrading projects realized in Rio de Janeiro, as part of the IDB-sponsored Favela Bairro program in the 1990s, which understood participation as a modality of static consultation. These programs in effect disguised top-down decisions as the result of participation.

In this context, CAMPO explored a revised mode of participation that stresses the importance of having an effective influence on educating stakeholders—be them institutional or from society—in order to create effective channels of communication.[5] This process highlights the necessity to better calibrate communication channels, instead of remediating urban policies

Local fishermen arriving early in the morning with fresh catch that will be cleaned and sold directly from their boats.

and form as short-term attempts to resolve apparently clear demands. One of the major issues identified with participation is linked to inadequacies in communication and vocabulary, which consequently privileges the governmental institutions by reducing the empowerment of the community. The issue at stake here is not merely about revising terminology, but rather about finding ways to incorporate planning and design issues as linguistic components in the participatory process. Further, these issues need to be incorporated into the early stages of urban regeneration plans instead of as end results. How can we empower a community to make informed decisions in an alien process? Can planning and design be effectively assigned a political role in participatory processes, avoiding a merely allegorical role? How can form be present and relevant in forums of social and political participation?

Architects as Enablers

In Brazil, for the past three to four decades, planning and design have had less and less influence in broader social and political debates. The rejection of physical-behavioral determinism indicative of modern masterplanning—the allegedly "scientific ability" to foresee the future that planners and designers imagined—has proven to be flawed in many occasions. This issue can be easily seen in the case of slum-upgrading projects, which operate within quintessentially informal contexts (that exists outside of institutional planning boundaries), and typically disrupt planning forecasts.[6] Such impossibility of "planning the informal," led us to critically engage the problem in Canto de Itaipu in a manner wherein rigid top-down planning decisions—as is usually done for the sake of urbanizing the informal—are left aside in favor of a collaboration between community and governmental agencies to elaborate their own local sets of guidelines and needs.

This process effectively repositions the role of the architect as the facilitator of participatory processes—where the roles of planner and designer are synthesized. The architect has a unique ability to reconcile the abstraction and universality of policy, and the materiality and specificity of form. This setting enables the spatialization of policy and regulations into form, allowing all stakeholders to understand the repercussions of legal planning. The architect (as well as urbanists, landscape architects, etc.) is especially valuable in this context not only because of their inherent professional capacities, but also because the discipline holds the key to the continuous understanding of the repercussions of policy and planning regulations onto the territory. Architects could be enablers of participatory conversations, instead of solely executing ideas. This enabling strategy implies that architects need to revise their naturalized top-down biases through the development and implementation of an equalized vocabulary, as common denominators for all stakeholders.[7] This approach requires

Designed public spaces
Special urbanization
Transportation
Bike paths and ecological trails
Environmental recovery
Spatial regulation

LIMITS
SECTORS
legal housing units
informal settlements / fishermen
social meeting places
unrestricted public spaces
restricted public spaces
controlled access
listed site / building

a methodological repertoire that negotiates the technocratic (top-down) and the social-political (bottom-up) dimensions of space, by using planning and design to foster political agreement—reformulating briefs and adjusting the legal and political stages of urban regeneration plans.

Specific Context

The Canto de Itaipu fishing community was founded in the early 1800s, when the area was still a secluded beach, despite the fact that Niterói had already been a well-established capital for the State of Rio de Janeiro. Most of the current members of the community descend from the original families that founded the village. Initially self-governed through their own internal set of rules that overlooked governmental, urban, and environmental regulations, in time, the village slowly integrated the city's infrastructural network. As it became more connected, it also was subject to both the benefits and harms of urban dynamics. Today, it suffers from, among other things, unplanned growth and severe real-estate speculation practices due to its desirable location.

In order to overcome the conflicting planning regulations and to define clearer roles, the plan tied distinct urban and landscape design intervention sites to specific planning and regulation institutions.

Different scopes derived from the sectors defined by institutional responsibility. These results were used to initiate discussions with local and governmental stakeholders in order to determine what would later become the actual design commissions within the renewal plan.

Being part of both the neighboring Itaipu Lagoon Protection Area and the Tiririca State Natural Park, over the years, the area got entangled in a myriad of conflicting environmental regulations. Further, the presence of heritage listed buildings and sites in the area—such as the old Santa Teresa Motherhouse, where the Itaipu Archeological Museum is now housed, and the Duna Grande (Big Dune), a former indigenous burial site—have inserted an additional layer of complexity through restrictions. The presence of the natural parks, museum, and the dune establishes a series of perimeters whose occupation is extremely regulated. Such regulations define rigid occupation indexes to deter (or exert complete control of) construction, be they either publicly or privately owned. Over the years, divergent issues among these regulatory agencies painted an almost impossible picture for future planning in Canto de Itaipu. Superimposing, mutually exclusive and incompatible planning regulations, created a context that is only useful in creating barriers for any debate or action on the urban regeneration of the area. All active community and government stakeholders continuously undermine one another, creating distress and preventing any form of action.

Among the numerous conflicts in the area, it has become routine for those in the fishing industry to sue the government to more actively regulate predatory tourism and real-estate speculation in the area. On the other side, the National Heritage Institute (IPHAN), due to illegal construction on listed heritage sites, sues the community. The list of disastrous and unresolved pairings such as these are endless and their seemingly impossible resolution actually triggered the development of a method to empower stakeholders for effective dialogue through planning and design. For this to occur, it was necessary to synchronize discussions on policy and regulations with their actual spatial outcomes. The proposed way to achieve this established a common lexicon was based on form.

Consultation versus Participation

There is a tendency to mistake participation with public consultation, which are in fact conceptually different. It is deceptive to understand participation as a synonym to consultation, and accept that whatever a given social or political entity voices is a valid truth. Society in general—and some politicians, planners, and designers as well—tend to blindly stress the values of listening as a means to compose a list of demands. It is an equally illusory idea that top-down technical knowledge is able to individually make informed decisions, being impermeable to any local input.[8] Unfortunately, participatory processes tend to fluctuate towards these extremes without yielding any positive long-term results. One of the most pressing challenges in implementing participation in planning and design is precisely to find a balanced ratio between adequately prepared local knowledge and technique. Lazy deliberators from both sides tend to assume often-biased *a priori* positions, which remain impermeable to debate or negotiation.[9]

The key to overcome this initial paralysis lies in shifting participation from mere consultation to a process of establishing effective channels of communication among all the stakeholders involved. It is necessary to understand that achieving a balanced ratio is not necessarily just avoiding one side from outnumbering the other (local versus technical). But it is more important to guarantee that there are equal numbers of stakeholders within each side prepared to fully understand the consequences of their discussions. Ideas and concepts have different meanings to different people, and for an effective conversation to take place, it is necessary for everyone to calibrate vocabulary around the same common object. The act of knowing, as a concept, is crucial in this context.[10] If we agree that knowledge is invariably connected to the way it is reproduced and shared, the first step is to be conscious of what knowledge really is. Stakeholders need to know what is being negotiated in order to overcome pre-existing biases. In the case of Canto de Itaipu, enabling dialogue was essential. The participatory method employed the idea that knowledge is formed from an active engagement with what is being studied. This means that taking action is needed to know something: to study, to investigate, to draw, and above all, to communicate. This led to the decision to educate and encourage stakeholders to appropriate design and planning visualization strategies, in order to actively engage with the spatial outcomes of participatory debates.

Playing Serious Games

Carlos Nelson dos Santos' 1980s project for the Brás de Pina slum, in Rio de Janeiro[11] remains a fundamental precedent for this process. Santos led a team of architects who were hired directly by the community (working pro-bono), to set up an office inside the favela and promote design workshops with the community, something unimagined at the time. It was the first time that a slum was not considered something ephemeral and readily prone to eviction, and instead was regarded as a valuable neighborhood with important social and cultural assets.

Santos argued that all planning operations were subject to games of power that invariably took place in space (a term he used generically as a synonym to the city), be it real or imaginary.[12] The material presence of the context (or space) was, therefore, a necessary parameter to be tackled. While stating that "it is not by renouncing the responsibility to give form to spaces, falling into the comfortable neutrality of diagnostics and plans[13] that only take care of generalities, that we will find ways."[14] Santos points out the necessity of urban plans to effectively embrace the dimension of local form as an active mechanism for debate and political expression.

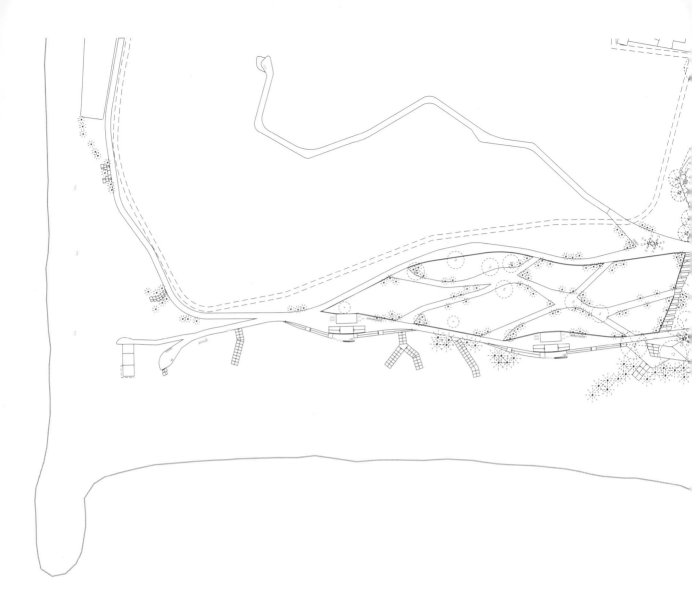

This experience eventually made him focus on the scale of the neighborhood and the spatial expressions of its everyday life.

Having become an avid reader of Michel de Certeau, especially his works on the power of the everyday,[15] Santos derived his participatory methodology from conceptual distinctions between tactics and strategies. Santos argued that the everyday use of urban form—specifically through the fundamental dialectics of house versus street and public versus private—was the ultimate expression of social solidarity[16], and how communities reproduced their ideals of order. Strategy was, in his interpretation of de Certeau, "organized from a postulate of power," while tactics were determined precisely by its absence, or a way that the everyday was able to permeate and recreate any spatial framework of a given community.

Clearly advocating in favor of local communities in their struggle against top-down decisions, Santos proposed added power be given to local tactical capabilities by incorporating design and planning techniques. With this in mind, Santos established what he usually refers to as the "deck of cards of urbanism."[17] By claiming that tactical actions (community) must be paired with strategic ones (public or private institutional powers) in order to create true participation, Santos developed in Brás de Pina what was called at the time the "community workshops." In the workshops, community members of all ages and social groups discussed their expectations and desires being mediated by the architects in a type of rudimentary design education environment, a quasi design studio. The team led by Santos would train local stakeholders in using basic architectural representation to evaluate and materialize their claims. Measurements, dispositions, locations, times, were all elements that had to be identified and discussed through drawings, collages, or models.

All deliberations had to be based on the actual spatial expressions of a given demand. The

area was as problematic as the community's ability to voice their concerns. Miscommunications among institutions also had to be resolved, as well as their interfaces with the community. The challenge was to use participatory processes to conceive both the pieces of a game, and more importantly, the different boards where they would be played.

Game Boards as Territorial Mediators

The game board was directly analogous to how the project had to initially resolve unwanted redundancies among the different roles of regulatory institutions in Canto de Itaipu. The overlapping regulations in place had immediate territorial and local repercussions that needed to be visualized and shared to enable negotiations. Communication "noise" was present not only between community and institutions, but also among institutions in different governmental levels. The workshops, initially conceived by Santos as tools exclusively for communities, would now also bring institutions to the common table. It was necessary to disclose the implications of the institutional presence in spatial and visible terms. This disclosure is what crafted the game board. The game boards were a series of maps rendered by the documentation of legal territorial constraints through the realization of community and institutional meetings in Canto de Itaipu. However, unlike the propositional nature of following workshops—closer to the spirit of the ones realized by Santos—the game board workshops aimed at clarifying the institutional scope (both local and governmental) and the future contexts of actions. That set the condition wherein all the game pieces (individual proposals developed in community meetings) could move about more efficiently while being aware of possibilities, duties, and rights. The composition of the boards was handled with three informational levels: sectors, articulations, and phasing. Such parameters organized the development of cartographic exercises in the workshops. The use of maps was particularly important for both pedagogical and symbolic reasons. As instruments of planning and design almost exclusively handled by technicians, maps usually distances stakeholders from the spatial frameworks at stake. Instead the process empowered the community and institutions to recognize themselves and their issues through maps.

The first level of mapping, sectors, identified the institutional presence and their physical boundaries in the area with respect to responsibilities and scopes. This level built a model of mediated and jointly liable collaboration between institutions and community. To a certain extent, this layer persisted and matured throughout all of the work phases. The second level, articulations, cross-referenced the sectors and their expected functions within the governmental scope. At this level, the possible location of future proposals had to be collectively identified within the workshops. By determining functions and potential

Detailed plan of the public parks and recreation areas on the edges of the beach, dune, and lagoon. Such parks also play the role of forming concrete borders to different areas under specific institutional responsibility and surveillance—guaranteeing that liabilities and boundaries are visible through urban design interventions.

drawings, and the frameworks they represented, became cards in a game. As with cards in a regular deck, their constraints, combinations, and powers were defined to enable discussions. Replies or counter arguments had to be equally represented. The collaborative environment of the workshops, where the community was made aware of the rules involved by the team and trained to react, was key to empowering them to take part in discussions with institutional stakeholders on balanced terms. It allowed the development of a regeneration plan that was attentive to the micro-negotiations in place, which were, in return, conscious of the legal and institutional frameworks where they co-existed. Tactics and strategies were mutually aware of each other. Building on this experience, the Canto de Itaipu project proposed the expansion of Santos' card game analogy to the idea of a field of actions defined by the game and visualized on a game board. As mentioned before, the maze of regulations and unclear responsibilities in the

Shared Grammars, Individual Desires

Aerial photograph show-
ing the current condi-
tion of Canto de Itaipú.
PHOTO: COURTESY OF
GABRIEL DUARTE / CAMPO

Illustration highlight-
ing the implementation
of the first urban design
and planning interven-
tions, as well as new
supporting architecture.
IMAGE: COURTESY OF
GABRIEL DUARTE / CAMPO

Expected outcomes ten
years after the full
implementation of the
plan, including the
recovery of the natural
vegetation and ecologies
of the dune, lagoon,
and beach.
IMAGE: COURTESY OF
GABRIEL DUARTE / CAMPO

synergies between different issues, it was possible to establish a synchronized set of actions for intervention and management. The third level, phasing, established the specific demands for the implementation of future proposals. Data collected and discussed in this level clearly defined the areas to be designed, which had among their goals the exact edges of each area and their institutional link to ensure that certain activities and uses were clearly delimited.

The initial participatory process to conceive of the game boards transformed the entire project in a way that was not anticipated by the team. Game board discussions and developments became by-products of both tactics (bottom-up) and strategies (top-down). The game boards took on the role of territorial mediators in specific discussions to clarify the limits and roles of the various spaces and stakeholders. The framework (game boards) that would later enable proposals to be conceived, had to have a definition in order to initiate negotiation. This created a positively paradoxical condition of feedback, wherein specific issues pertaining to both policy and design forced a revision of limits and regulations, and vice-versa. The community became architects; the architects became government; and government became community. Even in their development stages, the game boards provided the team with a series of unexpected micro-anchors that allowed the project to progress. Amidst the institutional chaos that existed in the area before, where no voice was heard nor understood, design-oriented negotiations enriched the participatory process. Unlike initially expected, stimuli through design was necessary to catalyze effective negotiations. Among other things, this process revealed that participation proved to be a game that needs to be constantly played, in order to be created.

Gabriel Duarte is a founding partner in CAMPO architecture and urban design, based in Rio de Janeiro, and a professor at the Department of Architecture of the Catholic University of Rio de Janeiro (CAU PUC-Rio), where he runs design studios that investigate the intermediate scales between landscape and architecture.

Notes

1   This process has been developed by CAMPO, an architecture and urbanism office based in Rio de Janeiro, and led by Gabriel Duarte, Renata Bertol and Ricardo Kawamoto.
2   Judith E. Innes, "Planning Through Consensus Building: A New View of the Comprehensive Planning Ideal." *Journal of the American Planning Association* 62 (1996): 460.
3   In Judith E. Innes, "Consensus Building: Clarifications for the Critics." *Planning Theory* 3 (2004): 5.
4   Prefeitura da Cidade do Rio de Janeiro. *Favela-Bairro: monitoramento e avaliação, Cadernos Favela-Bairro*, vol. 4 (Rio de Janeiro: Rio Prefeitura, 2005).
5   Judith E. Innes, "Consensus Building: Clarifications for the Critics." *Planning Theory* 3 (2004): 5.
6   Remy Sietchiping, "Prospective Slum Policies: Conceptualization and Implementation of a Proposed Informal Settlement Growth Model." Paper presented at the Third World Bank Urban Research Symposium on Land Development and Poverty Reduction, Brasília, Brazil April 4-6, 2005.
7   Dick Urban Vestbro, editor. *Are architects and planners obstacles to slum upgrading?* Stockholm: Universitetsservice Kungliga Tekniska Högskolan, 2008: 5
8   Linda Fox-Rogers and Enda Murphy, "Informal Strategies of Power in the Local Planning System," *Planning Theory* 13 (2014): 244.
9   Nikhil Kaza, "Tyranny of the Median and Costly Consent: A Reflection on the Justification for Participatory Urban Planning Processes," *Planning Theory* 5 (2006): 255.
10   Edward Tufte, *The visual display of quantitative information*, Chesire: Graphics Press, 2001.
11   Carlos Nelson, who had been a Visiting Researcher at the Department of Urban Studies and Planning (DUSP) in MIT in 1971 and a Professor at the Federal Fluminense University (UFF), in Niterói, documented his participatory planning experiences in two seminal books: Santos, Carlos Nelson Ferreira, and Vogel, Arno, and Silva, Marco Antonio. *Quando a rua vira casa*. (São Paulo: Projeto Arquitetos Associados, 1985), (When the Street becomes Home: The Appropriation of Spaces of Collective Use in Neighborhood Centers), which makes an interdisciplinary analysis of the appropriation of urban spaces by comparing a traditional neighborhood in Rio's Port Area (Catumbi) with a new area entirely planned according to parameters and modern conceptions (Selva de Pedra); and Carlos Nelson Ferreira Santos, *A cidade como um jogo de cartas* (Niterói: Universitária, 1988). Translated as "The City as a Game of Cards," it proposes negotiation methods for urban planning allied to design decisions through the analogy of card games strategies.
12   Carlos Nelson Ferreira Santos, Arno Vogel, and Marco Antonio Silva, *Quando a rua vira casa* (São Paulo: Projeto Arquitetos Associados, 1985), 12.
13   As dictated by the methodology applied by most public planning institutions in Brazil, urban plans are required to be preceded by official 'urban diagnostics', which often must obey institutionally prescribed items and scope of analysis. However, such prescriptions are rarely attuned with the reality of the areas subject to urban plans, negatively distancing architects/planners from the actual issues at stake. This idea—actually an analogy to medical practices—is a reminiscent of the supposedly scientific approach developed by modern planning ideals of neutrality, which still govern many planning operations in Brazil.
14   Translated by the author from the original (in Portuguese): "*Não é pela renúncia à responsabilidade de dar formas aos lugares, caindo nas neutralidades cômodas dos diagnósticos e dos planejamentos que só cuidam de generalidades, que iremos encontrar saídas.*" in: Carlos Nelson Ferreira Santos, Arno Vogel, and Marco Antonio Silva, *Quando a rua vira casa* (São Paulo: Projeto Arquitetos Associados, 1985), 17.
15   Although Michel de Certeau is credited with the theoretical maturity of the notion of everydayness, other thinkers, such as Henri Lefebvre, Martin Heidegger, Antonio Gramsci, among others, initially discussed the concept. However, this work is interested on the notion of Certeau's practice of everyday life, which he refers to as the ways in which the individual "individualizes" mass culture, turning popular elements into something of their own; and lived experiences are transformed by turning the everyday into critical knowledge. See: Michel de Certeau, *The Practice of Everyday Life* (Berkeley: University of California Press, 1984).
16   Carlos Nelson Ferreira Santos, Arno Vogel, and Marco Antonio Silva, *Quando a rua vira casa* (São Paulo: Projeto Arquitetos Associados, 1985), 26.
17   Ibid., 51

WITHIN GENERIC ARCHETYPES AND CROSS-SUBSIDIES: PRODUCTIVE HOUSING IN GUATEMALA AND CENTRAL AMERICA

Posconflicto Laboratory

Towards a Productive Housing Program

With the signing of the peace accords between the Government of Guatemala and Unidad Revolucionaria Nacional Guatemalteca (URNG) in 1996, Central America's last armed conflict came to an end.[1] Despite post-conflict plans and policy efforts, Central America has yet to overturn the structural issues associated with its housing deficit. Recalling Roque Dalton's *Acta*, this situation necessitates an urgent project to rethink architecture, the city, the territory, and the idea of the political, to guarantee access to housing for all.[2] The Productive Housing Program was established to instigate the construction of a local and overall Central American housing policy, rooted in the principle of subsidy. With a pilot project in Guatemala City, the large-scale housing initiative leverages the financial mechanism of cross-subsidies to promote the integration of both marginalized low- and middle-income social groups living in infra-urban and suburban conditions. The initiative goes beyond policy to operate spatially—introducing a housing archetype that is capable of adapting to differing urban fabrics and their associated densities. Most significantly, the program aims to provide adequate housing in central urban areas with close proximity to public transport. Working from within the generic, the community's form follows the self-managed cooperative and associative housing, and is comprised of a community development center, a patio-portico, and prototypical housing units. Utilizing a laboratory methodology, architecture is a pro-active agent for the urgent provision of housing in Guatemala and Central America.[3]

Rethinking the Public(s)

The staggering retreat of the public and the rise of neoliberal urbanization have radically influenced the diffused growth of Central American cities. Fueled by speculative markets, urbanization's pacifying force has further advanced the precarious nature of labor, and colonized all aspects of city life, re-qualifying class and ethnic contradictions as an "all-inclusive" marginalization.[4] In this context, there are two primary subjects that struggle to find adequate housing in the city, which we will call *Subject A* and *Subject B*. *Subject A* is

Photomontage of "Glorious Victory" (Diego Rivera, 1954; photo: Secretariat of the Presidency, Republic of Guatemala) and housing units at Lafayette Park, Detroit (Ludwig Hilberseimer and Mies van der Rohe, 1956). Starting from architecture, Lafayette Park proposed a crossed subsidy model with market apartments and housing cooperatives. A parallel history, the 1954 coup d'état—a CIA covert operation codenamed Operation PBSUCCESS—brought an end to ten years of progressive democratic reform in Guatemala. A thirty-six year internal armed conflict followed (1960–1996).
IMAGE: COURTESY OF A—C—T—A

an individual currently living in an infra-urban condition of poverty whose monthly income is between one and four times the minimum wage per household. *Subject B* is an individual currently living in marginalized suburban conditions whose monthly income is between five and fifteen times the minimum wage per household. *Subject A* is more and more about less and less. *Subject B* is less and less about more and more. As precarious subjects, however, both are always about less and less. The Productive Housing Program acknowledges *Project A*'s target social group—*Subject A*—as the segment of the population with no access to market housing; and Project B's target social group—*Subject B*—as the segment of the population with very limited options in accessing the housing market and currently renting in the city's periphery.

The aim of the housing program is to leverage subsidies, public land, and communal living to design affordability into the market. Land for both *Project A* and *Project B* sites are publicly owned, yet indefinitely managed on a right-of-use basis by cooperative and associative legal entities. Communal living in central urban areas is supported by a project-based economic regime, and is made possible through monthly installments. While all project members are required to make below-market financial contributions, *Project A*'s self-managed cooperative members additionally participate in building as a form of contribution and mutual-aid. Both housing projects provide each community organization with designated productive spaces, in addition to co-managing the usufruct rights of commercial and service spaces at ground level. As a non-speculative alternative within the market, the returns generated by *Project B*'s associative development provide the necessary capital counterpart to subsidize *Project A*. *Project A* then allows *Subject A* to access adequate housing and at the same time develop productive activities on-site, while integrating into central urban areas. *Project B*, who provides the subsidy, allows *Subject B* to access quality housing in central urban areas in close proximity to public transportation. In light of the daunting failure by the national Central American (re)publics in articulating a comprehensive and inclusive housing policy, housing as a project critically demands an alternative strategy from within the production of the city.

Project, Dissent and Action

The Productive Housing Program takes cues from La Ceiba IV, a community and neighborhood association in Guatemala City's Zone 18. Having occupied a municipal plot for eleven years, and with the intention of regularizing their tenancy status, La Ceiba IV is composed of fifty-six families. Urban managers and designers, with support from social workers, arranged three participatory workshops to learn about the neighborhood of La Ceiba IV and foster a dialogue with local residents. The first workshop reconstructed the community's recent history and collective memory through mapping the living and working

Subject A's urbanization
is *more and more about
less and less.*

A

Subject B's urbanization
is *less and less about
more and more.*

B

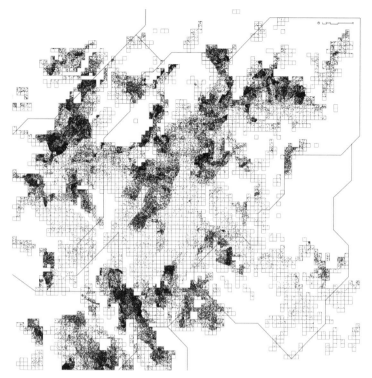

Mapping the housing deficit in the Guatemala City Metropolitan Area.

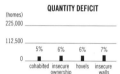

QUANTITY DEFICIT

(homes)
225,000
112,500
0

5% cohabited
6% insecure ownership
6% hovels
7% insecure walls

QUALITY DEFICIT

(homes)
225,000
112,500
0

14% waterless
15% drainless
0.33% insecure roofs
8% earth floors
38% over-crowded

HOUSING DEFICIT

Quantity deficit (16%)   Quality deficit (35%)   Total deficit 723,000 (100 %)

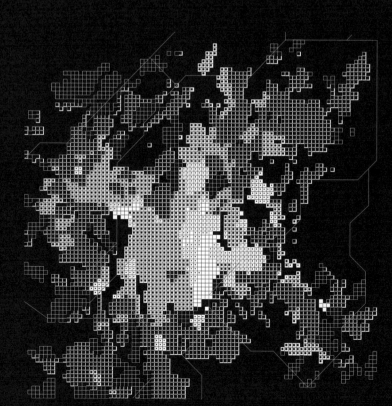

Mapping land value in the Guatemala City Metropolitan Area.

AREA BY LAND VALUE

(has)
5.000
2.500
0

6% $72
39% $148
33% $290
16% $510
6% more

HOMES BY LAND VALUE

(homes)
112,500
56,250
0

9% $72
53% $148
30% $290
7% $510
1% more

LAND VALUE

$ / sq m

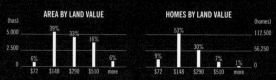

$72 $148 $290 $510   more

Project A's productive
housing archetype,
or self-managed cooper-
ative housing operation.

Project A's housing
prototype units or cell
possibilities.

community development center

patio-portico

housing prototype

productive housing archetype

PROJECT A
The Co-Operation

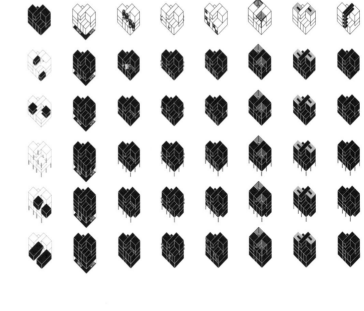

Project B's productive
housing archetype,
or associative market
housing operation.

Project B's housing
prototype units
or cell possibilities.

communal facility

patio-portico

housing prototype

productive housing archetype

PROJECT B
The Market Operation

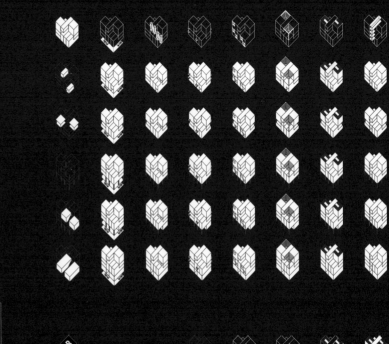

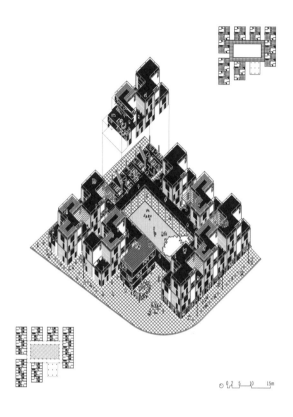

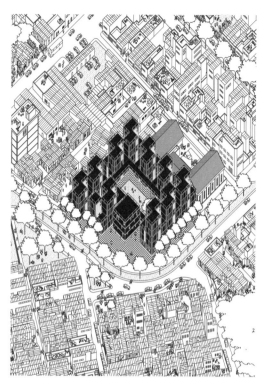

Pilot Project A is composed of prototype housing units, a patio-portico and a community development center.

Pilot Project A at La Ceiba IV, Zone 18, Guatemala City.

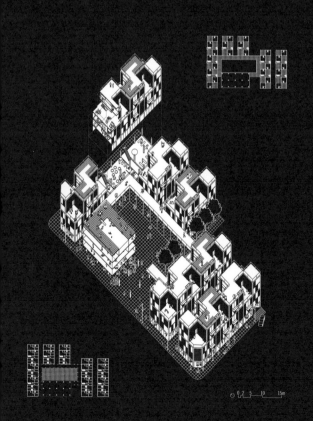

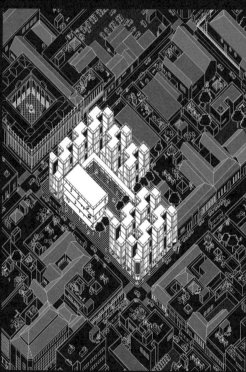

Pilot Project B is composed of prototype housing units, a patio portico, and social facilities.

Pilot Project B at 9th Avenue, Zone 1, Guatemala City.

Project A's productive
housing archetype
or self-managed cooper-
ative housing operations
in Guatemala City
and Central American
capital cities:
Belmopan, San Salvador,
Tegucigalpa,
Managua, San José, and
Panama City.

Inauguration Day
at Project A, Guatemala
City.

Project B's productive
housing archetype
or associative market
housing operations
in Guatemala City
and Central American
capital cities:
Belmopan, San Salvador,
Tegucigalpa,
Managua, San José, and
Panama City.

Picture for Women
at Project B, Guatemala
City.

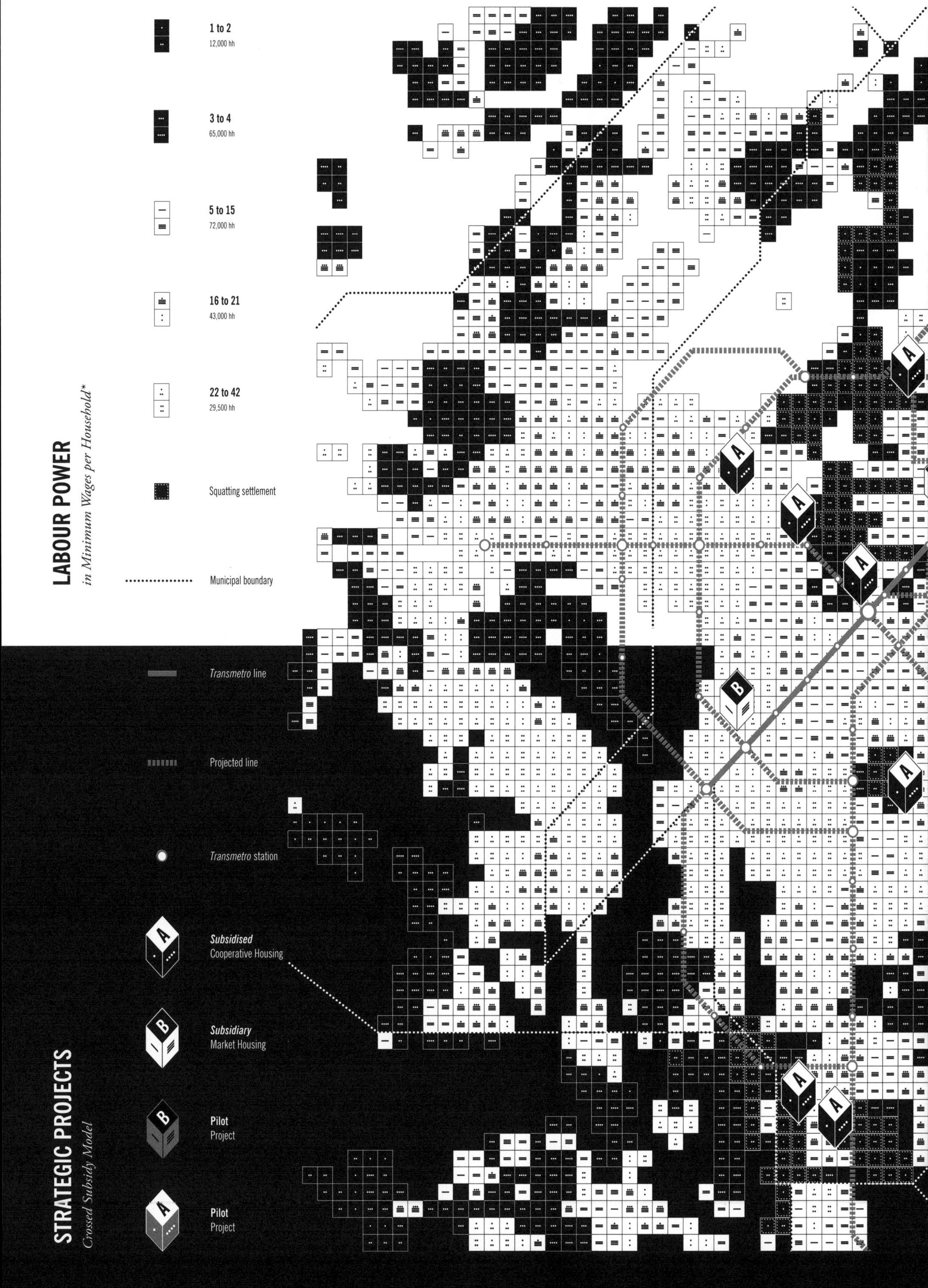

LABOUR POWER
in Minimum Wages per Household*

- **1 to 2** — 12,000 hh
- **3 to 4** — 65,000 hh
- **5 to 15** — 72,000 hh
- **16 to 21** — 43,000 hh
- **22 to 42** — 29,500 hh

Squatting settlement

Municipal boundary

Transmetro line

Projected line

Transmetro station

A *Subsidised* Cooperative Housing

B *Subsidiary* Market Housing

B **Pilot** Project

A **Pilot** Project

STRATEGIC PROJECTS
Crossed Subsidy Model

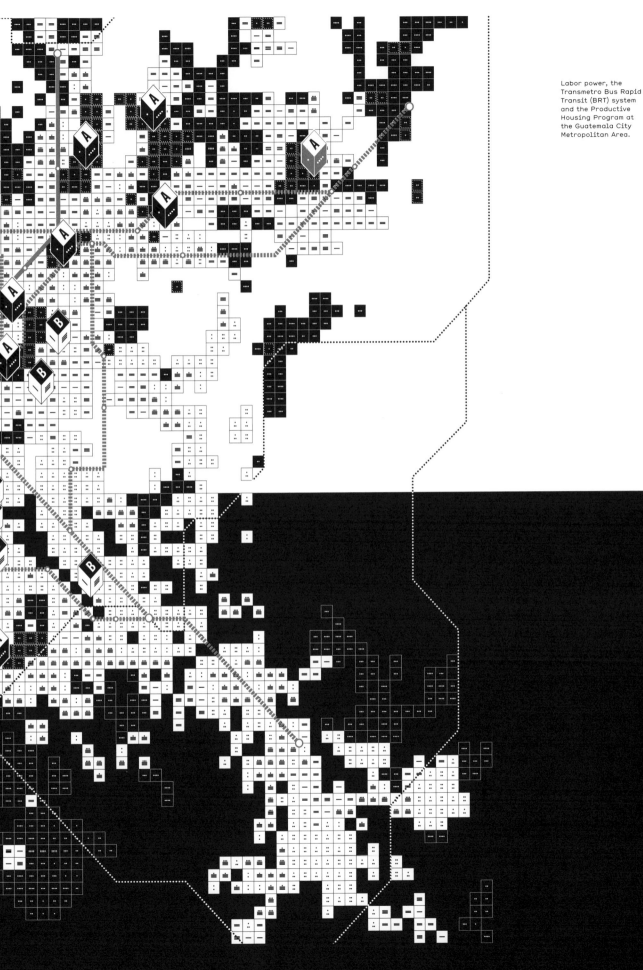

Labor power, the Transmetro Bus Rapid Transit (BRT) system and the Productive Housing Program at the Guatemala City Metropolitan Area.

conditions in space and time. To deepen the discussion on the neighborhood's basic needs, the goal of the second workshop was to emphasize the possibility for shared productive spaces.
As a result, the community prioritized the need for a cultural space, followed by a recreational area, a meeting hall, and a place for local production. Working with scaled models, the final workshop aimed at envisioning space and land-use scenarios. While these workshops were an initial step into understanding the desires of local residents, the pressing need for tangible property, combined with an advanced legal process for individual plot regularization, undermined the significance of a collective housing project, bringing the process to an end.[5] Despite this setback, the methodological and practical knowledge gained from registering the community's conflicting demands of private ownership and the possibility for common spaces, significantly contributed to the articulation of collective and adaptive housing archetypes.

As a publicly initiated housing project driven by conflicting bottom-up demands and top-down plans, the process at La Ceiba IV ultimately articulated the need for architecture as a common paradigm, promoting a design based on collectively self-identifiable, self-programmable, and self-scalable generic forms.[6] As a large-scale initiative, the possibility to prioritize common design, production, and management goals brought architecture into the foreground as a language to reinforce and strengthen a common ethos. By establishing a working agreement with the self-managed cooperative housing movement, with IDESAC and We Effect (formerly the Swedish Cooperative Center) as supporting organizations, a new process for the creation of *Project A*'s first self-managed cooperative —Cooperativa Integral de Vivienda y Esperanza (COINVE)—is underway. All belonging to vulnerable social groups, the cooperative's member households were pooled from municipal social programs. With alleged access to the program's central public land and having agreed on the project's minimum design rules, cooperative members initiated a comprehensive self-education process with support from social workers and technical assistance from designers, urban managers, and other specialists. In this regard, the productive housing archetype, with its community development center, patio-portico, and prototype housing units, emerged as an apparatus of dissent (and consent), enabling cooperative members to collectively program and self-manage their demands, while allowing the newly created public agency, Empresa Metropolitana de Vivienda y Desarrollo Urbano (EMVDU), to account for projected social milestones. Action in the form of renewed programmatic and spatial conflict exercised between cooperative members, social workers, designers, urban managers, legal advisors, and politicians has pushed pilot *Project A* to a convened a project implementation plan. While the self-managed cooperative housing movement, organized under Coordinadora Centroamericana

Autogestionaria de la Vivienda Solidaria (COCEAVIS), continues to gain strength in the Central American region, the strategic struggle for access to central urban land has only begun. Today, further political action is required for the Municipal Council to support the vital creation of the Productive Housing Program's municipal land bank, and similarly, to activate its crucial cross-subsidy technique for an inclusive and expanded productive housing project in Guatemala City.

Posconflicto Laboratory is both a project and a collective research platform centered on housing and post-conflict regions in Central America.

Project Team
Posconflicto Laboratory /
URBANÍSTICA—Empresa Metropolitana de Vivienda y Desarrollo Urbano (EMVDU) and Asociación Centroamericana Taller de Arquitectura (a—c—t—a)

Direction
Roberto Soundy and Álvaro Véliz; Deputy-Direction: Rossana García Ovalle and Silvia García Vettorazzi; Urban Management: Ana Cintrón; Housing Programme: Eva Campos; CounterSite General Design: Erick Mazariegos; Communications: Werner Solórzano; Design Participants: Frank Carrascoza, Gustavo González, Hans Schwarz, Felipe Vásquez and Jorge Villatoro. Housing Programme Implementation: Silvia Aldana; Social Urban Management: Cristina Dulcey. Other Collaborators: Rafael Aycinena, Diego Castillo, Mónica Santos and Emilio Vargas.

Notes
1 Several armed conflicts took place in Central America during the last three decades of the twentieth century (Guatemala 1960–1996, Nicaragua 1974–1990, El Salvador 1980–1992) leaving more than 330,000 people dead. Although armed conflicts in the region have ended with peace accords, several root causes remain unaddressed.
2 Dalton denounces private property and effectively anticipates Central America's armed conflicts during the Cold War. Roque Dalton, *Acta* (El Salvador, 1961; Carrie Comer, trans., 2011).
3 "Posconflicto Laboratory: Making City + Productive Program in Guatemala & Central America" was presented as part of the main exhibition at the 5th International Architecture Biennale Rotterdam (IABR) in 2012. 530/703.html.

4 Paolo Virno, *A Grammar of the Multitude* (Los Angeles: Semiotext[e], 2004), 50. According to Virno, rather than politics conforming to labor, it is labor that has acquired the traditional features of political action.
5 The majority of people at La Ceiba IV, overwhelmingly women and children, favored the Productive Housing Program. A small dominating group against the proposal had intentions of capitalizing on the regularizing of individual land plots.
6 Giorgio Agamben, *The Signature of All Things* (Brooklyn: Zone Books, 2009), 31. Paradigm is understood as "a form of knowledge that is neither inductive nor deductive but analogical. It moves from singularity to singularity."

FAction situates a particular constituency
and interrogates how these groups
act internally as well as interface with
other groups. These articles and projects
foreground the commonality of the
subject to consider specific forms of
action. In what way is the formation and
emergence of sub-collectives informed
and empowered by design?

ACTION

PRECARITY AND POWER

Neeraj Bhatia

What does the current political moment of low-voter turn out, general indifference, desensitization, and a lack of culpability to political action suggest for democratic governance? If we understand the ability to *act* as a distinct characteristic of democratic governance, we must question if contemporary democracy is enabling and empowering citizens to act. This article will explore the ramifications on action through the shift from a political public realm to a hierarchical society to a neoliberal globalized world. My contention is that feeling powerless to change, adjust, or critique a system is not only a call to rethink the effectiveness of democracy, it also suggests that new modes of generating power are required. How power is created, fostered, and maintained is arguably an act of spatial design, for it is when we come together in space and acknowledge what we share in common that we harness power.

From Action to Behavior

Exactly sixty years since its original printing, Hannah Arendt's *The Human Condition* is as pertinent today as ever. Arendt's treatise lists action, along with labor and work as the fundamental activities of the human condition. She defines action as taking initiative and setting something into motion.[1] It is action that reveals the distinctness of individuals and accordingly is dependent on the continual presence of others. Action becomes a critical component in the negotiation between distinct individuals and shared collective goals, and is thereby the *conditio per quam* of all political life.[2] For Arendt, the political realm arises directly from people acting *together*. The significance of action lies in its relational potential to create something new and unpredictable, as Arendt posits, action "always establishes relationships and therefore has an inherent tendency to force open all limitations and cut across boundaries."[3] In this reading, action becomes a fundamental element for a functioning democracy —it has the capacity to adapt and transform political governance, incited by individuals acting in concert.

Arendt's notion of action is intimately linked to her concept of pluralism, which she defines as a dialectic condition of distinction—each individual with their own capacity to speak and act—and equality—the recognition that a common world with shared values exists simultaneously. The continual mediation between the individual and collective is not only at the center of politics, it defines the robustness of the public realm. Because action reveals distinctions and requires the presence of others, it is fundamental to forming and ensuring the existence of the public realm. The loss of the ability to act therefore threatens the very essence of the political public realm.

It is not surprising that freedom and equality are the precursors to Arendt's notion of action. Using ancient Greek civilization to model her argument, she reveals a stark separation between the role of the private and public realm. And while much criticism has surfaced in response to this delineation, particularly in terms of the characterization of the private realm, it is worthwhile outlining Arendt's argument for our purposes, which centers more overtly on the public realm. For Arendt, the private realm in ancient Greece operated through strict hierarchy and attended to the necessities of life. It ensured the reproduction of life. Only once necessities were attended to, could one be fit for engagement with the political public realm. As one left their private household and entered the public realm, they entered a realm of equality, freedom, and politics, as she states, "The realm of the polis, on the contrary, was the sphere of freedom, and if there was a relationship between these two spheres, it was a matter of course that the mastering of the necessities of life in the household was the condition for freedom of the polis."[4] Freedom was a critical tool to ensure that citizens were able to act. Further, while the private realm operated through a hierarchical framework, in the public realm citizens existed as equals, albeit each with a unique vantage point that was revealed through action and speech. Arendt termed this moment where the public realm coalesced the "space of appearance," which was comprised of action, speech, power, and permanence.

The transformation from a political public realm to the organization of society entailed the blurring of the roles of public and private realm. In Arendt's assessment, society was formed through producing a "superfamily" that operated through hierarchy and addressed private necessity in public, as she posits: "The emergence of society—the rise of housekeeping, its activities, problems, and organizational devices—from the shadowy interior of the household into the light of the public sphere, has not only blurred the old borderline between private and political, it has also changed almost beyond recognition the meaning of the two terms and their significance for the life of the individual and citizen."[5] The creation of society dissolved the traditional family unit and absorbed it into social groups that operated as one enormous family with a unified opinion and interest.[6] Through this transformation, action was replaced by behavior, as Arendt states, "It is decisive that society, on all its levels, excludes the possibility of action, which formerly was excluded from the household. Instead, society expects from each of its members a certain kind of behavior, imposing innumerable and various rules, all of which tend to 'normalize' its members, to make them behave, and to exclude spontaneous action or outstanding achievement."[7] By absorbing the hierarchical organization from the private sphere and inserting it into the social sphere, namely to organize labor, a society of laborers and jobholders was formed. Labor is now a fundamental requirement to sustain life and its hierarchical organization in society has produced radical inequalities in the distribution of resources.[8] The superfamily of society foreshadowed by

Arendt, Marx, and others, transformed the role and effectiveness of action, as Arendt argues, "While we have become excellent in the laboring we perform in public, our capacity for action and speech has lost much of its former quality since the rise of the social realm banished these into the sphere of the intimate and the private."[9] Within this account, society not only created an organizational structure based on hierarchy and uneven distribution of resources, it protected this very system by limiting and replacing action with normalized behavior.

The inequalities in contemporary society are easily witnessed in wealth distribution and class division. While we are now all too familiar with the statistics on the uneven allocation of resources within our contemporary condition of advanced capitalism, nowhere are Arendt's warnings more evident then in the rise of a new class-in-the-making, the *Precariat*. This product of late capitalism's neoliberal global agenda is quickly growing from a minority to majority group.

Precarity

The term precariat is a neologism that combines the proletariat and precarity. It has been used to capture the material and psychological uncertainty felt by a class-in-the-making, which is a byproduct of neoliberal transformations in labor[10] practices within advanced capitalism. Terms such as creative labor, network labor, service labor, affective labor, immaterial labor, etc. reveal the diverse practices of labor that have emerged through globalization and information technology. These labor practices have caused an increasingly large sector of the population to live in precarity—referring to, "all possible shapes of unsure, not guaranteed, flexible exploitation: from illegalised, seasonal and temporary employment to homework, flex- and temp-work to subcontractors, freelancers or so-called self-employed persons. But its reference also extends beyond the world of work to encompass other aspects of intersubjective life, including housing, debt, and the ability to build affective social relations."[11] Moving beyond traditional social status divisions, the insecurities of the precariat are both objective and material as well as subjective and emotional. Precarious work does not provide the economic security to support the necessities of a household and the reproduction of life, threatening amongst other things, the ability to act in public.

Signs of the social crisis of precarity emerged during the first May Day parade (now grown into the Euro May Day parade) in Milan in 2001, where students and young activists gathered to protest their conditions of labor and life. Since then, we have witnessed a string of events such as the burning of the Paris suburbs, street battles and protests in Athens, demonstrations in Madrid, and the Occupy Wall Street Movement that have attempted to give a voice to the precariat. The economic crisis of 2008 and recession in subsequent years has radically increased flexible labor; for instance in 2010, ninety-seven percent of the

Another Green World,
2015, Nicole Eisenman
COURTESY THE ARTIST AND
ANTON KERN GALLERY, NEW YORK
THIS ARTWORK IS IN THE
PERMANENT COLLECTION OF
THE MUSEUM OF CONTEMPORARY
ART, LOS ANGELES.

jobs created in the United Kingdom were temporary. The precariat has been growing steadily with recent figures suggesting that forty percent of the adult population in Japan, Korea, Greece, Spain, Italy, Australia, and Sweden are living in precarity, with the largest group residing in China.[12] It is not a coincidence that we are seeing a rise in this almost-class as they are a direct product of neoliberal reforms.

While precarious labor has always existed, its dramatic growth was incited by neoliberal market reforms beginning in the late 1970s. From Reagan to Thatcher, visions of a liberalized global market also entailed the strategic dismantling of social institutions that "weakened labor's bargaining power" precisely because they stood against the market,[13] as summarized by economist Guy Standing:

> In the 1970s, a group of ideologically inspired economists captured the ears and minds of politicians. The central plank of their 'neo-liberal' model was that growth and development depended on market competitiveness; everything should be done to maximize competition and competitiveness, and to allow market principles to permeate all aspects of life. One theme was that countries should increase labor market flexibility, which came to mean an agenda for transferring risks and insecurity onto workers and their families. The result has been the creation of a global "precariat," consisting of many millions around the world without an anchor of stability.[14]

Most of the sectors of labor that foster precarity—hospitality, construction, agriculture, retail, cleaning, journalism, information technology, design—are dominated by multinational companies whose priority is to their shareholders.[15] With the integration of China and other developing economies into the world labor market, there has been a downward pressure on wages in all Organization for Economic Co-operation and Development (OECD) countries.[16] It is important to note that the precariat is not a sub-class, but rather a pivotal group in a global neo-liberal economy. As precarious labor moved from a peripheral position under Fordism to a central position in late capitalism, flexible and uncertain work is being habituated over a larger swath of the population. Global capitalism necessitates a workforce with the precariat's nimble characteristics to operate within the volatility of the market.

The precariat is difficult to precisely group together, as precarious work cuts across a series of markets and subjects—from migrants to housewives to entrepreneurial creatives among others—that are joined by their temporary and contingent relationships. One of the more consistent factors within this heterogeneous group is age—which disproportionately puts young and older workers at risk. At entry and exit points from the labor market, young and older workers are increasingly in precarious positions for longer periods of time.[17] In France, Germany, Sweden, Spain, and Portugal, over fifty percent of jobs for those under twenty-five years of age were temporary contracts.[18] It should be noted that these conditions are not new—in fact higher numbers of youth, women, and immigrants (particularly third-country nationals) have traditionally been subjected to labor insecurity. What has transformed, however, is the sheer number of people living without labor security and certainty.

Insecurity among the precariat manifests in several material and psychological ways, which can broadly be discussed in terms of their relationship to labor and the state. Precarious work often relies on volatile money wages in flexible, short-term contracts. As average wages have stagnated in the United States, France, Germany and other OECD countries in the past thirty years, it has put pressure on the precariat to live in debt, often unsustainably, or what Standing refers to as a systemic form of rental extraction.[19] This changes the way we understand their economic sufficiency, as the precariat's net income is well below their gross income. Moreover, precarious work requires other forms of labor that are not recognized or compensated—learning new skills, updating job profiles, networking for jobs, etc.—which leads to a feeling of continually being out of control of time.[20] These transformations to this type of labor are compounded by increasingly privatized relationships to traditional forms of state security. As governments continue to pursue competitiveness through policies of labor flexibility, it makes labor more insecure—positioning the precariat as the first class in history to be losing acquired rights—whether cultural, civil, social, economic or political—reducing this group to being supplicants, and confirming the Latin root of precariousness to "obtain by prayer."[21] This is to say that precarious workers are more likely to not have social rights and non-wage benefits—access to decent affordable housing, health care, pension, education, etc.—and the absence of these keeps individuals in precarious work.[22] The psychological effects of living in uncertainty manifest in different ways. Standing argues that the precariat has no occupational identity or narrative to give their lives, creating an existential insecurity, which is witnessed in the unprecedented fact that many people have educational levels that exceed the type of labor they can expect to obtain.[23] The "financialization of daily life" fosters anxiety and insecurity while making it difficult to predict one's fate, build a future, construct a life, and be politically active.[24]

The precariat is currently not a class in the Marxian sense, but they are a class-in-the-making—approaching a consciousness of common characteristics. It is difficult to identify the precariat, as the factors that lead to temporary work and insecure futures are manifold, and the political effects are just as divergent. Standing has focused on identifying and defining this group in order for it to identify itself. According

Precarity and Power

to Standing, the precariat is composed of four sub-groups. The first is the "lumpenproletariat," an often criminal minority with no class-consciousness and thereby not politically active. The second faction consists of migrants and minorities, who are most likely to keep their heads down and focus on survival. They are often denizens and denied rights from everywhere. The third group consists of older workers—the original proletariat—who have lost material and social security due to transformations in labor. This sub-group often perpetuates myths that foreigners are responsible for the decline of their security—fostering nationalistic, xenophobic, and racist agendas. Finally, the fourth subgroup consists of young, educated people who are unable to achieve financial or social security. While being deprived, this group overlooks neo-facists and instead aspires to create a society based on equality, freedom, and ecological sustainability.[25] What these four groups share is the inability to provide for necessity and thereby enter a political realm of freedom and equality.

If we understand democracy as a form of governance that requires shared responsibility, neoliberal policies are pushing more people into precarious conditions, which requires competition for security and status—transforming a collective responsibility to an individual responsibility.[26] This is to say that while democracy comes with the promise of absolute freedom, it also requires responsibility that is shared and divided equally. As espoused by governance and political scientists Sofia Näsström and Sara Kalm: "the production of precarity that is operative in many democratic countries fosters a privatization of responsibility that corrupts the public core of democracy. Instead of encouraging commitment to democracy, the emphasis on individual ambition, competition and distinction runs the risk of producing a 'market for monarchy.'"[27] As more people enter the precariat, it poses a direct threat to democracy as expressed by Chomsky, "Another feature of a capitalist democracy such as the United States is the inequity in distribution of resources, which translates into vast differences in the ability to participate in a meaningful way even in the narrow margin of decisions that remain with the political system."[28] Our ability to act and be political is largely dependent on our security—materially and psychologically— as well as access to resources.

Identifying the precariat as a group with shared characteristics and goals is the first step to acting together as a collective, which would transform the group into a class-for-itself. This is crucial to recognizing what is shared and common across the diverse subjectivities, and creates a basis for common political action. The struggles of the precariat require new forms of social organization that differ from social state models, trade unions, or Fordist structures to respond to new labor practices that are more contingent in nature, yet do not need to compromise the securities required for democratic action. This alternative future needs to be created for and

by the precariat, requiring this class to aggregate power to create a countermovement. In essence, if the precariat can identify as a class, it could also eradicate itself. As more people associate with the characteristics of the precariat, we can recontextualize the protests, marches, and uprisings in the past years as primitive rebels —where an emerging class unifies around what they are against, but not as certain on what they are for. These early stages are important for this group to identify as a class-for-itself and form a countermovement to restructure the redistribution of resources—from reconceiving labor unions and regulating flexible labor to reforming migration policies and introducing universal basic income. The uniting of this group allows its members to recognize that they are bigger than a group of strangers, and together they can create power.

The Production of Power: Living Together
The organization around common action is intimately tied to the production of power. According to Arendt, power is the human ability to act *in concert*. An individual cannot possess, hold, or store power, it is always a potentiality—whenever people gather—and only converted to actual power through acting and speaking *together* and vanishing as soon as people disperse.[29] Arendt's definition of power stands in distinction to strength and force, which are individual in nature and can be possessed or applied.[30] Most importantly, power entails a temporary agreement between acting individuals, requiring plurality to reify. Because this is tied to the condition of plurality, power is both an egalitarian and non-hierarchical relationship between individuals, with the caveat that these individuals must possess freedom. Accordingly, Arendt's concept of power is an extension to her notion of action, as power preserves the space of appearance, and is thereby the lifeblood of the human artifice.[31]

While power can only be produced between individuals acting together, the potential for creating power is always greatest when people are together, as stated by Arendt, "The only indispensable material factor in the generation of power is the living together of people. Only where men live so close together that the potentialities of action are always present can power remain with them, and the foundation of cities, which as city-states have remained paradigmatic for all Western political organization, is therefore indeed the most important material pre-requisite of power."[32] This is to say that the potential of producing power is greatest where we have density. At an architectural scale, this potential is highest when individuals truly live together.

The project of living together has witnessed a resurgence in cities recently, which is not surprising given the increasing precarity of urban dwellers. New typologies of commoning domestic spaces—communes, co-living, cooperatives, among others—have emerged to create affordable domestic spaces that more precisely respond to nomadic lifestyles, alternative family units, the need for meaningful social units, and the yearning for a form of luxury without economic burden.

In the North American context, living together was most actively demonstrated by the commune movement in the 1960s and 1970s, at the height of the free love and anti-establishment era. Rooted in Northern California, the commune was a critical invention for a group of people to define their own particular family unit, way of living, and politics, that often sat outside or adjacent to the dominant system. Moreover, several communes valued notions of shared property, labor, and liberation from consumerism—all of which are sources are inequality. During this time, estimates suggest that over 5,000 communes existed in the United States and housed close to a million residents.[33] The majority of these communal experiments emerged in California with hundreds of communes in the Bay Area alone. While this social legacy still remains, most of the communes have disbanded. There are a series of reasons (and theories) for why they did not persist—from the challenges of living together and increased rental prices, to legal issues surrounding building occupation and the habits of residents. With relatively little trace of the original movement, it could be argued that the tactical growth of communes did not scale-up into a strategic vision. This is inherently challenging—to scale-up a type that emerges from power at the bottom. As Garrett Hardin's influential (but often mis-interpreted) critique suggests, management and accountability of the commons becomes increasingly challenging at a larger scale.[34] Not surprisingly, the majority of California's communes from the countercultural moment to present day, house between ten and thirty residents. As communes scale-up, while the potential for power also increases, local control, governance, and accountability become more difficult. If we understand living together as a critical mechanism in the creation of power, scaling up the commune could be a critical instrument in addressing the growing precarity of the population.

While projects to scale-up the commune were rare, they did occur. In addition to the well-documented *Whole Earth Catalogue* was The Kaliflower Commune, which examined ways to aggregate power across communes. *Kaliflower* started as a weekly inter-communal newsletter in April 1969, reaching over three hundred communes in the Bay Area.[35] Printed in the basement—which soon became known as the Free Print Shop—of the Sutter/Scott Street commune in San Francisco, the newsletter ran until December 1971. The newsletter contained a multitude of information —it was a bulletin board for sharing between communes, a how-to manual for a range of topics revolving around sharing, from editorial opinions to poetry. In addition to the newsletter, the The Kaliflower Commune organized the Free Food Conspiracy where around 150 communes pooled food stamps to acquire large volumes of food that were then distributed based on need. In essence, The Kaliflower Commune recognized the potential power of aggregating communes into a shared network. As one issue of the newsletter put it, "Nuclear family members don't usually buy and sell to each other, are in fact communistic, and we wanted nuclear family intimacy among the communes."[36] By creating a super family that enabled local forms of power to aggregate into larger forms of action, The Kaliflower Commune's initiatives provided a glimpse of how to scale-up the commune while retaining local governance. While the legacy of The Kaliflower Commune is clearly embodied in the altruistic rhetoric of the current sharing economy, there are more recent examples of communes that leverage new tools to aggregate the potential for power.

Within this context, the Embassy Network is a unique contemporary case study in how to maintain the benefits of stewardship in smaller communities while embracing other scales of sharing across a network of communes. This net-work of San Francisco communes began as a retrofit of an eleven-bedroom Edwardian mansion —now called the Embassy commune—that hosts between seventeen and twenty-three residents, some of whom are temporary. The commune leverages technological platforms such as Slack, Loomio, and Cobudget to help mediate relations within a governance structure they call a "do-ocracy." The local Embassy Network includes two other locations in San Francisco, which allows residents to move easily between locations, acknowledging our increasingly nomadic and transient lifestyles. An intentional community, revolving around values of curiosity, questioning, and engagement, the house has commoned most spaces and also reached outwards to the surrounding community—hosting public events, engaging with the adjacent school, as well as working with marginalized groups such as ex-convicts. Locally, the Embassy Network is part of the Haight Street Commons, a group of communes in close proximity in San Francisco. Beyond sharing domestic space, this connection to other communes adds a larger scale of sharing— between communes—of goods, services, and resources that are more seldom required. At a still larger scale, the commune has leveraged the entrepreneurial spirit of the Bay Area to form an international Embassy Network—a digital platform to expand their spatial and social footprint of commons globally. With additional locations in Berlin, The Netherlands, Greece, Costa Rica, and Haiti, this network enables residents to move between locations and countries for different periods of time. Unlike most membership-based living models that leverage digital networks, the Embassy Network is created and controlled by the residents themselves (not a corporation), providing a promising template of how to strategically scale-up the commons, while retaining local control. Power in this case can be aggregated between individuals and distributed amongst a network.

The California communes—particularly in urban contexts—have largely reappropriated the hardware of a city built for different values. Ironically in San Francisco, several communes are housed within structures once built for bourgeois nuclear families. Given the limited trace of the original 1970s movement, one wonders how sustainable the reappropriation of the existing urban fabric is to the long-term development and evolution of this movement. Let us not forget the primary elements that comprised Arendt's space of appearance include action, speech, power, as well as permanence. Permanence was put forth by Arendt to ensure the public realm remains in existence and that we are connected to a longer lineage of collectivity—that which we inherited and will pass down. If the commune is to grow and develop as a project for the city, it must go beyond being a reappropriation "software" and actually reformat the hardware of the city.

Without purpose-built architectural projects to reflect new values, governance structures, family types, and ways of sharing, the experiments of living together can vanish as quickly as they emerged. Using design as a vehicle to evolve ideas of living together, a series of new architectural experiments on how to live together can reify new governance structures into form. From the German experiments in *baugruppen* ("building groups") to the Asian Share-House, international models of concretizing relationships of collective living are promising.[37] Most importantly, these architectures can be a strategic weapon in reifying power and forming a new lineage of collective living experiments. The commune challenges the strict divisions between the public and private realm, reconceiving the domestic world as less private, more equal, and shared. Instead of the separation of private realm of necessity and the public realm of politics, living together addresses both economic need and political action. Within the commune, power can be produced from the intimate world, yet scaled up in a network fashion. Most importantly, the commune reminds us that within the space of appearance, even the most precarious can act and possess power.

Notes

1   Hannah Arendt, *The Human Condition*. (Chicago: University of Chicago Press, 1958), 177.
2   Ibid., 7.
3   Ibid., 190.
4   Ibid., 31.
5   Ibid., 38.
6   Ibid., 39.
7   Ibid., 40.
8   Ibid., 46.
9   Ibid., 49.
10 Arendt would refer to this as "work" as opposed to "labor" which ensures the reproduction of life.
11 Brett Neilson and Ned Rossiter, FCJ-022 From Precarity to Precariousness and Back Again: Labour, Life and Unstable Networks, The Fibreculture Journal : 05, (2005), 1.
12 "The Precariat: The New Dangerous Class," posted on October 27, 2014, https://workingclassstudies.wordpress.com/2014/10/27/the-precariat-the-new-dangerous-class/.
13 Guy Standing, "Meet the precariat, the new global class fueling the rise of populism," published November 9, 2016, https://www.weforum.org/agenda/2016/11/precariat-global-class-rise-of-populism/.
14 Guy Standing, "The Precariat: The new dangerous Class," (New York: Bloomsbury, 2011), 1.
15 Study on Precarious work and social rights, Carried out for the European Commission (VT/2010/084) Working Lives Research Institute Faculty of Social Sciences and Humanities London Metropolitan University.

16 Standing, "Meet the precariat."
17 Sonia McKay, Steve Jefferys, Anna Paraksevopoulou, Janoj Keles, "Study on Precarious work and social rights," Working Lives Research Institute & London Metropolitan University Carried out for the European Commission (London, 2012), 7-8.
18 "Youthful members of the full-time Precariat," *Vox Europ*, published Sept 15, 2011, http://www.voxeurop.eu/en/content/article/953511-youthful-members-full-time-precariat.
19 Ibid.
20 Ibid.
21 Ibid.
22 McKay, et al., "Study on Precarious work and social rights."
23 Standing, "Meet the precariat."
24 Randy Martin, 2002. See: Brett Neilson and Ned Rossiter, FCJ-022 "From Precarity to Precariousness and Back Again: Labour, Life and Unstable Networks," The Fibreculture Journal: 05, (2005, 1).
25 Guy Standing, "The Precariat: The New Dangerous Class," Working Class Perspectives (October 27, 2014) https://workingclassstudies.wordpress.com/2014/10/27/the-precariat-the-new-dangerous-class/
26 Näsström and Kalm, "A democratic critique of precarity," *Global Discourse*, 2014, 1-18. 10.1080/23269995.2014.992119.
27 Ibid., 568.
28 Noam Chomsky, *On Power and Ideology* (Chicago: Haymarket Books, 2015), 152.
29 Arendt, *The Human Condition*, 199.

30 It is important to understand Arendt's definition of power in distinction to strength, force, and violence, which are often casually interchanged in contemporary discourse. For Arendt, strength is a property inherent in an object or person, and is individual in nature, whereas force refers to the energy released by physical or social movements. Finally, violence is an instrumental character that is related to strength—it is the multiplication of natural strength and in this sense is distinct from power, as posited "Power and violence are opposites; where the one rules absolutely, the other is absent. Violence appears where power is in jeopardy, but left to its own course it ends in power's disappearance… Violence can destroy power; it is utterly incapable of creating it" (Arendt, "Communicative Power," 71)
31 Arendt, *The Human Condition*, 204.
32 Ibid., 201.
33 Matthew Roth, "Communalism in San Francisco," *FoundSF*, accessed October 30, 2017, http://www.foundsf.org/index.php?title=Communalism_in_San_Francisco.
34 Garrett Hardin, "The Tragedy of the Commons," *Science*, Issue 162, December 13, 1968, 1243-48.
35 Roth, "Communalism in San Francisco."
36 Chris Carlsson, and Lisa Ruth Elliott, *Ten Years That Shook the City: San Francisco 1968–1978*, (San Francisco: City Lights Books, 2001), X.
37 In addition, see for instance Dogma's article in this volume.

HOUSING RESISTANT FORMS-OF-LIFE: HOUSING PROJECTS AND SOCIAL MOVEMENTS IN TEHRAN, 1941–53

Hamed Khosravi

In the landscape of the Central Asia, or particularly, the larger Iranian Plateau, the original form of life is nomadism. The nomadic way of life is characterized by movement, which is in vital balance with the ever-changing environment. This harmony can be achieved through the extensive control and management of natural forces. To maintain their mobile way of life, nomads cannot only rely on the temporarily found resources of water, food, and energy; they make use of environmental forces to produce necessary resources. Such performance requires a high level of changeability and resilience, which exists in contrast to rigid and static boundaries. Indeed this interaction is not for absolute dominance over external forces, but rather is a dialectical state that drives and supports nomadic life. This form of life exists in a permanent state of conflict. For nomads, the ideal form of living is only possible by having a communal life. Aristotle defines "communal life" as the response to the political nature of humans (as they desire to live together).[1] The political significance of communal life reveals itself when it is in antagonism with stabilizing forces of the state. Settlement of those nomadic lives, presupposes a land-appropriation and a land-division that is determined by a broader stable order, applied by the state. Historically this order was conducted through both spatial and juridical apparatuses: making frames that bounded life to a territory in order to regularize it. It has undergone many changes in its more than three thousand year history, while in this transition, some of those tamed lives have tended to reclaim their original way of living even in the spatial configuration of the permanent living space.

A historic architectural model that successfully facilitated communal life can be found in the medina.[2] Medina describes a habitat within a frame, a city that is structured and defined by edges. This frame performs three successive functions. Initially, it establishes a certain group of people by will power, then it excludes and therefore defines the group in opposition to the others, and ultimately by holding those lives, it establishes a relation between the people, the territory, and the (legislative) power. In this way, medina not only accommodates the "community of faithful," but by separating believers from non-believers it forms the political community. This model informs well-known typologies such as mosques, caravanserais, schools as well as traditional Iranian housing units, serai,[3] that remains as a very dominant typology from the Bronze Age onwards. In its historical development as a dwelling space, serai offers a delimited form whose walls are inhabitable; the chambers are set in a rectangular shape around a void. This dwelling model became one of the most successful and easily achievable architectural means to celebrate the nomadic form of life; it mediates between open and closed, inside and outside, and more abstractly, between action and re-action, or forces and resistance.

Islamic Revolution, February 1979. People occupied an unfinished building, waiting for Ayatollah Khomeini.
PHOTO: ALAIN DEJEAN; IMAGE: SYGMA/CORBIS

This form of spatial organization, an inhabitable wall enclosing a void, was historically conceived as a "terrestrial paradise."[4] As an analogon of the state, the enclosure is a micro-cosmos recapitulating the collective organization of the political body. Thus, the Iranian house embodies many meanings: it is a theological entity outside history and the mythical foundation of the Islamic state; at the same time, it is the engine of production and the theatre of everyday resistance.[5] The socio-political significance of the Iranian house (*serai*) became evident in the twentieth century, when political projects explicitly targeted domestic spaces. These attempts abandoned the traditional housing archetype, established new housing models, and ultimately manipulated the interior space of the house to avoid political tension and stabilize the dwellers' lives. And, with this, the house once again became the epicenter of social movements and the core of the resistance.

In Tehran, during the post-second World War period, the urgent need for massive reconstruction not only resulted in developing new construction techniques, but also paved the way for direct and fast implementation of both foreign and domestic political projects. Many of these attempted to instrumentalize modern technology and planning concepts on behalf of particular ideologies to tame the socio-political tensions. This period could be characterized by secularization. At the center of the secularization project was the issue of domestic space. It happened not only through large-scale planning apparatuses, but was also initiated in the careful engineering of the form of living in domestic spaces. The intent was to administer and govern the Iranian society at large.

The Anglo-Soviet invasion of Iran, which occurred on August 25, 1941, inaugurated an interregnum that lasted twelve years. It ended Reza Shah's undisputed control of the army, bureaucracy, and court patronage. It initiated a period in which the new monarch maintained control of the armed forces, but lost control over the bureaucracy and the patronage system. This interregnum lasted until August 1953 when Mohammad Reza Shah, through a coup engineered by the Americans and the British, re-established royal authority, and, thereby, recreated his father's regime to act as an executive monarch for the next twenty-five years. In these years power was not concentrated as before. On the contrary, it was hotly contested between the royal palace, the cabinet, the parliament, and most importantly the urban masses—organized first by a socialist movement and then by a nationalist one.[6] The mass, which was mainly constituted of the urban middle-class and working class, formed a major threat to the Pahlavi dynasty.

The first real challenge to the notables came from the socialist movements. Within a month of Reza Shah's abdication, a group of recent graduates from European universities and former political prisoners announced the formation of the Iran Communist Party on September 29, 1941.

The party was called Tudeh, or the party of the masses. By early 1945, the party had managed to create the first mass organization in Iran's history. It became the party of the masses in more than name; in its first manifesto published in September 1944, in the Tudeh party's newspaper *Rahbar*, they claimed, "our primary aim is to mobilize the workers, peasants, progressive intellectuals, traders, and craftsmen of Iran."[7] Besides their political activities in the form of demonstrations and gatherings, they aimed to train and educate the public, specifically the working and middle-class. Henceforth, the discourse of domesticity was at the center of their political thesis to activate urban society, and addressing women in particular as a forgotten half of the active political mass. Within a few years, the organization was published in various newspapers, pamphlets, and books through which it not only attracted workers and peasants but also drew support from urban wage earners and the salaried middle class—especially the intelligentsia. Among the members were famous writers, artists, politicians, and architects. They were not only active members of the Tudeh party but also they increased by establishing unions, organizing professional associations, and artists' groups in line with the party ideology. Among them was the Society of Iranian Architects, which remained vital to the Iranian architectural movements during the second half of the twentieth century.[8] These architects and the political activists were the initiators and designers of many housing projects between 1948–1953. Their projects introduced new forms of domestic environments and were influential in perpetuating social and political movements.

One of the main issues of resistance was domestic life. In 1948, three members of the Society of Iranian Architects, Ali Sadegh, Manouchehr Khorsand, and Abbas Ajdari, designed the first large-scaled housing project in Tehran, known as *chaharsad dastgah* (400-Unit Housing).[9] In contrast to the traditional Iranian courtyard house typology, they proposed a new dwelling type that allocated rooms to specific functions, such as bedrooms, dining room, and living room. The proposal limited the traditional way of living in the house into specific uses. Instead, through its spatial configuration, it aimed at encouraging the inhabitant to go out of the house and occupy the city for their socio-political activities. The feature that the architects incorporated in the proposal was a central open space intended to be the locus of public activities. Although the *chaharsad dastgah* seemingly followed the international post-war housing typologies, by placing it within the socio-political context of Iran, it aimed at domestic reform to generate mass mobilization.

The project was designed based on three housing typologies. The first was a single-story house with three major rooms: a bedroom, living room, and dining room, along with a kitchen, storage, and a courtyard. The second was a two-story dwelling made up of five rooms: two on the basement floor, which was one meter lower than ground level and therefore received light from the courtyard, and a first-floor level with two bedrooms, a kitchen, storage, and a courtyard. The third typology was designed for the one- to five-room apartments that connected to the courtyard and contained a street-facing shop. Contrary to the traditional Iranian housing typology, the separation of functions and divided spaces of the new apartment plans imposed a new lifestyle. For example, kitchens remained separate from living rooms and often combined with storage spaces or bathrooms. In fact the Iranian woman's role as a housewife, which had been central to the spatial dynamism of a home, became marginalized in these new typologies. Previously, all rooms were multifunctional, and living spaces could easily be adapted for different activities of the household. The logic of the proposed apartments dictated not only very specific activities, but also a controlled family size and lifestyle. The city and houses, which since the mid-1940s had mushroomed in the urban periphery, had been depoliticized through rational planning. While the previous attempts at public housing had failed for either financial or political reasons, with the support of the Ghavam's government, who at the time had the support of leftist parties, especially the Tudeh party, *chaharsad dastgah* was completed between 1944–46. It became a prototypical model in design, planning, and materialization of future projects.

Following on the experience of *chaharsad dastgah* project, the Mosaddegh government (1951–52), who at the time had full support of Nationalist, Leftist, and Islamist groups,

launched the largest housing projects in the city. In 1951, the Law of Land Registration came into effect and large plots of land around Tehran became the possession of government as public property. At the same time, members of the Society of Iranian Architects, with the support of the government, founded the Construction Bank (*Bank-e-Sakhtemani*) that was responsible for providing affordable housing units. As a first step, the bank allocated 17,000 small plots of land for the purpose of accommodating the middle-class and working class. Accordingly, two of the largest housing projects of Tehran started in the neighborhoods of Kuy-e Narmak and Kuy-e Nazi Abad.

The lands of the Kuy-e Nazi Abad project were bought by the Construction Bank in 1951. The project is situated in the south-west, between the railway station and the military Qalemorghi Airport, and covers an area of nearly three hundred hectares. In the first phase, 2,800 building plots of two hundred to six hundred square meters were allocated for building low-income housing. These plots, due to the financial situation of their owners, were later subdivided into much smaller plots of eighty square meters. As a result, the housing units in this area are primarily two-room flats including a small store together with limited services.[10] However, in the beginning, the government provided housing for the working class, who were concentrated around the railway station and factories in the south of the city. In the late 1960s, the second phase of the project started to accommodate the middle-class groups, mainly teachers and railway company employees. Eight apartment blocks, each containing between twenty-four to thirty-two dwelling units, were constructed. The plan of the units were strictly divided and minimized into the functional cells. A uniform eighty square meter layout was used for all the apartments: each unit had three by four-and-a-half meter rooms, which were two bedrooms and one living room, with a balcony attached. The kitchen was an enclosed unit placed between the living room and the bathroom. Contrary to the traditional housing typologies, the Nazi Abad project applied a very rigid and rationalized framework for life, limiting the domestic space to the essential biological needs. By eliminating the courtyard, this project forced inhabitants to go out in the city in order to exercise communal life.

In 1951, parallel to the Kuy-e Nazi Abad, the Mosaddegh government bought a six hundred hectare plot of land. On this large site, 8,000 plots sized between two hundred and five hundred square meters each eventually supported one-story villas with small gardens. This residential district was divided into one hundred sections, each with open spaces and equipped with power supply and well water. About a third of this area, or two hundred hectares, was allocated for administrative buildings, services, as well as roads connecting the area. After two years of plot divisions and land allocation the construction started

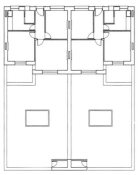

Single-Story Apartment

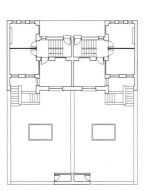

Two-Story Apartment, Ground Floor

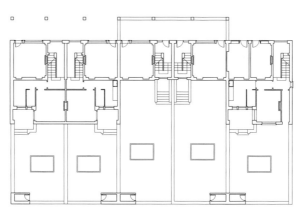

Two-Story Apartment with Shops on Ground Floor

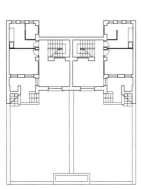

Two-Story Apartment, First Floor

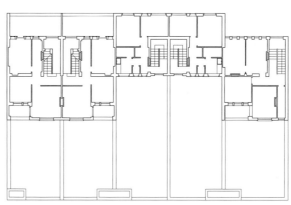

Two-Story Apartment, First Floor

0 1 2   5   10 m

0 1 2   5 m

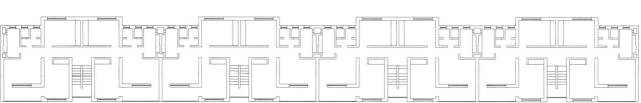

Kuy-e Nazi-Abad Four-Story Apartment Typology

in 1953. To accelerate the process of construction, the Construction Bank commissioned a French company to produce prefabricated concrete modules. Based on standard concrete panels (1.10 meter wide), various typologies were designed. Members of the Society of Iranian Architects, headed by Nasser Badie and Iraj Moshiri, led the design and planning of the housing complex. Following the master plan and the allotment of the area, they provided initial designs of three-, four-, and five-room typologies. The clients were free to choose between the given typologies or buy the plot and build their own house according to the schedule imposed by the bank. In the later, they had to follow the general construction regulations provided by the planners. The bank constructed four hundred apartments in the northern part of the area as model houses, which was named after the French company, Kuy-e Calad. In 1961, the population of this residential district was almost 70,000, while in 1966 it exceeded 90,000.[11]

Despite the ever-growing housing needs of Tehran, housing projects seemed to also carry a political agenda. They were designed to instigate the public to fulfill their political duties. The seeds of a revolution were planted in those domestic spaces. One of the main goals of these housing projects was to reform the traditional role of the housewife. By separating the functions and reducing the flexibility of the space, women were encouraged to go outside the house and work alongside men. Paradoxically, this approach not only criticized the traditional role of Iranian women in Islamic society but also targeted the new Western role model, which was promoted by the state. The architecture of domestic space was not, in fact, the only instrument for this project, it was widely expressed through the leftist media.

In the October 1944 article "Home and Its Limits in the Modern Age," published in *Bidari-e Ma*—the feminist bi-monthly publication of the Association of Women—contributor Farah Laqa Alavi emphasized that most of women's traditional responsibilities should now be assumed by the society at large rather than confined to the home. In step with early Soviet ideology, the main concern of *Bidari-e Ma* was to get women out of the house.[12] Ironically, these publications also accused the Pahlavi regime for its Western Modernization Project, which tried to free Iranian women from domestic traditions.[13] In another article in *Rahbar,* the writer claimed that the pro-Western political project of Reza Shah was to follow the German slogan of "Kinder, Küche, Kirche, und Kleid" (children, kitchen, church, and clothing),[14] and put the Iranian women back in the role model of the "good housewife."[15] As the movement got closer to the USSR, the promoted image of the woman increasingly resembled a Communist ideal. In an interview published in *Bidari-e Ma*, Said Nafisi, the Iranian Marxist writer, portrayed Soviet women as open-minded and active in the public sphere. The magazine also reported that despite their simple look and modest outfits, Soviet women possessed a unique beauty that surpassed women of other nations.[16] These visible Marxist-leanings, within the context of the global Cold War, was an alarm for the Shah and his American allies, which consequently instigated an American project.[17]

The same spatial devices of neutralization and control activated the political subjects (citizens) and triggered a series of counter-projects. Through these projects the concept of citizenship was reinforced and emerged to drive mass movements during the 1950s. For the first time in Iranian history, people went out of their houses and mass street demonstrations eventually became a common form of protest. On November 3, 1951, the speaker of the royalist fraction of the parliament criticized Mosaddegh's policies and described this new condition as:

Statecraft has degenerated into street politics. It appears that this country has nothing better to do than hold street meetings. We now have meetings here, there, and everywhere—meetings for this, that, and every occasion; meetings for university students, high school students, seven-year-olds, and even six-year olds. I am sick and tired of these street meetings … Is our prime minister a statesman or a mob leader? What type of prime minister says, "I will speak to the people" every time he is faced with a political problem? I always considered this man to be unsuitable for high office. But I never imagined, even in my worst nightmares, that an old man of seventy would turn into a rabble-rouser. A man who surrounds the *Majles* (parliament) with mobs is nothing less than a public menace.[18]

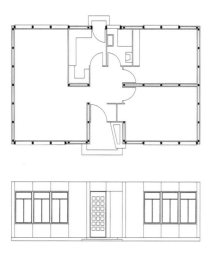

Four-Rooms Type A (Calad System)
Area: 84.9 sqm

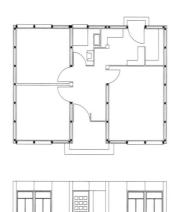

Three-Rooms Type A (Calad System)
Area: 65.8 sqm

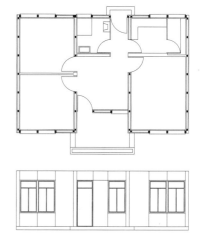

Four-Rooms Type B (Calad System)
Area: 75.6 sqm

0 1 2   5m

Kuy-e Narmak, construction of the pre-fabricated houses, or Calad system.
IMAGE: MOHSEN MA'AREFI, "ONE-YEAR OLD CITY," REVUE DE LA BANQUE DU CONSTRUCTION 7-8 (1958), 55.

Kuy-e Narmak, four- and five-rooms housing typologies, or Calad system.
SOURCE: RECONSTRUCTED BY THE AUTHOR BASED ON THE PLANS AND DESCRIPTIONS PUBLISHED IN "CONSTRUCTION OF THE FIRST 5-ROOMS APARTMENTS (CALAD SYSTEM) IN KUY-E NARMAK," *REVUE DE LA BANQUE DU CONSTRUCTION*, DÉCEMBRE 6 (1957), 10-20.

This social mobilization that started in the early 1950s went beyond the political agenda of the Left and attracted large number of people of any ideology. In one of the largest demonstrations, on July 21, 1952 in support of Mosaddegh's anti-Shah sentiment, thousands of people promptly poured into the streets, and after three days of general strikes and bloodshed, forced the Shah to back down. The crisis became known as *Si-e Tir* (July 21). In memory of those days Mosaddegh named Kuy-e Narmak as Kuy-e Si-e Tir. These riots and demonstrations became widespread movements throughout the country during the 1960s and 70s while the Islamists had the leading role in those years. It ultimately resulted in the Islamic Revolution of 1978-79. Although there is no immediate and direct effect of the spatial configuration on social behavior, specific spatial conditions of those architectural projects helped the middle-class and working-class reclaim their social cohesion. In fact, there seems to be a link between the form of life in domestic spaces and the political engagement of those people in the city.

Contrary to the historical forms of ruling states in Iran as theological powers, since the mid-nineteenth century, the state has tended toward secularization in order to tame the socio-political tensions. Carl Schmitt exemplifies this difference between the two forms of power as the one of statesman and shepherd. He writes, in the nomadic society, "the shepherd (nomeus) was the typical symbol of rule," which stands opposite to the statesman.[19] He rules over the flock with the nourishment by which he regulates their lives. While, the statesman does not stand as far above the people he governs; "he only tends to, provides for, looks after, takes care of."[20] In this way, the shepherd mirrors the image of God and the divine rule.[21] While shepherd performs through the mechanism of command and obedience, the statesman rules in a dialectical manner. This clash of forces, however, has not always been destructive; in particular periods, the conflicts have enabled and activated life in evolutionary processes. The nomadic way of life has been overcome by instrumentalization of the idea of the house as legal and spatial framework through which the state manages and controls lives of the subjects. The conflict between the stabilizing forces of the state and the form of life that escapes it, is held within the four walls of the domestic space. While these walls establish an elementary distinction between inside and outside, and between rules, rituals, and orders, the nomadic way of life maintains its dialectical opposition to static forces. It is characterized by constant movement and change, and is unfettered by systems of spatio-temporal organization. Through the spaces of the house, living becomes an act and tends to exceed the boundary of the house and overcome the city.

The ever-present possibility of conflict becomes the permanent state in which life was held. In this way, the architecture of domesticity holds life

Kuy-e Narmak,
aerial view.
IMAGE: MARTIN SEGER,
TEHERAN (WIEN AND NEW YORK:
SPRINGER, 1978), 229.

within a dialectical conflict, and deliberately gives rise to confrontation and struggle. This spatial configuration retains the possibility for the form-of-life to emerge within this dialectical process. Once this architecture, as a frame, houses the subjects, it holds conflict; a moment in which action and reaction, movement and resistance emerges. It is precisely through this relationship that the idea of citizenship is conveyed. The house becomes a frame for casting life in an on-going process of resistance.

Hamed Khosravi is an architect, researcher, and educator. His works mainly reflects on the relationship between political and formal aspects of the architecture of the city.

Notes

1 Giorgio Agamben, *The Highest Poverty: Monastic Rules and Form-of-Life* (Stanford, CA: Stanford University Press, 2013), 11.

2 Etymologically, the term "medina" derives from the Akkadian root *dinu* (or *denu*), which stands for "law," "right," and "judgment" and appears as *din* in Aramaic. In its exclusive occurrence, *din* is politically loaded and borrowed primarily in Hebrew and Arabic as the root of two fundamental words: *din* as "judgment" or "law," and *medina* as "city." There is, however, another translation of *din*, which provides further meaning: in Persian, *din* means "religion." These three readings—legal, political and religious—construct the deep meaning of "medina," a term which affirms the formation of a city or a settlement defined and controlled by theological power through construction of limits and borders.

3 *Serai* stands for spatial configuration of living space. Etymologically the word is from the Indo-European root *tra* as boundary or limit, which appears in Avestan as *thraya* (to protect), and Persian *serai* as a *bounded space* or a *house*. In its historical development *serai* offers an architectural layout; a delimited space by inhabitable chambers. It becomes suffix in shaping words like caravanserai, which eventually addresses a temporary communal housing.

4 Terrestrial Paradise here refers to the common concept of an earthly garden. This idea is shared in most of the religions and has been historically an instrumental spatial model for cities, and building typologies. See: Hamed Khosravi, "The City as Paradise, Spatialisation of Sovereignty in Early Iranian Cities," in Valentina Bandieramonte, et al (eds.), *The Next Urban Question* (Rome: Officina Edizioni, 2013), 270-285.

5 Janet Afary and Kevin B. Anderson, *Foucault and the Iranian Revolution: Gender and the Seductions of Islamism* (Chicago and London: University of Chicago Press, 2005).

6 Ervand Abrahamian, *A History of Modern Iran* (Cambridge: Cambridge University Press, 2008), 99-100.

7 Ibid., 108.

8 The Society of Iranian Architects was also a politically active organization that along with the leftist movement during 1940s and 1950s. It had a central role in mobilizing the intelligentsia. Among the early members of the Society of Iranian Architects were Noureddin Kia-Nouri, which at the time was the active member of the central committee of the Tudeh Party and later became the secretary general of the party, Mohammad Mosaddegh who was the leader of the National Front of Iran and later became the Prime Minister, Fereydoun Keshavarz, active member of the Tudeh Party fraction in the Parliament and later became the Minister of Culture, other who at the time were either members of the communist party or sympathizers. See the full list of members in "News," *Architece* 1 (1946): 39.

9 The head architect of the project was Ali Sadegh, who studied first at the Ghent University and then at the Académie Royale des Beaux-Arts (1932–36) in Brussels. There he was influenced by the modern movement and particularly the discourse of minimum housing. After returning to Iran in 1937, he incorporated those experiences, such as the protocol of CIAM 1929 in his practice of architecture. While Sadegh's architectural style was, perhaps, less distinctive than some of his contemporaries, he made significant contributions to the architectural environment of his time; perhaps his most influential contribution was the promotion of mass housing projects in Tehran as vice-president of the board of Mortgage Bank. Together with Iraj Moshiri, Naser Badie, and others, he established the Society of Iranian Architects in the mid-1940s, where he served as vice-president and then president.

10 Hushang Bahrambeygui, *Tehran: An Urban Analysis* (Tehran: Sahab Books Institute, 1977), 120.

11 Ibid., 119.

12 Pamela Karimi, "Dwelling, Dispute, and the Space of Modern Iran," in Aggregate (eds.) *Governing by Design: Architecture, Economy, and Politics in the Twentieth Century* (Pittsburgh: University of Pittsburgh Press, 2012), 121.

13 For example between 1936–41 Reza Shah ran a movement called "Women Awakening." This movement sought the elimination of the Islamic veil from Iranian working society. Supporters held that the veil impeded physical exercise and the ability of women to enter society and contribute to the progress of the nation. This move met opposition from the religious establishment.

14 The phrase originally appeared in writings in the early 1890s when Wilhelm II denoted the role of women: "Let women devote themselves to the three K's, *die Küche, die Kirche, die Kinder* (kitchen, church, and children)." The phrase then was used multiple times throughout the 1890s in liberal writing and speeches. In August 1899 the influential British liberal, Westminster Gazette elaborated on the story, mentioning, as well, the fourth 'K' as *kleid* (clothing). This slogan later repeated by Hitler with less emphasis on *Kirche*.

15 "Central Committee—The Association of Women, Women Movement in Iran." *Rahbar*, no. 829 (October 2, 1946), 8.

16 Pamela Karimi, 123.

17 Point four program.

18 Jamal Emami, *Parliamentary Debates*, 16th Majles, November 3, 1951.

19 Here Schmitt refers to the Plato's Statesman 'In Statesman, Plato distinguishes the shepherd from the statesman: the *nemein* of the shepherd is concerned with the nourishment (*trophe*) of his flock, and the shepherd is a kind of god in relation to the animals he herds. Carl Schmitt, *The Nomos of the Earth* (New York: Telos Press Publishing, 2006), 340.

20 Ibid., 340.

21 "The true shepherd could only be a divine shepherd." Cornelius Castoriadis, *On Plato's Statesman* (Stanford, CA: Stanford University Press, 2002), 101.

CULTIVATE COLLECTIVE: HOUSING FOR A CONTEMPORARY SUBJECT IN CHINA

De Peter Yi

In 2010, news outlets in China, and soon around the world, began reporting on a population of young college graduates who had formed a critical mass living on the outskirts of Beijing. Stories of these graduates focused on their living arrangements, which revealed both the social marginalization and economic hardships they faced, as well as the unique collectives they had organized to continue pursuing opportunities within the city. Accompanying photos portrayed the graduates in nondescript rooms, surrounded by belongings that hinted at their individual interests and ambitions. The news outlets sensationalized the stories by terming these graduates the "ant tribe," coined by Beijing University social scientist Lian Si.[1] While dehumanizing as a metaphor, the term accurately described the lowly status of the individual members that made up this population, as well as how they had banded together to survive. In the process, these graduates had generated a way of life in which they pursued individual goals through collective action—qualities indicative of an emerging contemporary subject with the potential to define China's next generation. Set within the domestic sphere, this form of action evokes a lineage of architecture that developed new forms of housing befitting of emerging subjects. A renewed project of cultivating a subject through collective housing, drawing both from historical precedents and the sociology of the graduates, positions architecture to bridge the social and physical changes facing China today.

Modern and Pre-Modern Subjects in Chinese Collective Housing

All architecture is a political act—simply by the way a building organizes and distributes human activity and relationships. Housing is arguably the most overtly political building type, due to its simultaneous influence on both an individual subject and the collective body. Canonical collective housing models constructed during different periods of Chinese history point to a tradition of balancing the individual and collective, unit and whole. These models have also served a range of subjects, both self-defined and imposed by top-down societal forces. Wildly different in historical contexts but similar in ambition, these models serve as important precedents for how contemporary housing can generate reciprocal relationships between the subject and the deployment of form.

Top:
The largest remaining tulou, Chenqilou, contains several additional rings of units and communal spaces in its courtyard.
PHOTO: DE PETER YI

Middle left:
In the lilong, the kitchen of one row of units face the entrance courtyards of another row of units, activating the lane with a mixture of domestic activity.
PHOTO: DE PETER YI

Middle Right:
The carved stone entryways to individual lilong units add distinctive character to different neighborhoods.
PHOTO: DE PETER YI

Bottom left:
A subway under construction obstructs the view of Anhualou, the last remaining model urban commune in Beijing.
PHOTO: DE PETER YI

Bottom Right:
While the lobbies in Anhualou have lost their original luster, their generous proportions hint at the attention given to communal space.
PHOTO: DE PETER YI

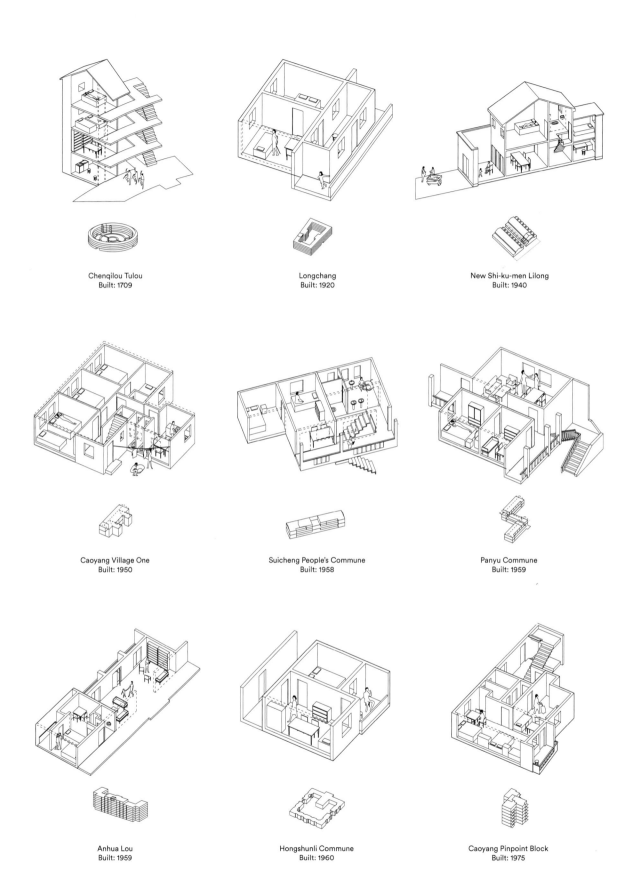

Chenqilou Tulou
Built: 1709

Longchang
Built: 1920

New Shi-ku-men Lilong
Built: 1940

Caoyang Village One
Built: 1950

Suicheng People's Commune
Built: 1958

Panyu Commune
Built: 1959

Anhua Lou
Built: 1959

Hongshunli Commune
Built: 1960

Caoyang Pinpoint Block
Built: 1975

During most of pre-modern China, the immense scale of the country was controlled through a hierarchical system of imperial rule, leading to an adherence to the family clan unit at the lowest level of hierarchy. The *tulou* arose as a vernacular housing typology to collectivize groups of family clans. These earthen buildings were constructed in southeast China beginning in the 14th century, with thousands still surviving. They can be seen as precursors to the modern housing block: the largest *tulou* still in existence has over four hundred rooms and has housed fifteen generations.[2] The buildings are easily identified by their distinctive platonic shapes and single enclosed courtyards. In the wide-open hills of southeast China, the *tulou* form and its endless variation of clustering, created an inward organization of communal clan life and projected distinctive outward identities for its subjects.

Modern history in China can be broadly split into two time periods— before and after the 1949 founding of the People's Republic of China. Each period saw its own efforts by rulers to modernize society following centuries of imperial rule. As Shanghai was one of the first cities that opened up to the West in the mid-19th century, it was also the birthplace of the modern urban subject in China. *Lilong* settlements, which literally means "neighborhood lanes," were developed as a model of organization for housing the new worker populations arising in the city. The *shikumen lilong* merged the Chinese courtyard house with the Western rowhouse, redirecting the domestic activity, which traditionally revolved around the courtyard, out into narrow pedestrian streets. The lilong form filtered and contained an intimate microcosm of urban life within a single city block, and allowed the emerging modern subject a way to build distinctive neighborhoods in a tabula rasa condition.

The very nature of the Chinese modern subject changed in 1949, when its total collectivization became the primary political agenda of the Communist party. It is impossible to talk about this transformation without understanding its direct precedent—the period of societal restructuring in Russia, following the Bolshevik Revolution of 1917.[3] During that time, the Russian avant-garde pioneered an architectural project of using housing to empower a new subject, often working hand-in-hand with government organizations to establish the cultural materializations of untested socialist principles. It was in such an environment of productive dialogue between politics and the arts that the architect Moisei Ginzburg formed the Union of Contemporary Architects (OSA) to test and implement new housing block designs.[4] These buildings were termed the *dom kommuna* (communal houses), the most well-known of which is Narkomfin, which still stands in Moscow today.[5] With Narkomfin, Ginzburg parsed out the pieces of the nuclear familial notion of domesticity, reinvented each component for the socialist worker subject, and reassembled them in a cohesive form that clearly celebrated collectivity as the new social order.

The efforts of the OSA group fell into disfavor alongside the increasing influence of Joseph Stalin, who deemed their ideas too radical and instead favored the propaganda-laden architecture of socialist realism.[6]

However, the true significance of the OSA resided in the capacity they bestowed on architecture for the reorganization of society. OSA's ideologies influenced China's own post-revolution period of cultural redefinition starting in the 1950s, which had been delayed by decades of war. A brief and euphoric period of utopian planning that mirrored the earlier Russian avant-garde period peaked in 1960, and was subsequently cut short when poorly planned and implemented economic policies decreed by party Chairman Mao Zedong plunged China into decades of poverty and cultural regression.[7] It was enough time, however, for Chinese architects to produce a wealth of designs that imagined new living solutions at the unit, building, and urban scale. The most ambitious and optimistic undertaking occurred in 1960 with the construction of three model urban communes in Beijing. The only one surviving today is Anhualou, an imposing nine-story structure located near the center of the city.[8] For the residents of Anhualou, life was almost completely collectivized as the architects shifted the organizational focus of the building away from the unit to the canteen, which occupied the entire ground floor and was large enough to serve all residents. Furthermore, the building opened up the domestic realm to a range of programs, including a general store, washrooms, kindergarten, gym, shared kitchens, and communal living rooms, in order to collapse social barriers between life, work, and recreation.[9] Embedded within the mass of units, all of these functions were contained in a symmetric, monumental form that towered over its surroundings—proudly proclaiming the bold new way of life harbored behind its façades.

Despite their inception at different points in China's history, all three housing models—the *tulou*, *lilong*, and urban commune—created new subject-form relationships to demonstrate how architecture can identify, define, and empower emerging subjects. China's present combination of rapid modernization, coupled with the social strains such efforts have produced, has once again created the backdrop for the emergence of a contemporary subject. While each of the aforementioned housing types still exist today, the subjects they serve are based on outdated definitions and have long been replaced by more relevant, more urgent needs. What are the characteristics of the ant tribe that define them as a contemporary subject? What is the ideal subject-form relationship for this constituency to enable their empowerment?

The Contemporary Subject

The graduates that comprise the ant tribe have a series of characteristics that indicate the emergence of a contemporary subject. Firstly, they are communal. With few resources, they have learned how to share and live together. Secondly, they are hopeful. Driven by the optimism of being the first generation in their family to receive college degrees, this group has typically migrated from poorer inland areas to China's prosperous coastal cities.[10] Finally, their mobility arises out of the clash between China's traditional societal structures and its rapid move towards more open forms of economic development. China's current laws make it difficult

The facade of the proposed housing block acts as a canvas for the creation of symbolic associations that lead to identity generation.

takes action

Cultivate Collective 183

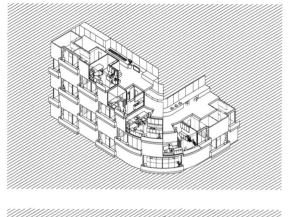
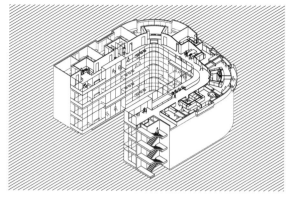

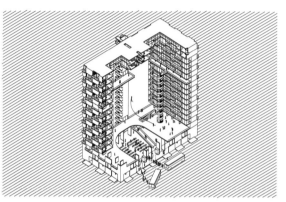
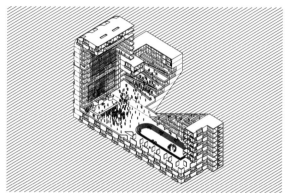

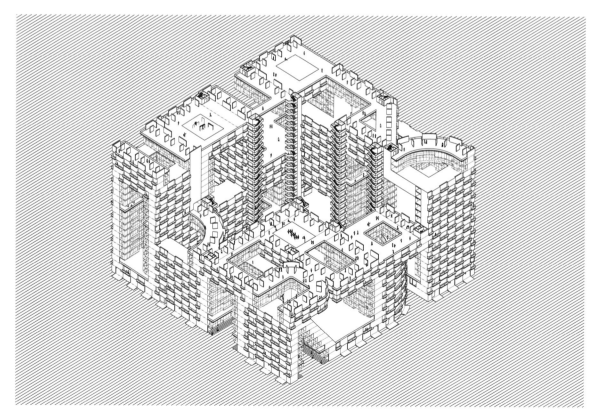

Top left:
The unit is the smallest
scale for taking action
within the housing block,
and satisfies the grad-
uates' need for mobility
and self-development.

Top right:
The interlock apartment
allows the individual
resident to form an
intimate network based
on personal or profes-
sional relationships.

Middle left:
The gateway is a perma-
nently programmed void
that acts as the meta-
phorical and functional
doorway of the housing
block.

Middle right:
The forum for content
and discontent fosters
internal agreement and
dissent in service of
productive initiatives.

Bottom:
The transfer plate is
a switchboard for
circulation and ideas.
Four transfer plates
stack to enclose
the central courtyard
of the building.

for migrant populations to find permanent footing in large cities.[11] However, the graduates have directed that uncertainty towards beneficial means, as they are socially nimble, adaptable, and quick to pursue new opportunities. This third characteristic puts the ant tribe in an overlapping category with what Pier Vittorio Aureli has identified as the "precariat" population—the rising mass of young, creative professionals.[12]

While the Russian avant-garde was addressing a singular proletarian collective, the qualities of the ant tribe (communal, hopeful, and mobile) have driven them to self-organize as a multifarious collective—one that operates within a wide range of goals, identities, and dreams. A multifarious collective achieves individual initiatives through their ability to form collectives of varying sizes and intensities—ranging from finding a single roommate to help cover the rent, to forming a collaborative of people with similar interests to develop a web start-up, to staging a large-scale organized protest to demand better bus routes to the center of the city. As the news articles reveal, the graduates have exhibited the potential for action, but their current ad hoc housing arrangements confine them to poor living conditions, lack the spatial resources for them to act on their desires, and make them susceptible to continued marginalization in the city. A housing block designed specifically for the graduates can better equip them to take action and establish identities for their fluid collectives. The Russian avant-garde demonstrated that an architectural project can cultivate a subject through reorganizing their daily inter-actions. As a single building encompassing a range of ideas, the Narkomfin communal house was perhaps the best treatise for OSA's vision of how subjects relate to form within the post-revolution Russian context. Adding and updating this lineage, a new housing block proposed for the ant tribe lays out four subject-form relationships for contemporary China.

I. Identity

Identity is key to a subject's capacity to organize itself, as well as for society at large to recognize and legitimize a subject. For example, the different shapes, sizes, and orientations of the *tulou* created distinct identities for the clans and their self-organized groups. The ability of a group of *tulous* to relate to each other through their streamlined organization, scale, and materiality, enabled the production of identities that could scale up as needed. A tight cluster of *tulous* could anchor the territory of several close-knit clans, as seen in *Tianluokeng* (affectionately nicknamed as "four dishes and a soup"), whereas a group of *tulou* clusters defined a village. The proposed housing block for the ant tribe borrows from, and fully develops, the *tulou*'s method of generating identity. The building brings together an array of voids in a single volume—articulating platonic shapes in the mass of units. The symbolic tendencies of these shapes are updated so that an audience can read them for their geometries and potential functions, with references to familiar building elements such as roofs, vaults, windows, and steps. The graduates can use this reciprocity between the generic and the specific as a canvas to project their own symbolic associations and build identity for themselves, the groups they form, and the actions these groups take. The form of the housing block is the vessel through which the graduates develop a stronger sense of belonging to the city, augmenting their confidence and ability to take action. At once a whole and an accumulation of parts, the building's form simultaneously conveys an image of permanence and harbors the potential for a multitude of readings—communicating the graduates' presence and ambitions to the city at large.

II. Mobility

The contemporary subject exemplified by the graduates is nomadic—partly because of their youth, partly because of the fluidity with which they must adapt to unexpected changes, and partly because they are in constant pursuit of fleeting opportunities. Despite its static nature, a building form can make it easier for a subject to be mobile within a given framework. Conversely, a building can also transform the act of mobility into more substantial experiences. In the *lilong*, for instance, the lanes adjacent to the units provided an overflow space for domestic activity—children playing hopscotch, elderly fanning themselves in lawn chairs, mothers washing their vegetables—to breathe and intermix in the same space. In Narkomfin and Anhualou, the more collective components of home life are relieved from the unit and reassembled elsewhere in the building, encouraging their subjects to foster relationships through increased encounters. In the proposed housing block, taking action begins with empowering the individual to be mobile at various scales, starting with the unit. The units range in size, orientation, and shape, but are all based on the same L-shaped spatial logic, allowing the graduates to easily move between, and adapt to, new units as their circumstances and relationships change. Drawing from the *lilong*, the corridors that allow access to the units become communal apartments, which graduates can share with an intimate network of friends, coworkers, or collaborators. The apartment form interlocks with an array of units, akin to the two sides of a zipper, creating nooks to accommodate the spillover of private life into communal territory. At a larger scale, the complexity of moving residents in and out of a massive building is solved by dividing the circulation into major cores, which bring residents from the city up to one of four transfer plates distributed throughout the building. From here, a series of secondary cores move residents from the transfer plate directly into their apartments. The role of the transfer plate as a switchboard for circulation is fully exploited for its ability to generate encounters.

III. Activity

A housing block can expand the range of activities that comprise the domestic sphere to better accommodate the needs or wishes of a subject. The activities that the ant tribe graduates engage in also form the basis for action, and by combining and sharing skills and resources, they are more readily able to capitalize on China's growing economic opportunities.

As China moves increasingly towards an innovation-based economy, the graduates are keen to develop and market their skills for a new crop of jobs. Furthermore, the graduates would be able to take advantage of the incentives created in such an economy to start their own business ventures. Already across China, there are stories of entrepreneurs building successful businesses from almost nothing, which would have been impossible just a decade ago. While Narkomin and Anhulaou expanded the domestic realm of the modern subject to include child-caring, group exercise, and other highly specific activities that emphasized the bonds created through shared labor, the activities that the ant tribe partakes in are driven by individual initiatives and are highly fluid. Therefore, instead of using program to predetermine activity, the proposed housing block uses form to suggest a possible range of activities. Shaped through the mass of units, the building's many voids are adaptable for different modes of collaboration. As the voids also connect at each transfer plate, these platforms are not only for the exchange of bodies, but also for the collision of ideas.

IV. Perception

Perception is perhaps the most important link between subject and form, in the proposed housing block. Perception is also the most lacking quality in the graduates' current living conditions, as many live in cramped rooms subsumed within chaotic makeshift villages of Beijing's periphery. In this environment, they are offered little chance to perceive, build an awareness for, and therefore act upon, the social bonds they have built. A building form can help its subject comprehend the relationship and role between the individual and the larger collectives they form. In the *tulou*, the courtyard was encircled by all the individual units, ensuring that residents were constantly aware of their position in relation to others within the building. This provided a way for the residents to determine how to assemble themselves in daily life and also how to re-organize when faced with more drastic, long-term changes. The potential of the courtyard to perceptually identify a collective, is magnified as a formal tool in the proposed building block for the graduates. The building rejects the typical linear organization of a housing block for a nested radial organization. Each unit clusters around a communal room. A number of communal rooms aggregate around the widened corridor of the apartment. Eight apartments stack around a void. Multiple voids aggregate above the transfer plates. Finally, the transfer plates encircle a central courtyard inside the building volume. At each scale, perception is manifested in a different spatial experience that caters to the collective, but maintains legibility and coherence through its centripetal force. The building's central courtyard, where an intensity of views is concentrated, is prone to being appropriated for the most contentious of collectives. The graduates face many grievances due to being migrants and holding uncertain status in the city. News articles have reported on their lack of sufficient transportation to the center of the city and threats by the local government to displace them to even farther reaches of the periphery.[13, 14]

To voice their shared concerns and demands, the graduates can organize protests within the courtyard. The government is particularly wary of large-scale organized protest as such events threaten its image and power. However, officials must balance these fears with a sensitivity to the graduates' needs, as further agitation to their livelihoods may provoke greater social unrest and sympathy for the graduates' cause.[15] The form of "contained protest" that occurs in the courtyard allows the graduates to collectively voice their concerns without being perceived with the intention of spreading social unrest beyond the physical boundaries of the building.

In an article for the World Economic Forum, Winston Wenyan Ma describes an encouraging and surprising assessment of how the graduates that make up the ant tribe may move forward from their current predicaments.[16] He states that their promise lies in their greater potential to define what the "Chinese Dream" may be, influencing the youth that will take over the reins from the previous generation to determine how to distribute China's newfound wealth.[17] China is in a period of economic and political transition, and as the government rewrites the rules that define their own actions, the current generation can have a decisive voice in the future of the country. Because of the hardships they have encountered while learning to harness China's growth, the graduates can lead China to a more sustainable model as it becomes a developed country—one that considers how the concepts of sharing and collaboration can be factored into its unique blend of capitalism and socialism. The subject-form relationships put forth through the proposed housing block recognizes this potential and places architecture firmly in a role of cultivating this emerging subject, in the vein of the Russian avant-garde project and informed by archetypal collective housing precedents throughout Chinese history. Explicitly political, housing is capable of becoming the setting where specific subjects take action towards their respective goals, and in doing so, redirect the rest of society towards a better future.

The housing block cultivates a contemporary subject that takes action through their day-to-day lives, generating a new way of life and identities that represent that way of life.

De Peter Yi holds a Master of Architecture from Rice University and a Bachelor of Science in Architecture from the University of Michigan. His current work engages architecture with the effects of cultural change invoked by globalization.

Notes

1 Chen Jia, "Despite Better Educations, 'Ants' Still Struggling," *China Daily*, December 14, 2010, http://www.chinadaily.com.cn/china/2010-12/14/content_11696624.htm.
2 Edward Wong, "Monuments to Clan Life are Losing Their Appeal," *The New York Times*, March 22, 2011, A5, New York edition.
3 Ian Beckett, *The Great War, 1914–1918* (London: Pearson/Longman, 2007), 528.
4 Alan Colquhoun, *Modern Architecture* (New York: Oxford University Press, 2002), 127.
5 Paul Reuber, "Moscow: Do Workers Prefer Cake?" *The Canadian Architect* (November 1998): 40.
6 Victor Buchli, *An Archaeology of Socialism* (Oxford: Berg, 1999), 76.
7 Dongping Han, "Farmers, Mao, and Discontent in China: From the Great Leap Forward to the Present." *Monthly Review*, vol. 61, iss. 7 (December 2009), http://monthlyreview.org/2009/12/01/farmers-mao-and-discontent-in-china/.
8 Sang Ye and Geremie R. Barme, "Lieux de Memoire," *China Heritage Quarterly*, no. 17 (March 2009), http://www.chinaheritagequarterly.org/articles.php?searchterm=017_lieux.inc&issue=017.
9 Ibid.
10 Andrew Jacobs, "China's Army of Graduates Struggles for Jobs," *The New York Times*, December 12, 2010, A1, New York edition.
11 Ibid.
12 Pier Vittorio Aureli, "Labor and Architecture: Revisiting Cedric Price's Potteries Thinkbelt," *Log* 23 (2011): 97.
13 Ralph Jennings, "China's "Ant Tribe" Poses Policy Challenge for Beijing," *Reuters* (February 17, 2010), http://www.reuters.com/article/2010/02/18/us-china-middleclass-idUSTRE61H0220100218.
14 Nelly Min, "Ant Tribe Swarms to New Villages," *China Daily* (August 12, 2010), http://www.chinadaily.com.cn/2010-08/12/content_11150579.htm.
15 Peter Ford, "China's Ant tribe: Millions of Unemployed College Grads," *The Christian Science Monitor* (December 21, 2009), http://www.csmonitor.com/World/2009/1221/China-s-Ant-Tribe-millions-of-unemployed-college-grads.
16 Winston Wenyan Ma, "The Future of China's Ant Tribe," *World Economic Forum* (March 13, 2010), http://forumblog.org/2013/03/the-future-of-chinas-ant-tribe/.
17 Ibid.

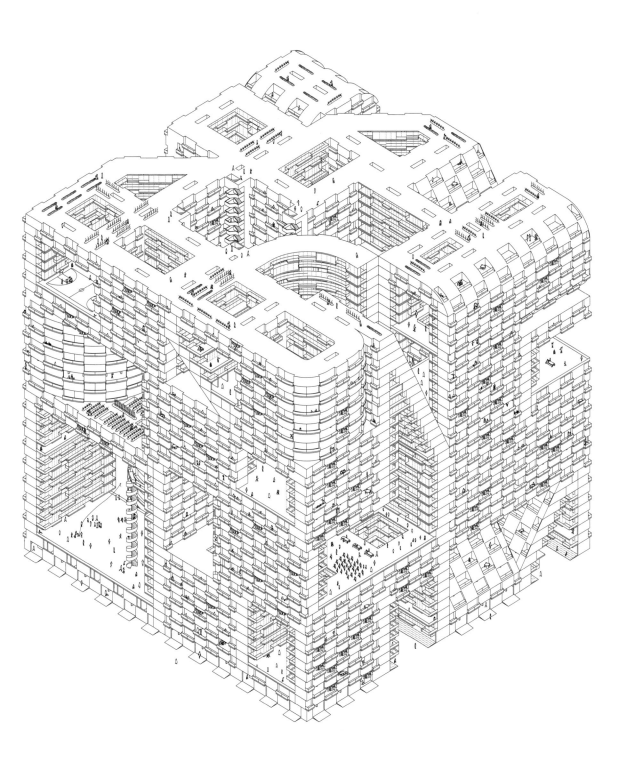

SPACES OF CONFLICT

Lori A. Brown

As polarizing an issue as abortion is in various parts of the United States, it provides a platform to consider the complex relationships of space, the autonomy of a body in space, varying degrees of governmental control, and the fluid and ever-shifting geography of reproductive healthcare access. Integral to abortion is how clinics intersect with the public sphere and the First Amendment of the United States Constitution; guaranteeing an individual the right to freedom of speech and peaceful assembly.[1] The intersections between the public realm and abortion-access interrogate the role and manipulation of space through legislating the literal geography around buildings, bodies, and healthcare access.

When considering what spaces are inherently contested and politicized, abortion clinics are an obvious choice, often transforming these sites into unstable environments.[2] The politicization of abortion is not an abstract idea solely debated within our legal system, but also in and around actual clinics located in the world. Over decades, local and state legislatures in combination with the Courts have established literal dimensions around buildings and bodies in response to the clinics' security concerns, which are commonly weighed against the limits of protestors' free speech. For example, in the Supreme Court decision of *Hill v. Colorado*, the court upheld the 1993 Colorado State measure creating a one hundred foot fixed-zone of protection around a health care facility's entrance and an eight foot

floating bubble zone around a person entering or exiting this fixed-zone. These measures were in response to the severity and magnitude of protests and the difficulty of access to the clinic.[3] Legislated distances make sense on paper and, one would imagine, result in safer zones surrounding the clinic. However, when one actually walks through a wall of protestors in order to reach a clinics' entrance, these legislated dimensions are all that some people have in protecting their access. This is especially true when local law enforcement is often not doing their job in some of the most restrictive statess. Numerous reports of officers allowing protesters unmitigated control of the sidewalk, as patients are being accosted by protestors en route to the clinic's front door, have been made. While there continues to be an increase of state restrictions being passed across the country, these restrictions produce abortion access that varies greatly from state-to-state. Currently, women in New York fare far better than women in Mississippi or Texas.

Within this political climate, the abortion clinic is inextricably a politicized space having real life consequences for those who seek reproductive healthcare and for those who serve these patients. As for the built environment, what can examining the wide range of influences that both directly and indirectly shape spaces like abortion clinics provide for the broader discipline of architecture and design? How does

examining such spaces broaden and deepen
the way people understand our built environment
and what value is placed on such spaces? What
is the potential agency within these spaces and
how are people who use these spaces able to
capitalize upon this potential and as a result alter,
reorganize, or subvert existing power structures
and the spaces that reinforce them? The discipline
of architecture should, and could, have a far
greater impact on these charged spaces.

The Public Sphere

Access to abortion reveals a highly politicized
and charged space that is being contested
in the public sphere. Utilized and active public
spheres are vital for democracy to function,
as witnessed recently in the Arab Spring, the
Occupy movement, the Hong Kong democracy
protests, and the national marches against
racial inequality in the United States. All these
protests visibly transpired in the public,
occupying our public spheres. It is precisely the
publicity of action that is critical. This is how
individuals come together to create action and
put pressure on political actors.

The public sphere is crucial in different ways
for abortion clinics. Anti-choice advocates regularly exercise their First Amendment freedoms
by protesting in front of abortion clinics across
the United States. This right is part of the freedom
individual citizens of the United States have to
publicly speak out against issues, providing legal

protection for protestors. State and federal courts
have ruled both in support and in opposition to
certain abortion rights cases; weighing free speech
against abortion access. This has produced a
variety of legislation differing dramatically from
state-to-state—controlling and manipulating the
actual geography and physical boundaries around
clinic properties, buildings, and people's bodies.[4]
This remains an ongoing debate and in June 2014,
the Supreme Court unanimously struck down
the constitutionality of the thirty-five foot buffer
zones around abortion clinics in the state of
Massachusetts.[5] This buffer zone had been created
in response to severe protests around Boston
clinics and the killing of an abortion doctor.
Weighing free speech and safety, the Supreme
Court declared safety is less of a concern than
the limiting of free speech.[6]

Privacy, the basis of the Supreme Court's
legalization of abortion, is deeply entrenched
within "[w]estern political theories of freedom,
personal autonomy, patriarchal familial sovereignty and private property."[7] The distinctions
created through many of these rulings rely
on the problematic gendered division of public
and private space historically associating men
with the public realm and women with the
domestic realm. But as the geographer Nancy
Duncan has so elegantly articulated, these
binaries, entrenched within political philosophy,
law, popular discourse, and general spatial
practices, are used to legitimate oppression,

regulate and exclude sexuality and sexual difference, and preserve more traditional structures of
patriarchal and heterosexist power.[8]

As Duncan has noted, not all spaces are so
easily divided into the public or private realm.[9]
We can trace the lineage of this binary structure
through Jürgen Habermas' instrumental theories
on the public sphere. His work is based on
discursive interaction wherein citizens debated
common issues separate from the state.[10] In his
seminal work, *The Structural Transformation
of the Public Sphere*, he begins by positing
how "the usage of the words 'public' and 'public
sphere' betrays a multiplicity of concurrent
meanings."[11] These meanings have evolved over
millennia and his book dives into great detail to
unpack this historical evolution. Habermas notes
that stemming from Greek antiquity, "the public
sphere was constituted in discussion (*lexis*),
which could also assume the forms of consultation
and of sitting in the court of law, as well as
in common action (*praxis*) ... [T]he reproduction
of life, the labor of the slaves, and the service
of the women went on under the aegis of the
master's domination... immersed in the obscurity
of the private sphere. [T]he public sphere [was]
a realm of freedom and permanence."[12] In the
sixteenth century, more modern binaries between
public and private were established, although
clearly not so far removed from their Greek roots.
During this time, "public" was associated with
the state—an absolutionist entity of power
and authority. The "private" became equated with
the exclusion from all that was state related.[13]
Although the meanings of these terms have
evolved somewhat since then, our usage of public
and private remain deeply indebted to their
earlier referents.

Habermas, however, is not without his critics.
In her essay "Rethinking the Public Sphere," critical theorist Nancy Fraser responds to Habermas'
intention of presenting a new form of public
sphere in order to retrieve its critical function.[14]
She establishes a different history, shedding
insight into several key omissions by Habermas.
The first of these being that although Habermas
argued that this public space was open and accessible to all, where "inequalities of status were
to be bracketed ... discussants ... to deliberate
as peers," in fact, this wasn't completely true
in practice. Gender served as means for exclusion
to participation. For example, in France, the
new republic's public sphere was established in
"deliberate opposition to that of a more woman-
friendly salon culture."[15] Additionally, in Britain
and Germany, the societies, clubs, and associations
were all based upon this new bourgeois class
formation. They were incredibly exclusionary and
served as "training grounds" for the rising "universal
class" that would eventually come to power.
Embedded within this structure is the separation
of public and private spaces where bourgeois
women were becoming associated both philo-
sophically and spatially with this newly defined
private domestic realm.

Fraser argues against the following four
assumptions by Habermas. First, the need for
the public sphere to be bracketed in order for
political democracy to happen through societal
equality. Second, that a single comprehensive
public sphere is preferable to a nexus of multiple
publics. Third, that public discourse should
only focus on the common good and discourse
should deny the inclusion of private interests
or issues. Lastly, that a functioning public sphere
necessitates a sharp separation between civil
society and the state.[16]

Her alternative approach to theories of the
public sphere comprise "a plurality of competing
publics to better promote the ideal of participatory parity"[17] in contrast to Habermas' single
public sphere. She acknowledges when there
are societal inequalities, the less powerful
groups will not have the same power of speech
and representation as the dominant groups,
but contends that this would be further
exacerbated if there is only one public sphere
where all engage. She refers to these new spaces
as "subaltern counterpublics" signifying "they
are parallel discursive arenas where members
of subordinated social groups invent and circulate
counter discourses, which in turn permit
them to formulate oppositional interpretations
of their identities, interests, and needs."[18]
These new publics increase discursive space
and contestation requiring that their once
unheard voice must be publicly acknowledged
and debated.[19]

The political theorist Iris Marion Young puts
forth a different notion about the public sphere.
She defines publicity as an actual space or a
precise indoor or outdoor location "for communicative engagement and contest"[20] open to all.
Inextricably combined with the idea of location
is one's ability to invite the public to this space
for such activities. Second, publicity refers
to a plurality of citizens "with varying interests,
priorities, values, and experiences."[21] Due to
the multiplicity of citizens, or 'actors' as she refers
to them, the public is exposed to a diversity

The queue of pre-Easter
protestors outside
of the EMW Women's
Surgical Center in
Louisville, Kentucky.
PHOTO: NELSON HELM (2012)

of viewpoints and attitudes and as a result "has little control over how the public will take up, interpret, and act in relation to what they see and hear."[22] The third aspect of publicity refers to the type of expressions made public. These need to be made in such a way that they can be understood by anyone.

In contradistinction to Habermas and Fraser, Young argues for a public sphere that incorporates elements from both of their theories. She agrees with Habermas' idea that "a single continuous public process or 'space' is necessary if the idea of public sphere is to be helpful in describing how a diverse, complex, mass society can address social problems through public action."[23] Young also acknowledges Fraser's idea of subaltern counterpublics as a way to create space "where members of subordinated groups develop ideas, arguments, campaigns, and protest actions directed at influencing a wider public debate, often with the goal of bringing about legal or institutional change."[24] Both theories are required because without the ability of smaller groups to organize and publicize their concerns, the unified public will exclude and disenfranchise some actors. Where Young then diverges and reframes the argument is through the way she defines democracy. She questions a democracy where "élite decision-makers are elected and subject to the rule of law" because this definition does not address the influence of regular citizens. Democracy, for her argument, is "a process that connects 'the people' and 'the powerful,' and through which people are able to significantly influence their actions. Democracy is more or less as strong and deep as the strength of these connections and how predictable that their influence is."[25]

This primary connection is the public sphere. A healthy public sphere is a space of "opposition and accountability … and policy influence."[26] Through their various methods, political actors can help instigate change. Their power resides in the ability to uncover, expose, publicize and even shame powerful actors. In so doing, ordinary citizens' use of the public sphere is one way to "limit power and hold powerful actors accountable."[27] Because power hides in often hard-to-find places, it is even more critical for diverse citizen groups to do their utmost to expose abusive power. As Young states, "[c]reative acts of civil disobedience often force power to become naked."[28] She acknowledges that it takes great will by the excluded to get their message heard and for these reasons, the public sphere will "be a site of struggle—often contentious struggle."[29]

The public space around the abortion clinic has become a subaltern space. Here, citizen actors, primarily from the anti-choice side, protest and project their beliefs about abortion and have been successfully exerting political pressure for decades. This use of public space supports the heterogeneity of citizen positions as advocated by both Fraser and Young. Ideas of difference can and should be publicly declared and acted out for

we want and support an active and contentious public realm where dissension can be articulated and visible. However, what happens when one side becomes so successful protesting out in front of clinics and lobbying inside legislative bodies to the effect of more restrictive and unbalanced reproductive healthcare laws? There are more restrictions now than at any time since *Roe versus Wade*, the Supreme Court 1973 decision that legalized abortion. Slowly and methodically, the right to access an abortion continues to be chipped away. The pro-choice side has failed to keep the pressure on those opposed to abortion. Only four years after *Roe versus Wade*, the *Hyde Amendment* was passed, which prohibited federal financing for abortion except in cases of rape, incest, or to save the life of the mother.[30] Even more recently, with the *Affordable Healthcare Act* (ACA), abortion coverage is purposively excluded in any of the healthcare packages and therefore, individual state marketplace packages are not required to offer abortion coverage. States are also allowed to not include any abortion coverage in any of their state marketplace plans.[31] If coverage is provided, the financial streams are required to remain completely separate from state received federal monies. If offered, additional abortion coverage may be purchased through a separate state rider. However, this rider option is not a state requirement that must be provided.[32]

So although federally guaranteed, abortion continues to become more and more difficult to access, especially for poor women of color. In conjunction with the difficulties of access, these contested spaces have become culturally normative. Young's ideas of civic action and even disobedience are critical to a thriving democracy, but what happens when one set of actors are so successful in curtailing women's legal rights to autonomy and control over their own body? Abortion is the only medical procedure so highly legislatively regulated. Abortion is not a decision made lightly. However, one can only infer from the growing list of restrictions including such things as required waiting periods, state mandated information a women must either read or be read to, required ultrasounds with descriptions of what is on the monitor, to restrictions on healthcare coverage for the procedure,[33] that legislatures believe women are either incapable of making this decision without intervention or do not seriously consider the decisions they do make. There is very little autonomy in this process. The space of the public, the private, and the body are con-tinually contested, invaded, and fought over for control. This is what happens when the state intervenes too much.

As Duncan writes in *BodySpace: Destabilizing Geographies of Gender and Sexuality*, "feminists are … exploring the far-reaching implications of a new epistemological viewpoint based on the idea of knowledge as embodied, engendered, and embedded in the material context of place and space."[34] This situated knowledge is one

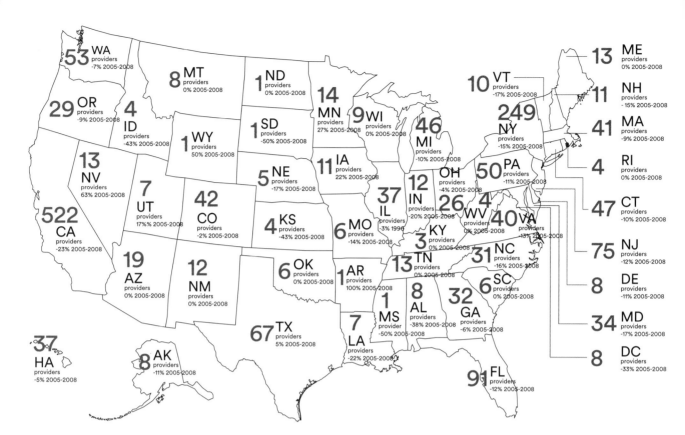

United States Counties with providers: This map illustrates where, within the United States, there are reproductive healthcare providers. The gray denotes counties with providers compared to the white where vast swaths of the country do not have access to a provider.

based in awareness of social, cultural, and geographical sets of relationships and are spatially "constructed and negotiated" and integral to place. Duncan believes that space is both controlling and confining of power and yet has the potential to disrupt these power relations.[35]

Duncan argues for a drastic rethinking of the deeply rooted public/private division. She believes there needs to be de-territorializing and more "progressive geographies" created, which are open-ended and empowering, to provide resistance to the normative and homogenizing policies currently in place. Studying the public space of abortion clinics raises important questions about the control of such spaces, the legislating of our public realms and the relationship of these spaces to free speech. Architecture has been mostly absent from designing these spaces. The providers are the ones who have creatively employed spatial tactics and been at the forefront of progressive geographies all in order to remain accessible. What was interesting is that through interviews and clinic visits, discussions rarely centered on the formal qualities or aesthetics of these spaces. Rather, the conversations often turned to the tactics that have been employed to create safe and secure medical spaces. These tactics were almost always stopgap measures. For example, this occurred through installing privacy fences or shrubs, wrapping of fences with dark plastic sheeting to prohibit views, the intentional elevating of noise levels through music or industrial fans, and even installing and then activating lawn sprinklers at precisely the moments when protestors are limiting physical access to a clinic's front door. All of these various and

sometimes even outlandish tactics produce places of access. Rarely was an architect or designer consulted in these build-outs and renovations. It was clear when one had been involved because the spatial layout, patient flow, and general environment was dramatically better. Imagine the possibilities if the disciplines of spatial practice became more engaged? Imagine how security technologies could be more sophisticatedly integrated, how new materials could be used to provide greater privacy and noise reduction, and how these clinics could become more aesthetically a part of their contexts?

As previously mentioned, a few states have legislated distances protestors must stand away from clinic entrances or to those approaching and exiting such facilities. These laws have been generally upheld by the Supreme Court, however the recent case ruling Massachusetts's thirty-five foot buffer zone illegal in *McCullen v. Coakley* is not an encouraging sign.[36] More broadly however, the right to free speech overrides all other concerns. Combined with ongoing restrictive state legislation, this produces situations where many women seeking reproductive healthcare services find it quite difficult and sometimes even inaccessible. Interestingly, there are several legal precedents where free speech has been legally restricted. These include zones around polling stations, the Supreme Court building, and military funerals.[37] The question must now be asked: why not around abortion clinics?

Spaces of Possibility

If the hope for architecture is not to just rely on its given modes of production but to create

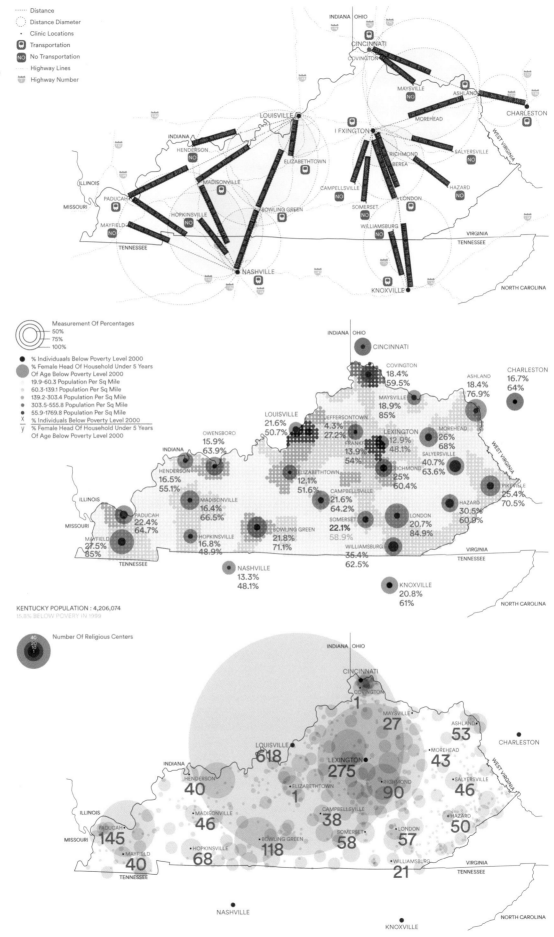

Kentucky Clinic Distances: Location and distances across the state to gain access to clinics.

Kentucky Poverty Rates: Using 1999 Census data, this diagram compares poverty statistics for individuals (small dark circles) to single women head of household with children under five (FhdH c<5) (larger dark circles) against population (smaller background gray dots). You will notice how large the percentage of FhdH c<5 are statewide.

Kentucky Religious Institutions: This map documents the large prevalence of religious institutions throughout the entire state.

Distance
Distance Diameter
Clinic Locations
Transportation
No Transportation
Highway Lines
Highway Number

Measurement Of Percentages
50%
75%
100%

% Individuaals Below Poverty Level 2000
% Female Head Of Household Under 5 Years Of Age Below Poverty Level 2000
19.9-60.3 Population Per Sq Mile
60.3-139.1 Population Per Sq Mile
139.2-303.4 Population Per Sq Mile
303.5-555.8 Population Per Sq Mile
55.9-1769.8 Population Per Sq Mile
X % Individuals Below Poverty Level 2000
Y % Female Head Of Household Under 5 Years Of Age Below Poverty Level 2000

KENTUCKY POPULATION : 4,206,074
15.8% BELOW POVERTY IN 1999

Number Of Religious Centers

something outside architecture's typical sets of responses, what enables this to happen? What other ways can architecture be conceived, produced, and politically engaged? As Philosopher Elizabeth Grosz writes, "[i]nsofar as architecture is seeking not so much 'innovation,' not simply 'the latest fad,' but to produce differently, to engender the new, to risk creating otherwise ... How to keep architecture open to its outside, how to force architecture to *think*?"[38] She goes on to posit, "Can [architecture] become something—many things—other than what it is and how it presently functions? If its present function is an effect of the crystallization of its history within, inside, its present, can its future be something else?"[39] For our built environment to improve, design professionals must be involved at all levels. Currently we are not. We ignore vast swaths of our built environment. We must expand how we utilize and bring our expertise to the larger public.

Case Study: Kentucky
With only three abortion providers throughout the state, Kentucky is one of the more difficult states for women to exercise their legal right to abortion. Ninety-eight percent of counties are without a provider and according to the *Guttmacher Institute*, seventy-four percent of women live in these counties. With so few providers, women must travel greater distances to a clinic. If someone does not own a car, then how are clinics accessed? Because there is a mandatory 24-hour delay law in Kentucky, a woman will need to pay for another round-trip ticket or spend the night in the clinic city, either way increasing the cost of the procedure. In many of the smaller towns, there are no bus or train services available requiring her to seek alternative modes of transportation.[40]

At the time that data was collected, Kentucky's average poverty level was just under sixteen percent compared to the national average of thirteen percent. Where greater disparity is revealed is when examining female head of households with children under five years of age (FHDH c<5) living below the line of poverty. Several examples illustrating this include: Louisville, the most populous city in the state, 21.6 percent of individuals live below the line of poverty compared to 50.7 percent of FHDH c<5 live below the line of poverty; Bowling Green has 21.8 percent of individuals and 70.1 percent of FHDH c<5 living below the line of poverty; Paducah 22.4 percent of individuals and 64.7 percent of FHDH c<5 live below the line of poverty. In less populated and remote areas such as London, 20.7 percent of individuals and 84.9 percent FHDH c<5 live below the line of poverty. Combine this data with Kentucky's restriction of public funding of abortions as well as prohibiting publicly owned hospitals and facilities to provide abortions unless to save a woman's life. This demonstrates an alarming rate of women where women in the greatest need are provided fewer resources to access reproductive healthcare.[41] It must also

be noted there are over six thousand religious institutions across the state. Although not as high as some of the other neighboring southern states, religion is a strong and persuasive force within state legislative circles and abortion restrictions are a direct reflection of this power.

Conclusion
No space is neutral. Place and space are created through various agents of power and influence. These complex relationships are understood more clearly through the data of a state like Kentucky. Spatial practices are producing extremely reconfigured spatial landscapes by a vast range of spatial tactics. Several examples include: anti-choice groups protesting every single day outside clinics; clinics attempting to register online for noise permits before protestors do in order to have a quiet work week; doctors being required to have admitting privileges even though clinics already have agreements with local hospitals in cases of emergency; and state legislatures defining new and more difficult building restrictions that other outpatient medical facilities are not required to follow.[42]

And yet, the owners, providers, doctors, and medical staff continue to create ways to do their job. Sometimes they have used political will to their advantage. They have filed injunctions against unnecessary and biased laws; they have patient escorts in greater numbers than the protestors; and often confront state agents such as local law enforcement or judicial departments for not doing their job to uphold the law. These actions provide alternatives and are challenging the effects, distortions, and manipulations of power by governmental and private groups and the media's exploitation of these efforts.

By making abortion so publicly an issue, something the pro-choice movement did so successfully prior to *Roe versus Wade*, the anti-choice groups have garnered visibility, voice, and political power. They have been far more effective in transforming their agenda into legislation that directly effects and limits physical and geographic access. Both anti-choice protestors and abortion providers are thinking of architecture differently. Architects, however, could enable a far more radical rethinking of these relationships all the while enhancing spaces in and around abortion facilities. This requires architects to become active citizen agents as well as members of local government zoning and building code departments. We must be active and in public, as Arendt writes. Who better than architects to be responsible for developing governance of our built environments, facilitating public discussions about why design matters for all, and taking direct action to improve the design of our world?[43]

Lori Brown is an associate professor of Architecture at Syracuse University and is a registered architect in the state of New York. Her research focuses on architecture and social justice issues with particular emphasis on gender and its impact upon spatial relationships. She is the co-founder and co-director of ArchiteXX, a women and architecture group working to bridge the academy and practice in New York City.

Notes

1   "The United States Constitution." (n.d.).

2   This essay is part of a larger research project recently published in Lori A. Brown, *Contested Bodies: Abortion Clinics, Women's Shelters and Hospitals* (Surrey, England: Ashgate, 2013).

3   *Hill v. Colorado* (2000), http://caselaw.findlaw.com/us-supreme-court/530/703.html.

4   Madsen v. Women's Health Center (1994) upheld noise restrictions during certain times of certain days. The FACE law (1994) protects anyone exercising their right to reproductive services and First Amendment religious freedoms and makes unlawful to intentionally damage or destroy facility property or places of worship. Schenck v. Pro-Choice Network of Western New York (1997) upheld a 15-foot fixed zone around door-ways and doorway entrances, parking lots entrances, driveways and driveway entrance of the clinic facilities. Hill v. Colorado (2000) upheld 100-feet fixed zone around health care facilities and 8 feet bubble zone around someone entering and exiting a clinic. See: http://caselaw.findlaw.com/us-supreme-court/512/753.html

5   See Milton J. Valencia, "Justices question Mass. abortion clinic buffer zones," *Boston Globe*, January 15, 2014, http://www.bostonglobe.com/metro/2014/01/15/mass-abortion-clinic-buffer-zone-law-debated-supreme-court/ikxyOs71IvK3KdUOHDyhPL/story.html; Robert Barnes, "Supreme Court justices question size of buffer zones around Massachusetts abortion clinics," *Washington Post*, January 15, 2014, http://www.washingtonpost.com/politics/supreme-court-justices-question-size-of-buffer-zones-around-mass-abortion-clinics/2014/01/15/834f21c4-7e02-11e3-95c6-0a7aa808 74bc_story.html; and Nina Totenberg, "Supreme Court Considers Legality of Abortion Clinic Buffer Zones," *NPR News*, January 15, 2014, http://www.npr.org/2013/12/20/255870199/supreme-court-considers-legality-of-abortion-clinic-buffer-zones.

6   There is a body of literature that has analyzed the Courts interpretation of free speech in protests and various other uses of the public realm. For example see Don Mitchell's body of research in this area such as: *The Right to the City: Social Justice and the Fight for Public Space* (2003); co-authored with Lynn Staeheli, *The People's Property? Power, Politics, and the Public* (2008); articles include: "Property Rights, the First Amendment, and Judicial Anti-Urbanism: The Strange Case of Hicks v. Virginia," *Urban Geography* 26 (2005), 565-586; Don Mitchell and Lynn Staeheli, "Permitting Protest: Constructing—and Dismantling—the Geography of Dissent in the United States," *International Journal of Urban and Regional Research* 29 (2005), 796-813; "The S.U.V. Model of Citizenship: Floating Bubbles, Buffer Zones, and the Rise of the 'Purely Atomic' Individual," *Political Geography* 24 (2005), 77-100; "Political Violence, Order, and the Legal Construction of Public Space: Power and the Public Forum Doctrine" *Urban Geography*, 17 (1996), 152-178.

7   Nancy Duncan, "Renegotiating Gender and sexuality in public and private spaces," in *BodySpace* ed. Nancy Duncan (London: Routledge, 1996), 128.

8   Ibid., 127–8.

9   Ibid., 129.

10   Jürgen Habermas, "Preliminary Demarcation of a Type of Bourgeois Public Sphere," *The Structural Transformation of the Public Sphere: An Inquiry into a category of Bourgeois Society*, trans. Thomas Burger and Frederick Lawrence (Cambridge: MIT Press, 1989).

11   Ibid., 1.

12   Ibid., 3-4.

13   Ibid., 11.

14   Nancy Fraser, "Rethinking the Public Sphere: A Contribution to the Critique of Actually Existing Democracy," *Social Text*, no. 25/26 (1990), 57-58.

15   Ibid., 59.

16   Ibid., 62–3.

17   Ibid., 66.

18   Ibid., 67.

19   Ibid., 66–7.

20   Iris Marion Young, *Inclusion and Democracy* (Oxford: Oxford University Press, 2000), 168.

21   Ibid., 169.

22   Ibid.

23   Iris Marion Young, *Inclusion and Democracy* (Oxford: Oxford University Press, 2000), 168-169.

24   Ibid., 171.

25   Ibid., 172.

26   Ibid., 173.

27   Ibid., 174.

28   Ibid., 172–3.

29   Ibid., 174–6, 178.

30   Lori A. Brown, *Contested Bodies: Abortion Clinics, Women's Shelters and Hospitals* (Surrey, England: Ashgate, 2013).

31   Alina Salganicoff, Adara Beamesderfer, Nisha Kurani, and Laurie Sobel, "Coverage for Abortion Services and the ACA, *The Henry J. Kaiser Family Foundation*, 3-4, (September 2014), http://kff.org/womens-health-policy/issue-brief/coverage-for-abortion-services-and-the-aca/.

32   Kinsey Hasstedt, "Abortion Coverage Under the Affordable Care Act: The Laws Tell Only Half the Story," *Guttmacher Policy Review*, vol. 14, no. 1, 16, 19 (Winter 2014), http://www.guttmacher.org/pubs/gpr/17/1/gpr170115.html.

33   NARAL Pro-Choice America for state-by-state list of restrictions, http://www.prochoiceamerica.org/government-and-you/state-governments/.

34   Nancy Duncan, "Introduction," in *BodySpace* ed. Nancy Duncan (London: Routledge, 1996), 1.

35   Ibid., 3, 4–5.

36   McCullen v. Coakley, 573 U.S. __ (2014), http://caselaw.findlaw.com/us-1st-circuit/1200297.html.

37   For example, see Adrian Walker, "Right to access in balance in Supreme Court," *The Boston Globe*, (January 20, 2014), http://www.bostonglobe.com/metro/2014/01/20/free-speech-rights-protesters-should-not-limit-women-access-abortion-clinics/XyLL5POyvyXmTgUnSyrytI/story.html; J.K. Trotter and Abby Ohlheiser, "You Can Still Protest the Supreme Court," *The Wire*, (June 13, 2013), http://www.thewire.com/politics/2013/06/you-can-still-protest-supreme-court/66225/; Abby Ohlheiser, "The SCOTUS 'Buffer Zone' Case Isn't Just About a Grandmotherly Abortion Protestor," *The Wire*, (January 15, 2014), http://www.thewire.com/national/2014/01/scotus-buffer-zone-case-isnt-just-about-grandmotherly-abortion-protester/357041/. For a broader understanding of the control of space in regards to free speech using Washington State see the ACLU Washington State's "Street Speech: Your Rights in Washington to Parade, Picket, and Leaflet," https://aclu-wa.org/news/street-speech-your-rights-washington-parade-picket-and-leaflet.

38   Elizabeth Grosz, *Architecture from the Outside: Essays on Virtual and Real Space* (Cambridge: MIT Press, 2001), 64.

39   Ibid., 70–71.

40   NARAL Pro-Choice America. List of Kentucky State Restrictions: Unconstitutional and criminal abortion bans, State prohibits certain state employees or organization from receiving state funds from counseling or referring women for abortion services, TRAP, state subjects providers to burdensome restrictions not applied to other medical professions, Physician-only restriction; state prohibits certain qualified health care professionals from performing abortions, State restricts insurance coverage of abortion, State prohibits use of public facilities for performance of abortions, State allows certain entities to refuse specific reproductive health services, information or referrals, State restricts post-viability abortions, Women are subjected to biased counseling requirements that can be done via telephone, State requires mandatory 24-hour delays before receiving an abortion, State requires mandatory parental consent, and State prohibits public funding for women eligible for state medical assistance for general health care unless procedure is necessary to preserve the woman's life, or the pregnancy is the result of rape or incest or fetal abnormality incompatible with live birth. Please see: http://www.prochoiceamerica.org/government-and-you/state-governments/state-profiles/kentucky.html.

41   Lori A. Brown, *Contested Bodies: Abortion Clinics, Women's Shelters and Hospitals* (Surrey, England: Ashgate, 2013), 121.

42   Based upon ambulatory surgical center requirements, some of these spatial changes, often quite expensive and unnecessary for abortion care, could include such things as increased dimensions of hallways, increased closet sizes and doorway openings, build new locker rooms for doctors, greater fire safety requirements including the installation of sprinkler systems and the upgrading to complex ventilation systems. For more see: Mike Cason, "Alabama House Republicans seek new restrictions on abortion clinics," *Alabama.com*, (January 29, 2013), http://blog.al.com/montgomery/2013/01/alabama_house_republicans_seek.html; National Abortion Federation, "The TRAP: Targeted Regulation of Abortion Providers," http://www.prochoice.org/about_abortion/facts/trap_laws.html; Laura Bassett, "Anti-Abortion Laws Take Dramatic Toll On Clinics Nationwide," *Huffington Post Politics*, (August 26, 2013), http://www.huffingtonpost.com/2013/08/26/abortion-clinic-closures_n_3804529.html.

43   Carla Corroto, "When Will Architects Speak Up for Women's Rights?" ArchDaily. (July 1, 2013), http://www.archdaily.com/?p=395639.

DELIRIOUS ACTIONS: GENDER TACTICS IN PUBLIC SPACE

Serafina Amoroso

In 2003, theorist Jane Rendell defined critical spatial practice as occupying the "triple crossroads: between theory and practice, between art and architecture, and between public and private."[1] In her essay "Critical Spatial Practices," Rendell traces a map of the recent evolution of architecture's engagement with gender difference, identifying five themes—collectivity, alterity, interiority, performativity, materiality—that she considers specific to a feminist approach to critical spatial practice.[2] In the article "Delirium and Historical project,"[3] theorist Teresa Stoppani sets out to redefine "delirium" in architecture by engaging it with Tafuri's historical project,[4] identifying a sort of filiation from Tafuri's legacy in the work of a group of women architectural theorists, whom she refers to as *mulieres delirantes* ("delirious women"). Taking a cue from these two positions, this essay intends, first, to examine the expanded implications for the terms "delirium," "gender," and "tactics"; and, second, to focus on the modes, methods, and concerns of a gender-based approach to spatial practice. In particular, its ability to incite political and social actions through the analysis of the works of two feminist practices: muf architecture/art based in London and atelier d'architecture autogérée based in Paris.

Delirium
Beyond its etymological sense of transgression from linearity and its Freudian meaning as intentional censorship and erasure, delirium embodies a key concept to comprehend the new relationship between theory and practice, and thought and action. The delirium refers to a way of thinking that blurs the boundaries of identity and architecture as a discipline in order to return to architecture after considering ideas and concepts generated in other disciplines. This modus operandi has been shared for decades by a wide group of women architectural theorists and practitioners, above all with respect to their way of going beyond the contingency of professional practice. Recovering philosopher Jean-Jacques Lecercle's[5] notion of *délire*, architectural theorist Jennifer Bloomer affirms that it "is the name and the condition of the overlay."[6] Quoting Lecercle, she specifies that *délire* is a particular form of delirium, through which the patient attempts to go beyond the limits of his psychosis, introducing method into it.

In psychosis, *délire* is a sort of "patch" on psychic fissures; it's the fracturing of the ego state that provokes *"la disolución de las barreras identificatorias ante el otro"* ("the dissolution of the identifying barriers towards others").[7] A psychotic's necessity to construct new worlds stems from this situation. The construction of new realities of psychotic certainties doesn't provoke a loss of reality, but rather an unshared reality through which the psychotic subject produces himself or herself through new identities. In his or her search for a lost subjectivity, the subject turns delirium into rationality, which ultimately is the other side of delirious thinking. In such a context,

muf architecture/art,
Shared Ground
(Southwark Street,
London, 1996–2001).
Detail of the new pave-
ment constructed in
cast in situ aggregate
using Thames shingle.
PHOTO: COURTESY OF
MUF ARCHITECTURE/ART

rationality is meant to be an extended rationality in which there is room for other notions, such as justification to be added to demonstration, and probable truths to be added to certain truths.[8] This kind of delirious openness to change and chance goes beyond the limits of a discipline—working in an interdisciplinary, collective, participatory, and cooperative way. For example, working together with experts from other disciplines and local communities, beyond any fixed identity or set of rules, can be considered as a distinctive aspect of a gender perspective in architectural practices.

Gender

Architecture constantly needs to question and renegotiate its disciplinary boundaries in order to remain involved in the challenges of the present and provide an effective framework for human actions. Today, architecture has to engage with a wide range of contingencies in order to minimize the risk of marginalization as compared with disciplines such as economics or engineering, which tend to dominate the formulation of possible future urban and environmental developments. Architecture's core activity is no longer the design and production of buildings. The role of writing, drawings, buildings and the hybridization among them as different and interdisciplinary modes of practice have already been explored by feminist practices. Jane Rendell provides a definition of interdisciplinarity that relates to a way of working across, between, and at the edge of different

disciplines, so that specialists can be engaged in the procedures and operating paradigms of each other's in order to question them.[9] This approach to interdisciplinarity comes directly from a particular understanding of the relationship between theory and practice: practice is neither the application of theory nor its inspiration. Theory and practice are relational concepts that provide a common ground for exchanging ideas and experiences from different areas of knowledge and expertise. Liza Fior, partner at muf architecture/art, has stated: "The commissioned project is itself the site and opportunity for research and theoretical / critical reflection; it is the means by which theory, as the framework for practice, is produced. For muf that theoretic framework is the means by which the status quo is challenged, and new modes of practice are tested which rebalance the relationship between the commissioned professional and the end user. So the theory is enmeshed within the making of the project, it's the continual standing back framing, questioning, considering."[10]

Fior's words make explicit the main aspects of a feminist—and, in general, of a gender and social justice—agenda in architecture, which includes a commitment to participatory principles and an inextricably intertwined link between theory and practice, design and performative actions, "expanding knowledge and taking action."[11] Seen from this point of view, as argued by Despina Stratigakos, "feminism remains an inherently positive approach" to architecture, because women's concerns belong to everyone.[12] The fact that some issues are no longer visible as gender approaches cannot overshadow their genealogies. There will always be a gender dimension to architectural practice, but now the process is run in a more subtle, implicit, and indirect way.

The feminist and the feminine notion can be considered together, though feminine notions can also be separated from the feminist. An independent view of reality from a gender-based and delirious perspective is still necessary to establish distance from dependence on reality and to develop new views on urgent social and political issues. Thanks to the work of some radical urban geographers[13] and to the sharing of some key inherent concerns,[14] close ties can be maintained between gender perspectives and other post-colonial spatial studies in relation to the fight against global inequalities, the individual experience of oppression, the situation of disabled people, the condition of immigrants, refugees, erased memories and identities in urban areas and post-colonial contexts.

Tactics

It is possible to draw connections between Michel de Certeau's notions of strategies and tactics, and the definitions of representations of space and representational spaces elaborated by Henri Lefebvre. De Certeau's distinction between strategies and tactics is based on the fact that while strategies comply with abstract models that produce conceptualized spaces, tactics "can only use, manipulate, and divert these spaces."[15] Tactics "do not obey the law of the place, for they are not defined or identified by it."[16] They focus on the ways of using a place (modalities of action and formalities of practices), while strategies deal better with what is used. Strategies produce spaces, while tactics can only use or re-use them.

Lefebvre's spatial model is articulated in three modes:
1. spatial practice, which produces and masters social space; it is a perceived space, empirically evaluated, and related to daily and urban realities;
2. representation of space, which he qualifies as "the space of scientists, planners, urbanists, technocratic subdividers, and social engineers."[17] It is a conceived, a conceptualized space;
3. representational space, which is a space described (by users, inhabitants, artists, philosophers, writers) and directly lived thorough symbols, images, interpretations; it's a symbolic dimension which overlaps with physical space.

This spatial triad makes clear the interaction and interdependence of social and spatial relations: on the one hand, space is a social production; on the other hand, social relations are a spatial construction. "[...] the lived, conceived and perceived realms should be interconnected, so that the 'subject', the individual member of a given social group, may move from one to another without confusion."[18]

De Certeau's tactics and Lefebvre's representational spaces are, both of them, time-based rather than space-based practices. Strategies "[...] privilege spatial relationships"[19] rather than temporal ones, while tactics privilege time, for they are "procedures that gain validity in relation to the pertinence they lend to time-to circumstances."[20] Tactics and representational spaces are temporal modes of space activation and transformation. Unlike strategies and representations of space, which works from the imaginary position of a panoptic eye, they favor the analysis of the fragmentation and the locality of social phenomena and spatial settings, thus providing only partial—but, at the same time, plural—knowledge. Tactics and representational spaces are styles of operating, instructions for use; they take advantage of certain spatial situations into which they inextricably interweave new levels of meaning and functioning, new ways of using spatial constraints; they foster a deviation from the rules of a system without leaving it. In this way of resisting from within the dominant pre-established social rules—continuously question existing orders and attempting to make room for creativity, invention and imagination—and of consciously trespassing preexisting boundaries and constraints, it's possible to identify some common cross-cutting issues, strategies and priorities shared by gender perspectives and concerns.

Strategies are the result of the distortion of spatial and temporal issues caused by a functionalist approach according to which temporal articulations are reduced to spatial sequences. This typical attitude of modern architecture postulates the existence of marked definitions which attempt to delimit a proper place for architecture, against the existence of a usually threatening exteriority. The main character of the proper is autonomy, associated with a sense of mastery of time. An autonomous space is at the same time a readable space, which can be controlled. By contrast to this conception of strategy, a tactic is an action without a proper location, without exteriority, without autonomy.

The notion of action referred to here is an expanded definition of Hannah Arendt's usage.[21] Arendt's action is synonymous with agency which referrers to "who" acts—that is to say to the agent—rather than to "what" is the effect produced by action. Neither imposed by necessity nor by utility, action is the impulse to set something new in motion, to introduce change and novelty in the world, both through words and deeds. Arendt doesn't indulge in political metaphysics: "the political" is not an inherent quality of an action; it's rather a consequence of the conditions of living together with others, with a human plurality of unique beings. Therefore, action is always acted among the others, is an inter-action; it establishes relationships and is always in concert.[22] Its key components—freedom and plurality—link the notion to a participatory

muf architecture/art, *Pleasure Garden of the Utilities* (Stoke, 1998). The domestic and intimate dimension of the street.
PHOTO: COURTESY OF MUF ARCHITECTURE/ART

–>
muf architecture/art, *Altab Ali Park* (Whitechapel, Tower Hamlets, East London, 2011). View of the park and of its elements.
PHOTO: COURTESY OF MUF ARCHITECTURE/ART

Practice: architects as curators

As defined by the Oxford English Dictionary, practice is the "actual application or use of an idea, belief, or method, as opposed to the theory relating to it."[24] But the relationship between theory and practice is indeed more complex. Deleuze states that "Practice is a set of relays from one theoretical point to another, and theory is a relay from one practice to another."[25] Jane Rendell, referring to Deleuze's words, says that many feminist architectural practices consider only the useful and productive aspects of theory. It's possible to detect in the way these feminist practices dismiss the "traditional" role of the architect as the sole and undisputed producer/demiurge—pursued by working as curators, advisers, space activators, and other producers—a sort of delirious drift towards an expanded dimension of architecture, which calls into question what architecture is. Dismantling the paradigm of the building as the *conditio sine qua non* of architectural production, testing, and questioning some of the most consolidated and accepted categories of architectural practice (such as the role of the author, the concept of disciplinary boundaries, the gap between builders and theorists), many women architects have subverted the relationship between theory and practice, pointing out that writing, drawing, model-making, and designing are all specific forms of architectural thought and practice.[26] These approaches enable the production of spatial arrangements, whether built or not. Architects act as enablers for making changes and transformations possible: the project is therefore a process, an action taking place rather than a designed spatial solution. Architects as curators expands the traditional scope of architecture by imbuing the thinking and design process with issues from other disciplines (such as art, politics, social science, gender issues, philosophy), combining their approaches within an interdisciplinary methodology.

Redefining the Brief: muf architecture/art

Muf is a London-based collaborative practice founded in 1994 by Liza Fior, Katherine Clarke and Juliet Bidgood. Muf's works demonstrate the possibility of thinking differently about urban planning and the existence of more effective tools for directing (urban) design. Their feminist approach unfolds in the openness of the planning process in which the clients' brief is continuously questioned and renegotiated to make room for end users' needs and requirements. New modes of practice are tested and investigated; they suggest creative and inventive solutions that raise new questions rather than only offer design outcomes. Their attitude of questioning the brief has, on some occasions, brought the extreme—but ethical—situation of dissuading their clients from building. They believe that architecture without building is possible; going beyond the notion of the building as a single object, they believe that "buildings have edges that extend beyond their property line, that they are networks of relationships."[27]

dimension and to the city as a political organization of people living together rather than as a physical environment/space. The city, intended as the "public" realm *(polis)*—as opposed to the "private" sphere *(oikos)*—is, according to Arendt, the only specific setting for action. Feminists have long criticized both this rigid distinction and the agonistic dimension of her politics, pointing out that, since women, both in ancient Greece and in early bourgeois republics, were confined to the domestic realm alone, they were prevented from taking part in political life and public sphere, which were consequently ruled by individualistic and masculinist practices. If, on the one hand, Arendt's schematic private/public dichotomy is quite incompatible with contemporary late capitalist societies, where things are much more complex, on the other hand, it's possible to rescue Arendt for feminism just because of the concerted, pluralistic, participated dimension of her account of political action.[23]

Close ties can be created between the concept of "action in concert" and the methods, modes, and concerns of a gender-based approach to architecture and its relationship with the city, which blurs the traditional disciplinary role and mastery of the architect, focusing on the social production of space. The most challenging issue is to activate spatial potential rather than providing design solutions, thus making urban spaces a continuous project open to change and transformations.

In the "Shared Ground" project (1996–2001), in spite of the conflicts that emerged during the consultation process, the final design,[28] thanks to its "inclusive sensibility,"[29] was able to manage a great number of residents', visitors' and local workers' demands, matching their expectations. In the "Pleasure Garden of the Utilities" project (1998), a domestic and intimate dimension was implemented in the design of an urban space by inserting small-scale interventions. Ceramic benches were designed and manufactured by a fireclay team from the local Armitage Shanks factory in order to celebrate and make visible a local tradition. In the "Altab Ali Park" project (2011), muf planned on-site actions, such as painting, and other temporary transformations, involving both artists and inhabitants in the design of the park, stimulating awareness of their own cultural traditions. The site, from a cultural and historical point of view, was a multi-layered space made up of different—and often conflicted and divergent—constituents. Muf's work aimed at creating a homegrown shared space between generations and genders so that everyone could fully enjoy it as a positive and collective experience. The partners at muf in writing on the project state that "Use Predicts Use, making shared space as a means to test the emerging design."[30]

Activating Spaces: aaa
(atelier d'architecture autogérée)

Atelier d'architecture autogérée (aaa) is a Paris-based practice founded by Constantin Petcou and Doina Petrescu in 2001. It usually acts as a catalyst for participation; it operates as a platform and network for collaborative and participatory research and action, carried out together with other partners (NGOs, universities, institutions, artists and other specialists, end users). They create and provide an infrastructure that enables local residents to assume ownership of projects, which consists of the reactivation of disused and abandoned urban spaces that are converted into self-managed spaces.

aaa's "Passage 56" project (2006) embodies construction as a social and cultural action itself. An urban interstitial space in the east of Paris, which was a neglected passageway between two buildings, has been converted into a self-managed collective space, becoming a node inside a wider cultural network of vicinity, productive interaction, and proximity relationships.

The project has been conceived as removable. The bottom-up design approach began by gradually engaging local residents through their interaction with small temporary devices and mobile installations (shade canopies, information panels, exhibition panels showing local residents' ideas, small potted plants). Step-by-step, these objects were converted into the first construction inputs of the collaborative process of spatial reactivation. A number of participatory activities, which local residents could get engaged in, were carried out—including training sessions on green/eco construction techniques (such as energy

autonomy, recycling, and a compost laboratory) —in order to enable inhabitants and local organizations to manage the site on their own.

The "Ecobox project" (2001–2009) in the La Chapelle area of northern Paris—consisting of gardens made by using recycled materials— represents an example of a small-scale urban intervention aiming at developing a critical, creative, and active approach to misused and underused spaces. Aaa members were the initiators of this experience that involved local residents and external experts. After the initial activation of this space, local residents assumed responsibility to carry on transformation of the space and integrated activities on their own until they decided to relocate the garden elsewhere.

What is most striking about these methodologies is their tentative dimension and approach. Architects have gradually realized that the project, if intended as an erasure of what exists in order to pursue another reality based on abstract and deterministic models and quantifiable data, is an arbitrary and ruinous style and design exercise. Aaa act as activators of social interests and actions, taking care to leave enough room for users, residents, and collaborators to establish responsibility.

Conclusion

Our ordinary, everyday life activities take place within the framework of a dialogical dimension oscillating between two states: behaviors governed by rules often merge with those shaped by contingencies. The preparation for actions implies the production of plans, but due to the growing complexity of contemporary life the static and traditional notion of plan needs to be expanded to encompass the possibility of change. In a similar manner, if architecture wishes to substantiate its contribution to today's challenges, it should transform the way it has always performed in front of reality. It should overcome the impossibility of architectural forms and morphology to accommodate urban scale and the complexity of urban spaces by rethinking plans and projects not so much as a design instruments and close-off

atelier d'architecture autogérée (aaa), *Passage 56* / Eco-interstice (Paris, 2006). PHOTO: COURTESY OF ATELIER D'ARCHITECTURE AUTOGERÉE

systems, but rather as evolving processes and devices that allow the unpredictable to take place. The openness to change should become an inherent quality of design, being embedded into it; emphasis should be put on both the final product and the process, beyond a traditional object-driven design. The complicated and unresolved relationship between ideology, theory, practice and our present concerns in relation to the city openly defy the conventional disciplinary boundaries and the operational scopes of architecture.

Our understanding of urban spaces is often based on the experience of segregated and controlled spaces, which we used in an almost mechanical way. But space is more than a physical product: it is generated by emotions and shaped by affective relations and dialogue. In my opinion, thinking deliriously can mediate (even though not conciliate) the discrepancy between the specificity/partiality of the project and the incompleteness of the city, that is to say the social consciousness of its necessary and continual process of re-structuring. It's impossible to master space completely. The project requires narrowing its field of action in order to be put into practice, being obliged to mark its boundaries, but there is a new awareness of their tentative and uncertain dimension.

Gender spatial practices implement delirious tactics, which encourage inhabitants, users and other producers' actions. Their works are able to enhance the hidden potentialities of contexts and people, changing both spaces and subjects involved. On the one hand, while working at the coalface of practice, women architects actively devote themselves to create exchange-based relations in order to transform, undermine, and subvert norms, rules and received meanings. On the other hand, representing the interface between final users and authorities/institutions, they become deeply and often emotionally entangled in the transformations and processes they are fostering. These examples are prototypes that cannot be replicated anywhere, but similar protocols, agendas, and processes could be adapted to new contexts, and new forms of governance and management could be invented in order to foster a more ethic and sustainable use of urban space.

Serafina Amoroso is an Italian architect. After graduating in 2001 in Florence, where she began to develop her first professional contacts, in 2006 she got a PhD degree in Reggio Calabria. Between 2011 and 2012, she obtained a Master degree in Advanced Architectural Design in Madrid (ETSAM). She is currently working in Florence as a lecturer under contract in an architectural design studio and as a middle school teacher.

Notes

1 Jane Rendell, "A Way with Words: Feminists Writing Architectural Design Research," in *Design research in architecture: an overview*, ed. Murray Fraser (Burlington: Ashgate, 2014), 119.
2 See: Jane Rendell, "Critical Spatial Practices: Setting Out a Feminist Approach to some Modes and what Matters in Architecture," in *Feminist Practices: Interdisciplinary Approaches to Women in Architecture*, ed. Lori A. Brown (Surrey and Burlington: Ashgate Publishing Limited, 2011), 17-57.
3 Teresa Stoppani, "Delirium and Historical project," *Thesis, Wissenschaftliche Zeitschrift der Bauhaus-Universität Weimar, Heft 4* (2003): 22-29.
4 Tafuri's "historical project" defines the historical space of "production" of ideas (both theoretical an historical) where complexity and multiple meanings are allowed in order to question continuously its own limits. The historical project is an open-ended issue, a work to be continued. It isn't an *ex post* discourse or finite (hi)story of the past; it's a project made up of many possible "provisional constructions" continuously re-engaging with the present, being embedded and implied in it. See: Manfredo Tafuri, *The Sphere and the Labyrinth—Avant-Gardes and Architecture from Piranesi to the 1970s* (Cambridge: The MIT Press, 1987).
5 Jean-Jacques Lecercle, *Philosophy through the Looking Glass: Language, nonsense, desire* (London: Hutchinson, 1985), 44-45.
6 Jennifer Bloomer, *Architecture and the text: the (s)crypts of Joyce and Piranesi* (New Haven: Yale University Press, 1993), 120.
7 Fernando Colina, "Diez tesis sobre el saber delirante," *Revista de la Asociación Española de Neuropsiquiatría*, vol. 4, no. 9, 1984: 35.
8 See: Chaïm Perelman and Lucie Olbrecht-Tyteca, *The new rhetoric: A treatise on argumentation*, trans. John Wilkinson and Purcell Weaver (Notre Dame: University of Notre Dame Press, 1969).
9 Jane Rendell, "Critical Spatial Practices: Setting Out a Feminist Approach to some Modes and what Matters in Architecture," in *Feminist Practices: Interdisciplinary Approaches to Women in Architecture*, ed. Lori A. Brown (Surrey and Burlington: Ashgate Publishing Limited, 2011), 17-57.
10 Liza Fior (muf architecture/art), e-mail to author, March 10-11, 2014.
11 Katja Grillner, "Design Research and Critical Transformations: situating thought, projecting action" in *Design Research in Architecture: An Overview*, ed. Murray Fraser (Burlington: Ashgate, 2014), 89.
12 Despina Stratigakos, "Why architects need Feminism," *Design Observer*, http://places.designobserver.com/feature/why-architects-need-feminism/35448/.
13 Such as Edward Soja's "spatial triad," borrowed from Henri Lefebvre, and David Harvey's "right to the city." See: Edward Soja, *Postmodern Geographies: The Reassertion of Space in Social Theory* (London: Verso, 1989); David Harvey, *The Condition of Postmodernity* (Oxford: Blackwell, 1989); David Harvey, "The Right to the City," in *The Emancipatory City?: Paradoxes and Possibilities*, ed. Loretta Lees (London: SAGE Publications Ltd., 2004), 236-240.
14 Such as: a commitment to the competition for egalitarian rights to inhabit space; a critical, casual, explanatory and interpretative approach to reality; the awareness of the plural, unstable dimensions of the construction of identities (class, sexuality, gender, religion, race), whose more or less invisible boundaries need to be constantly contested and renegotiated.
15 Michel de Certeau, *The Practice of Everyday Life*, trans. Steven Rendall (Berkeley: University of California Press, 1984), 29-30.
16 Ibid., 29.
17 Henri Lefebvre, *The Production of Space*, trans. Donald Nicholson-Smith (Oxford: Blackwell, 1991), 38.
18 Ibid., 40.
19 de Certeau, 38.
20 de Certeau, 38.
21 For the philosopher Hannah Arendt, "action" is one of the three essential conditions of our being-in-the-world and the highest realization of the "vita activa." See: Hannah Arendt, *The Human Condition* (Chicago: Chicago University Press, 1958).
22 See: Bonnie Honig, "Toward an Agonistic Feminism: Hannah Arendt and the Politics of Identity," in *Feminist Interpretations of Hannah Arendt*, ed. Bonnie Honig (University Park: Penn State Press, 1995), 156-160.
23 Arendt's rise of the "social," provoked by the blurring of boundaries between public and private, has been further demoted to bureaucracy and conformity, which erase plurality turning individuals into passive recipients of administrative tasks and compliances. Citizens have become consumers and the social realm has been transformed into a surveillance and voyeuristic society.
24 Oxford Dictionary, http://www.oxforddictionaries.com.
25 Michel Foucault and Gilles Deleuze, "Intellectuals and power: a conversation between Michel Foucault and Gilles Deleuze," in *Language, Counter-memory, Practice: Selected Essays and Interviews*, ed. Michel Foucault and Donald F. Bouchard (Ithaca: Cornell University Press, 1977), 206.
26 See: Francesca Hughes, ed., *The Architect: Reconstructing Their Practice* (Cambridge, Mass.: The MIT Press, 1996).
27 Florian Heilmeyer, "muf architecture/art, Interview," http://www.baunetz.de/talk/crystal/index.php?lang=en&cat=Profil&nr=27.
28 At first, muf were commissioned to design a one hundred meter-long pilot project, consisting of the creation of a footway equipped with lighting, planting and urban furniture on the sunny side of a street, whose generous width was obtained winning back space to the detriment of the traffic lane; later, money were found to redesign the remaining six hundred meters.
29 See: Ellis Woodman, "Architecture: Southwark: walking back to happiness," http://www.independent.co.uk/arts-entertainment/architecture-southwark-walking-back-to-happiness-1085327.html.
30 Muf architecture/art, "Altab Ali Park," http://www.muf.co.uk/portfolio/altab-ali-park.

HELLINIKON AND THE QUESTION OF THE LARGE URBAN VOID

Aristodimos Komninos

Aristodimos Komninos

"The effort to reclaim the city is the struggle of democracy itself"
—Michael Sorkin[1]

Since the 2008 economic crisis, the privatization of public land has found traction across the struggling European South. Greece is leading in privatization of public land in Southern Europe, and Athens' former airport, Hellinikon, is one of the most debated recent examples.[2] This design project examines the processes behind the private development and explores an alternative model of urbanization based on radical forms of collective governance through urban design.

The rapid transformation of urban space is one of the most critical problems arising from capitalist crises and affects the post-crisis generation's use of space. Investments that occur during recession periods, because of their fast-tracked and highly deregulated development, offer little, if any, relief to the real economy. The result is often the widening of social inequity and an exploitation of the natural environment. For instance, during the recent state fire sale in Greece, the Canadian mining company Eldorado Gold Corporation acquired 26.4 hectares of land in Skouries, Greece for extracting gold.[3] This region of rare natural beauty (a Natura 2000 site) is an invaluable natural asset and serves as an integral part of the native touristic product.[4] According to a recent report from the School of Agriculture in Thessaloniki, the ongoing mining operations will trigger long-term and irreversible damages to the natural systems and agricultural activity, thus undermining the future of the area and the wellbeing of its inhabitants.[5, 6]

In the midst of the current economic crisis, prime urban land and their voids are threatened by development. Ten kilometers south of downtown Athens, along a four-kilometer stretch of Aegean coastline, lays Hellinikon, the former international airport of Athens that ceased operations in 2001. Fourteen years of government commitment for the development of a public Metropolitan Park were eventually cast aside by privatization efforts and consequent acquisition in 2013 by a multi-national investment conglomerate. The sale of Hellinikon triggered many reactions regarding the legitimacy and transparency of the privatization tender. The primary argument behind these claims was that the state revenues were far lower than the original estimates, calling into question the neoliberal

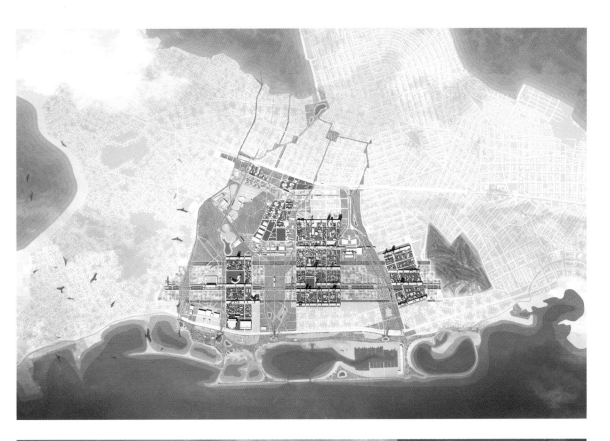

TRADING SPINE /
OLD RUNWAY

URBAN
PATCHES

AGRICULTURAL
BELT

THE COLLECTIVE
SUPERSTRUCTURE

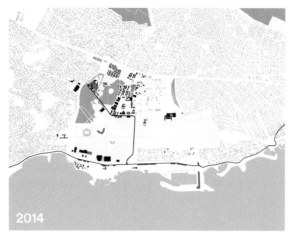

2014

2020

2035

2050

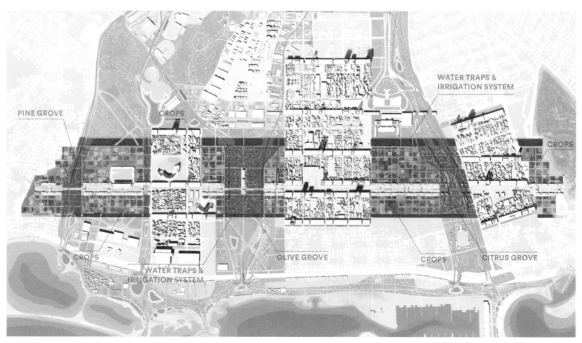

PINE GROVE

CROPS

WATER TRAPS & IRRIGATION SYSTEM

CROPS

CROPS

OLIVE GROVE

CROPS

CITRUS GROVE

WATER TRAPS & IRRIGATION SYSTEM

2014:
Current state on the
site with red indicating
the active buildings
and areas, including the
urban farm, the social
clinic, the aviation
museum, the air-traffic
control tower, some
sporting facilities, the
tram's terminal station
and some scarce admin-
istrative buildings.

2020:
In the next phase,
squadrons occupy
inactive buildings on
the north sector of
the site and establish
the first community,
creating scarce agri-
cultural plots.

2035:
The urban patches
expand, building up
successive rows of new
community centers.
Squadrons occupy exis-
ting Olympic venues and
airport facilities, and
transform them into the
civic buildings for the
community. The tramline
reaches the third patch,
and the waterfront
continues to evolve.

2050:
The community reaches
its maximum capacity,
the waterfront park
is completed, and
the collective super-
structure enters its final
steady-state phase.

Bottom:
The agricultural belt
is a strip of farming
land deployed along the
airport's former runway,
and is the main tool
for the community's
self-sufficiency in food.
The agricultural belt
is able to sustain
a community of seven
thousand people.

->
View of the community
center and the adjacent
public space.

competitiveness of privatizing state assets.[7, 8] Even more troubling, how-ever, was the proposed multi-million euro investment in luxury housing, boutique retail, yacht marinas, and casinos, announced by the new owner of Hellinikon. With unemployment at thirty percent and an abandoned downtown district, the city has immediate needs for affordable housing, health care facilities, and large open spaces.

Historically urban voids, whether abandoned buildings or vacant lots, have acted as breeding grounds for social activism and grassroots movements.[9] In 2010, environmental activists in West London founded the Grow Heathrow movement and occupied the site of Heathrow's future runway as a reaction against the environmental threat posed by the airport's expansion.[10] Similarly, and long before Hellinikon's sale in 2013, a handful of people reclaimed the former airport site as a platform for social prosperity through acts such as voluntary tree planting as well as the founding of a community clinic, a civil aviation museum, and an informal cooperative urban farm.[11] Despite these initiatives falling short of providing a holistic viable solution of equal force to combat the model of privatization, their emergence and resilience have raised critical questions about the appropriate uses of public urban land.

The Collective Superstructure

This proposal is predicated on the belief that a coalescence of social action with radical urban design can transform large urban voids into an alternative space that questions traditional developmental practices. The scenario of this design proposal assumes the scaling-up of bottom-up practices in Hellinikon and investigates the manifestation of the shift from grassroots movements to an organized autonomous community, described here as the collective superstructure. Autonomy, as defined by contemporary Greek philosopher Cornelius Castoriadis, is the condition of creating one's own laws and is the basis of a truly democratic society.[12] In contrast, heteronomy, is the appropriation of this authority by extra-social institutions. In the case of Hellinikon, heteronomy aligns with the ongoing privatization agenda whereas autonomy engenders the possibility of a new community with the capacity to define its social and spatial being—its self-institution. The role of the collective superstructure is to provide the spatial platform for the new community's self-institution. It utilizes the physical, social, and natural infrastructure currently found on Hellinikon as a departure point for the design of the new community that is based on two strategies: urban autonomy and environmental resiliency.[13]

Urban Autonomy

This project identifies local self-sufficiency in and the provision of social services as the pillars towards urban autonomy. Drawing inspiration from the Metropolitan Community clinic and the cooperative urban farm in Hellinikon, this project envisions the expansion of this social and production model, enabling equal access to food, housing, and employment, as well as a safe urban environment.

**URBAN PATCH AND
THE COMMUNITY CENTER**

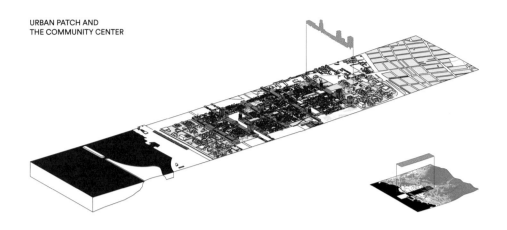

**ANALYSIS OF COMMUNITY CENTERS'
DEFENSIVE MECHANISMS**

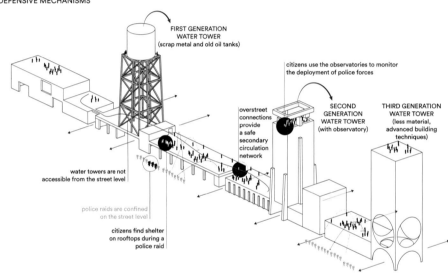

FIRST GENERATION
WATER TOWER
(scrap metal and old oil tanks)

citizens use the observatories to monitor
the deployment of police forces

overstreet
connections
provide
a safe
secondary
circulation
network

SECOND
GENERATION
WATER TOWER
(with observatory)

THIRD GENERATION
WATER TOWER
(less material,
advanced building
techniques)

water towers are not
accessible from the street level

police raids are confined
on the street level

citizens find shelter
on rooftops during a
police raid

**WATER MANAGEMENT SYSTEM
SECTION ALONG THE URBAN PATCH**

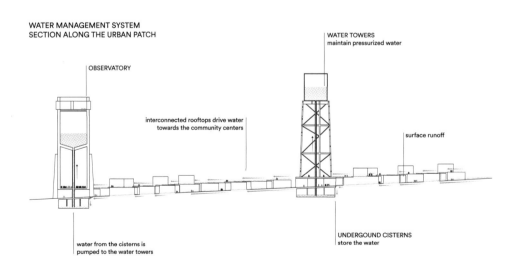

OBSERVATORY

WATER TOWERS
maintain pressurized water

interconnected rooftops drive water
towards the community centers

surface runoff

water from the cisterns is
pumped to the water towers

UNDERGOUND CISTERNS
store the water

Environmental Resiliency

The critical location and scale of the site as well as its decommissioned facilities provide an opportunity for a large-scale environmental strategy. This strategy is driven by the intention to reconnect the nearby mountain to the waterfront through public parks and green corridors. Not only does this gesture provide the community with natural resources for its self-sufficiency, but it also returns to the city the long-anticipated Metropolitan Park while protecting an accessible waterfront. With this as a starting point, the design proposal re-imagines the abandoned airport buildings as the community's administrative and cultural facilities. Moreover, extensions of existing transportation networks and the re-use of the former runway are proposed to establish a domestic transportation system that ties the community back to the city of Athens. Accordingly, the new urban and social construct does not remain an enclave, but rather extends its influence to the existing city.

More often than not, urban utopias avoid the clash between the existing and alternative city. Renowned examples of utopian settlements such as Drop City in Colorado, or Auroville in India—both built far away from existing cities or towns—vividly illustrate the shortcoming of ideal cities to address pressing problems of the neoliberal urban age. The collective superstructure asserts that developing utopian urban models away from current social realities is not enough. It is also necessary that new models of living are built by scaling up practices emerging from the city itself. With Athens' protagonist role to the never-ending drama of the Eurozone crisis, Hellinikon seems to set the ideal stage. And while its recent privatization seemed like the final act, the collective superstructure aims to offer a counter model. Rather than seeking supranational solutions to questions related to the urban topos, this urban design narrative claims that the answer lies with the post-crisis cities and the active local communities.

Aristodimos Komninos is an architect, researcher and educator. His works mainly reflect on the relationship between political and formal aspects of the architecture of the city.

Notes

1 Michael Sorkin, *Variations on a Theme Park: The New American City and the End of Public Space* (New York: Hill and Wang, 1992), XV.
2 A Publication of Privatization Barometer, "The PB Report 2013 /2014" (2013), http://www.privatization barometer.net/PUB/NL/5/3/PB_AR 2013-2014.pdf.
3 Evangelia Apostolopoulou and William M. Adams, "Neoliberal Capitalism and Conservation in the Post-Crisis Era: The Dialectics of 'Green' and 'Un-Green' Grabbing in Greece and the UK," *Antipode* 47, no. 1 (January 1, 2015): 15–35.
4 Hellenic Ornithological Society, "Our National Heritage at a Bargain Price," http://www.ornithologiki.gr/ page_cn.php?tID=79183&aID=1461.
5 Apostolos Apostolidis et al., "Report of the Teaching and Research

Faculty Board of the School of Agriculture of the Aristotle University of Thessaloniki" (Aristotle University of Thessaloniki, School of Agriculture, 2012), 17, https://soshalkidiki.files. wordpress.com/2012/11/geoponiki.pdf.
6 Naomi Klein, *This Changes Everything: Capitalism vs. the Climate* (Toronto: Simon and Schuster, 2014).
7 The Press Project, "Anti-Corruption Prosecutor Launches Investigation into Privatisation Deal for Former Airport," http://www.thepressproject.net/ article/70508/.
8 Klaus Busch, et al., "Euro Crisis, Austerity Policy and the European Social Model," http://www.academia. edu/download/30582208/austerity_ policies_and_the_esm.pdf.
9 Claire Colomb, "Pushing the Urban Frontier: Temporary Uses of Space,

City Marketing, and the Creative City Discourse in 2000s Berlin," *Journal of Urban Affairs* 34, no. 2 (May 1, 2012): 131–52.
10 Sarah Dooling and Gregory Simon, *Cities, Nature and Development: The Politics and Production of Urban Vulnerabilities* (Burlington: Ashgate Publishing, Ltd., 2012), 121–123.
11 Polina Prentou, "More Athenian Sociospatial Injustice in the Works? Creating a Metropolitan Park at the Former Hellinikon International Airport of Athens" (AESOP 26th Annual Congress, Ankara, Turkey, 2012).
12 "An Interview with C. Castoriadis," *Telos*, no. 23 (April 1, 1975): 131–55.
13 Aristodimos Komninos, "Hellinikon and the Question of the Large Urban Void" (SMArchS Thesis, Massachusetts Institute of Technology—School of Architecture and Planning, 2013).

BORDERLANDS: AN EXPLOITATION OF THE U.S. POLITICAL GEOGRAPHY

Cesar Lopez

The El Paso and Ciudad Juarez borderland is a trans-national metro-politan region situated around the faint trickle of the Rio Grande River, which demarcates the boundary between the United States and Mexico. Throughout history, these two cities have thrived as a closely-tied community; forging bonds through a shared culture and an integrated economy of trade and local commerce.[1] However, today the region is among the most contentious in the Americas as a vicious drug war sub-sumes Ciudad Juarez. This has transformed Ciudad Juarez into one of the most dangerous cities in the world, while El Paso has simultaneously stagnated. A robust political geography led by a unilateral approach to the United States border security has severed the two cities; producing economic, social, and environmental issues that challenge the equilibrium this borderland has relied on.[2] A series of actions can be drawn from the historical moments that have led to the aggressive enforcement of the El Paso–Ciudad Juarez border with the aim of reversing and restructuring the United States-Mexico political geography into an accessible region for trans-border residents, commuters, and trade.

Before the territory was complicated with settlement, the Rio Grande River naturally divided the region into a north and south bank, making it the nexus of continual boundary claims. Throughout the 1800s, these banks became subject to Spanish governance, the First and Second Mexican Empires, the United Mexican States, the Texas Republic, and briefly, the republican forces of the exiled Mexican government. Although the Rio Grande River was declared the official boundary in 1848, effectively demarcating the northern bank as United States territory and the southern bank as Mexican territory, disputes and revolutions still continued well into the twentieth century.[3] The sense of ambiguity created by the various changes in governance allowed the region to develop strong cultural and economic ties that remained unaltered by the emerging political geography.

When prohibition struck in the 1920s and 1930s, El Paso became a major port of entry for smuggled liquor originating from Ciudad Juarez. Acknowledging the minimal border security, the United States began to enforce the region's first real border policies that reified in the forms of physical artifacts, which divided the territory with check points, walls,

The hydrological character of the Rio Grande River—traced historic river paths that led to the Chamizal Dispute (Fig.01a); the Rio Grande River and watershed—transition from river to political boundary (Fig.01b); the regulating system of dams restraining the Rio Grande River's natural hydrological cycles (Fig.01c).

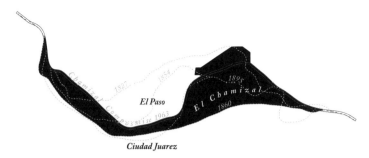

Fig01A: Rio Grande River & The Chamizal Dispute

Fig01B: Rio Grande River Watershed & Territory

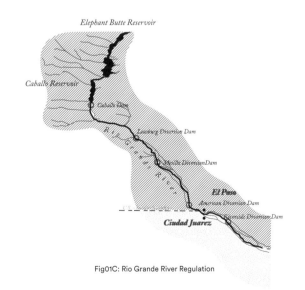

Fig01C: Rio Grande River Regulation

and fences. Despite the spatial robustness of the separation, circum-venting flows of people and goods still persisted. In fact, national differences in law positioned Ciudad Juarez as a popular destination to experience what was considered illicit and immoral activities in the United States.[4]

Concurrently, the Rio Grande River's dynamic hydrological cycles caused major flooding, which constantly re-adjusted the river's path, thus making a static legal boundary unobtainable. By 1873, the river/border migrated south, defecting over six hundred acres of Mexican land to the United States. The uncovered territory was named El Chamizal and its incorporation into the United States was contested in courts for several decades. In 1963, the United States and Mexico agreed to split the El Chamizal land and channelize the Rio Grande River to solidify an artificial divide between El Paso and Ciudad Juarez.[5] Due to these actions, the river is now a drought-ridden trickle that, with further channelization, is prone to completely drying up—endangering dependent reservoirs and production.[6]

By the late twentieth century, El Paso and Ciudad Juarez shared an integrated economy through trade and a trans-border labor market. The large volume of daily commuters and tourists proved to be one of the most critical interactions between the two cities.[7] However, when the outbreak of the Mexican cartel war occurred in 2008, claiming 5,400 lives; the steady rhythm of crime Ciudad Juarez had always been known for, quickly escalated to a violent insurgence of weapon- and narco-trafficking. As a result, many Ciudad Juarez residents and businesses decamped to El Paso, leaving behind a sea of abandoned homes, buildings, and public spaces.[8] The vacancies have since become the breeding ground for the Mexican cartel's colonization of Ciudad Juarez, occupying buried voids within the centers of city blocks to obtain seclusion from the public and law enforcement. The U.S. State Department reacted to the violence by dissuading casual crossing into Mexico and, over time, enforced strict unilateral border policies that limited Ciudad Juarez resident's from entering El Paso. This had the affect of drastically reducing the social and physical contact needed to sustain the trans-border economy each city had become dependent on.[9]

Fig02 A: Territorial Operation I

Fig02 B: Territorial Operation II

Fig02 C: Territorial Operation III

Territorial Operations I, II & III disables the American Diversion Dam immediately located upstream from central El Paso-Ciudad Juarez, expanding and dupli-cating the Rio Grande River's boundary through vacant struc-tures to create an extra-territorial space.

Borderlands is a proposal that leverages the El Chamizal dispute as a precedent to explore the reconfiguration the river-border between El Paso and Ciudad Juarez, with the aim of constructing a territorial gray-space. To address the rigid boundary and the regulated river system, the abandoned structures are considered as potential hosts to an expanded river network, thus erasing the negligent spaces while multiplying the border. A deregulated Rio Grande River could, in time, be restored to its natural ecological state through a series of hydrological cycles, while blurring the border throughout the region. In order to re-activate the watershed and protect surrounding reservoirs and production, the Rio Grande River must be dechannelized while a system of tributaries is constructed to facilitate the river's natural hydrological cycles. Over time, the river's diminished ecosystem can be reversed, producing new biodiversity through riparian edges, recharged grasslands, and bosques.[10] While these actions primarily seek to keep the Rio Grande River and its ecology from further deterioration, they will also resituate the border from a singular static line to a field of duplicated and overlapping boundaries.

Meanwhile, as the river's footprint increases, it will require additional tributaries to protect the surrounding cities from flooding. The demands for space to facilitate the increasing number of tributaries serve as an opportunity to reverse Ciudad Juarez's cartel colonization, by rezoning abandoned structures. New policies enacted by border patrol agencies could deploy the removal of concealing walls, barriers, and entire structures, thus exposing the hidden spaces of the cartel trafficking network. The International Water and Boundary Commission, responsible for the Rio Grande Rivers maintenance, can excavate the uncovered grounds, reinforce the remaining context to act as channel walls, and used them to circulate the river's expanded form; transforming the collection of cartel-run spaces into a river network. Although, the Mexican cartel is resilient and will always find methods to operate, the intent of these design strategies is to eradicate their hidden occupations thereby offering a new way to self-police the city's vacant spaces. This will give way to a new era of unfettered access, as any subsequent increase to border security will need to integrate the multiple crossings and its commuting publics.

Public space can now be expanded into the river/border tributaries revealing multiple ways to circumnavigate the border region, reestablishing a contiguous landscape that promotes the trans-border activities. These spaces could become migration routes, gathering spaces, black markets, as well as ecological habitats, whereas other areas could potentially become exploited—thus returning to its historic character. While acknowledging that these spaces may present their own vices, these actions succeed in diversifying public use outside of the strict political definition of space. The success in the flow of goods and exchanges, whether they are legitimate or otherwise, has always relied upon the circumvention of the geography. The gray-space leverages

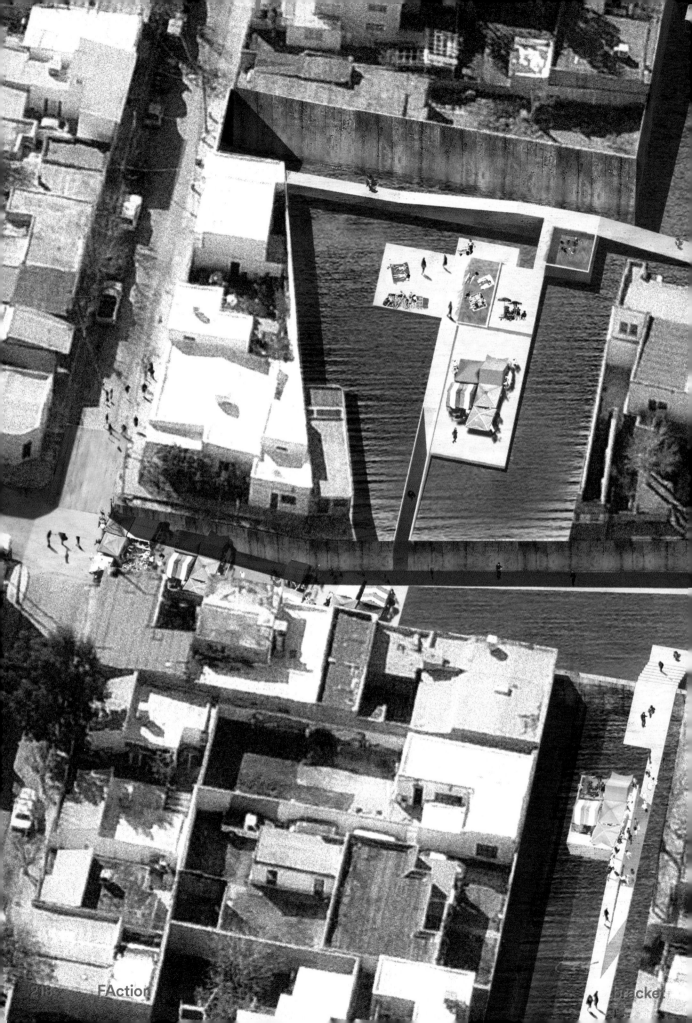

FAction

bracket

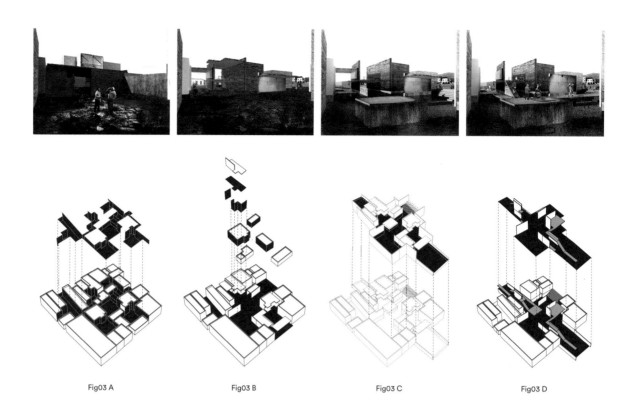

Fig03 A   Fig03 B   Fig03 C   Fig03 D

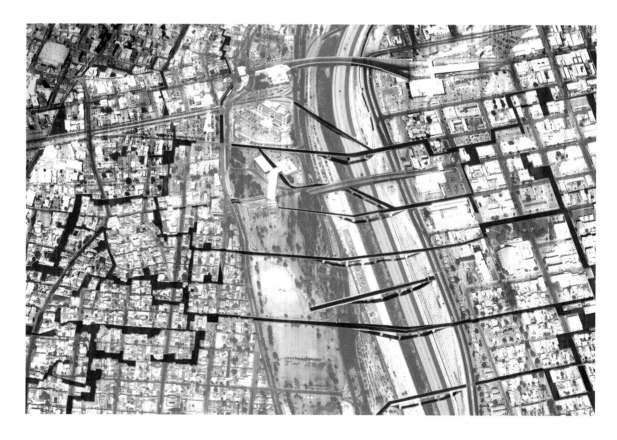

A series of architectural acts are employed to subvert and repurpose negligent vacant structures to facilitate the increasing number of Rio Grande River tributaries and circulation for trans-border publics.

The imposition of the Rio Grande River's natural hydrological cycles produce a gradient of territory as the U.S./Mexico boundary is expanded into a gray-space.

a platform that allows these publics to reprise an economic empowerment that was maintained even through a riddled history of territorial claims.

The resuscitation of the Rio Grande River and the diversion of seasonal hydrological flows through reclaimed delinquent spaces creates a blurred border, an altered state, which enables new ways to conceive the political geography and its devices. Moving from a line to space, a new sense of contact through unaffiliated spaces allows the trans-border publics to re-engage in social and economic exchanges. Despite the fact that an El Paso–Ciudad Juarez border will always exist, overlaying the complexities of a natural river on the boundary creates an experience that no longer affirms separation. *Borderlands* subverts the devices that separated the region—river, channel, and barrier—and reconfigures them into a dispersed experience in which one is always crossing borders.

Cesar Lopez is a designer at The Open Workshop and Studio VARA in San Francisco, California. His work focusses on the parallels between urbanism and political structures.

Notes

1 John F Dulles, "Impacts of Federal Immigration Law Enforcement on Border Communities" *Federal Immigration Law Enforcement in the Southwest: Civil Rights Impacts on Border Communities* (Darby, Pennsylvania: Diane Pub, 1997), 12-21.
2 Robert Buffington, "Prohibition in the Borderlands: National Government—Border Community Relationships," *Pacific Historical Review* 63, no. 1 (1994): 19.
3 Wilbert H. Timmons and David J. Weber, *El Paso: A Borderlands History* (El Paso, Texas: Texas Western Press, 1990), 74-75.
4 Oscar J. Martinez, "Prohibition and Depression in Ciudad Juarez-El Paso," in *U.S.–Mexico Borderlands: Historical and* .

Contemporary Perspectives (Wilmington, Delaware: Scholarly Resources, 1996), 151-152.
5 Gladys Gregory and Sheldon B. Liss, "CHAMIZAL DISPUTE," *Handbook of Texas Online,* Texas State Historical Association (June 12, 2010), http://www.tshaonline.org/handbook/online/articles/nbc01)
6 Roger A. Dural, Jean W. Parcher, Dennis G. Woodward, "A Descriptive Overview of the Rio Grande-Rio Bravo Watershed," *Journal of Transboundary Water Resources*, vol. 1 (February 2010): 159-177.
7 Gordon Hanson, "U.S.–Mexico Integration and Regional Economics: Evidence from Border Pairs," *Journal of Urban Economics*, vol. 50 (2001): 259-287.

8 Bowden, Charles, and Julia Cardona, *Murder City: Ciudad Juárez and the Global Economy's New Killing Fields* (New York: Nation Books, 2010), 111, 204, 235.
9 Cesar M. Fuéntes and Serjio Péna, "Globalization, Transborder Networks, and U.S.-Mexico Border Cities," in *Cities and Citizenship at the U.S.–Mexico Border: The Paso Del Norte Metropolitan Region*, ed. Kathleen A. Staudt, Julia E. Monarrez Fragoso, and Cesar M. Fuentes (New York: Palgrave Macmillan, 2010), 1-20.
10 Kevin Bixby (Executive Director of the Southwest Environmental Center in Las Cruces, New Mexico) in discussion with the author, January 2013.

InAction is a way of acting by not-acting. From squatting and loitering to waiting lands, in particular contexts, inaction has proven to be an effective way to sidestep, undermine, or identify loopholes within a system. How might design engage socio-political change with the least means necessary?

AC
TION

PRODUCTION/ REPRODUCTION: HOW TO LIVE TOGETHER

Pier Vittorio Aureli and Martino Tattara (Dogma)

The modern capitalist city has historically been planned and built by establishing spatial and juridical pairs, such as public and private or production and reproduction.[1] Many scholars and social movements, such as the feminist movement, have often challenged this division.[2] In recent years, we have become increasingly interested in domestic space, as it is a space that enables us to move beyond these pairings, thus positioning it—oppositely to what it is usually thought of—as the core space of politics and production.

We think of domestic space as a political space because, more than any other space, it best represents the *ethos*, or the "habitual"[3], namely a pattern of daily routines that defines the formal structure of life. For this reason, domestic space can be assumed as the most accurate seismographer of the political condition of our time. Furthermore, with capitalism, reproductive labor has been split off—relegated to a separate, private domestic sphere—which has obscured its social importance. Social reproduction—the forms of provisioning, caregiving, and interaction that produce and maintain social bonds—forms capitalism's human subjects, their *habitus*, and the socio-ethical substance. These activities are absolutely necessary to the functioning of capitalism and, as such, are an indispensable background condition for the possibility of capitalist production.

Despite the constitutive necessity of the social reproduction for capitalist production, or precisely because of it, within the rise of the modern city, domestic space has been reduced to an appendix of the workplace, reinforcing its role as a refuge from the harsh and promiscuous reality of work and as a retreat from production. In reality, the house is the very core of production since a population can be productive only if life is maintained and reproduced. For this reason, the advent of "immaterial labor"[4], or a labor that produces the informational and cultural content of a commodity and thus expands production far beyond the traditional workplace, makes domestic space the epicenter of production. Within immaterial labor, essential human faculties such as language, affect, and the entire spectrum of social relationships, become a means of production, while production and reproduction are no longer just complementary conditions but overlapping. It is within immaterial production that Marx's definition of labor as "labor power" (labor not as a finished product, but as potential) gains truth; labor is the aggregate of those mental and physical capabilities existing in the physical form—the living personality—of a human being.[5] Immaterial labor is not just a new form of production, it is rather the emergence of a latent condition: life itself as production.

In the *Grundrisse* (1857–61), Marx addresses capital's exploitation of not just the physical power of the body, but of the general social knowledge spread throughout society and embodied in each individual, what he referred to as the "general intellect"—the diffused social knowledge of

Fontenelle Monastery,
9th Century

1 Church
2 Narthex
3 Dorter
4 Camera
5 Refectory
6 Cellar
7 Archive
8 Library

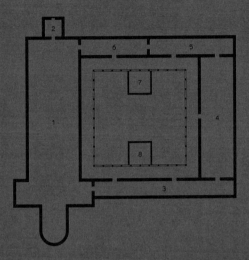

0   30m

society. He goes beyond the designation of the worker as labor power (or living labor), revealing instead a future that has become our present: the subsumption of society into productive powers for capital, which involves the incorporation of all subjective potential, the capacity to communicate, to feel, to create, to think, or to establish relationships. Production takes place outside of the factory or the office and now situates itself in various social relationships. This is why these relationships, their organization in space, and the *ethos* they produce are not only important, but the quintessential element to understand if we are to identify new modes of living that can counter the effects of capitalism.

In what follows, we propose a critical survey of domestic spaces where the overlapping of living and working becomes manifest. By doing so, these domestic spaces counter dichotomous conditions such as private/public, living/working, production/reproduction. The examples are often expressed through specific architectural spaces, while sometimes they exist in the form of dwelling that can appropriate existing spaces. Even within their controversial nature, these experimental models of organizing domestic space lead to modes of living together and thus to alternative ways to organize the political.

Monastery
The modern movement transformed the house from a symbolic space into what Le Corbusier defined as a "machine for living." Interestingly, this vision of domestic space was rooted in the architecture of a pre-industrial institution: the monastery. It is well known that Le Corbusier's rationalization of living space was greatly inspired by his fascination for monastic life. During his formative *voyage d'Orient*, Le Corbusier not only spent three months in the monastery of Mount Athos but also visited the Carthusian Monastery of Val d'Ema near Florence, which deeply influenced his vision of living space.[6]

Monasteries were not built for contemplation alone, but also as an apparatus to regulate life in all its physical and mental aspects. Within the monastery, one's entire existence, including laboring activities, were considered an *opus dei*. The organization of living and working became the focus of an unprecedented meticulous organization, which anticipated disciplinary institutions such as the school and the modern factory. Every order defined a form of life clearly prescribed according to a rule, that is to say, a precise program. The goal of this organization was not to replace life with abstract standards or schedules (such as our daily routines) but rather, to make the rule so consistent to life that the rule would almost disappear.[7] This aspect of monasticism is made evident in the simplest monastic rule ever presented, which is Augustine's *dilige et quod vis fac* ("love and do what you want"). Unlike the logic of disciplinary institutions that were inspired by the rigor of monastic life, within the latter the

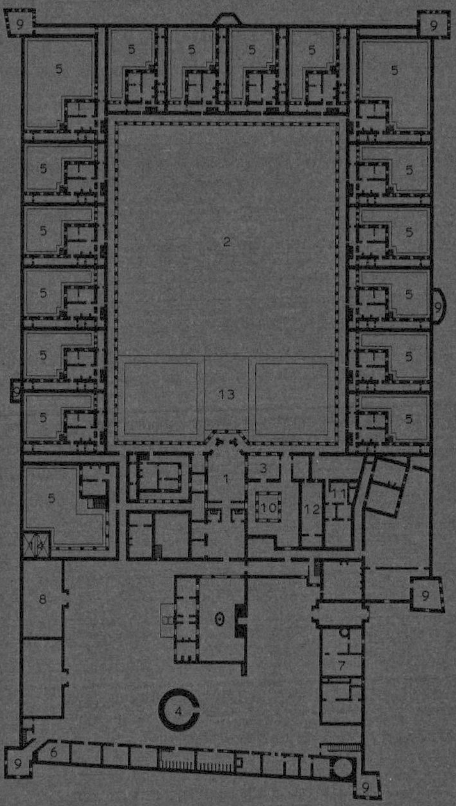

The Carthusian
Monastery

1 Church
2 Great Cloister
3 Chapter House
4 Dovecote
5 Individual Cells
  with Gardens
6 Stables and Rooms
  of Laymen
7 Guest-House
8 Barns
9 Watch Towers
10 Small Cloister
11 Kitchen
12 Refectory
13 Cemetery
14 Prison

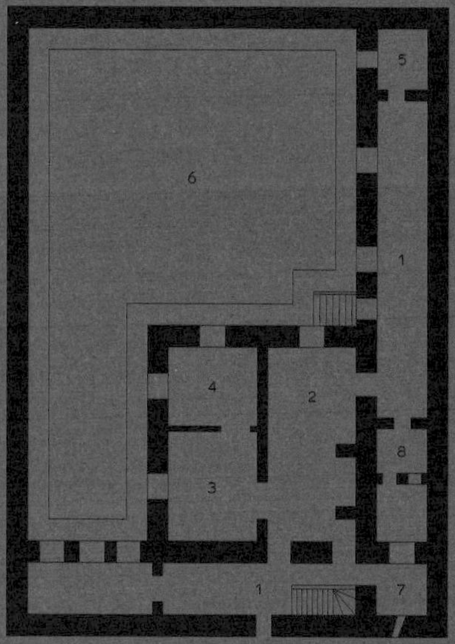

0   30m

The Carthusian Cell

1 Corridor
2 Ante-Room
3 Main Room
4 Second Room
5 Latrine
6 Garden
7 Aperture
8 Larder

0   5m

ends do not justify the means; rather, means and ends coincide. For this reason the associative life of the monastery is assumed by the monks not as "natural" (like within the family or the clan) but as voluntarily accepted. In order to make means and ends coincide, every program or moment of the day is defined by a clearly recognizable space. This is visible, for instance, in the Frankish Monastery of Fontanelle in Normandy, which was founded in 822 AD. The plan of this monastery represents the distinction of different functions such as sleeping, praying, eating, and studying as a sequence of corridor-like rooms built along the four sides of the central cloister. The gallery along the cloister guides the path of the monks through the course of the day: from the communal dorter, or dormitory, on the western side of the cloister, down to the stairs into the transept of the church for prayer, onto the northern side to the cellar and the refectory for eating, and finally to the eastern arm for study. All activities are communal and separated by the quadrangular shape of the cloister: sleeping in the west, praying in the north, eating in the east, and studying (a form of work) in the south. The four realms of life and work are made into singular experiences to be lived in four different environments. In this way, architecture gives physical form to the life lived according to the rule. Architectural space is therefore not simply functional but also ritualistic, and it is precisely this character that ensures the possibility of a communal life. The history of monasticism can be understood as an *experimentum vitae*, in which what is at stake is the fine-tuning of collective life with the possibility of being alone.

Monasticism has evolved through different forms; such as the eremitical, where the hermit chooses a life of solitude away from communities ("monk" comes from the ancient Greek *monos*, which means alone); the semi-eremitical, where hermits live together in an un-prescribed way; and the *cenobitic* (from the Greek *koine bios*, "common life") in which the monks not only live in the same place but also share the same monastic rule.[8] The Carthusian monastery combines the eremitical and cenobitic model, and thereby is organized through a series of small independent cells that are gathered around a large cloister, highlighting with utmost clarity the tension between communal life and the possibility of being alone. The Carthusian cell is a small house for one person, where a monk lives and works. The cell embodies the monastic condition itself: it is solitary and yet communal, meditative yet laborious, and silent yet socialized (since all monks live in the same condition). Each cell contains a garden, a domestic unit made of three rooms, and two corridors. While a short inner corridor acts as acoustic isolation from the noise of the cloister, the longer corridor contains the services, such as the larder and the latrine. And yet, even in its radical isolation, the monk is not independent but shares a number of facilities such as the kitchen. The Carthusian monastery thus realizes what for

Roland Barthes was the main factor for communal life: the possibility for "idiorrhythmy" (from the Greek *idios*, "particular" and *rhythmos*, "rhythm, rule"), living together according to one's own rhythm of life. In this condition, monks or nuns would be both isolated from, and in contact with, one another in idiorrhythmic clusters.[9] Within the clusters, living together would not completely impinge on the possibility of being alone. Le Corbusier regarded the Carthusian cell as an early example of the rationalization of space; a machine for living that regulates and balances the necessities of life but that, at the same time, provides the occupant with a sense of relief from the burden of domesticity. This duality addresses the fundamental dilemma of living together, which is the stress that comes from collectivity. Living together requires a high degree of reciprocity between the collective and the individual, which can only occur if we have the possibility of being alone.

The Phalanx
As it is well known, Friedrich Engels was critical towards Charles Fourier's notion of communal living since, according to the German philosopher, Fourier did not ground his proposal on an overall critique of capital political economy. Yet, seen from the vantage point of today's organization of labor, in which affectivity and sociability play a central role, Charles Fourier's proposal for a large living and working unit known as the Phalanstery seems much less utopian then when it was introduced. There is no doubt that the starting point of Fourier's idea was not just social justice but the maximization of productivity. To achieve this goal, Fourier proposed to bypass the organizational structure of the family with a community of 1,600 members, living and working together. The term, "Phalanx," is of military origin and describes a community that works around one industrial branch and whose products are exchanged against those fabricated in other Phalanxes distributed over the territory.

According to Fourier, the large number of inhabitants of each unit would enable a certain economy of scale that would not only make production more efficient and profitable, but also liberating. Not only would people be freed from the burden of work, but also women would be liberated from their confinement to domestic labor. The objective of the project was ultimately to transform work into pleasure, therefore making the inhabitants not only happier, but also more productive. To this end, Fourier proposed a rule of his own—dividing the day into one and a half hour intervals in order to diversify the activities, avoid routine, and make labor more interesting. To this rhythmic sequencing of time, corresponded a precise spatial choreography enacted through the space of the *rue galerie*, which played the role of interiorized streets. Heated in the winter and cooled in the summer, the *rue galerie* would permit an efficient transition from one realm to another, while offering the possibility of encounter and exchange.

Production/Reproduction

The Phalanstery was organized around a central court where silent functions were located (the apartments, the stock-exchange, and the post office). Two wings departed from this central court, with loud activities such as workshops, carpentry, metallurgy, and nursery schools on the one side, and the guestrooms of the Phalanstery on the other. This planimetric organization conferred a new form to the unfolding of life and reinvented the spatial sequencing of activities from the monastic "circular" model to a radial one. The center supported the private and individual character of life, while the periphery accommodated labor, which was considered a highly collaborative activity. Similar to the Carthusian monastery's spatial organization, the organizing principle of life in the community was based on the wing surrounding a court and connected by galleries. The relationship between the monastery and the Phalanstery is suggestive of the conceptual search to give form to the management of life. Fourier's model was ultimately to encourage varied opportunities for social encounters; the carefully scripted life of the inhabitants would be informed by a total coincidence of work and socialization, production and personal interests.

Dom-komuna

Similar to the Phalanx, housing experiments during the early period of Soviet Russia have always been considered to be utopian gestures that are devoid of practical consequences. Yet, they are worthwhile to examine as they represent an attempt to reform society starting from the realm of the habitual. The transformation of *byt*, or the "way of life," was one of the priorities of the new governing elite after the 1917 shift from Tsarist autocracy to Soviet socialism. After the October Revolution, Soviet leaders planned to industrialize their rural and technologically-rudimentary nation. This ambition necessitated the mass displacement of populations to urban areas and therefore the construction of new housing. This need for mass housing brought about an opportunity to replace what was seen as the individualistic and *meshchanskie* ("petty-minded bourgeois")[10] character of the Russian city—mainly composed of single-family townhouses—to accommodate the *perestroika byta*: a restructured way of life. The entry of women into the labor force, the nationalization of private property, and the urbanization of rural populations were all to be gradually accommodated in new forms of housing and work spaces. A series of experiments of various scales and scopes, grouped under the label supercollectivization, attempted to provide a spatial response to the new societal order.[11]

Critical of the totalizing supercollectivization put forward in the form of large communal-houses, Ivan Leonidov (1902–1959) suggested a different organization. In his proposal for a Garden City at Magnitogorsk, Leonidov imagined a loose form of collectivization by grouping small communities on geometrically organized plots arrayed along a wide transportation artery and bordered by lateral plots providing recreational facilities on one side, and cultural services on the other. The plots could be filled with eight low-rise buildings, or two towers, so as to produce formal variations. Not convinced by low-lit interior corridors, Leonidov avoided galleries and chose the ground floor as the place for collective life. In his view, inhabitants would freely appropriate the green space provided, engaging in recreational, sporting, and cultural activities that required exterior movement. In this sense, we could say that Leonidov's diagram departs from the previous organizations of the monastery and the phalanx as it is neither centripetal nor radial but rather distributed in parallel strips, providing the necessary infrastructure for the practice of a particular sphere of life: reproduction, health, and culture.[12] The disciplinary character of supercollectivization is dissipated and diffused into a rhythmic induction to life. Small enclosures and narrow corridors are replaced by an open landscape punctuated by residential or public buildings. Leonidov's proposal for Magnitogorsk interprets collectivism as the framework for a gradual transformation of life, giving enough space to the scale of the individual, the family, and the community respectively.

Similarly, the Organization of Contemporary Architects (OSA Group) attempted to facilitate the work of the Soviet Construction Committee by proposing standardized, economical, and rational living units for workers and their families, which permitted a balance between sharing and privacy. Some of the most innovative models were suggested by Moisei Ginzburg (1892–1946) and would later be deployed in the 1928 project of a communal house for the workers of the People's Commissariat of Finance in Moscow—the Narkomfin. It is based on two main types of duplex units catering to either individuals or families.[13] Each of the types was provided with a living room and built-in kitchen. The residential area was annexed to a four-story building with a canteen, kindergarten, library, and gymnasium lying adjacent to a two-storey building comprised of laundry and repair services. This communal house formed a social condenser as it brought together people engaged in a wide range of activities. Spacious and well-lit corridors connected the living spaces to the collective social encounters. However, the inhabitants were allowed the option for complete intimacy, as the units were fully equipped. The presence of domestic facilities in both the apartments and in the collective building was an attempt to gradually accommodate the new socialist *byt*—stimulating collectivism without dictating it. The spatial organization of Narkomfin reflects the concept of the medieval charterhouse, although materialized in a more communal form. As in the charterhouse, privacy and self-sufficiency do not diminish, but rather support the collective dimension of the socialist *byt* offered by the shared services—canteen, kindergarten, or library. The Narkomfin represents an attempt to solve the issues of

The Phalanstery,
Charles Fourier,
19th Century

1 Main Square
2 Winter Garden
3 Interior Courtyards
4 Main Entrance
5 Theater
6 Church
7 Large Workshop,
  Stores, Granaries,
  Sheds
8 Stables
9 Dovecotes

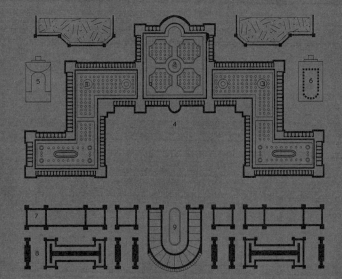

0   500m

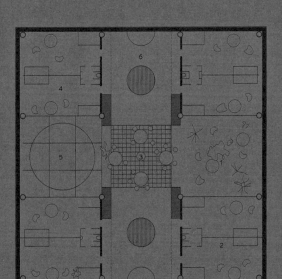

Magnitogorsk Proposal
for an Industrial City,
Ivan Leonidov, 1930

1 Garden
2 Public Seating
3 Interior Seating
4 Rest Room
5 Terrace
6 Hall

0   10m

Narkomfin Housing
Complex, Moisej
Ginzburg, 1928

1 Gallery
2 Living Units
3 Laundry and Canteen
  Service Building

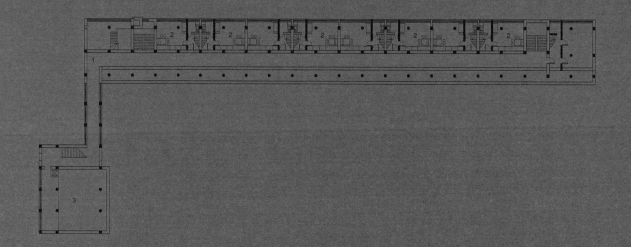

0   10m

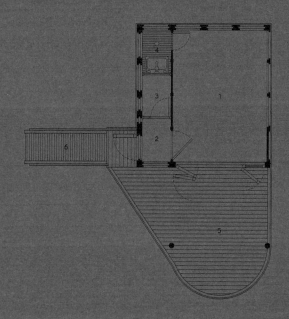

The Single-Cell of
the Green City

1 Living Room
2 Vestibule
3 Rest Room
4 Washroom
5 Covered Terrace
6 Stairs

0   2m

supercollectivization by allowing a certain degree of privacy while introducing the possibility of collective living. As in Fourier's case, circulation becomes the hinge of this transition, and the corridor takes on an important role that is not only functional but also eminently social.

In 1930, Ginzburg would again tackle the theme of supercollectivization with his "Green City" project, a proposal that went beyond the scope of living and leisure—already at the center of the Narkomfin model—to also address the spheres of production and consumption.[14] Ginzburg imagined a muscovite suburban neighborhood centered along a street with galleried paths streaming towards strips of inhabitation cells. The inhabitants would be employed locally in industrial and agricultural complexes, walking to work through greenery punctuated by collective services such as sports facilities, canteens, and libraries. The inhabitation cells would accommodate an individual, a family, and groups of families respectively. The single-cell was designed as a square house for one inhabitant, and comprised of a twelve-and-a-half square meter room, a vestibule, a shower room, a toilet, and a covered terrace. The wall facing the terrace was composed of framed glass panels that could be folded to extend the room onto the deck. The room was detached from the ground as if not to disturb the natural landscape, a leitmotif, in Ginzburg's projects. The manual of assembly for the single-cell, with its prefabricated elements, alludes to the economic advantages of the standardized, generic model. Akin to Leonidov's Magnitogorsk project, the spacing of the strips of the single-cells and of the collective services leading to the street conferred the life rhythm. Rejecting even small community buildings, Ginzburg parcelizes the settlement into individual living houses and provides life independence and privacy, but obliges the occupiers into the socialization of domestic labor as their private houses lacked kitchens. Rather than large communal estates, the works of Leonidov and Ginzburg represent a shift from early housing experiments in Soviet Russia, and re-focus on the architecture of the habitual in order to reform society.

Exodus

While in Soviet Russia the reinvention of housing aimed to abolish private property, the capitalist welfare state not only encouraged home owner-ship for workers, it also organized society within the framework of the nuclear family. Today, we nostalgically celebrate the generosity of the welfare state because we are confronted by the violence of neo-liberal budget cuts. And yet, we should not forget that from its inception, the welfare state aimed to define a population eager to consume and thus fit into predictable social conventions of the middle class, in which the family and owning one's home were the funda-mental tenets. It was precisely against this ideology of welfare, that new forms of life beyond home ownership and welfare consumption were invented at the beginning of the crisis of the welfare state between the 1970s and 1980s.

Living in a place without renting or owning it is traditionally defined as squatting. Today, squatting is considered an illegal way of appropriating an abandoned building. The illegality of squatting derived from the fact that the regime of property ownership is the fundamental datum of the juridical and political order to the city. Historically, the practice of squatting was considered an essential way to survive, as in ancient times, the idea of leaving a place and settling in another one was often considered the ultimate act of resistance towards oppression. Perhaps, the archetype of squatting can be found in the vicissitudes of the people of Israel narrated in the book of Exodus. To escape the condition of enslavement under the Pharaoh's rule, the people of Israel decided to not fight against the Pharaoh but to leave in search of land where they could live freely. A similar strategy of exodus was pursued by the early monks in the face of the institutionalization of the Christian church as a state apparatus during the late Roman Empire. These monks took refuge in the isolation of the desert where they would find the opportunity not only to be closer to God, but also to start an alternative way of life. More recently, the practice of exodus occurred in the early days of industrialization in the United States, where communities of people escaped the alienation of factory work and formed spontaneous communities often driven by religious ideals. All these exoduses implied the principle of squatting—the occupation of land and thus the possibility of breaking away from existing power.

In the 1970s, exodus resurfaced as a strategy of escape, this time from the state and capital. One of its most radical manifestations was the 1977 Italian movement known as *Autonomia*. Largely made of young people, one of the political tenets of this movement was the refusal of work.[15] This refusal was not a denial of one's creative and productive powers, but the rejection of the capitalist exploitation of these powers.[16] Here, exodus consisted of leaving capitalist rule by rejecting the wage system. This refusal manifested itself in new ways of affirming creativity and self-organization against the paternalism of state-driven welfare. Such political and economic emancipation was put forward by the *Autonomia* movement as a process of self-valorization.[17]

The theory of self-valorization was introduced by autonomist thinkers such as Antonio Negri and Mariarosa Dalla Costa, as a worker's strategy to reclaim one's productive potential from capitalist command. Within capitalistic society, value depends not only on the accumulation of production surplus, but also on the capacity of capital to manage class relations to achieve total control over the life of the worker. Against this process, a worker's self-valorization was the attempt to reclaim margins of autonomy out-side value-forming labor. In the 1970s and 1980s, this process transpired through the idea of independent production within culture and the arts. Particularly within music, with the rise of punk and hip-hop, self-valorization attempted to escape the ubiquitous commodification of life that made creativity increasingly commercial.

In Italy, experiments of self-organization took place in many cities through squatting in buildings, which became famous as Centri Sociali Autogestiti. Often abandoned, yet architecturally prominent industrial buildings or defense structures, these Centri Sociali were governed by small councils composed of the same people that occupied them.[18] Although many of these centers were not living and working spaces, their functioning went beyond the schedule of a normal recreational center in order to contest the idea that creative activities such as music or the arts are what occur beside work. In the 1980s and 1990s, the popularity of these centers exceeded their underground circuits, as they became important epicenters of counterculture that resisted the process of depoliticization and the commodification of life that was typical of these two decades. Ironically, the success of the Centri Sociali made them an attractive model for the nascent creative industry and the idea of diffused production outside the wage system became the harbinger for neoliberalism's systematic precarization of work in the early years of the 2000s. It is especially within this framework that the practice of squatting and self-valorization acquires its ambivalent social meaning. On the one hand, the practice of squatting is depicted by media as aggressive and illegal because it breaks the fundamental principle of capitalistic society: the right to private property. While in the 1980s, many European states were somehow tolerant of the squatting of disused buildings, in the last decade property speculators have been successful in lobbying governments to ban squatting as a socially dangerous activity. At the same time, many of the cultural trends initiated within these centers— such as co-working spaces and mixing of working and social activities—have been coopted by both municipalities and developers. Termed "incubators," flexible working spaces resemble the atmosphere of self-organized squatting, but are rented as a commercial workspaces.

After the 2008 recession that left numerous vacant buildings, the practice of squatting was adopted by building owners for the temporary occupation of vacant properties against the threat of occupation by real squatters (which the media now terms "bad squatters"). Within this ambiguous framework, many of the self-valorizing processes started in the 1970s have become mere survival strategies encouraged by post-crisis austerity policies. It is in this context that many movements, especially within the cultural industry, were forced to rethink the possibility of exodus not as generic claim, but as the social and political recognition of creative work against the state of precarity in which capitalism has forced the workers through this form of production.

One of the most emblematic initiatives of this new wave of squatting movements was the short-lived occupation of the Torre Galfa in Milan in 2012.[19] Organized by a collective of creative workers called "Macao," the occupation intended to reclaim a 1950s high-rise office building in the center of Milan as a collective social space open to all. The occupation was both symbolic and practical. On the one hand, it wanted to symbolize, once again, the right of workers to self-organize and expose the crucial problem of unpaid labor within cultural work. On the other hand, it was a solution to the challenge of finding proper work-space in a city where speculation is one of the primary economic activities. Once a symbol of speculation and corporate capital, with the occupation of Torre Galfa the typology of the office tower was reclaimed as a social condenser placed in the heart of the productive metropolis. The high-rise office typology offered the occupants three main advantages: the neutrality of a plan that could be easily organized according to ad-hoc forms of occupations, the density of a tower that could accommodate a vast number of people (and thus strengthen the political power of the community), and enhanced visibility. During the first night of the occupation, Macao was able to use a neon lighting installation left in the building for an advertisement campaign in order to illuminate the transparent volume of the tower and its potential emptiness. Suddenly this immense empty space appeared in the city and made visible to the possibility of free space to work and share production outside of the rental system. The symbolic power of this occupation was so strong because the act of self-valorization did not develop at the margins of the city or in some "terrain vague," typical of occupations in the 1970s and 1980s. As such, it immediately made visible the possibility to use abandoned properties as productive spaces. For this reason, the occupants of the tower were evicted only a few days later, but the symbolic impact of the occupation has remained within the city and has animated a series of diffused initiatives where living and working are not just exploitative conditions, but pursuit to live together towards a better life.

Conclusion

The cases illustrated here do not exhaust the range of experiments, possibilities, and realities that have animated the history of collective living and working spaces. Above all, what needs to be emphasized is the experimental nature of these case studies. Even if they often failed in the short term, in the long term they have influenced and inspired many communities to self-organize their own life and work. These examples show how self-organization is, far from being a spontaneous process, a carefully choreographed ritual. The question that arises is what is the role of architects in this process? This question forces us—as architects—to look back at our position vis-à-vis social issues such as the problem of housing and access to welfare facilities within the city. In the postwar period, the welfare state offered to

Galfa Tower, Melchiorre
Bega, 1956

1 Gallery
2 Workshop
3 Storage
4 Stairs
5 Elevators

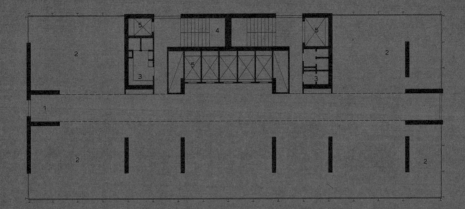

0   10m

architects the possibility to design social projects on an unprecedented scale. Often commissioned by the public sector, these projects allowed architects not only to have work, but to feel that their work had a clear social mandate. With the dismantling of the welfare state, this situation transformed dramatically, and starting from the 1980s the only social significance architects could gain—at least in Europe—was from commercial commissions such as museums, luxury housing, or corporate buildings. Moreover, architects increasingly find themselves no longer in the condition of confident professionals, but rather in that of precarious workers. To work on social projects in this condition implies that architects do not look at these social projects from an outside position, but from the point of view of their own social condition as part of the once celebrated creative class that has now become precarious. This means that even before designing new typologies of living and working space, we need to imagine new forms of dwelling and inhabiting space starting not only from our professional knowledge, but also from our dwelling experience as inhabitants. The examples presented here took the form of clear architectural strategies, but the social and cultural impetus came from the possibility of imagining new forms of life. Perhaps it

is precisely the professional insecurity within which architects find themselves that may force them to re-consider living space not just as a condition to provide design solutions. Instead, these spaces offer the possibility of a social and political framework within which architects may be able to reinvent their mandate and, in doing so, find new ways in which we can live and work together. Above all, we need to remember that work, when it is a self-fulfilling activity, is not bad. Work becomes bad when it depends on debt and rent, when we work in order to fulfill external forces that extract their value from our work. In this way, the alternative forms that domestic space can offer to the organization of a life, freed from productivity as an alienated condition, as well as the possibility of worker's self-valorization, can position it as the core space of politics and production.

Pier Vittorio Aureli is an architect and educator. His work focuses on the relationship between architectural form, political theory, and urban history. Together with Martino Tattara, he is the co-founder of Dogma.

Martino Tattara is the head of research and teaching at Studio Basel: Contemporary City Institute at the Swiss Federal Institute of Technology in Zurich (ETH). His main theoretical interest is the relationship between architecture and large-scale urban design. Together with Pier Vittorio Aureli, he is the co-founder of Dogma.

Notes

1   This refers to Hannah Arendt's distinction between *labor* and *work*. While *labor* is the sheer unending business of our species reproduction (such as eating, sleeping and cleaning, giving birth to and raising kids, cleaning of the household), *work* concerns the production of lasting materials.
2   In "Behind Marx's Hidden Abode," Nancy Fraser argues that the division between social reproduction and commodity production is not only central to capitalism, but is its artifact. See Nancy Fraser, "In Behind Marx's Hidden Abode," *New Left Review* 86 (2014), 55-72.
3   The word derives from the Greek *ethos*, meaning the habitual character and disposition, habit or custom. See Online Etymology Dictionary.
4   On the concept of immaterial labor see: Maurizio Lazzarato, "Immaterial Labor" in Paolo Virno, Michael Hardt, eds., *Radical Thought in Italy. A Potential Politics* (Minneapolis: Minnesota University Press, 1996), 241-259.

5   Karl Marx, *Capital: A Critique of Political Economy* (New York: Vintage books, 1977), 270.
6   See: Giuliano Gresleri, *Viaggio in Oriente* (Padua: Marsilio Editore, 1984).
7   Giorgio Agamben, *The Highest Poverty: Monastic Rules and Form-of-Life* (Redwood City: Stanford University Press, 2013).
8   For a comprehensive historical overview of monasticism see: C.H. Lawrence, *Medieval Monasticism: Forms of Religious Life in Western Europe in the Middle Age* (London: Routledge, 2014).
9   Roland Barthes, *How To Live Together: Novelistic Simulations of some Everyday Spaces* (New York: Columbia University Press, 2013).
10   Caroline Humphrey, "Ideology in Infrastructure: Architecture and Soviet Imagination," *Journal of the Royal Anthropological Institute* 1, vol. 11 (March 2005): 39.
11   Andrei Ikkonnikov, *Russian Architecture of the Soviet Period* (Moscow: Raduga Publisher, 1988).
12   P.A. Aleksandrov and S.O. Chan-Magomedov, *Ivan Leonidov* (Milano: Franco Angeli Editore, 1975).

13   The two types are referred to as the K Type and the F Type
14   See *Architecture Contemporaine: Sovremennaja Architektura* (London: RIBA Publications, 2010), 1-2.
15   On the Autonomia movement there is a lot of literature. For an overview of the Movement available in English see: Sylvere Lotringer, Christian Marazzi, *Autonomia: Post-Political Politics* (Los Angeles: Semiotext(e), 2008).
16   See: Mario Tronti, "La Strategia del Rifiuto," in *Operai e Capitale* (Turin: Einaudi, 1966), 234-252.
17   On the concept of self-valorization see: Antonio Negri: *Marx Beyond Marx: Lessons on the Grundrisse*, (London: Pluto Press, 1992).
18   On the rise of the Centri Sociali see: Robert Lumely, *State of Emergency: Culture of Revolt in Italy, 1968-1978* (London: Verso, 1990).
19   On the occupation of Torre Galfa in Milan see: Martina Angelotti, "Macao. L'occupazione della Torre Galfa a Milano" in *Doppiozero*, http://www.doppiozero.com/materiali/fuori-busta/macao-loccupazione-della-torre-galfa-milano.

POST-SQUAT NL: REPROGRAMMABLE CITY

David Eugin Moon

From 1971 to 2010, the Dutch government mandated an urban experiment in reprogramming its cities. In dealing with the crisis of an overwhelming amount of vacant spaces, aging structures, and an incompatible set of needs, the citizens of Holland were legally allowed to squat in buildings that were vacant for more than a year, if a user could enter a space bringing only a bed, desk, and chair.[1] The result of this new and unique set of conditions were often bizarre anomalies that contested preconceived notions in architecture and urbanism including programming, prescribed functionalism, form-making, as well as ownership models, and the boundaries of individual rights in the city. Young, middle-class professionals, and recent college graduates were suddenly able to occupy entire floors of empty office buildings; vacant blocks became temporary hotels; new centers of subversive culture spontaneously formed and institutionalized.

Many of these occupancies flourished undocumented until 2010, despite strong public demonstrations and student strikes in major cities throughout the Netherlands. This unusual period of collective experimentation poised between the formal and the informal represents the active involvement of many Dutch citizens. Their actions creatively reconceptualized and manipulated the existing urban infrastructure to its needs, partaking in untested modes of spatial organization on a national scale. Select aspects and examples

from this forty-year period will be outlined here, to re-frame a discussion on ownership, design processes, and professional paradigms in the reprogramming of the city. Suggesting the possibilities of spatial organization that mediate the provocative nature of spontaneous occupations and the necessity for the agency of architecture, the Dutch squat and its post-squatted progeny provide a reconsideration for the making and remaking of cities.

House Rights

It was the Dutch Supreme Court's ruling under the "House Right" in 1971 that established the squatters as legal occupants protected from forceful intrusions.[2] A fundamental discussion in the debate was the right to ownership versus the citizen's basic rights for habitation. At stake was the city's right to control private property and the responsibility to regulate it. As described by the conservative Bastiaan van 't Wout in the booklet *Black Book of Squatting* from 2008, the opponents of squatting continue to argue for the unconditional rights of private owners; as an analogy, they offer the premise of appropriating a neighbor's vehicle as not defendable in any circumstance, despite its underuse.[3] The opposing viewpoint in the subsequent *White Book of Squatting* (2009) represents the position that squatting advocates have been holding since 1971 and argues for the rights of the individual with a narrative similar to Henri Lefebvre and David

Bicycle-in-Office Tower "House," 2007.
PHOTO: INÊS CATARINO CABRITA

Harvey's "right to the city," and furthermore, for the civic responsibilities to protect such basic rights through legislation and policy.[4] The debate became more relevant because of the abundance of vacant spaces and the estimated seven-year waiting list for a social housing unit.[5] Beyond the ethical debate, are associations and portraitures of the squatters who some described as undesirables and the marginal, while conversely, they are also the creators of culture and positive actors for dysfunctional parts of the city. Further fueling controversy, the practice of the "anti-squat" became prevalent. This still exists today as a low cost housing solution or a start-up opportunity in which property owners—with the sole intent of keeping the squatters away—actively recruit occupants who would pay an exceptionally low rent to temporarily occupy a space. The anti-squatters surrender many of their basic rights as occupants, inhabiting a gray area in the market.

Feasible Utopias

With the legalization of squatting, the possibilities of the previously unknown experiments in urbanism became available to the Dutch general public who were no longer subject to the normal approvals process, public consensus,[6] and administrative procedures of the city.[7] These freedoms, without the limitations imposed by the traditional spatial disciplines and management regimes, allowed for an autonomy in redesigning the city, similar to the descriptions by architects Alredo Brillembourg, Hubert Klumpner,[8] and the sociologist Richard Sennett.[9] This prompted a kind of reprogrammable city, which did not involve modernism's singular vision for a new perfectly planned and structured, compart-mentalized, static city. In contrast to the familiar urban planning paradigms that were selected and standardized from the Athens Charter or from the work of architects and urbanists such as Tony Garnier, Ebenezer Howard, or Le Corbusier, the Dutch squat offered a more dynamic model of the city that had no hierarchical framework or plan (other than the city itself) and was constrained only by the immediate resources of a marginalized or adventurous public. As a whole, the degree of dynamism—as well as the limitations—of the Dutch squats imply the speculative urban megastructure proposals of the architects Yona Friedman, Cedric Price, and Eckhard Schulze-Fielitz, or Archizoom's infinite exterior-interior multi-material and mirrored models of "weak modernity" from the 1960s, which immediately preceded the period of legal squatting in Holland. The squats became representative of the utopian ambitions of plug-in and self-empowered projects wherein users were also creators. The squats were the sites where the individual or group's programmatic experimentation, as suggested in the example of weak modernity, played a key role in adjusting the mismatched demands of a population and the existing built city.

(A)Typical Plan

Shifting between the projective and the actual, programmatic experimentation can foster a compelling manipulation of space, from the generic Koolhaas-like "typical plan" to the context-rich city of Rotterdam, a complex landscape of post-war constructions, historical remnants, and urban voids.[11] The spontaneous self-initiated programmatic experiments by the squatters sometimes resulted in strange scenes or seemingly inappropriate program-to-space and program-to-form relationships, such as the singular occupant in the tower (as photographed by Inês Catarino Cabrita) posing both puzzlement and incitement. Such real but unlikely scenarios challenged notions of the typical program, allowing for incredible mismatches in type, form, and use that redefine ideas of the home and its constituent parts. As writers and architects such as Amanda Reeser Lawrence and Ashley Schafer have noted, indeterminacy of program and the flexibility of forms have been the motivator of seminal works, and this is also evident in the spontaneously squatted spaces in Holland.[12]

Destination, Spectacle, and Institution

Due to their unusual nature, some of the successful squats inevitably became centers of voyeuristic spectacles, as well as touristic and eventually financial interests, tightly integrated into the various systems of the formal city. Originally initiated by informal groups of artists and ad-hoc associations, one of the most well-known squatted structures in Amsterdam was an abandoned grain silo, also known as *de Silo* (the Silo). The 270-hectare site, located along the IJ River, declined in use after the relocation of port operations closer to the sea. The former grain silo was first squatted in 1989 with its primary program as housing, despite the peculiarity of its towering industrial structure, which was predominantly windows-less. As one of the most stringent and limiting programmatic types, the infiltration of the housing program into the silo made for an unexpected development, contrary to any typical notions of existing housing typologies or conventions. Started from a group of one hundred inhabitants who traded skills and services to meet basic everyday needs, by the late 1990s it became the location and the framework for an acclaimed performance venue, as well as art galleries, cafes, and bakeries, serving as a must-see "alternative" tourist destination in the Amsterdam harbor area. Combined with its reappropriated monumental iconography and programmatic diversity, *de Silo* became a landmark in the city. It was nominated for the World Heritage list of UNESCO, and was declared a national monument in 1996.[13] In 1998, the squatters were evicted for a condo development, though they would later move towards a more formalized strategy in initiating a project called NDSM after the ban.

Similarly, in creating new opportunities outside of existing conventions, OT301 is as an unlikely formation and legitimization of an institution through squatting. OT301, an artist collective, was initiated at the site of an abandoned film school, and is an exemplary precedent of an informal, self-organizing group that appropriated existing structures, before eventually becoming institutionalized. The old film school was endowed with a small stage that was converted into a bizarre infrastructural zone, open-ended, yet programmed for a specific set of uses throughout the week. The new group of occupants benefited from "inheriting" all of the amenities of the old school, none of which were used as originally programmed. OT301 follows the recurring theme in Holland of a culturally grounded squatted space that became a legitimized, fully-owned (and incorporated) institutional space, supported by various public and private funds. As a funded institution since 2007, OT301 wrestles with its changing identity, constituencies, and its public presence. During its transformation, cases like OT301 highlight the improbable self-organization and creation of institutions despite a hierarchical and often inaccessible urban infrastructure.

Occupation

While squatting was a necessary alternative housing solution to many, the act of squatting has also been a highly visible form of dissent and resistance against the conventions and hegemonies in Dutch society. In the early 1970s, when a new construction project was proposed in the Nieuwmarkt neighborhood that required demolition to make way for a new highway and a new underground subway line, protest groups organized to strategically squat vacant houses in these areas of redevelopment. The act of squatting was not only a way of preserving the current fabric through a physical and legal presence—what sociologist Hans Pruijt calls "conservational squatting"—but also was an act of protest and representation. The development plans were eventually cancelled and some of the protestors' demands were met in the form of a return to the original street plans and the addition of a new housing block that would prevent any such future thorough-fares.[14] Many of the squatted areas in Amsterdam were eventually replaced with low-income housing and in those cases, Pruijt notes that the squatters usually left voluntarily when develop-ment was planned.[15] The intervention of the squatters challenged the normal operations of state and industry in the space of the city, permanently effecting the future development of the city in an unusual example of role reversal in societal power.

Culmination (and Ban)

A national debate surrounding the squat ban was part of a broader conflict in Holland involving a resurgent conservative political party and the changing demographics of the population, which included an ever-growing minority of immigrants, and the lack of support of integration and cultural assimilation. After forty years of progressive policies, and towards the end of this discrete period in Dutch history, Holland had begun to encounter a resistance to many of the liberal policies that helped establish and maintain the famously tolerant society. These changes also coincided with the economic turmoil of 2008 that brought about increased societal tension and dramatic shifts in attitude away from support for important public institutions and programs, and growing intolerance with its immigrant population—most easily observed through the popularity of the highly conservative Geert Wilders and the Freedom Party.[16] Despite its potentials, squatting remained a contentious issue. On October 1, 2010, squatting was banned by the Dutch Parliament and the decision was met with riots, protests, and a national petition. The squatters who violated the new law were met with severe penalties including up to one to two years in prison. By 2011, many of the squats had already disappeared and by 2012, only twenty-three squats remained in Amsterdam down from its peak, with an estimated 20,000 squatters, in the 1980s.[17]

Afterword, "Self-made City"

NDSM, a so-called "self-made city" in the Amsterdam harbor, started in 1998 when some of the former squatters of the Silo submitted a winning proposal for an open competition for the re-use of the wharf of NDSM (*Nederlandse Droogdok en Scheepsbouw Maatschappij*, or Dutch Dock and Ship-building Company). Today, the development is still expanding and developing in a continual process, for example through the latest 2015 plans for an energy-neutral wind farm. A former shipyard and foundry converted into a city within a box, NDSM is one of the many progeny from squatting, where an informal system is reproduced with formal processes. Located across the river from the old central district of Amsterdam, and reminiscent of the aforementioned utopian megastructure projects of the past that were never realized (albeit as a much more realistic and grittier inter-pretation), the 37,000 square meter complex was remade into a large three-dimensional adjustable infrastructure that allows for each individual artist, store owner, and others to design their own unit or "plot" within the larger steel armature with each owner responsible for their own approvals and permissions to the municipality.[18] Similar to some of the squats of the earlier generations, the activities are diverse and inclusive, but organized through a system of city streets, internalized blocks, and public "squares." NDSM and similar projects take an aggressive approach in the individualization and modification of space, reshaping and reform-ing existing volumes, structures, and envelopes

Squat Protest in
Amsterdam, 2009.
PHOTO: JOS VAN ZETTEN

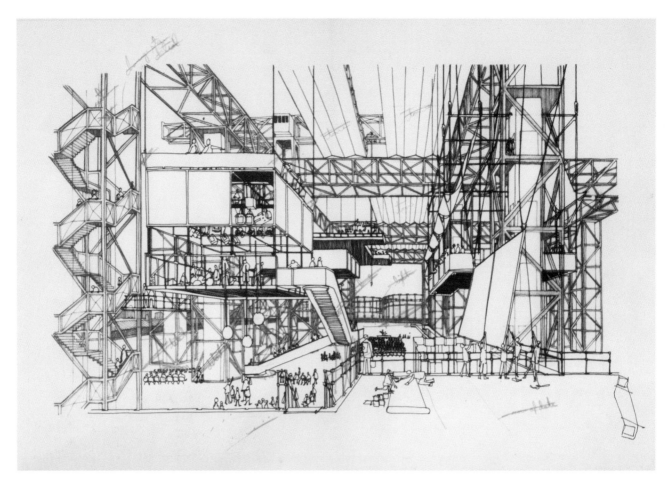

Cedric Price, Fun Palace:
Interior Perspective,
ca. 1960–1964.
IMAGE: COURTESY CEDRIC PRICE
FONDS, COLLECTION CENTRE
CANADIEN D'ARCHITECTURE/
CANADIAN CENTRE FOR
ARCHITECTURE, MONTREAL

while positing pressing questions regarding the hard distinction between and classification of the formal and informal, or the programmatically determinate and indeterminate. The original plan by Dynamo Architecten continues to thrive today, led by its visionary co-founder Eva de Klerk and others, with four hundred companies in-house and a year-round event schedule.

Post-Squat NL: Reprogrammable City

The official mandate for the Dutch experiment in the self-organized reprogramming of the city had ended with the squat ban in 2010 and the transformations in Dutch cities would have to continue through other means. Despite the disappearance of the myriad of squatted buildings and sites (and some of the squatters themselves who moved on to other aspirations), many of the remnants and resultant networks, institutions, and post-squat projects remain. In retrospect, the notion of a reprogrammable city could have many interpretations in that any city may be considered reprogrammable to some extent. However, the particular social and political circumstances in Holland point towards the possibility where the proactive actions of the citizenry could play a role in a larger vision of a more dynamic urbanity. As suggested by others, urban propositions are often best synthesized through the research of the existing city and the distillation of these unexpected and provocative observations, so that they might produce new architectures or new implementations of the familiar.[19] In order to distill ideas and concepts for a post-squat Netherlands from squatting, and consider relating the actions of spatial production and articulation to that of occupation and appropriation, what is necessary is not an advocacy to return to the past, nor a fetishization of any aesthetics of informality. Instead, these observations and insights suggest that program and its reappropriation can be a moderator between on the one hand, the civic desires and aspirations relative to a social, political, and economic context and on the other hand their realities at a particular moment. Moving away from the irresponsibility and ineffectuality of universal flexibility or total informalism, the work of a post-squat NL can suggest the investigation into the potentials in the re-established abilities and responsibilities of the disciplines. In the contemporary context of severe social, political, and economic limitations, the research continues the disciplinary investigations and experimentations in program, typology, and indeterminacy, and articulates their roles as facilitators of architecture in the city.

David Eugin Moon is a partner at N H D M and teaches at Cornell University Architecture Art and Planning. N H D M is a New York-based design and research collaborative, founded in 2010.

NDSM Wharf Interior,
2011.

PHOTO: JASON ANDRE

Notes

1 Hugo Priemus, "Squatters and
municipal policies to reduce vacancy:
Evidence from the Netherlands," paper
presented at the *Enhr Conference*,
Toulouse, France, (July 5-8, 2011).

2 Hans Pruijt, "Is the Institutionalization of Urban Movements Inevitable?
A comparison of the Opportunities for
Sustained Squatting in New York City
and Amsterdam," *International Journal
of Urban and Regional Research* 27.1
(2003): 145.

3 Tino Buchholz, "To Use or Not Use
Urban Space" paper presented at the
4th International Forum on Urbanism,
Amsterdam/Delft (November 26-28,
2009), 213-214.

4 Ibid.

5 Hans Pruijt, "The Logic of Urban
Squatting," *International Journal
of Urban and Regional Research* 37.1
(2013): 29.

6 Markus Miessen, *Markus Miessen:
The Nightmare of Participation (Cross-
bench Praxis as a Mode of Criticality)*
(Berlin: Sternberg Press, 2011), 20.

7 Hans Pruijt, "Is the Institutionalization of Urban Movements Inevitable?
A comparison of the Opportunities for
Sustained Squatting in New York City
and Amsterdam," 145.

8 Michiel Dehaene and Saskia Sassen,
*Power: Producing the Contemporary
City* (Rotterdam and New York: 010
Publishers, 2007), 188.

9 Jonathan Hughes and Simon Sadler,
*Non-Plan: Essays on Freedom, Partici-
pation and Change in Modern Architecture and Urbanism* (Oxford and Boston:
Routledge, 2000), 12.

10 Rem Koolhaas, Bruce Mau, and
Jennifer Sigler, *Small, Medium, Large,
Extra-Large* (New York: Monacelli
Press, 1998), 334-353.

11 Ewout Dorman, et al., *Post.Rotterdam
Architecture and the City after the
tabula rasa* (Rotterdam: 010 Publishers,
2001), 16-44.

12 Amanda Reeser Lawrence and
Ashley Schafer, "Re:programming,"
Praxis (2006), 4.

13 Bert Hogervorst and Peti Buchel,
*Turning Tide: The Users Role in the
Redevelopment of Harbour Buildings
in North-West Europe* (Amsterdam: Art
Data, 1998), 2, 7-9.

14 Hans Pruijt, "The Logic of Urban
Squatting," 14-18.

15 Ibid.

16 Steve Erlanger, "Amid Rise of
Multiculturalism, Dutch Confront Their
Questions of Identity," *The New York
Times*, August 13, 2011.

17 "Amsterdam no longer a city of
squatters," *DutchNews.nl* (June 25,
2012), http://www.dutchnews.nl/news/
archives/2012/06/amsterdam_no_
longer_a_city_of.php.

18 Christer Bengs, et al., *Temporary
uses as resource of urban planning*
(Helsinki: Publications in the Centre
for Urban and Regional Studies,
2003), 69.

19 Dana Cuff and Roger Sherman,
*Fast-Forward Urbanism: Rethinking
Architecture's Engagement with the City*
(New York: Princeton Architectural
Press, 2011), 2.

TAKE ME, I'M YOURS: RECLAIMING FREE SPACE IN THE CITY

Jill Desimini

"Buildings eventually fall, but ground plans remain; elevation is the least durable element of urban form, but plot forms its longest lasting element."
—Denis Cosgrove, *Geography and Vision*

Land and economy are inextricably linked. Not only does land represent a significant value in the United States—estimated at $4.5 trillion just a few years ago—but land development and land prices also react to economic cycles.[1] Land is typically seen as a safe investment, but what happens when land loses its economic value, when it is foreclosed upon, when it and its neighborhood are abandoned, or when it becomes something that a person or a city cannot give away, much less sell?

Growth and privatization models dominate land economy in the United States, making conditions of loss and abandonment extremely problematic. The privatization of property has a fundamental influence on American development and culture. The promise of land ownership and control underlies the country's foundation and fuels its continued attraction.[2] Land ownership is traditionally tied to representation. It brings economic and, for some, political liberty. There is still some contention on the relationship between land and property ownership, democracy, and citizenship.[3] Still, there is a freedom implicit in owning land—the freedom to do whatever you want on it, within the given regulatory parameters. The undeniable rights of the Declaration of Independence—life,

liberty, and the pursuit of happiness—descend from a Lockean idea of life, liberty, and property and land still lurks in the sentiment. But there are times when the freedom is revoked, when land becomes a liability rather than an asset.

Land in the United States, and in most Western countries, is a bundle of rights. It is the soil, air, and water, and the right to control, access, harvest, develop, sell, lease, trade, and give it away. To own land is to be established. Central to the economics of land ownership is the expectation that housing and property will appreciate, and that the demand for land will increase with time, resulting in a certain ingrained growth imperative. The common perception is that land is both a status symbol and a safe investment. Despite these assumptions, American land value depends on market demand, and is highly variable both across the country and within metropolitan areas. The value of a home is divided between the costs of the structure and the value of land. In the first quarter of 2012, land value in Detroit equaled $5,234, representing a five percent share of the home value, whereas land value in San Francisco for the same period was $565,181, a 73.4 percent share.[4,5] Within the New York City metropolitan area alone, the land value per square foot varied between $0 and $12,647.53.[6] Within the home value equation, residential land price accounts for most of the variation in housing price.[7] Location dependency and market fluctuation means that control over property value in the long-term—

Land Banking Cycles and Strategies: Diagrams describing the formal and informal land banking practices in Flint, Michigan and Youngstown, Ohio. Free land patterns are depicted, showing the perforated base condition of aggregating land (frozen temporarily in 2011), the transfer of land from private to public control, and the developing landscape practices (adopt-a-lot, long-term leases, garden and habitat creation) designed to promote greater social and ecological use.

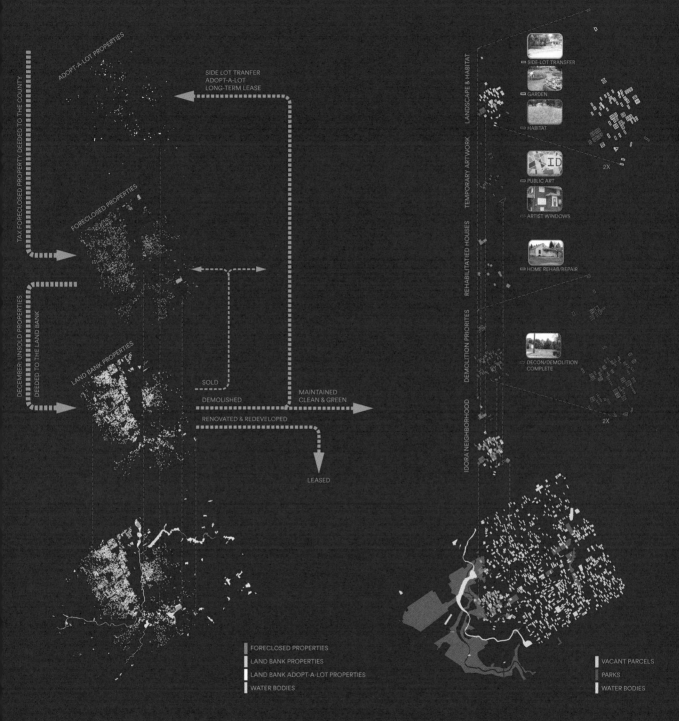

ADOPT-A-LOT PROPERTIES

SIDE LOT TRANFER
ADOPT-A-LOT
LONG-TERM LEASE

TAX FORECLOSED PROPERTY DEEDED TO THE COUNTY

FORECLOSED PROPERTIES

DECEMBER: UNSOLD PROPERTIES
DEEDED TO THE LAND BANK

LAND BANK PROPERTIES

SOLD

DEMOLISHED

RENOVATED & REDEVELOPED

MAINTAINED
CLEAN & GREEN

LEASED

LANDSCAPE & HABITAT

SIDE-LOT TRANSFER

GARDEN

HABITAT

2X

TEMPORARY ARTWORK

PUBLIC ART

ARTIST WINDOWS

REHABILITATIED HOUSES

HOME REHAB/REPAIR

DEMOLITION PRIORITES

DECON/DEMOLITION
COMPLETE

2X

IDORA NEIGHBORHOOD

FORECLOSED PROPERTIES
LAND BANK PROPERTIES
LAND BANK ADOPT-A-LOT PROPERTIES
WATER BODIES

VACANT PARCELS
PARKS
WATER BODIES

THE GENESEE COUNTY LAND BANK
DATA FROM thelandbank.org + conversation with planning staff at the Land Bank, 10.12.2011

YOUNGSTOWN NEIGHBORHOOD DEVELOPMENT
DATA FROM YNDC

because the land is a non-duplicable good—is not normally subject to increases or decreases based on the actions of the owner, but instead is subject to external influence.[8] There is a tension then between the individual owner and the public, where the owner holds title to the land but cannot control the greater economic, social, political, and environmental systems affecting its future value. Through regulation, community organization, and activism there is some power, but it is limited. Greater economic forces and political decisions mean that formerly valued land may lose its value, and this loss may continue slowly over decades. To address continued disinvestment in certain areas, the needs of the individual and the collective must be seen together—and the regulatory frameworks must better support the recognition of limited economic and social resources. Otherwise, inequity will likely prevail as land development decisions cater to market and political trends.

Valuation, Dispossession, and Use

Where value is concerned, location matters above all, with housing prices being more susceptible to decline than housing quantity. In fact, the behavior of the housing market can help explain the persistence of declining prices.[9] Because housing is durable, a decrease in demand leads to a drop in price rather than a decrease in quantity, which means that the housing stock stays constant despite the market change. For this reason, decline is not the opposite of growth. Where possible, houses are built quickly when demand for them increases but they remain largely extant when demand for them drops. To compensate for the discrepancies in supply and demand, housing prices drop. If housing prices descend to levels that are below the cost of construction, it can be inferred that the population of the surroundings has also declined.[10]

So what can owners do when formerly valued private land loses its market value? One option is to abandon it. With the freedom to do whatever you want with your land, comes the freedom to dispossess yourself of it. This is not a perfect freedom, however, as the only way to dispossess yourself of your land is to transfer ownership of it, and if there is no market value, there is no market, and no buyers or takers. The freedom becomes a burden—a burden that either rests with the landowner or is passed on through the foreclosure process to a bank or municipality.

In an urban context, this errant land might be briefly de-privatized, joining a municipal land bank, the adoption agency for unwanted lands. Typically, long-term plans for this type of common land do not exist, only the hope to find it a suitable owner as quickly as possible—someone who will agree to take care of it. The Genesee County Land Bank Authority (GCLBA) in Flint, Michigan is at the forefront of the land banking practice in the United States. Following a statewide change in the handling of foreclosed properties in 1999, the GCLBA has been acquiring tax-foreclosed properties since 2002.[11] Prior to the adoption of the new tax law, foreclosed properties faced legal limbo, evading taxes for up to seven years while simultaneously harboring speculation—placing existing homeowners at risk and contributing to continued property devaluation. Under the new law, property title is transferred to the county after two and a half years of unpaid property tax. Unlike most land banks, the GCLBA does not actively transfer property back into private hands, as there is a dearth of suitable owners. The properties are vulnerable to speculation, what the *Flint Journal* editorial board likened to out-of-town leeches who hang onto abandoned properties, sometimes selling them sight unseen through internet auction houses for profit. This happened as recently as November 2010, when foreclosed properties went through a two-part auction process—going from the GCLBA to an Illinois-based investment company whom purchased a 58-house package for $25,350. A few months later, one house had garnered a bid of $92,800 on eBay.[12] The GCLBA works to fight property predators, despite continued growth in the number of properties requiring management and declining resources. The county cut a significant portion of the GCLBA's funding in September 2011, a decision that renders the immediate future for the errant lands bleak.

From a long-term perspective, however, the incremental transfer of urban land from private to public ownership offers the potential for a new property model and with it, new modes of design. Cities looking for ways to transform themselves physically have their hands tied by property law. The slow accumulation of land could open up opportunities over time. Foreclosed properties are inherently not paying taxes. Private owners have no incentive to look into alternative property uses, as even if they grant free access to their land, they maintain liability. In the case of commonly held land, alternative maintenance, use, and lease models are viable. Lands can be kept open in the face of indeterminate futures. They can support innovation, assuming a role as a form of future commons.

Presently, the idea of an indeterminate future for land, especially for vacant—or more aptly named *latent*—urban land, is met with great anxiety. Re-engaging private ownership remains the goal of most resource-strapped municipalities. In Flint, Michigan, when a homeowner is situated next to a lot that has been abandoned, title may be transferred to them for a nominal fee. Like the Homestead Act, a federal law enacted in 1862 in which qualified applicants were given 160 acres of farmland and a mule free of charge, land is given away to upstanding citizens, which in this case means tax-paying residents. The GCLBA encourages this practice as much as possible. If you live next to a land bank property, expect a postcard solicitation, to come claim another five thousand square feet. With the Homestead Act, grantees were required to build a home, work the land, and live on it for at least five years. Now, the only obligation is monetary—to keep current on the taxes. Physical improvement is at the

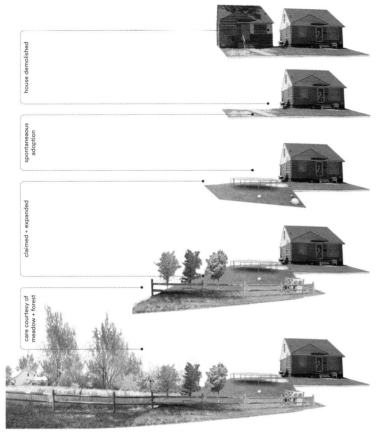

house demolished

spontaneous adoption

claimed + expanded

care courtesy of meadow + forest

An illustration of the spontaneous side-lot transfer process, where residents of an occupied house and volunteer plants have appropriated adjacent abandoned plots. A gradient is created, from residential yard to meadow and forest. The differential land management optimizes limited economic resources while fostering ecological and social health.

discretion of the individual. The side-lot transfer process has been given a moniker. "Blotting" is a portmanteau of block and lot, created by the planning and design firm Interboro in 2006, to describe local practices witnessed in Detroit.

Detroit is the poster child of the United States shrinking cities, with roughly forty square miles of vacant land within its city limits. The vacant lands are no longer contiguous, as they were in 1862, and modern-day Detroit homesteaders are aggregating their lands one parcel at a time. Interboro observed this blotting practice, further characterizing it as "New Suburbanism," where neighbors assumed control, responsibility, and even ownership for adjacent abandoned properties.[13] Through investigation, they realized that this land acquisition was often done by legal means as the land was purchased rather than appropriated. The result is a morphological shift in the block's structure, reorienting the building-to-lot configuration, and altering the floor-area-ratio or proportion of building to land.

Planners find optimism in the local, incremental adoption of land. In Youngstown, Ohio, the Youngstown Neighborhood Development Corporation (YNDC) is turning the concept behind blotting into a neighborhood stabilization strategy. Targeting Idora, a neighborhood with strong internal leadership that is located adjacent to a vibrant county park, the YNDC is utilizing a menu of transformation options pinpointed to local parcel conditions. For example, on streets with only a few vacant structures, YNDC is sponsoring the rehabilitation of houses and placing

them back on the market. For vacancies next to occupied homes, YNDC is creating blots by demolishing homes and giving the cleared lots to neighbors. For mid-block vacant lands, community gardens are being organized. And for parcels next to the metropolitan Mill Creek Park, the city is demolishing homes and removing infrastructure to plant meadows and tree groves. Parkview Avenue has morphed almost entirely into parkland. Intersections are marked with stop signs and fenced recreational meadows on all four corners. Eco-seeds mixed with the spontaneous, abundantly growing Queen Anne's lace have assumed responsibility for the lands.

Absent an adjacent property owner willing to adopt the lands municipalities often manage land inventory through periodic mowing. Deemed "blight control," lots are tamed by seeding lawns and mowing to keep volunteer vegetation at bay. The Pennsylvania Horticultural Society (PHS) runs the most established of these "clean and green" programs, maintaining eight thousand lots representing ten million square feet of land and one hundred jobs.[14] The program is widely respected, with benefits toward improving visual perceptions, safety, and even land value around the sites. But the long-term potential is limited.[15] The program manages a form of banal stabilization, branded as a short-term improvement, until development returns. It is palliative rather than projective.

The New Orleans Redevelopment Authority (NORA) is experimenting with alternatives to the trap of continued mowing—which in the case of New Orleans where the vegetation grows quickly, amounts to eighteen mowings annually at a 450 dollar expense per lot. The agency currently owns and maintains nearly 2,500 lots scattered across the city and has begun some small pilot projects to test alternative maintenance strategies on properties with the least market value.[16] These include meadow implementation, with twice yearly mowing to arrest sucession, and canopy plantings on aggregated lots to rebuild the urban canopy. NORA plans to monitor the ecological performance and public perception over time in order to adapt the intial experiments into a larger strategy.

In Detroit, the city council recently approved the purchase of an 140 acre area for a tree plantation project called Hantz Woodlands. Through a combination of sapling and mature tree plantings, a local investor is pushing his version of an urban forest—straight trees in straight lines—as a way to address expanses of fallow urban land.[17] He is jump-starting a process that happens when land sits dormant with time. For example, a robust woodland has emerged on the lands of the former Pruitt-Igoe housing site in Saint Louis, forty years after demolition. With resource limitations, transformation can be managed incrementally to leverage ecological process while embedding social agendas. The wholesale clearing of lots and planting of trees in the Hantz Woodland project does not make sense from a resource standpoint while the unfettered growth and cultural unease renders the Pruitt-Igoe site both vulnerable

and socially irresponsible. Hybrid models are required, ones that are economically, socially, and ecologically defensible.

Action is fueled by the desperate need for a caregiver, and care comes in many different forms. As these examples indicate, some responses include social spontaneity through property transfer from the city to a tidy neighbor; others can be deemed palliative care, sustained with mowing by the "weed and seed" community team that comes periodically to maintain the lots; and a third group can be described by ecological assertion, by minimally maintained meadows, or even ecological dominance, by a forest that emerges when land is left alone for a long time. In these instances, where the land market value has dropped significantly, the ecological, aesthetic, or social value of the land ultimately outweighs its economic value.

The actions can be categorized as forms of maintenance, means of aid, support and assistance, rather than as acts of alteration and insertion. The promotion of social and ecological value is sustained through the means of providing the necessities required for subsistence. In the case of ecological function, these are minimal—air, water, soil, and space. For social function, the needs are more complex, but security, cleanliness, bewilderment, and space are paramount. Design, in this context exists, but it does not take the form of a one-time physical insertion. It is not about construction or capital improvement.

Instead, design is achieved through reformulation and sustained upkeep. Design is a support system for the abandoned, not an economic panacea, but a spatial advocate. It allows for fundamental alteration through tactical acts of maintenance. The acts of maintenance appear minimal or non-existent on the surface but the sub-surface enables transition and transformation into alternative visions of public space. The fence, the lawnmower, the goat, the Queen Anne's lace, and the Sumac—directed and engaged through careful deployment and spatial organization—are the actors and materials of design that support social and ecological engagement.

While these examples emerge and operate in contexts of market devaluation, they point to the potential for alternative and viable forms of land valuation that could be applied to and alter development in other contexts. While the large swathes of non-tax paying land are problematic for municipal operation, they also provide an urban condition where ecological and social functions could coexist. Land value is usually tied to market value, or the potential capital that could be generated through rent or sale. Exchange value is given high importance. Assessed value, the taxation basis of the property, usually reflects market value, with a time lag, as assessments cannot keep up with market fluctuation. In some instances, where a certain use is desired, the use value may affect the assessed value of the property. Farmland preservation is a good example. With an expansion

A bird's eye view of the wild urban woodland at the former Pruitt-Igoe housing site, showing the haunting power of the thirty-three acre tract within its urban context. The woodland is ecologically robust but, to date, socially unresponsive. Without citizen buy-in and a clear cultural agenda, the site is under-performing.
PHOTO: COURTESY OF AUTHOR

of the cadre of highest and best use, the value assessment can be altered to reflect alternative and locally specific uses. The adage invoked earlier of location matters, can be diversified to reflect the bio-geophysical, cultural, and social parameters of location. This benefits locations where economic capital has vanished but human and ecological capital remains. Through non-market valuation, concepts of land value—and its associated bundle—shift.

When market forces vanish, land typically goes from being a symbol of freedom to being that other sort of free, the sort that is met with suspicion. People are leery of land that comes at no cost— what is the catch? But in the case of abandoned land, despite any suspicion, it still performs. Abandoned land is like an electronic device, left curbside, with a note attached, saying 'it works'. Many people walk by, and choose not to take the free item, some because they truly do not want it but others because there is risk associated, coupled with imperfect information. There is no way to test the device in situ; and there are questions about why someone would give away something for free. Why not sell it if it works? Why not keep it? There is a supposition that goods given away for free could be damaged. Only when the context of their situation is made clear, as in the case of samples at the grocery store, is that which is free embraced. Further, there is a stigma associated with taking or relying on free goods. Being able to negotiate a deal is seen as clever, but taking things without paying, especially if done frequently, can be viewed as dependence. In this case, free is no longer associated with independence but rather a lack of financial freedom and a reliance on aid. Free is then not a choice but a need.

To return to the electronic device left curbside, there are times when the advertising is true. When plugged in, it turns on. The risk pays off. Here, there is a relevant analogy with the abandoned urban land. This land works too. It has ecological value and social potential, attributes not usually valued by the market, but important for urban function. The land suffers from imperfect information, where a negative reading is tainting its perception. Through visual decoding and data support as evidenced by the long-term planning, outreach and pilot initiatives of the Detroit Future City project, the efforts of data collection by Data Driven Detroit,[18] the perspective of the Unreal Estate Guide to Detroit,[19] and the evidence-based studies of the PHS "clean and green" program effects, arguments can be made for inclusion of this land within the urban fabric, as a fully functioning, highly flexible, connective tissue.

Yet there is another tension with the free urban land because much of the land is being transferred from private to public hands. Currently, there is not a viable economic model for this type of un-settlement. Both taxation and public funding depend on human occupation of land. Beyond pure economics, there is a tendency to view this transformation as regression, rather than part of a reproductive cycle. Production is linear, unidirectional towards growth. But while overall growth occurs, with ever-expansive urbanization, some land is left behind in the wake of capital's process. And land cannot be simply thrown away. There is an imperative to find a way to restructure the land market to remove the stigma of the free, to see the potential in maintenance, to provide the information necessary to convince both public and private entities to take action and permanently adopt the unwanted lands.

Don't wait for development. Go ahead. Plug the land back into the city.

Jill Desimini is assistant professor of Landscape Architecture at the Harvard University Graduate School of Design. She holds Master of Landscape Architecture and Architecture degrees from the University of Pennsylvania. Her research focuses on design strategies for abandoned urban lands.

Notes

1 Joseph B. Nichols, Stephen D. Oliner, and Michael R. Mulhall, "Commercial and Residential Land Prices Across the United States 2010–16," *Finance and Economics Discussion Series*. Divisions of Research & Statistics and Monetary Affairs, Federal Reserve Board, Washington, D.C. (2010), http://www.federalreserve.gov/pubs/feds/2010/201016/201016pap.pdf.
2 Harvey M. Jacobs, "Claiming the Site: Evolving Social-Legal Conceptions of Ownership and Property" in *Site Matters: Design Concepts, Histories, and Strategies*, ed. Carol J. Burns and Andrea Kahn (New York and London: Routledge, 2005), 20.
3 Ibid., 22.
4 Morris A. Davis. and Michael G. Palumbo, "The Price of Residential Land in Large US Cities," *Journal of Urban Economics*, vol. 63, issue 1 (2008): 352-384.
5 Lincoln Institute of Land Policy, *Land and Property Values in the U.S.*, http://www.lincolninst.edu/resources/.
6 Andrew Haughwout, James Orr, and David Bedoll, "The Price of Land in the New York Metropolitan Area," *Current Issues in Economics and Finance: Second District Highlights*, vol. 14, no. 3 (April/May 2008), http://www.newyorkfed.org/research/current_issues/ci14-3.pdf.

7 Morris A. Davis, Michael G. Palumbo and Jonathan Heathcote, "The price and quantity of residential land in the United States," *Journal of Monetary Economics* 54, Issue 8 (2007): 2595-2620.
It is interesting to include Davis and Heathcote's statement on their data: "Note that we do not directly measure the price of land, but rather infer it from data on house prices and structures costs. With the exception of land sales at the undeveloped fringes of metro areas—where land is relatively cheap—there are very few direct observations of land prices from vacant lot sales, because most desirable residential locations have already been built on. Our indirect approach allows us to circumvent this potentially intractable measurement problem."
8 Wolfgang Kantzow and Philipp Oswalt. "Property: Whose City?" in *Shrinking Cities: Volume 1 International Research* (Ostfildern-Ruit. New York: Hatje Cantz, D.A.P./Distributed Art Publishers, 2005), 694.
9 Edward L. Glaeser and Joseph Gyourko. "Urban Decline and Durable Housing." *Journal of Political Economy*. vol. 113, no. 2 (April 2005): 345-375.
10 Ibid., 345.
11 Genesee County Land Bank, '*About Us*', http://www.thelandbank.org/aboutus.asp

12 Longley, Kristen, "Package of 58 Flint houses for sale on eBay," *M live*, January 8, 2011, http://www.mlive.com/news/flint/index.ssf/2011/01/package_of_58_flint_houses_for.html.
13 Tobias Armborst, Daniel D'Oca and Georgeen Theodore. "Improve your Lot," in *Cities Growing Smaller. Urban Infill no. 1*, Steve Rugare and Terry Schwarz, eds. (Cleveland: Cleveland Urban Design Collaborative, Kent State University, 2008), 46-64.
14 Pennsylvania Horticultural Society, "LandCare Program," http://phsonline.org/greening/landcare-program.
15 Charles C. Branas, Rose A. Cheney, John M. MacDonald, Vicky W. Tam, Tara D. Jackson, and Thomas R. Ten Have, "A Difference-in-Differences Analysis of Health, Safety, and Greening Vacant Urban Space," *American Journal of Epidemiology* 174, no. 11 (2011): 1296–1306.
16 New Orleans Redevelopment Authority, "Land Stewardship," http://www.noraworks.org/land.
17 Laura Berman, "Planting a Walk in the Woods," *The Detroit Press*, October 15, 2014.
18 For more information see: http://detroitfuturecity.com; http://www.dcdc-udm.org; and www.datadrivendetroit.org.
19 Andrew Herscher, *The Unreal Estate Guide to Detroit* (Ann Arbor: The University of Michigan Press, 2012).

WHAT A BODY CAN DO: THE POLITICAL AS GENERATOR OF A COMMON SPATIALITY

Lucía Jalón Oyarzun

***Elks Parade, Harlem**, 1938*

Jack Manning was eighteen years old when he took this photograph. He was a member of Aaron Siskind's Feature Group, part of the New York based Photo League, since 1936. The Feature Group was working, in collaboration with sociologist Michael Carter, on a cultural analysis of Harlem through photography.[1] The once bourgeois neighborhood in Upper Manhattan was now one of the worst slums of the northern United States. In 1939 a report published by the Citizens' Housing and Planning Council of New York outlined the main problems affecting Harlem—overcrowding, skyrocketing rent-prices, and aging buildings—all underscored by a growing racial segregation. In 1940, *Look* published "244,000 Native Sons," a feature illustrating this situation with the work of the Feature Group alongside Carter's texts. Manning's *Elks Parade* image was chosen as its cover. If Siskind's focus was on the relationship between formal composition and social criticism, the younger Manning was fascinated with the interactions between the people of the neighborhood. For two years he had explored the neighborhood, conversed with the neighbors, and gotten to know its workings, the unfolding of its days, and the intermingling of its lives. Through these wanderings he came to grasp Harlem's paradoxical condition. The neighborhood was alive and exciting, but also a slum trapped within the unwritten segregation found in the North.

Elks Parade was taken in the summer of 1938, during the annual parade of the Elks. Manning must have stood on the western side of 7th Avenue looking east, to the block between 129th and 130th Streets. There is joy and wonder in the situation, in the stance of the bodies—from the tiptoeing children to the sitting elders—in the cohesion between groups and conversing neighbors, and in the careful proximity of those watching on their own and everyone's expecting gazes. The multitude's joy expressed in the photograph, the fleeting configuration of a singular spatial organization born out of the materiality of the everyday, turns Manning's piece into a photographic translation of the Spinozist expression that we don't know what a body can do: there is always an uncharted dimension of our body's actions and passions that radically unsettles the premise of modern politics.

Those bodies, defined "by what they can do, by the affects of which they are capable—in passion as well as in action," are producing a common spatiality capable of expressing their political presence outside of the officially designated political arena from which they have been extracted.[2] They have been forced to acknowledge that the publicness of the square or any other officially designated political arena, is not something given but produced, and that it is therefore their collective doings that "collect the space itself, gather the pavement, and animate and organize the architecture."[3] Thrown out of the political sphere of American liberal democracy, with no possible participation in the game of representation, another kind of political expression comes forward,

Elks Parade, Harlem, 1938, Jack Manning (1938).
PHOTO: COURTESY OF THE JACK MANNING ESTATE

one based on the political potential implied in the body's material presence. A presence that defines a "non-epic politics" where taking action does not imply a revolution to seize power, but the sustained battle for survival in an endless quotidian actualization of the body's agency[4]: its inherent potential for action. An action threaded across the temporalities and rhythms of the everyday. Accordingly, a new concept of space as multiple corporeality arises: a field of relations in which we discover ourselves enmeshed and not just placed emerges from the body's doings. The role of the formal is radically transformed as the limits between inside and outside or public and private stop functioning as borders and turn into common bonds. Space is no longer a Cartesian static scenario but constituent movement in which the individual bodies are constantly responding and reacting to each other through their actions, and consequently endlessly reconfiguring new forms of a common spatiality.

In order to develop his politics, Spinoza felt the urge to go back to ethics. He needed physics to understand the constitution of everything that comes into being, the ways in which material reality constantly composes and decomposes, emerges and changes. What would happen if, rather than thinking of architecture as the codified builder of scenarios for the unfolding of modern politics that treat the bodies as recurring guests, it is thought of through the physics of the bodies, an active agent within the production of their commonly produced spatial organizations?

Nowhere (I)

The block, number 1914, photographed by Manning was built for middle-class families in the last decades of the nineteenth century. Back in 1880, when the train reached the north of the island and real construction in the neighborhood began, realtors sought to attract people from the overcrowded neighborhoods of the south by offering working class housing, as in the dumbbell tenements built east of 3rd Avenue as well as the upper

and middle-class housing to the West. Though this intense construction period was stopped by the 1904 recession, almost all of Harlem had been already built by then. Unrestrained speculation flooded the market with vacant houses and the prices dropped. Under these circumstances, and against the resistance of its white residents, landlords started renting apartments to a rapidly growing black population. The Great Migration, the largest displacement of population to ever take place on American soil, brought 1.6 million people to the northern cities of the country. Among them, Harlem was imagined as a new El Dorado: "there was money, good money, to be made in the North, especially New York. New York; the wonder, the magic city. The name alone implied glamour and adventure. (…) And so, it was on to New York, the mecca of the New Negro, the modern Promised Land."[5] But, the new arrivals soon discovered that, while fleeing the South's de *jure* segregation, they had found its *de facto* northern version. However—and therein lied the paradoxical condition that so fascinated Manning—the neighborhood was to give rise to the 1920s Harlem Renaissance, a thriving cultural movement exploring the new racial pride expressed in the figure of the New Negro.

Ralph Ellison unveiled the profound dimension of this paradox in "Harlem is Nowhere," when he noted how it all read "like the legend of some tragic people out of mythology, a people which aspired to escape from its own unhappy homeland to the apparent peace of a distant mountain; but which, in migrating, made some fatal error of judgement and fell into a great chasm of mazelike passages that promise ever to lead to the mountain but end ever against a wall."[6] The problem of black identity was still at the core of Harlem life in 1948, even though it had been almost twenty years since the Great Depression and a continued economic and social segregation had put an end to the New Negro movement. This identity of one's own was not understood as a category to find comfort, but a strategy to organize one's relation to the surroundings, mediating between the chaos within and beyond the individual self. "Who am I, What am I, Why am I, and Where?" were the questions organizing Harlem's everyday, wrote Ellison; questions mirrored in the answer to the more routine "How are you?": "Oh, man, I'm nowhere." This answer expressed the lack of a "stable recognized place in society, (for) one's identity drifts in a capricious reality in which even the most commonly held assumptions are questionable. One 'is' literally, but one is nowhere; one wanders dazed in a ghetto maze, a 'displaced person' of American democracy."[7] Ellison's expression, "one 'is' literally," implies a material body that wanders the streets, but it is a body that occupies no place and has no voice within the political sphere of representation. American democracy becomes a realm that exists beyond matter just as representation displaces presence.

Ellison's expression "being nowhere" shows its disquieting proximity to Bartleby's "I would prefer not to."[8] They are both formulas[9] to render inoperative the system of normalcy wherein they are uttered. "Being nowhere" opens up a crack in which the nowhere of representation becomes an everywhere of presence, both a field of immanent production where identity is made present/presence as common production of the multitude, and an active denial of former transcendent, officially granted and perfectly bounded categories in which to belong. "Nowhere" implies both the plane where that common production unfolds and the spatial —material—dimension defining it. This relational field produced by the body's agency turns the architect into an agent, versed in the production of spatial organizations, as well as their processes, concepts, triggers, rhythms, and opportunities. Consequently, taking action implies assuming the political dimension, not so much of architecture as a codified discipline, but of an *architectural intent* as practical art conceived for the organization of the world that surrounds us, that turns the production of our common identity into a need.

Sounds

The parade is not what interests Manning, and though the marchers and bands are lost outside the frame, their sound isn't. The soundscape of Harlem meant "a distinctive and valuable culture," a significant part of that produced identity and, consequently, a claim for a physical space they could not own.[10] But that soundscape was only a single thread of nowhere. Ellison's "nowhere" meant, not so much a counter-public sphere but a different kind of common realm outside the modern notions of publicness. An unbounded common spatiality produced by the interaction between the layout of the Manhattan grid, the formal conditions of west Harlem architecture, and it's growing black population. This distinctive sphere made out of sounds, minor practices, common languages, shared rooms, partaken meals, and folk traditions did not relate through representation—through the public roles of its inhabitants, for there was no real recognition of those—but through their material presence and everyday production. "Nowhere" seeped in throughout the blocks, running through the narrow corridors of rooming houses, shared bedrooms, and communal kitchens, adjusting temporalities and rhythms of use, overflowing the streets through open windows, or reigning unbounded through its rooftops.

Far from romanticizing this state of things, we need to acknowledge them as the survival strategy they were. The streets, fire escapes, or rooftops were occupied out of necessity. As the rent prices skyrocketed, doubling those of the rest of the city, apartments were systematically subdivided and blocks became cramped. But it wasn't just the interiors that flowed outwards. Since the streets had a steady presence of police officers—patrolling the neighborhood, dispersing any kind of gathering, and serving as a "constant reminder of the boundaries of acceptable conduct,"[11]—and the economic pressure as well as lack of public or available facilities and diversions put a strain into Harlem's social life, an inside-exteriority appeared too, from the "rent-parties" to the "buffet flats."

Exteriors

The title of Manning's photograph *Elks Parade* referred to the annual parade organized by the Benevolent and Protective Order of Elks. The Elks were the most important fraternal order, charity, and social club in Harlem, where they offered a network of support for many of its members, promoted educational programs, community services, and entertainment, such as dances, parties or parades.[12] These were common in Harlem. By 1930, the neighborhood was described as a parade ground because "during the warmer months of the year no Sunday passes without several parades. (...) Almost any excuse for parading is sufficient—the funeral of a member of the lodge, the laying of a corner stone, the annual sermon to the order, or just a general desire to 'turn out.'"[13] This "turning out" did not require any special occasion, and all day long the streets were crowded, Lenox and Seventh being "the two favorite avenues of Harlem where folks go a-strollin'" according to the *New York Times*.[14] This situation was captured in Palmer Hayden's *Midsummer Night in Harlem* [IMG04] where these streets, the real public squares of Harlem, could not be reduced to their imprint in the ground for they climbed façades, peered through open windows and made small talk in the fire escapes.

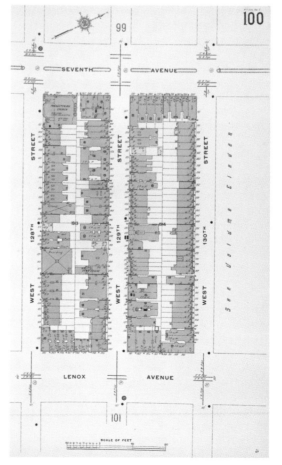

Manhattan v. 7, plate no. 100 (Map bounded by 7th Ave., W. 130th St., Lenox Ave., W. 128th St.); Insurance maps of the City of New York published by the Sanborn Map Company (1912).

Poster for the Tenement House Department of the City of New York advising that tenement house residents keep their fire escapes free of obstructions, Federal Art Project, 1936 or 1937.

Children on Fire Escape, Weegee (1938).
PHOTO: COURTESY OF THE INTERNATIONAL CENTER FOR PHOTOGRAPHY, NEW YORK

Fire escapes became a key element of the New York cityscape after 1901, when the Tenement House Act gave specific instructions for their construction in new buildings and their attachment to existing ones. In just a few years they were an essential part of Manhattan's urban experience.[15] They weren't just vantage points to observe the city, but also were spaces for storing, gardening, drying the laundry, among others. And in the hot summer nights when "the big barracks are like fiery furnaces, their very walls giving out absorbed heat (and) men and women lie in restless, swelter-ing rows, panting for air and sleep,"[16] they became outside bedrooms. The public realm was coated with intimacy when basic domestic practices over-flowed the buildings to create open-air interiors. Something similar happened in the rooftops of the city. The urban grid is inverted and while the streets become unwalkable, their public nature is transformed into a shared horizon where a com-mon use spreads beyond the boundaries of private property. Staircases, walls, and parapets become forms that offer protection, a hiding spot, a bench, or a vantage point to watch the parade.

Interiors

When *Look* magazine published Manning's photo-graphy in 1940, it appeared clipped and showed only the overcrowded fire escape balconies. By the end of the 1930s, 250,000 African Americans occupied an area of 262 blocks, which meant that more than one-tenth of New York's total popu-lation was packed in less than one-sixteenth of the island area.[17] The large apartments of west Harlem were systematically subdivided and turned into rooming houses or shared with lodgers. This meant a relentless and frantic activity happening within those apartments: "when bedtime comes, there is the feverish activity of moving furniture about, making down cots or preparing floor-space as sleeping quarters. (...) Even 'shift-sleeping' is not unknown in many places. During the night, a day-worker uses the room and soon after dawn a night-worker moves in."[18]

And still the rents doubled those of the rest of the city, a two-room unit in Manhattan averaged a $12 rent, but in Harlem it meant $24.50.[19] The reason was simple, nowhere else in the city were African Americans able to rent an apartment. Hence, in the 1920s many tenants began to throw "rent-parties" in order to meet the monthly payment. At first they were no more than the festive gathering of a few friends before the land-lord's visit. Soon, they spread quickly and you could find, every Saturday and simultaneously, "as many as twelve parties in a single block and five in an apartment building."[20] For twenty-five cents admission, families and tenants opened their houses and moved the furniture, but this time to accommodate a complete social event with food, music, and dancing: "It was so full of life, so much fun. People would be telling jokes... Folks would be chitchatting in the bedrooms, and, of course, lots of people would be congregated in the kitchen because that's where the food was. But the living room was where they did the dancing."[21] There were also "buffet flats," apartments that "in the evening, and after nightclubs closed, operated as a venue offering alcohol, music, dancing, prostitutes, and, commonly, gambling, and, less often, rooms to which a couple could go."[22]

Nowhere (II)

In Harlem, "nowhere" occurred as the interior took on the outside while the exterior overflowed inside—when publicness, unchained from the principle of political representation, was radically transformed and it's produced nature revealed. It is here that the full meaning of a politics of presence comes forward, a non-epic politics founded on the everyday practices of bodies; bodies within which lie the possibility of action. It is through the actualization of that potential that new situations and singular spatial configurations emerge. In Harlem, "nowhere" was produced through an entanglement of the bodies' doings, sayings and relations, comings and goings, events, parties and parades, routines and rhythms, racial and economic limitations threaded with strategies for survival, mixed traditions, and cultural (re)inventions. "Nowhere" was where the politics of the non-epic took place and where the political in relation to the architectural unfolded.

And still we don't know what a body is capable of, through its actions or non-actions, what orders, configurations, or turmoils it can create when, while remaining individual, it becomes multiple. We don't know what a body is capable of, and that is why the modern architectural discipline, born along the liberal state and its particular understanding and functioning of politics as the management and administration of life, fails to overcome its instrumental subjection to politics. It does not recognize the possibility of that uncharted remainder. "Nowhere" was but one of the many instances in which a different kind of political action, based on the body's agency, reclaimed a new relation to the sensible and opened up the way for a new understanding of architecture, not as codified technical knowledge, but as a critical practice integrated into the action of the multitude.

Lucía Jalón Oyarzun is an architect and Master in Advanced Architectural Projects by the ETSAM School of Architecture of Madrid, where she now teaches in its landscape specialty line. Since 2013, she is editor-in-chief of *displacements: an x'scape journal*. Her research interests focus on the relation between the political and the spatial construction of the common, and the relationships between body and the built environment.

Notes

1   See Elizabeth J. van Arragon, "The photo league: views of urban experience in the 1930s and 1940s," PhD diss., University of Iowa, 2006; Joseph Entin, "Modernist Documentary: Aaron Siskind's Harlem Document." *The Yale Journal of Criticism* 12, no. 2 (1999): 357-382; Aaron Siskind, Maricia Battle, and Ann Banks, *Harlem Photographs, 1932–1940* (Washington: National Museum of American Art, Smithsonian Institution Press, 1990); and Mason Klein and Catherine Evans, *The Radical Camera: New York's Photo League, 1936–1951* (New Haven, Conn: Yale University Press, 2011).
2   Gilles Deleuze and Claire Parnet, *Dialogues II* (New York: Columbia University Press, 2002), 60.
3   Judith Butler, "Bodies in Alliance and the Politics of the Street," *European Institute for Progressive Cultural Policies*, (September, 2011), http://eipcp.net/transversal/1011/butler/en.
4   The term "non-epic politics" is coined after Spanish philosopher Amador Fernández Savater's article "Notas para una política no estado-céntrica." He notes how, in the political realm, "little value or visibility [is given] to that which is not epic." This is due to a constant recurrence to "mental schemes of reference (the imaginary of revolution, etc.)" that put the weight of political action into a future that will solve all problems, rather than on the everday composition of a common world. "Notas para una política no estadocéntrica," *eldiario.es*, (April 11th, 2014), http://www.eldiario.es/interferencias/Notas-politica-estadocentrica_6_248535164.html. There is an English translation available: "Notes for a Non-Statocentric Politics," *Critical Legal Thinking*, (April 21, 2014), http:// criticallegalthinking.com/2014/04/21/notes-non-statocentric-politics/.
5   Frank Byrd, "Harlem Rent Parties," *American Life Histories: Manuscripts from the Federal Writers' Project, 1936 to 1940* (Library of Congress, Manuscript Division, WPA Federal Writers' Project Collection), http://www.loc.gov/item/wpalh001365.
6   Ralph Ellison, "Harlem is Nowhere," in *The Collected Essays of Ralph Ellison*, ed. John F. Callahan (New York: Modern Library, 1995), 323.
7   Ibid., 325.
8   Herman Melville, "Bartleby, the Scrivener: A Story of Wall Street," in *Billy Bud, Sailor, and Other Stories* (London: Penguin Books, 1985).
9   Gilles Deleuze, "Bartleby; or, the Formula," in *Essays Critical and Clinical* (London: Verso, 1998), 68-90.
10   Clare Corbould, "Streets, sounds and identity in interwar Harlem," *Journal of Social History* 40, no. 4 (2007): 859-894.
11   Ibid., 867-868.
12   Stephen Robertson, "Perry Brown: A Lodge member's life in Harlem," *Digital Harlem Blog*, (July 15, 2010), https://digitalharlemblog.wordpress.com/2010/07/15/perry-brown-lodge-member/.
13   James Weldon Johnson, "Black Manhattan," in *Writings* ed. Library of America (New York: Literary Classics of the United States, 2004), quoted in Stephen Robertson, "Parades in 1920s Harlem," *Digital Harlem Blog*, (February 1, 2011), https://digital harlemblog.wordpress.com/2011/02/01/parades-in-1920s-harlem/.
14   "Harlem's Streets Gay and Colorful," *New York Times*, September 6, 1931; quoted in Shane White and Graham J. White, *Stylin': African American Expressive Culture from Its Beginnings to the Zoot Suit* (Ithaca, NY: Cornell University Press, 1998), 220-247.
15   See Elizabeth M. André, "Fire Escapes in Urban America: History and Preservation," PhD diss., University of Vermont, 2006; Sara E. Wermiel, "No exit: The rise and demise of the outside fire escape," *Technology and culture* 44, no. 2 (2003): 258-284; and Thomas A. P. van Leeuwen, "Iron Ivy," *Cabinet Magazine* 32 (Winter 2008/09), http://cabinetmagazine.org/issues/32/vanleeuwen.php.
16   Jacob A. Riis, *How the Other Half Lives: Studies Among the Tenements of New York* (New York: Charles Scribner's Sons, 1890), 166.
17   Thorin Tritter, "The Growth and Decline of Harlem's Housing," *Afro-Americans in New York Life and History* 22, no. 1 (1998): 67; Neil Smith, *The New Urban Frontier: Gentrification and the Revanchist City* (London: Routledge, 1996), 136-162.
18   Byrd, 2.
19   Franklin O. Nichols in cooperation with the Committee on Inter-racial Problems in Housing, *Harlem Housing* (New York: Citizens' Housing Council of New York, 1939), 10-23.
20   Kathleen Drownee, "House-Rent Parties," in *Encyclopedia of the Harlem Renaissance*, ed. Cary D. Wintz and Paul Finkelman (New York: Routledge, 2004), 582-584.
21   Frankie Manning and Cynthia R. Millman, *Frankie Manning: Ambassador of Lindy Hop* (Philadelphia: Temple University Press, 2007), 25-27.
22   Stephen Robertson, "Harlem Undercover: Vice Investigators, Race, and Prostitution, 1910–1930," *Journal of Urban History* 35, no. 4 (2009): 486-504; See also "Harlem Undercover—the maps," *Digital Harlem Blog*, April 17, 2009, https://digitalharlemblog.wordpress.com/2009/04/17/harlem-undercover-the-maps/.

MOBILE LOITERING: PUBLIC INFRASTRUCTURE FOR A HIGHLY GENDERED URBAN CONTEXT

Mariam Kamara

Map of proposed route.

Niger's capital Niamey, as with many other cities in sub-Saharan Africa, is growing rapidly. The implementation of the government's current vision for the city—Niamey *Nyala*, or the "Niamey the Beautiful" plan— provides the impetus for this project. By navigating the line between formal and informal, and permanent and fixed, the city is calibrated to increase the participation of women of all ages in urban public life.

City Streets in Africa

Unprecedented growth is transforming many urban areas in Africa. Strict colonial planning has been overtaken by a complex network of informal infrastructure that has reshaped city streets to meet economic needs and satisfy social desires. Streets have become a large public space, but also a source of loopholes to be exploited by a city's inhabitants in imaginative ways.[1]

Streets in African cities cannot always be defined as "public" in the conventional Western sense, as their occupation is often segregated by class, gender, or age. In the context of a Muslim city such as Niamey, situated in a predominantly Muslim (albeit secular) country, a woman's presence outside of the home—for purposes other than running errands, conducting business, or going to school—is questioned by society. Mobile loitering is a tactic developed by women in Niamey to circumvent this type of public scrutiny. Women are able to inhabit the street by using their journey to and from social calls as a pretext, while enjoying relative privacy by remaining on the move. This practice allows them to loiter in public without fear of judgment. These *flâneries féminines* are a valued source of entertainment, through the spectacle of the street itself, and of knowledge in a city where little space is allocated for leisure or educational activities.

Designing Pretexts for Mobile Loitering

This design proposal formalizes the pretext of mobile loitering as a form of camouflage, offering women destinations as justification for occupying city streets. A lightweight infrastructure marks a path, establishing a framework for takeover actions similar to those observed in the informal areas of Niamey.

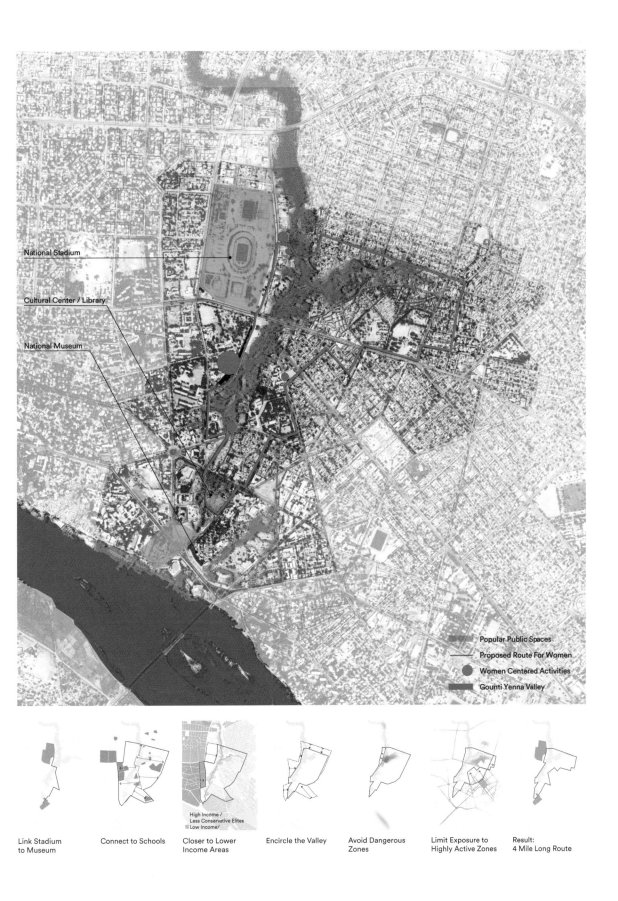

National Stadium

Cultural Center / Library

National Museum

Popular Public Spaces
Proposed Route For Women
Women Centered Activities
Gounti Yenna Valley

Link Stadium
to Museum

Connect to Schools

Closer to Lower
Income Areas

High Income /
Less Conservative Elites
Low Income/

Encircle the Valley

Avoid Dangerous
Zones

Limit Exposure to
Highly Active Zones

Result:
4 Mile Long Route

Stations for fitness, group study, health education, and shopping, punctuate the four-mile route, connecting major public spaces currently used by Niamey's youth. The route's hallmark trait is a shading system made of handmade woven mats, which hovers over open city streets. The primary spaces along the route are designed to be visible to the public, while still offering varying degrees of privacy through the layering of materials and changes in topographical levels. The activity stations are placed strategically to ameliorate access to certain areas for women, or to take advantage of favorable conditions at any given location. For instance, amenities such as markets or fairs are placed in less populated areas along the route in order to increase pedestrian traffic and safety in those zones. In densely populated areas with higher levels of foot traffic, structured community-led programs offer health education and mentoring for women of all ages. Mix-gender activities such as study carrels and fitness stations are situated along quiet streets on the route at regular intervals.

The proposed route establishes a subversive framework that opens up new possibilities for women of all ages in Niamey. Legitimizing, and thereby increasing, the female presence in public has the potential to change social prejudices over time.

Mariam Kamara is from Niger in West Africa, and has a Masters of Architecture from the University of Washington Department of Architecture. In 2015, she founded atelier masōmī, an architecture practice based in Niger, dedicated to finding appropriate contemporary expressions for local materials and traditional techniques.

Notes
1   Abdou-Maliq Simone, *For the City Yet to Come: Changing African Life in Four Cities* (Durham and London: Duke University Press, 2004), 65.

CONTESTED ENERGIES

Ersela Kripa and Stephen Mueller

Contested Territories

Recent transformations in domestic energy policy have instigated a new era of resource-based urbanism throughout the United States, fundamentally reshaping relationships between property, resources, and domestic space in newly contested territories. Embodied most visibly in the proliferation of hydraulic fracturing (fracking) sites across the Great Plains and western states, paradigmatic shifts in energy extraction technologies and transport logistics have conspired to inscribe volatile intersections between competing interests within newly domestic geographies. National policies aggressively promoting energy independence have opened new sites to energy exploration, enabling speculative investment in energy infrastructure by private companies, and a booming market for jobs in the energy extraction sector. This has catalyzed the development of new urban forms—negotiated environments born of necessity, hardship, and speculation. Once-sleepy towns in the Great Plains have been transformed, seemingly overnight, into centers of production, transport, labor, and housing, in support of the new domestic energy economy. Private property owners in areas targeted for exploration have incrementally relinquished vast areas to both federal and private interests, ceding easements and mineral rights, in some cases through pressure from energy interests and the use of eminent domain.[1] Split estates, kill zones, man camps, and carbon cemeteries are but a few examples of the emerging petro-industrial

spatial typologies, whose very nomenclature indicates the uneasy and often conflictual methods by which these transitions occur.

Across these contested territories, the proposed Keystone XL (KXL) pipeline cuts a definitive transect, representing a newly-minted intercontinental territory, and a site of potential existential and ecological risk. KXL is a proposed and partially completed oil pipeline originating in Alberta, Canada. The line is planned and maintained by TransCanada, a major North American energy company, which manages pipelines and other energy interests across the continent. If completed, the KXL pipeline will span seventeen hundred miles in length, making it one of the longest oil pipelines in the world. KXL will conduct crude oil extracted from Albertan Tar Sands (and additional supply from the Bakken Shale in the northern Great Plains) to advanced modern refineries in Texas capable of handling the new product. A majority of output would be exported to global markets, leaving a small percentage for domestic consumption. The United States would act largely as a bystander in this territorial transaction, its property given over as a conduit to global commerce and the flow of extra-territorial resources across its borders—in effect producing a form of "international easement." Debate over the future of the line has stalled its construction, after completion of its southern leg. The northern leg requires a "presidential permit" to cross the international border with Canada, but

An anatomy of equipment, operations, and tactics employed by Transcanada—obstructionist activists—and local authorities in and around the proposed Keystone XL construction easement in the 2012 East Texas Tar Sands Blockade.
IMAGE: COURTESY OF AGENCY; DRAWING: GARRET HOUSE

Sites of protest and obstruction related to the Keystone XL pipeline.
IMAGE: COURTESY OF AGENCY; DRAWING: GARRET HOUSE

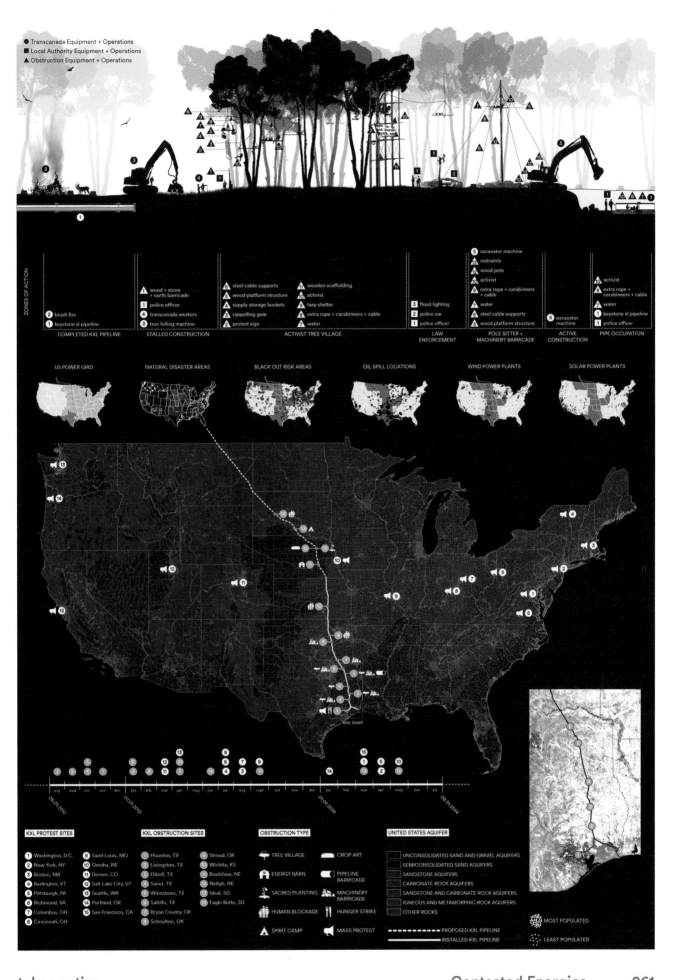

Transcanada Equipment + Operations
Local Authority Equipment + Operations
Obstruction Equipment + Operations

ZONES OF ACTION

COMPLETED KXL PIPELINE
2 brush fire
1 keystone xl pipeline

STALLED CONSTRUCTION
wood + stone + earth barricade
1 police officer
4 transcanada workers
3 tree felling machine

ACTIVIST TREE VILLAGE
steel cable supports
wood platform structure
supply storage buckets
rappelling gear
protest sign
wooden scaffolding
activist
tarp shelter
extra rope + carabineers + cable
water

LAW ENFORCEMENT
3 flood lighting
2 police car
1 police officer

POLE SITTER + MACHINERY BARRICADE
5 excavator machine
restraints
wood pole
activist
extra rope + carabineers + cable
water
steel cable supports
wood platform structure

ACTIVE CONSTRUCTION
5 excavator machine

PIPE OCCUPATION
activist
extra rope + carabineers + cable
water
keystone xl pipeline
1 police officer

US POWER GRID   NATURAL DISASTER AREAS   BLACK OUT RISK AREAS   OIL SPILL LOCATIONS   WIND POWER PLANTS   SOLAR POWER PLANTS

KXL PROTEST SITES
1 Washington, D.C.
2 New York, NY
3 Boston, MA
4 Burlington, VT
5 Pittsburgh, PA
6 Richmond, VA
7 Columbus, OH
8 Cincinnati, OH
9 Saint Louis, MO
10 Omaha, NE
11 Denver, CO
12 Salt Lake City, UT
13 Seattle, WA
14 Portland, OR
15 San Francisco, CA

KXL OBSTRUCTION SITES
1 Houston, TX
2 Livingston, TX
3 Diboll, TX
4 Sacul, TX
5 Winnsboro, TX
6 Saltillo, TX
7 Bryan County, OK
8 Schoolton, OK
9 Stroud, OK
10 Wichita, KS
11 Bradshaw, NE
12 Neligh, NE
13 Ideal, SD
14 Eagle Butte, SD

OBSTRUCTION TYPE
TREE VILLAGE
ENERGY BARN
SACRED PLANTING
HUMAN BLOCKADE
SPIRIT CAMP
CROP ART
PIPELINE BARRICADE
MACHINERY BARRICADE
HUNGER STRIKE
MASS PROTEST

UNITED STATES AQUIFER
UNCONSOLIDATED SAND AND GRAVEL AQUIFERS
SEMICONSOLIDATED SAND AQUIFERS
SANDSTONE AQUIFERS
CARBONATE-ROCK AQUIFERS
SANDSTONE AND CARBONATE-ROCK AQUIFERS
IGNEOUS AND METAMORPHIC-ROCK AQUIFERS
OTHER ROCKS

PROPOSED KXL PIPELINE
INSTALLED KXL PIPELINE

MOST POPULATED
LEAST POPULATED

aug sept oct nov dec jan feb mar apr may jun jul aug sept oct nov dec jan feb mar apr may jun jul
08.01.2012   01.01.2013   01.01.2014   08.01.2014

takes action

has been delayed pending review by the US Department of State. A forthcoming report will assess the project's contribution to the national interest, considering its potential impact on foreign policy, national security, global ecology, and the domestic economy. The project remains hotly contested along all of these vectors.

Concerns for the project are diverse, stemming largely from uncertainty surrounding the unprecedented scale and environmental impact of resource extraction in Canada's Athabasca oil sands. The carbon and water-intensive extraction process has already transformed millions of acres of Boreal forest and wetlands in Northeastern Alberta into a seemingly alien landscape of bitumen strip mines, populated by supersized hydraulic excavators, and four hundred ton heavy hauler trucks standing almost twenty-four feet high. These highly visible transformations feed the fears and rhetoric of concerned citizens and those living in its path, who conflate the transmission of environmental devastation from the resource's origin to the physical artifact of the pipeline itself, and extrapolate possible future disaster scenarios across the pipeline's territory. Since KXL would connect the domestic interior with the wild otherness of this extraction landscape, it can be read as an intrusion on the presumed sanctity of domestic territory, forging a radical continuity between landscapes of extraction and internal practices of consumption. The high visibility, and hyperbolic nature of this landscape present a radical shift in the domestic awareness of energy production, which for decades has been sourced in environments beyond the close scrutiny and daily attention of American consumers. The messy realities of energy production, once held at arm's length in the few quietly producing remaining interior oil fields, off-shore platforms in the outer continental shelf, and highly productive but highly contested fields of oil-rich nations in Latin America and the Middle East, are now brought decisively home. Opponents thus respond to the seemingly innocuous pipeline as a physical artifact of the desperation of late capitalist energy exploration, as a daily reminder of our dependence on scarce and inefficient resources, and our codependence on other nations and business conglomerates to support our carbon-intensive lifestyles.

Where the pipeline is already complete, it has a largely invisible, yet highly volatile presence—silently, but decisively, remapping property and human relations. The chemical composition of the transmitted crude (a particular composition known as diluted bitumen, or DilBit) is a highly corrosive and viscous mixture, which demands higher operating temperatures and pressures than required for conventional oil transmission. This poses new challenges to the integrity of the pipeline, which may fail with corrosion over time, or produce highly pressured leaks contaminating large areas above and below ground. Spectacular failures of other oil sands pipelines in the United States and Canada, and documentation of poor workmanship on completed segments of KXL, add to a climate of growing public skepticism for technologically risky energy endeavors since the Deepwater Horizon catastrophe in 2010.

In a position of readiness and anticipatory response, TransCanada has created a punctuated series of hierarchical control structures across the territory, enabling pervasive spatial protocols of surveillance and maintenance. The pipeline and its associated infrastructure manage the security of both resource and property, as the transmitted crude moves from extraction site through on-ramps, tank farms, and refineries. An industry-standard deployment of pump stations at fifty-mile intervals and notational mile markers along the line set up a new rhythm of spatial accountability across the Jeffersonian grid. Huge swaths of property are transformed as wide local easements for construction and access. This meting out of the territory also provides regular intervals for surveillance and monitoring of conditions, with robotic "smart pigs" conducting sweeps between pump stations—checking for defects in pipe integrity, chemical, and electromagnetic composition, which could signal tampering or systemic failure. Local wildlife and vegetation is monitored with periodic aerial photography to capture variations that could signal leakage or contamination. In the case of any leaks, larger mile-wide swaths are designated as voluntary evacuation zones,[2] inscribing a virtual no-mans-land imbued with the portent of potential disaster. Areas with high volume input, like those near natural gas production in the Bakken Shale, and potential high volume export, like the Gulf refineries, accumulate higher orders of security and transport infrastructure.

The final path of the pipeline is a result of intense, spatial negotiation between competing and often adversarial interests. The path marks

Pumping station in Steele City, Nebraska. These stations are operational for the existing Keystone pipeline and the southern leg of the Keystone XL, with new junctures, electrical facilities, and site offices installed throughout the territory as new segments come online.
PHOTO: COURTESY OF AGENCY

what, in the minds of its developers, advocates, and enablers is the path of least resistance, doing the least harm to those constituencies which pose a real threat of opposition. Its expedient march through depressed areas of the Great Plains has been described as a "map of power and poverty," and an example of "environmental racism."[3] Targeting those properties of the poor and disenfranchised, who have few resources and offer minimal resistance,[4] is a clear example of "disproportionate impact" on those with little alternative but to agree to the construction of the line.[5] In this way, realizing the pipeline has served to unearth the heterogeneous assembly of competing interests enmeshed in an otherwise passive territory, generating new sites for conflict and action.

Making and Acting in the Energy-Industrial Landscape

The contemporary energy practices which have enabled the pipeline's construction echo and reinforce longstanding preoccupations of the modern, elucidated with an astute skepticism by Hannah Arendt in *The Human Condition*. The modern's drive for absolute efficiency and increased production, in Arendt's terms, constitutes a making of the world—the design and execution of an explicit and controllable product or mechanism with limited or finite inputs and presumably predictable outcomes. For Arendt, making is an expedient substitute for acting, whereby an individual entity becomes uniquely empowered to control the outcomes of a situation.[6] This, she states, inhibits the political practice of plurality, a fundamental human condition whereby individuals with independent and often conflictual expressions constitute a "space of appearance which is the public realm."[7]

The makers of the contemporary energy-industrial landscape argue for the exploitation of untapped resources, the expansion of domestic extractive landscapes, and the proliferation of resource infrastructure, citing quantifiable outcomes in increased production, improved energy independence, and decreased costs to the consumer. The mechanisms they propose are economic, technological, and infrastructural, including tax credits and trade embargos, sonic cannons and seismic airguns, steam injection wells and transcontinental pipelines. They balance their argument, in Arendtian terms, both with the modern notion of "early concern with tangible products and demonstrable profits" and "its later obsession with smooth functioning and sociability."[8] The maker's relationship to their opponents is largely "antagonistic"—a binary politics of "friends and enemies," and not an "agonistic" plurality—where "adversaries," or "friendly enemies" might agree over principles but disagree about the means to achieve them.[9] "Drill, Baby, Drill!" is the clarion call of the makers, rejecting the public realm's "fiercely agonal spirit"[10] by collapsing plurality and casting the consideration of alternative voices as an impediment to progress. When the phrase was introduced by Michael Steele at the 2008 Republican National Convention, it promoted expanding domestic energy production by opening production on previously unexplored sites. This was suggested as a part of a strategy for voters to "put [their] country first,"[11] seemingly sacrificing individual agency for a pragmatic approach to a presumably consensual, desired outcome.

This ethos of making enabled by such rhetoric is further manifest in the construction of KXL. Yet, the spatial realities of making across the contested territory enable spaces for action within its blind spots. The maker's top-down instantiation of strategic energy-industrial spatial protocols promote a type of productive disequilibrium where the transect misaligns with existing structures and intersects adversarial population centers. The trans-political territory of the line is far-flung and overextended, leading to uncertainty, confusion, and oversight in its construction, maintenance, and in response to actions against it. As it crosses

The proposed path of the Keystone XL pipeline through Nebraska remains a hotly contested issue, with the project permit stalled as concerned citizens and organizations throughout the state protest the pipeline's path through ecologically sensitive areas, including the Nebraskan Sand Hills.
PHOTO: COURTESY OF AGENCY

The Keystone XL pipeline crosses several water bodies, including rivers and aquifers supplying the Great Plains with water for drinking and agriculture.
PHOTO: COURTESY OF AGENCY

juridical and political boundaries, the pipeline constitutes a new territory of misaligned and often uncoordinated interests. A range of actors and competing interests are unearthed and subsequently drawn together, including company executives, construction crews, local law enforcement, property owners, and activists. From the acts of mapmaking, to surveying, site clearance, and the actual laying of the pipe, the line is continuously negotiated, and constantly in flux. The proposed Nebraska segment has been redrawn multiple times in response to competing interests, largely due to concern over its transgression through the Ogalalla aquifer—one of the nation's largest supplies of drinking water—and the Nebraskan Sand Hills. Discussions with multiple property owners, including sovereign Native American tribes, have resulted in the line's recalibration and significant rerouting. These types of adjustments are to be expected, though others were unforeseen. Construction on the line has reorganized entire small towns, some of which have been nearly emptied of residents who leave for temporary jobs in pipeline construction never to return. While the deployment of seemingly regular and innocuous infrastructures across such a large and heterogeneous territory would attempt to produce a predictable stability, it has produced instead a new public realm, and novel constituencies, coincident with the polarization and amplification of existing stakeholders.

Obstructionist Spatial Practices
In its realization through conflict, the territory moves from its conception as prescriptive artifact of making to a pervasive, responsive condition of acting, enabling a range of creative spatial practices from the bottom-up. Bill McKibben, an environmentalist and staunch opponent of KXL, speaks readily about the pipeline's ability to galvanize action from a diffuse and heterogeneous set of environmental, economic, and political actors.[12] McKibben's organization, 350.org, has helped to construct the pipeline territory in the

public imaginary as a symbolic space of conflict. Through his work, and the work of countless others, the pipeline has been recast into a type of lightning rod for political activism of all sorts, and a cipher for a growing number of environmental and social injustices, incubating and attracting oppositional constituencies.

In this milieu, obstructionist and interventionist spatial practices abound. An anti-pipeline coalition in Nebraska built an "energy barn" in the pipeline's right-of-way as a type of didactic spatial demonstration of the pipeline's many failings. The project models an alternative use of clean energies, in the hopes of exploiting the backlash and negative publicity when the highly visible project is demolished. The Rosebud Sioux tribe built a "spirit camp" in the pipeline's path near Ideal, South Dakota, while the Ponca tribe planted sacred corn varietals near Neligh, Nebraska, similarly problematizing the line's construction before it begins. These and other tactical interventions along the line successfully anticipate and exploit the violence of making the pipeline's territory. The future path of the line is thus transformed into a site for opportunistic action, a field of potential where the public realm is enacted through the behaviors of autonomous individuals engaging in explicitly political practices.[13] Alliances are forged between constituents with disparate interests across space, aligned in their opposition and their intersection with the line. Activists from around the world have travelled to the pipeline to participate in shared action.

In 2012, a variety of resistance camps were organized and promoted by the Tar Sands Blockade (TSB), a coalition of activists who believed in "peaceful, sustained direct action"[14] as a primary means of stopping the construction of KXL. In September 2012, founders of the organization, many of whom were veterans of the Occupy movement,[15] established a "tree village" in the piney woods of East Texas. They occupied an area the size of a city block above a planned fifty-foot wide easement for over two and a half months.[16] The camps opportunistically exploited the uncertainty in the emerging legal framework surrounding the pipeline's construction, creating a productive space for action within the recently redefined legal boundaries of property and ownership. If McKibben's rhetoric had established the pipeline as a geography capable of galvanizing national attention, the direct actions in East Texas in 2012 were an experiment of KXL's capacity to serve as a site for sustained action.

Expanding the anticipatory logics of other interventionist practices on the line, the activists in East Texas would be forced to evolve their tactics in response to changing scenarios. Preparation for the occupation began in late summer. As TransCanada secured rights for KXL easements from landowners and obtained presidential approval of the southern leg running from Cushing, Oklahoma through Texas,[17] TSB planned its counteroffensive. Activists spoke with property owners who had second thoughts about the presence of the company on their land, and the questionable safety of petro-industrial infrastructure on their property. They found an unlikely partner in David Daniels, a property owner near Winnsboro, Texas who contributed his land and his labor to the cause, allowing the activists access to his property and helping them build the aerial encampment.[18]

The tree village draws on, and expands, technological legacies of civil disobedience and protest encampments, adapting these strategies to the particularities of the sites in East Texas and Daniels' own experience rigging high-wire circus acts.[19] Lessons learned from experiments in tree-sitting activism, rock climbing, and more common arborist equipment and techniques enabled the protesters to construct a minimal and flexible presence in the path of the proposed pipeline. The "village" has a sophisticated level of development for such a short-lived inhabitation. Described as a "web of tree houses, structures, and pulleys,"[20] the village is a series of aerial platforms seventy-feet above the ground, including a tree house built by Daniels himself. A small outbuilding serves as the headquarters, with a communal kitchen nearby capable of feeding fifty protesters. Days into the occupation, an outhouse was built by a local church. Water is carried in buckets and assorted containers. A makeshift shower is rigged for public bathing.[21] Tree sitters are supported by a band of support staff, including on and off-site medical, legal, and media assistance.[22] Training staff hold informational sessions for newcomers on "prusik knots" and "footloops" before they climb into position.[23]

The village is defined as much by the behavior of its inhabitants as the presumed and instigated behaviors of its detractors—that is, it embodies action as a spatial organizational device. It is critical to the campaign that a few activists are present and visible in the aerial encampment at all times, with the strategic movement of supplies and occasional substitution of exhausted occupiers orchestrating an aerial choreography of resistance.

The anticipated extraction methods of law enforcement prompt the design and embellishment of the tree village. Platforms are constructed out-of-reach of easily deployed extraction equipment like the ubiquitous "cherry picker," increasing the difficulty for law enforcement to remove the platforms and their occupants without specialized tools or specially trained operatives. As a failsafe, occupiers build devices resembling "squirrel guards," extended metal or wooden panels below the platform of an occupied tree to prevent a would-be extractor from accessing the platform from below.

The logistical complexities of life in the trees parallel difficulties throughout the contested territory. For the organizers, their operations scale up and connect them with a larger and underrepresented constituency, the activists' microbehaviors on site echoing larger regional concerns. As Grace Cagle, a biologist from Fort Worth, Texas and founder of TSB explains, "We had to haul up our own water, similarly to those who have to import water after their native sources have been contaminated by fracking and mining."[24] For the protesters, the ubiquitous presence of machinery on site is a fitting microcosmic re-enactment of daily life within the contested territory. The advance of machinery toward the site portends the inevitable advance of law enforcement and the protester's eventual extraction. It also replicates in miniature the machinations of surveillance and logistics that will be enabled by the sanctioned and prolonged presence of industry on and around private properties throughout the line. These types of inclusive interpretations of the environment, disseminated publicly and transparently via online posts, interviews, and live updates from the media team, contribute to the construction of the site as a site for action.

As the occupation wears on, activists are forced to find new means of spatial resistance to respond to changing scenarios. Along with the tree village, and its distributed occupation, parallel and more direct tactics emerge to more explicitly exploit the anticipated violence of dismantling, providing new and more visible confrontational boundaries between the protesters and law enforcement. A timber scaffold spanning the construction easement stood forty feet in the air, "a 100-foot-long wall lashed together with timber,"[25] providing a barrier to the advancing machinery. The scaffold was occupied by a small band of sitters, sporting a banner reading "You Shall Not Pass," delaying construction activities for several days. Actions of individuals were conceived and highlighted in TSB media outreach, providing a forum not only for the communal and sometimes anonymous behaviors of a masked, nameless, and camouflaged collective in the trees, but also for the explicitly attributable action of individuals.

Coincident with the growing media attention, the sites for action left the canopy and came out into the open. The movement began to have faces and names. On October 1, Houston resident Alejandro de la Torre locked himself to an underground cement block in the path of the pipeline near temporary construction about twelve miles north of the blockade, lying on the ground for about ten hours with his hand chained below the ground.[26] Also in early October, twenty-two year old Maggie Gorry occupied a one-foot by four-foot plank[27] atop a forty-foot pole, blocking construction for two days before her arrest. Blockaders had constructed her impromptu obstruction device under the cover of darkness.[28] Tethered to the ground with support lines in a highly visible clearing, the monopod construction temporarily stalled the advance. Upon their arrests, accounts of Gorry's and de la Torre's experiences are added to the growing list of direct actions highlighted on the TSB website, a veritable catalog of tactical practices evolved from sustained action.

Countermeasures, Coevolution, and Escalation

The increasing sophistication of obstructionist tactics in East Texas, and the relative ease with which they could adapt to changing pressures from law enforcement, sparked a type of obstructionist "arms race," transforming the pipeline territory into a laboratory of countermeasures. While the protesters took care to only engage in non-violent and non-destructive acts, their illegal occupation on newly minted company property began to wear on company representatives, who increasingly sought backup from local law enforcement to restore order to the territory and allow construction to continue. Both sides staked a claim for a right to action within the pipeline's easement. Young activists, having studied political and environmental science, sociology, urban planning, and law,[29] held training sessions for occupiers on the technical and legal aspects of disobedient spatial occupations. TransCanada, meanwhile, reportedly briefed local law enforcement on the tactics and identities of protesters, suggesting they reconsider the criminality of the use of certain protest devices, and even suggesting that the protesters' activities be designated as terrorist acts subject to federal prosecution. As evidence of the protesters' supposed transgressions, Transcanada presentations cited the vast geography of TSB's social-media based financial network, which funded construction and supply of the camps through the accumulation of small donations online, and the high level of education and organizational capabilities of the actions' leaders.[30] The sophisticated coordination of broad-based resistance across such a vast territory had made TSB's activities inherently suspect, their actions not only criminalized but disproportionately vilified in order to enable swift and decisive countermeasures.

A heightened response by law enforcement sought to quell the growing visibility of protestor tactics in the media, adopting an increasingly entrenched and militarized stance in the control of the site, and information surrounding the actions. From a company presentation to law enforcement, obtained through a Freedom of Information Act request, TransCanada expressed concern not only with the legality of the protester's actions, but also with the increase in media attention and the high profile these actions had generated.[31] Local law enforcement, encouraged by TransCanada representatives, adopted countermeasures to control the dissemination of information from the blockade. Police reportedly erected screens around sites of detainment to deter onlookers and journalists from seeing and recording their procedures, during the more exposed confrontations and arrests. Officers controlled the records and transmission of actions on the site through the confiscation of cameras and other recording devices, claiming the records were evidence in criminal investigations.[32] A temporary and reportedly "arbitrary" media boundary was put in place by TransCanada, and moved throughout the occupation to limit access to the site and the recording of its events.[33] Police shone floodlights on sitters at night, limiting sleep and creating an environment of ubiquitous surveillance. TransCanada later filed suit against Tar Sands Blockade and their allies, seeking damages and the forced eviction of protesters from company property and construction easements.[34] In January 2013, the protesters agreed to TransCanada's terms, prohibiting certain actions within the pipeline easement including "chaining, shackling, binding, or attaching any person's body, or any other object, article, or mechanism… to stop, halt, or arrest" Keystone construction.[35]

The limiting terms of the lawsuit, the state-sponsored control of information to support corporate activity, and the suggested reclassification of coordinated direct action and civil disobedience as analogous to terrorist activity, all serve as haunting precedents for future actions in contested territories of this sort. They are indicative of a general trend toward what Stephen Graham has called the "new military urbanism," whereby security protocols developed in military settings by occupying forces abroad are brought to bear on the daily operations of the domestic homeland.[36] The defensive posturing of our energy territory, developed in the name of domestic security, and redoubled in the face of obstructionist practices, has recast domestic constituents as extra-state actors and criminal entities. This belies the inherent vulnerability of our energy landscape, which fuels a politics of fear and a pragmatics of response. Action against our energy interests is seen as action against security, and labeled as such.

The escalation of response by the authorities in East Texas suggests a slippery slope, which could enable future possible over-reaches of state actors in dealing with action on and against the line. Just as future urban forms might be harvested from embryonic territorial logistics,[37] legal and authoritative precedents are seeded and calcified with accumulated decisions and actions in spatial practice. In today's climate of increasing scale and frequency of protests, the mutual escalation of protester and police tactics fuels the evolution of obstructionist tactics. In the 2014 Umbrella Revolution in Hong Kong, for instance, protesters and police were visibly coevolved, adapting their clothing, communications, and spatial organizational systems to each other's advances.[38] Similarly, in emerging coevolved models of urban warfare of the IDF and Palestinian guerilla fighters, each side adopts, and then adapts, the technologies and characteristics of its adversary.[39] The next generation of actions in newly contested territories will be equally coevolved, hardened by the experience of TSB, anticipating authoritative response.

As of this writing, the completion of KXL has been successfully stalled, due in some part to the actions in East Texas and other actions nationwide. As sites for direct action dry up, many of the organizers are moving from tactics of resistance to longer term strategic planning, including new community organizations centered on environmental and climate justice.[40] Ron Seifert, a climate activist who serves as a spokesperson for TSB suggests, "We need to ask ourselves as organizers, 'What does escalation look like? [...] Physically blockading infrastructure is a great place to start the conversation [...] we can still build and cultivate a culture of resistance and action, capable of escalating to the point of shutting this stuff down in the future."[41]

Arendt describes action as both a beginning and a realization.[42] While often warning of the unintended consequences and unpredictable outcomes actions might produce, she also details the process by which actions evolve, evoking the double-edged sword of longevity and permanence that might evolve from spontaneous, even intentionally temporary inputs. The processes Arendt describes are not the sequential optimizations of predictable outcomes that modern industry would prescribe, but rather the messy realization of accumulated actions operating within a public realm—some of which catalyze into sweeping historical and cultural transformations, others failing and fading into obscurity. We might better think of process as a chain reaction, or a chain of actions, able to be primed, evaluated, and opportunistically managed through the willful and prolonged construction of sites for action, both physically and intellectually. The first sites will be those like the easement in East Texas, recently redefined blind spots in emerging and evolving contested territories, whose ambiguity and contested nature provide a robust realm for action, debate, and design.

Ersela Kripa and Stephen Mueller are founding partners of AGENCY, an interdisciplinary practice engaging contemporary culture through architecture, urbanism, and advocacy. The partners currently teach at TTU-El Paso, a new satellite program conducting architectural experiments within the developing transnational context of the El Paso-Ciudad Juarez borderplex. Kripa and Mueller are winners of the Rome Prize in Architecture from the American Academy in Rome.

Notes

1 For a complete mapping of eminent domain filings by county related to the Keystone XL, see: "Keystone XL Eminent Domain Map," *Keystone Mapping Project*, http://keystone.steamingmules.com/maps/keystone-xl-eminent-domain-map.
2 "Voluntary Evacuation Zone," *Keystone Mapping Project*, http://keystone.steamingmules.com/gallery/voluntary-evacuation-zone.
3 Taylor Marsh. "Interview-Tar Sands Blockader," (December 12, 2012), http://www.taylormarsh.com/2012/12/tar-sands-blockader-grace-cagle-the-path-of-this-pipeline-is-like-a-map-of-power-and-poverty/.
4 Erin Flegg, "Using Her Body to Stop Keystone XL," *Vancouver Observer*, February 6, 2013, http://www.vancouverobserver.com/sustainability/using-her-body-stop-keystone-xl-biologist-texas-sits-tree-and-goes-jail.
5 Wen Stephenson, "The Grassroots Battle Against Big Oil," *The Nation*, October 28, 2013, http://www.thenation.com/article/176556/grassroots-battle-against-big-oil.
6 Hannah Arendt, *The Human Condition* (Chicago: University of Chicago Press, 1998), 220-230.
7 Ibid., 220.
8 Ibid.
9 Chantal Mouffe, *Agonistics* (London: Verso, 2013), 1-18.
10 Arendt, 41.
11 "Transcript of Michael Steele RNC Speech," *Free Republic*, September 4, 2008, http://www.freerepublic.com/focus/f-news/2074519/posts.
12 Samuel Avery, *The Pipeline and the Paradigm: Keystone XL, Tar Sands, and the Battle to Defuse the Carbon Bomb* (Washington, D.C.: Ruka Press, 2013).
13 Arendt, 7-8.
14 "Who We Are," Tar Sands Blockade, www.tarsandsblockade.org/about-2/who-we-are.
15 Stephenson, October 28, 2013.
16 Flegg, February 6, 2013.
17 Zoe Carpenter, "Tar Sands Blockade: The Monkey Wrenchers," *Rolling Stone*, April 11, 2013, http://www.rollingstone.com/politics/lists/the-fossil-fuel-resistance-meet-the-new-green-heroes-20130411/tar-sands-blockade-the-monkey-wrenchers-19691231.
18 Daniels' story is documented in the upcoming film, *Above All Else*, directed by John Fiege (2014; Fiege Films).
19 Joshua Holland, "New Film Destroys TransCanada's Sunny Keystone PR Campaign," Moyers and Company, May 20, 2014, http://billmoyers.com/2014/05/20/new-film-destroys-transcanadas-sunny-keystone-pr-campaign.
20 Dan Frosch, "Last Ditch Bid in Texas to Try to Stop Oil Pipeline, *New York Times*, October 12, 2012, http://www.nytimes.com/2012/10/13/us/protesters-gather-at-keystone-xl-site-in-texas.html.
21 Stephenson, October 28, 2013.
22 This detail from an account correcting perceived errors and omissions in the Frosch article above from Alexandra Mara. "The New York Times Got It Wrong With The Tar Sands Blockade," *New York Times Examiner*, October 15 2012, https://www.nytexaminer.com/2012/10/the-new-york-times-got-it-wrong-with-the-tar-sands-blockade.
23 Lorenzo Serna, "A Wall Against the Threshold of Collapse," Tar Sands Blockade, October 13 2012, http://www.tarsandsblockade.org/day20/).
24 Marsh, December 12, 2012.
25 Frosch, October 12, 2012.
26 Maria Gallucci, "Keystone Protesters Say They're 'Scared for Their Lives'; TransCanada Denies Wrongdoing," *Inside Climate News*, October 2, 2012, http://insideclimatenews.org/breaking-news/20121002/keystone-xl-pipeline-protesters-tar-sands-blockade-texas-arrests-transcanada-trees-civil-disobedience-oil.
27 "Action Video—Maggie Delaying KXL For Another Day," *Tar Sands Blockade*, October 3, 2012, http://www.tarsandsblockade.org/day10.
28 "Maggie Has Been Arrested After Sitting on a 40 Foot Pole to Delay Keystone XL Clear-Cutting for Two Entire Days," *Tar Sands Blockade*, October 4, 2012, http://www.tarsandsblockade.org/maggie.
29 Stephenson, October 28, 2013.
30 Full TransCanada presentation available from Bold Nebraska at http://www.scribd.com/fullscreen/147205465.
31 Mark Hefflinger, "TransCanada Calls Nebraska Ranchers Aggressive and Abusive, Talks of Terrorism," *Bold Nebraska*, June 14, 2013, http://boldnebraska.org/transcanada-calls-nebraska-ranchers-agressive-and-abusive-talks-of-terrorism.
32 Stephanie Fraser and Melanie Torre. "Pipeline Protestor Locks Self to Ground, ETX Sheriff Attempting Removal," KTRE, Oct 1, 2012, http://www.ktre.com/story/19686437/pipeline-protestor-locks-self-to-ground-etx-sheriff-attempting-removal.
33 Alexandra Mara. "The New York Times Got It Wrong With The Tar Sands Blockade," *New York Times Examiner*, October 15 2012, https://www.nytexaminer.com/2012/10/the-new-york-times-got-it-wrong-with-the-tar-sands-blockade.
34 Stephenson, October 28, 2013.
35 Laurel Brubaker Calkins, "TransCanada Wins Deal to Halt Keystone Protests in Texas," Bloomberg, Jan 28, 2013, http://www.bloomberg.com/news/2013-01-28/transcanada-wins-agreement-to-halt-keystone-protests-in-texas.
36 Stephen Graham, *Cities Under Siege* (London: Verso, 2010). XI-XXX.
37 Neeraj Bhatia, "Harvesting Urbanism Through Territorial Logistics," in *The Petropolis of Tomorrow* (Actar: New York, 2013), 272-287.
38 Infographic: Riot Gear—How Occupy Protesters and Police Stack Up," *South Morning China Post*, October 11, 2014, http://www.scmp.com/infographics/article/1614415/infographic-riot-gear-how-occupy-protesters-and-police-stack.
39 Eyal Weizman, *Hollow Land* (Verso: London, 2007), 185-218.
40 Stephenson, October 28, 2013.
41 Ibid.
42 Arendt, 177.

THE EMPTY CITY: BUILDING A NOMADIC INDUSTRIAL COMPLEX

Martin Sztyk

Emptiness can be a catalyst for intervention. The vast landscape known as the Qattara Depression has great potential; perhaps even the ability to redirect the fervor from political conflicts in the region. This was the thinking of the Central Intelligence Agency in 1957. The declassified CIA document is the genesis of the Empty City proposal as it suggested that flooding the Qattara Depression would bring stability, an altered climate, and economic development within northern Africa and the Middle East.[1] But the concept of the Empty City challenges the CIA's original plan of external influence. The action, instead, comes from local nomadic tribes and offers its own version of latent environmental exploitation.

The terrain of the Qattara Depression produces a natural border condition with its elevation 130 meters below sea level. It's a hostile environment that has discouraged human intervention. The Empty City relies on the surface mining of gypsum and exporting the rich mineral deposits from this prehistoric former sea. These basic ingredients condition the soil for agriculture, which serves as the vehicle for developing and sustaining surrounding regions. Building bacterially-calcified sand and gypsum domes contributes to the knowledge of fast and durable construction techniques in the desert. The proposal catalogues 200 years, showing the simple beginnings of the settlements to the fully mechanized mining operation. However, it is a nomadic endeavor, which is the way people have lived in the region for thousands of years. The working nomads mine resources and then move to the next site. The expanding desert eventually swallows their architectural artifacts and intrusions on the landscape.

The creation of the Empty City relies on the depletion of its resources. A hydro-electric facility floods the Qattara Depression, as it returns to its prehistoric state. The destiny of the nomadic people is intertwined with the industrial complex such that they will benefit from it for generations. Can this lessen the disparity and exploitation in northern Africa? The local endeavor makes the depression's proximity to populated cities worth exploiting.

The Empty City is not designed, but a deliberate and pragmatic intervention built by its nomadic workers. The workers cast the sand

The funicular railway arrives at the edge of the Qattara Depression.

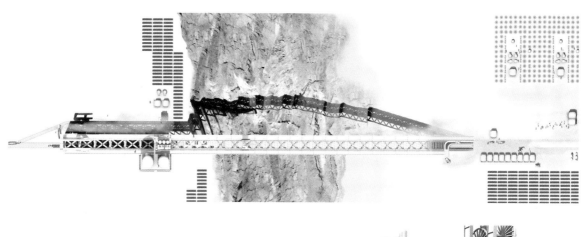

Overhead view of
the funicular railway
as it connects to
the nomadic camps.

A self-sustaining camp
oversees the
northwestern region of
the site, and functions
as a hub for the
transportation of mined
resources.

An underground mineral
depository reveals
the infrastructure of
the funicular system.

Typical nomadic housing
interior integrates
passive systems of light
and ventilation. The
structure is composed
of bacterially calcified
sand and gypsum cast
from pneumatic formwork.

mixture on pneumatic formwork, and when it hardens, the formwork is deflated and reused. The scale of its infrastructure is an accretion of smaller interventions. Specifically, the interventions include housing, industry, transportation, and agriculture, all built for temporary use. The action is a collective effort in response to the vastness of the site. What is learned through the Empty City can be applied to developing countries that experience desertification and the degradation of land used for agriculture, as the need to address the current model of the built environment and its outdated technical practice bring a new progressive measure.

Martin Sztyk is an artist and architect living in Los Angeles and currently holds the position of senior designer of exhibitions at the Los Angeles County Museum of Art.

Notes
1   Gale. 2009. Farmington Hills, MI: ATOMIC ENERGY COMMISSION, Document Number CK3100648275. Reproduced in "Declassified Documents Reference System," http://gdc.gale.com/products/declassified-documents-reference-system/.

Site diagram of Qattara Depression in proximity to the Mediterranean Sea.

RETRO

RetroAction includes projects and texts that center on the contemporary role of memory, memorials, and commemoration on our understanding of valuing and giving place to history. How do forms of action participate in the registration of memory and foster a sense of historical recollection?

ACTION

A LETTER TO ARCHITECTS

Vishaan Chakrabarti

With climate change fully upon us, a swelling global migrant crisis, widespread social inequity, a searing geography of racial injustice, and endless wars bolstered by a century of domination by the internal combustion engine, we must ask what actions the architect can take. This is particularly important in an era when the tools of the Enlightenment can no longer serve us and all that they defined for architectural agency have been rendered ineffective. The challenges architects confront today remain geographic, and therefore spatial, perhaps even more so than during the past two centuries; but are the tools, methods, and convictions of architecture revelatory much less relevant when they remain tethered to a bygone epoch? If architects are to be relevant to our own epoch, as Mies van der Rohe implored, is our discipline even operating at an effective scale of action given the vast territory that contemporary challenges engulf?

Populated by billions of municipal citizens connected by urban, rather than national, identities, cities represent an effective scale of action to confront these challenges, but their capacity is heavily reliant on precise definitions. True cities—as opposed to the vertical suburbs often mistaken for cities today—are built upon a well designed set of networks, be they social networks, street networks, public space networks, or the extensive network of space, materials, and systems that constitute architecture. Such networks provide the social glue that differentiates the *cosmopolis* from the mere metropolis, and offers its citizens the confluence of joy, empowerment, exasperation, and surprise.

If a metropolis is a geographic construct —a large urban region consisting of commerce, housing, and infrastructure, a cosmopolis is a cultural construct that encourages the mixing of social, cultural, and economic groups such that discursive space is enabled across its territory. Discursive space is an expansive definition of the civic realm, something that exists both physically and virtually, in which the public space of the city is seen as something other than a mere amenity. Urban spaces of discourse are critical because they enable the serendipitous exchanges that lead to social friction, allowing for the unplanned and uncontrolled elements that transform society. This may be true at the level of the individual, when an executive crosses a public plaza and confronts or denies the realities of a homeless person, or at the level of crowds, when protests in a public plaza bring down a national government or challenge policing tactics. Movements such as the Arab Spring and Black Lives Matter are reliant on the discursive space of the cosmopolis. By contrast, the Dubai metropolis is physically and socially incapable of hosting such discourse, regardless of how many gleaming airports, shopping malls, skyscrapers, and imported liberal western institutions it may build, because the platforms that generate social friction have been ignored, forgotten, or expunged.

Many architects, too often vainglorious, ignore this distinction between the metropolis and cosmopolis at their peril. While the majority of architectural practices espouse a dedication to the city, few seem willing to decline major commissions for dictatorial regimes regardless of the treatment of construction labor, the censorship of cultural content, or the inability to protest power within their projects. When the world continually sees many of the profession's leaders design opera houses without opera companies, stadia with slave labor, museums with curatorial suppression, windswept plazas in which dissent is illegal, and do so with disdain, greed, and willful ignorance, we need not wonder why architects have lost the credibility needed to address the urban issues of our age. Worse still is the defense of these actions under the neocolonialist guise of "experimentation," in which these practitioners argue that design unfettered by the constraints of accountability allow for a level of architectural freedom unavailable in their home territories. The notion that critical architectural expression necessitates operation outside of the bounds of transparent governance engenders the converse pondering by reactionary traditionalists of whether contemporary architectural vision is even appropriate, necessary, or desirable. But the more urgent question is whether critical architectural expression is possible within a framework of accountability, and to this question there must be a resounding "yes," if design can be something other than either a tired set of compromises defined by bureaucrats or a tired level of irrational exuberance desired by dictators. Projects such as Utzon's Sydney Opera House, OMA's Seattle Public Library, Snøhetta's Malmö Concert Hall and Conference Center, Thom Mayne's Caltrans District 7 headquarters in Los Angeles, and Diller Scofidio and Renfro's conversion of New York's Lincoln Center all demonstrate that this need not be a false choice—architecture can advance the cosmopolis without resorting to designing spaceships built by slaves in the sand. The fascinating commonality among these examples, all of which were executed in democratic municipalities often necessitating the successful navigation of painstaking bureaucratic processes, is the degree to which they remain open field conditions rather than their static object-building counterparts. This is inherent to the open nature of both the client and the context of the cosmopolis as opposed to the closed and deterministic nature of clients and architects who seek the iconic object as a fixed prize. The joy of architecture lies in its capacity for transformation through human agency, which is why the use of buildings over time is critical to the cosmopolis.

The cosmopolis thus requires an ecological network of empowered citizens, generous buildings, discursive public space, robust infrastructure, and a thriving natural environment. Architecture and urbanism are essential to this notion. The size of blocks, the intensity of infrastructure, the use of the ground plane, the connectivity of public space, the access to public institutions, the combinatory architectural art of materials, tectonics, and spatial flow are all critical factors that define whether a metropolis is in fact the cultural phenomenon of the cosmopolis. Architects can advance groundbreaking architecture projects that build the physical, economic, social, and cultural networks of our cities, with an emphasis on beauty, function, and user experience. We can focus on projects that form cultural, institutional, and social density. At the forefront of our process could be a constant emphasis on the lived experience of our work— whether by the inhabitants of our projects or the city's passersby—with the hope of uplifting both the functionary and the flâneur. Yet this demands that we define our work beyond the scale of the building. As some critics have observed, buildings serve as hardware while cities perform as software.[1] Like an iPhone, a Nest thermostat, or a Tesla, we can design beautiful, functional, and groundbreaking buildings, but in the parlance of our epoch, these are only examples of hardware enabled by software. Venkatesh Rao in his online technology series "Breaking Smart"[2] argues that not since the advent of writing and money has there been a technology as powerful as software, largely due to the ability of individuals to advance open-ended outcomes through trial and error. With substantial implications for the design of the cosmopolis, Rao advocates for a "promethean," versus a "pastoralist," attitude to design in which progressive ends are achieved incrementally, without an overly purist or formal mindset. Implicit in this advocacy is a strong critique of the Enlightenment approach to urban planning that dominated the field from figures such as Ebenezer Howard, Baron Haussmann, L'Enfant, Le Corbusier, Lucio Costa, and Robert Moses.

While the critique of deterministic urban planning is over fifty years old, Rao offers a new way to consider the advancement of the cosmopolis from outside of the design profession. He describes, for instance, the transformation of the automobile, once the symbol of the consumerist American Dream, into essentially a "smartphone accessory" that relies on software for its shared and more efficient use. Buildings are no doubt similar, with an ability to adapt and be shared based on the software that enables their use. Arguably that software is the city itself, in which the actions of design allow a wide use of buildings across time and space. Consider a major study[3] at Columbia University, which found that of the 300,000 new technology and media jobs created in New York City over the last decade, eighty-five percent were housed in structures built before World War II.

For the design of buildings and cities, this begs the question of how new structures can be equally flexible whether through their tectonics or their morphology. At the urban scale, this question brings to mind Albert Pope's work on grid- versus spine-based urban morphologies,[4] and the implications for fixed versus flexible planning for the cosmopolis of the future. Consider that despite Rao's critique of purist determinism, the grid systems of Manhattan's 1811 Commissioners Grid and Cerdà's plan for Barcelona have allowed a multiplicity of outcomes unforeseen by their original planners. While Rem Koolhaas, in *Delirious New York* (1978), delivers the most cogent critique of the real estate imperatives of Manhattan's grid, he simultaneously recognizes the sectional possibilities of New York's "culture of congestion," including its unplanned and unmediated outcomes.

Rao closes in part by discussing the distinction between purists who seek "civilizational goals" versus pragmatists who seek "civilizational capabilities." Our capacity for action is fundamental to this necessarily incomplete worldview, with the open understanding that civilizational goals are in continuous and iterative flux. This flux is the heartbeat of the cosmopolis, and as such the architect's impulse should not be to freeze the city into the static object—a methodology that reached its apotheosis at the close of the last century. Our civilizational capabilities, therefore, can be directed at this open-ended future, rife with challenges, yet brimming with the possibilities of action.

Notes

1   Markus Westbury, "Cities as Software," *Volume, #27: Aging* (2011).
2   Venkatesh Rao, *Breaking Smart*, 2015, http://breakingsmart.com/.

3   James Sanders, "Building the Digital City: Tech and the Transformation of New York," *Volume, #42: Art & Science of Real Estate*, 2014, https://www.academia.edu/8303446/Building_the_Digital_City_Tech_and_the_Transformation_of_New_York.
4   Albert Pope, *Ladders* (New York: Princeton Architectural Press, 1996).

WHAT IS A TOMB FOR?

Steven Chodoriwsky

Three Thresholds

There is a briskness to the ordeal. It starts by bringing the body to the family home. At the shrine in the alcove of the spare room, family members light incense and inform the neighbors. The person who has passed away is washed and dressed by the women. The men construct a box, and the washed, clothed body is set inside in a seated position, flexed at the hip. The seated figure's casket is then transported by a vehicle. In a village ceremony at the turn of the century it may have been a palanquin; perhaps it still is a variation of one if the house is in walking distance from the family's ancestral tomb. Today, it is a hearse fueled with oil, window-paned, and air-conditioned. Banners and tablets follow in procession. In the tomb's forecourt, relatives gather to offer prayers, the first of several times in coming years.

The casket is pushed through a small entrance, positioned on the lowest level in the center of its interior, and the hatch is resealed with mortar. The stage is set for the body's deterioration. Men and women leave separately, but not before placing sandals, staff, hat, cloak, lantern, and some food and drink nearby. The details seem trifling, but this is no time or place for improvisation. Succeeding death, according to Okinawan custom, the soul now wanders, without repose, in a space between tomb and home. There is still much to do: death alone does not assure membership in the multitude of ancestral deities. Relatives are required to provide especially vigilant care during this time, as the deceased is not yet truly dead but remains en route and at risk.[1]

Another threshold to death arrives on the forty-ninth day. The family gathers again in the open air of the court for "the separation of the soul," when then dead spirit is cleaved from living relatives. Belongings are redistributed—what is it of theirs that you might want to have?—and the burning of a mortuary tablet becomes the important milestone: now, truly dead, they have reached the other world.

Truly? Skip ahead several years, make a mark, and begin again. Female family members closest to the deceased return again to the tomb, unfurl an umbrella or tent to deter the soul from fleeing, pry open the door, and bring the coffin out. This exhuming commences the second, permanent burial. Act precisely. Barthes wrote: "The more formal the rite, the more pacifying its virtue … think that (private) ceremony leads to freedom, instead of requiring it."[2] Open the coffin. Divest the body of remaining soft matter: cleaning of soft parts is evidence that the dead has reached the level of deification due to good actions while alive. Use large chopsticks, rinse the bones thoroughly with water and again with a clear, distilled liquor. Take a vessel—a sturdy container, from local earth, finely shaped—and assemble the architecture of the body as it was once constructed: first feet and legs, then backbone, arms, and skull, and place on the lowest ledge in the left chamber. In time it will be moved up to make

Tomb in the environs
of Futenma Air Station
(southeast), Ginowan,
Okinawa, 2009.
PHOTO: COURTESY OF
STEVEN CHODORIWSKY

room for other jars. Face the skull's eyes tomb-ward: the deceased is "not inclined to leave if it cannot see outside."[3] Write the name and year on the inside of the lid.

A tomb encourages deep loss to be met regularly, repeated, and collectively maintained as a site of dialogue and mutual care. I wish to linger a while, in my description of these rites, on the steps that living bodies take to ferry a passed-away person to a new state, the state of *ancestor*. And when I wrote ordeal earlier, I can only imagine how harrowing an ordeal it is. Grief and the actions taken to process it are by no means limited to tiny islands in the Pacific Ocean called the Ryūkyūs, stretching in a chain between Japan and Taiwan; it is an ordeal that is shared and meted out in the largest of terms: How can living bodies act properly and decisively in such circumstances? And what do the deceased propose in return? In and around tombs such as this, a seam appears, where death and life clutch at one another for mutual support. As a dispersed network of small community spaces and practices, they mediate ordeals on both personal and collective scales, absorbing and including that trauma through the complexities of daily life.

Fields of Action
It was by the fourteenth century, amid a long tradition of cultural reciprocity with China, that ancestor worship as a practice was transposed to the Ryūkyūs.[4] The structures were built later.

In the seventeenth century, the so-called turtleback form in particular was adopted from crypts of the Fujian and Fuzhou provinces. They would be built to inter an extended kin-group of the paternal family line. Large and limestone-hewn, it is as though, to truly value a space of death, the container would need to rival the home in both size and construction cost. Smaller but still impressive in stature are the gable style tombs, especially when found in clusters. These became more prevalent during rapid twentieth-century urbanization.

At a now-distant point, upper-class tombs on the main island in particular would have been "the most prominent man-made feature" of Okinawa's agrarian landscape.[5] That illustrious crown now undoubtedly belongs to the archipelago of American military installations across the main island, obstinately present since the end of the Second World War. Indeed the island is still being shaped by the eponymous battle fought on its soil near the war's end, where twenty percent of the island's population died, "equaling the number at Hiroshima and Nagasaki combined."[6] The transformation of the landscape into a vast military garrison began thereafter, and all facets of daily life were affected with few structures—not least the funerary vaults—that escaped harm.[7] In addition to poverty, economic disarray, and individual loss of property, a major issue for survivors was taking proper care of the extraordinary number of casualties. In the war's aftermath

A collection of tombs in the environs of Futenma Air Station (southeast), Ginowan, Okinawa, 2009.
PHOTO: COURTESY OF STEVEN CHODORIWSKY

"anxiety and depression became common among Okinawans … compounded by their inability to physically inter the dead"—a key tenet of their religious practice.[8] The trauma of war and occupation was directly linked to unfulfilled social and familial obligations. It is in this vein that tombs continue to be sites of contested action, then as now. Beyond their physical presence in the landscape, their ongoing attendance and maintenance becomes a precise performance of citizenship and memory. Especially in the backdrop of both personal and historical shocks, they constitute, by their very survival, both "fields of action … and the basis of action, a reservoir of power from which the strength of the individual, household, and community derive, and into which they invest their energies."[9]

The Futenma Surrounds

An encounter with the urban environment on Okinawa's main island is an encounter with two competing impositions: American imperial-outpost space and Japanese urban sprawl, on an island strapped for buildable land. Throughout the Cold War and Vietnam eras, the reversion of American control to Japanese prefectural status in 1972, and after numerous incidents involving crime, conflict, and excess noise, Okinawa still shoulders three-quarters of the United States' Japan-based facilities despite being a fraction of the national land mass. With compensatory economic support from the Japanese central government, Okinawa's strategic peripheral location turns inside out to become a center for brisk United States military deployment, or, in general periods of standby, "pavement to park their warplanes."[10]

The most controversial—although not even the largest—site is Futenma Air Station, in the city of Ginowan. At a point where the 112 kilometer-long island narrows to six kilometers and built on prime agricultural land, the Futenma base is enclosed on all sides by twentieth-century urban expansion. Thus, while Futenma's size is comparable to New York's Central Park, absent is anything parklike whatsoever: the museums, the zoos, the views, or even the slightest freedom of any throughway vehicular movement. Instead, it is populated by American aircraft carriers, building facilities, and rotations of military service members, maintained by a leasing agreement between the United States and Japanese federal governments.[11] With plans for its relocation perpetually postponed, it remains a symbolic center of the ongoing struggle for Okinawa's stalled demilitarization.

Approaching its eleven-kilometer perimeter fence—amid the apartment blocks, auto shops, schools, parks, and soccer pitches—there are fleeting glimpses of pre-war agrarian terrain. And tombs: a significant number are located in Futenma's extended environs, and particularly in its southern section. Happening upon a tomb, knit into the city fabric, does not mean another is nearby: they will be where you expected a house, a parking lot, a plot of vegetables. Likewise, if

Tomb overlooking the
airstrip of Futenma
Air Station (southwest),
Ginowan, Okinawa, 2009.
PHOTO: COURTESY OF
STEVEN CHODORIWSKY

you expect a fallow field or a shed, instead there is a tomb. Due to the plateau-top placement of the airfield, much of its edge condition is sloped or terraced—the same desirable limestone topography as where generations of families have situated their ocean-view funeral plots. Scattered on either side of the fence, they do not recognize the base as a boundary—why should they?

In unique situations, city planning maps show the cadastral lines of the base transposed in places over time, allowing some tombs to be reincorporated by negotiating landowners, returning them, so to speak, to the city.[12] Elsewhere, newer, sentinel-like tombs are erected side-by-side on slivers of property directly abutting base grounds, hemmed in by chainlink backdrops. But in the most unsettled situations, plots are found fully enveloped in base territory, and families must secure special visitation arrangements. Here, cultures, geographies, and administrative regulations are superimposed: it suggests a place of slippage where inside and outside are not clearly marked, and there is the potential for a momentary *détente* between occupier and occupied. The intrusive qualities of the base, and the need to negotiate passage into it, brings into sharp relief the metonymic relationship between death and politics, and the necessary strategies for dealing with each.

Another portrait of tenuous spatial and cultural attitudes along this edge can be seen in an amateur video, circa 1987, portraying a young United States

soldier, walking down a road outside the base.[13] Off-duty, he giddily narrates his surroundings to his companion behind the camera's eye. The frame jumps and staggers along with the soldier's downhill skips and heel-clicks, as he points at everything he sees: "There's somebody's house. Somebody's cars. Somebody's washing the roof, yeah. We'll get a telephoto on that now." He zooms in. "Who's that?" A car passes. "Somebody who's working. Oh, my shoes untied." The camera cuts a brazen line out to the horizon and back to the untied shoelace, commanding the extremes of time and space. For a half-second, the frame pans hard right, and the soldier says the first thing that comes to mind: "Another Okinawan graveyard, whatever you wanna call it. It's something like that. There's only one person in there, [and] takes up an awful lotta space. They put these things wherever they want to, and they're almost in the middle of the road."[14]

Walking around Futenma now as then, the soldier's claims are easy to dispute: it is the bases, not the tombs that impose and interrupt. The current lack of progress in political issues related to American military presence is not just a point of contemporary context. It underscores patterns of gross interruption to Okinawan life over the past seventy years, and proposes that even a waning funerary culture, with its spatial legacy and prescribed routines, can provide inhabitants with some mechanisms for coping, some tools to combat imposition. Living in,

working around, and dealing with the shadow of the base, all states far from ideal, present a contemporary circumstance that may exist on the same continuum as prolonged funerary rituals—on one hand, a stance of collective resistance; on the other, a strategy to combat personal grief.

Interruption and Maintenance

Just as deaths impose upon lives, so too do the funerary rites infringe upon regular schedules— as though two unique rhythms superimpose to generate a more dense everyday state. Over centuries, the observances multiplied. Along with the 49th-day ritual native to the islands, the 100th-day, 1st-anniversary, and 3rd-anniversary rites were incorporated from continental practices. Still more the 7th-, 13th-, 17th-, 25th-, and 33rd-anniversary rites were included from mainland Japan, depending often on local particularities. These cyclical acts of condolence, appeasement, and communication, from several source traditions and integrated over time, pry open a seam between living and dead states, calling attention to the seam's architecture. In this sense, this architecture is as much literal and spatial as it is performative and emotional. On their own, this dispersed network of structures across the island waits, inert, but as a community invigilates, their architecture stirs.

These sites of commingled life-and-death matters seem to fall outside easy categorization:

is the tomb inside or out? Is it home or away from home? Is it a community center, post office, vestibule, or stage? Far from being a foreign place and far from solemn in atmosphere, family members are at ease here, having returned count-less times since childhood. In August, for the *obon* festival, they greet ancestral spirits and escort them back to their households. In April, for *shīmī*, families celebrate in the forecourts with colorful foods and strong drinks, burning stacks of paper money for ancestors to use in the upcoming year. With a tarp down and a tent up, a seated audience lingers there in open air, watching traditional dance accompanied by singers and the *shamisen*. This regular presence, humbly enacted, retains a long pact of interaction and engaged spatial practice across generations.

There is also the matter of physical upkeep. Another amateur video, more recent, illustrates a group of people repairing a tomb on the *tanabata* festival.[15] They perform miscellaneous tasks: tempering the encroaching wilderness, sanding down and replastering worn edges and ledges, removing trash and brush, digging out weeds from flowerbeds along the fringe. A camera operator pivots, left to right and back again across a frieze of bodies with their tools between the barriers embracing the forecourt area. The lens never tilts to the sky or to a panorama, or fixes upon the tomb partially obscured by a tent. To what or whom does this site orient? With an indirect gaze, it is a film of the movement of people working:

A row of tombs along the perimeter of Futenma Air Station (northwest), Ginowan, Okinawa, 2009.
PHOTO: COURTESY OF STEVEN CHODORIWSKY

the drones of machines fall in step with the camera's measured, unstill eye, pulled back and forth out of a desire to document a practice that is proving more and more difficult to maintain. It is precisely these types of discrete individual labors that link ancestral spirit to living body and span both traditional and contemporary space-making. As an ensemble of movements, they propose an active state of maintenance, and a pact to withstand the gross interruptions that individual deaths—or decades of military impositions—have brought upon a community.

Correspondence and Infrastructure

There is yet another beginning in the long progress from life into death. It is now the thirty-third year after a person passes away. If all goes to plan, observances will have been paid at five key anniversaries. This extraordinary suspension of time is the "socialization of the soul," echoing the approximate duration of an individual's upbringing to adulthood.[16] The tomb door is again unsealed. The jar, previously on a lower step, is opened, and its ossified contents are emptied into a collective area, commingling with the remains of the previously deceased.[17] It is an abundant, powerful gesture: now the deceased is a "full-fledged ancestor," and need no longer be singled out for individual treatment.[18] What remains is the soul matter.

Accompanying the dead person to this point is a delicate rite of passage and entails mutual responsibilities. If properly harnessed, the invisible crowd of the dead becomes a privileged source of spiritual sentiment, benevolent surveillance, and ardent support.[19] Between the two parties, a conversation occurs *over and over again*, and this over and over again is not from a loss for words. It is in the very predictability of encounter that assures certain basic, practical concerns be addressed—that living and dead are not at cross-purposes.[20] Death is thus drawn out, into life. However, this limestone structure threatens

to be something other than a shelter of repose. Without proper conduct, a deceased person will "preserve his personality" and is unable to proceed to the stage of ancestral deity, consigned to live, entombed, within the tomb.[21]

As a socio-spatial medium, the tomb type found on Okinawa is one that precedes, and endures past, the twentieth century shadows of war, occupation, and rampant modernization. However its requisite labors are not resigned to the purely "cultural"—that is, as if nostalgic, anachronistic, or politically mute. It is true that some aspects of mortuary rites are no longer carried out; the practice of bone-washing, for instance, is all but unpracticed on the main island although it still may be found in the villages on outer islands.[22] But a waning in practice is not a fading from psychic relevance, as the repercussions of these acts remain seated in the stories and the distributed architectures of the place. To borrow from David Graeber: "the things we think of as cultures might be better viewed as social movements that were to some degree successful in achieving their aims."[23]

Against all undercurrents of unease, whether personal, familial, or concerning Okinawa at large, the remnant tombs and their embedded practices could be said to collectively comprise an informal institution of ongoing resistance. In one sense, they adhere to an alternative type of planning that resists the colonial and military boundaries that have carved up the island during the twentieth century. But more than this: the sites of death remain alive, as replenishing wellsprings of support. In the prolongation of death through commemorative ritual, the tombs suggest a collective state of vigilance regardless of the source of hardship, cultivating an optimism that is a resistance to death itself.

Steven Chodoriwsky is an artist, designer, and writer. He lives and works in Los Angeles, and teaches architecture at Cal Poly Pomona.

Notes
1   For details on the content and sequencing of funerary rites in this first section, I have borrowed in several locations from: Evgeny S. Baksheev 2008. "Becoming Kami? Discourse on Postmortem Ritual Deification in the Ryukyus," *Japan Review* 20 (2008): 282-285.
2   Roland Barthes, et al., *The Neutral: lecture course at the Collège de France, 1977–1978* (New York: Columbia University Press, 2005), 123.
3   William P. Lebra, *Okinawan religion: belief, ritual, and social structure* (Honolulu: University of Hawaii Press, 1966), 200.
4   George H. Kerr, *Okinawa, the history of an island people* (Rutland, VT: C.E. Tuttle Co., 1958), 278.
5   Ibid., 218.
6   Matthew Allen, *Identity and resistance in Okinawa* (Lanham, MD: Rowman & Littlefield Publishers, 2002), 143-144.
7   During the war, family tombs were used—often futilely—as protective chambers for native Okinawans and, elsewhere, as pillbox locations for military combatants. This resulted in widespread destruction, vandalism and looting island-wide, as well as the loss of countless ancestors' remains.

For a graphic American account of the role of tombs during the war, see: Gerald Astor, *Operation Iceberg: the invasion and conquest of Okinawa in World War II* (New York: D.I. Fine, 1995), 62-64.
8   Allen, 143-44.
9   Christopher T. Nelson, *Dancing with the dead: memory, performance, and everyday life in postwar Okinawa* (Durham: Duke University Press, 2008), 139.
10   Mark L. Gillem, *America town building the outposts of empire* (Minneapolis: University of Minnesota Press, 2007), 17.
11   Local pamphlets for citizens and statistics documents, illustrated with cartoon maps and diagrams of the city, do their part to put a neutral spin on the situation, focusing on the dough of the city—school locations, cultural sights, parks, demographic information—and not the gaping doughnut hole of the Air Station. In headline news, it is the hole that—rightly and resoundingly—dominates discourse. But in the pamphlets, the airfield is portrayed innocuously enough, a thin strip of grey tarmac like a rural airport, surrounded by bucolic greenspace like a nature reserve.

12   One high-profile instance is the return of property of Michio Sakima, a prominent landholder in Futenma. Sakima negotiated the alteration of the base periphery so that the ancestral tomb would sit outside the fence. On part of the land, he also built the Sakima Art Museum, offering to the public both a poignant cultural space and a rooftop terrace that overlooks Futenma's vast expanse. See Nelson, 215-19 and http://sakima.jp.
13   "Walking down hill from main gate —MCAS Futenma (Summer 1987)," www.youtube.com/watch?v=Bj_TJxvQkd8.
14   Ibid.
15   "Haka no kaishuu kouji," www.youtube.com/watch?v=pEZ5VX1SX6M.
16   Baksheev, 281.
17   This number, depending on the stature of the family, could run into the thousands.
18   Lebra, 166.
19   Nelson, 138-40.
20   Nelson, 138-39.
21   Baksheev, 287.
22   Nelson, 149.
23   "Interview with David Graeber," *The White Review*, December 2011, http://www.thewhitereview.org/interviews/interview-with-david-graeber/.

CULTIVATING RESILIENCE

Karen Lewis

On the morning of December 14, 2012, Newtown, Connecticut, a town of 28,000, was suddenly impacted by an unimaginable tragedy. Twenty children aged six and seven and six women who educated, cared for, and protected them were violently killed at the Sandy Hook Elementary School by a member of the Newtown community.[1] It is no surprise that, "in the wake of a tragedy such as this, each and every member of a community is impacted."[2] The ripple effects of this violence was felt across all members of the community: the families who lost children and wives, mothers, sisters, aunts, grandchildren and grand-mothers directly; children and educators at Sandy Hook Elementary School; first responders and police, fire and emergency technicians who first arrived on the scene; clergy, health, and mental health providers who continue to work with families and the community; educators at Sandy Hook and across Newtown schools; the broader community who lost members of their swim teams, boy scout troops, or Sunday school classes.

Within days of the event, public officials established infrastructure to care for the community. Twenty-four hour mental health care services were provided for the entire town. Town churches, synagogues, and temples were opened and non-denominational services were made available. Thousands of people came to mourn and leave tributes, temporary memorials, signs, and notices, which filled almost every available public space. The town also made efforts to shepherd the visual representation of the tragedy. Within a week, the flags were raised again and within ten days, the temporary memorials were respectfully removed during the cover of night. It was understood that the language of the memorials, the constant visual reminder of the tragedy that filled every intersection, plaza, and public cross-road, reinforced the trauma for Newtown citizens. After eight months, the town politely declined any further special concerts or events. A post by first select-man Pat Llodra at OneNewtown.org suggests this decision was made to create space for all residents to move "into a quiet period of rest, recuperation, and healing."[3]

As the short-term measures of commemoration, healing, and community strengthening ebbed, the town transitioned to thinking about

Since the massacre, Newtown's community programming has focused on wellness. Free counseling sessions, therapy dogs, musical concerts, yoga classes, and non-demoninational religious events have been held throughout the town.

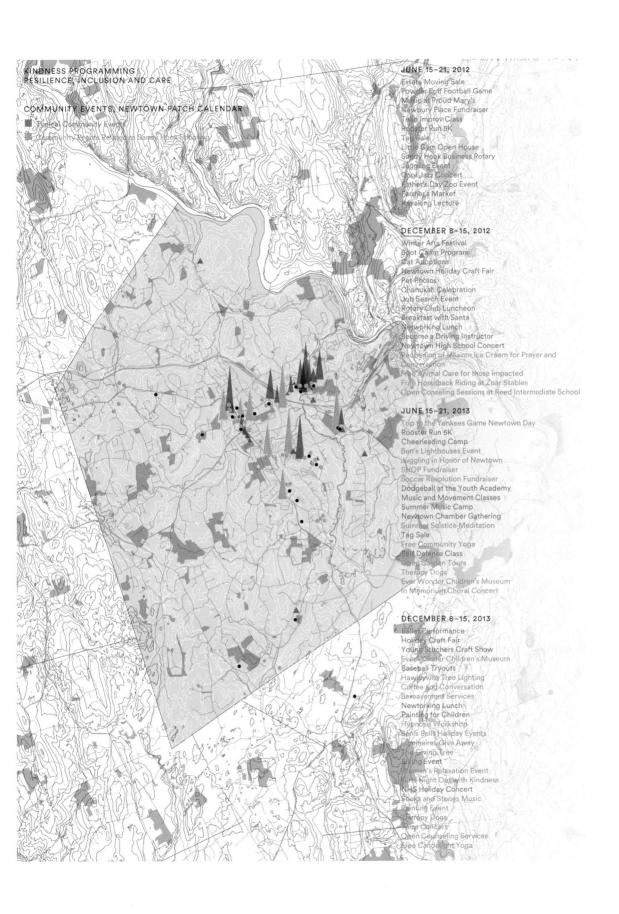

KINDNESS PROGRAMMING
RESILIENCE, INCLUSION AND CARE

COMMUNITY EVENTS, NEWTOWN PATCH CALENDAR

■ Typical Community Events
■ Community Events Relating to Sandy Hook Shooting

JUNE 15–21, 2012
Estate Moving Sale
Powder-Puff Football Game
Music at Proud Mary's
Newbury Place Fundraiser
Teen Improv Class
Rooster Run 5K
Tag Sale
Little Gym Open House
Sandy Hook Business Rotary
Juggling Event
Cool Jazz Concert
Father's Day Zoo Event
Farmer's Market
Kayaking Lecture

DECEMBER 8–15, 2012
Winter Arts Festival
Boot Camp Program
Cat Adoptions
Newtown Holiday Craft Fair
Pet Photos
Chanukah Celebration
Job Search Event
Rotary Club Luncheon
Breakfast with Santa
Networking Lunch
Become a Driving Instructor
Newtown High School Concert
Reopening of Heaven Ice Cream for Prayer and
Conversation
Free Animal Care for those impacted
Free Horseback Riding at Zoar Stables
Open Conseling Sessions at Reed Intermediate School

JUNE 15–21, 2013
Trip to the Yankees Game Newtown Day
Rooster Run 5K
Cheerleading Camp
Ben's Lighthouses Event
Juggling in Honor of Newtown
SHOP Fundraiser
Soccer Revolution Fundraiser
Dodgeball at the Youth Academy
Music and Movement Classes
Summer Music Camp
Newtown Chamber Gathering
Summer Solstice Meditation
Tag Sale
Free Community Yoga
Self Defense Class
Open Garden Tours
Therapy Dogs
Ever Wonder Children's Museum
In Memoriam Choral Concert

DECEMBER 8–15, 2013
Ballet Performance
Holiday Craft Fair
Young Stitchers Craft Show
Ever Wonder Children's Museum
Baseball Tryouts
Hawleyville Tree Lighting
Coffee and Conversation
Bereavement Services
Networking Lunch
Painting for Children
Hypnosis Workshop
Ben's Bells Holiday Events
Luminaires Give Away
The Giving Tree
Biking Event
Women's Relaxation Event
A Night Out with Kindness
NHS Holiday Concert
Sticks and Stones Music
Painting Event
Therapy Dogs
Faize Concert
Open Counseling Services
Free Candlelight Yoga

The memorial landscape
connects two of
Newtown's recreational
landscapes: Treadwell
Park and Rocky Glen
State Park. The memorial
extends the restorative
park network throughout
the town, creating a
space of contemplation,
reflection, and movement.

Creek Threshold   Family Groves

Treadwell Park   Treadwell entrance   Entry Meadow   Memorial Meadow
to Memorial Forest

Responders Spruce Grove

Memorial to Victims of Gun Violence

Temporary Memorials

Sandy Hook Firehouse

Former site of Sandy Hook Elementary School

Pootatuck River

Sandy Hook Center

Rocky Glen State Park

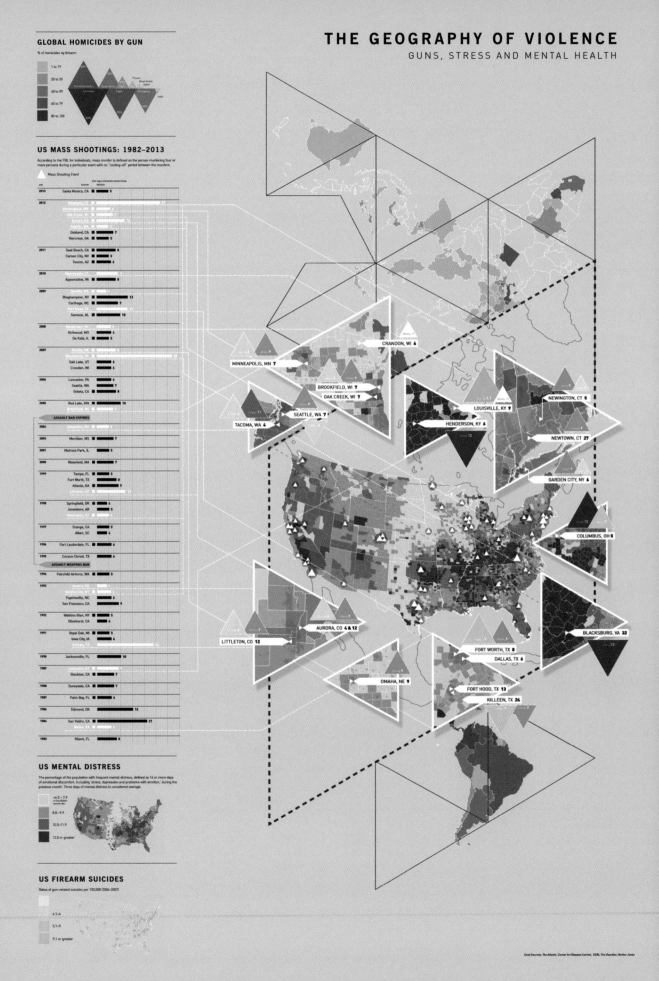

long-term mental health and wellness care. Newtown also began to discuss development of a permanent memorial to honor the lives lost at Sandy Hook. This was initiated by asking questions about how the memorial could integrate into the community. Recent memorials installed at Virginia Tech, Oklahoma City, and Columbine have documented traumas by demonstrating the number of lives lost: one plaque for each victim, one chair for each missing family member; one paver for each individual. These solid, permanent memories do not create space, nor do they offer a therapeutic environment. These memorials' emotional connection is based entirely in the inscription of one name on one solid element. They are fixed, immobile, and reference the typographic language of grave inscriptions. However, a memorial should do more than simply document statistics and lives lost. Instead, it can offer a place for gathering and cultivate an environment of wellness. This proposed memorial for Newtown, titled "Cultivating Resilience," develops a broader memorial landscape in conjunction with the town's goals of community support, health, and wellbeing.

What kind of civic spaces, restorative environments, and community landscapes foster recovery? How does the design of a memorial contribute to the restoration and healing of the community? How does the memorial recognize the event without reframing the trauma? "Cultivating Resilience" offers a living, therapeutic memorial that demarcates the event without reifying it as a singular tragedy.

Networking Civic Spaces

The environment where one builds community resilience is as significant as the memorial that commemorates the event. The "living" memorial aligns Newtown's proposed Sandy Hook Elementary Memorial with the broader community health goals of wellness, mental health, and compassion. It links together underused civic spaces by providing a landscape network between public parks, the Pootatuck River, Sandy Hook town center, and the state forest preserve. By connecting the memorial to other recreational spaces, the memorial fosters exploration, health, and community interaction.

Restoration versus Reminder

The memorial is discretely and respectfully located in the forest between Treadwell Park and the Sandy Hook site. In the aftermath of 12/14, the overwhelming temporary memorials located throughout the town were a constant, traumatic reminder of the event. This memorial site takes advantage of the existing roadways and parking, and is located discretely within a covered forest, giving the community the opportunity to connect to the memorial without being over-whelmed by its presence. The memorial is central to the town without defining the public space of the town; it integrates into the town's existing fabric, while simultaneously expanding and connecting its existing open spaces. As a living, therapeutic landscape memorial, the

The Memorial Meadow is surrounded by groves of birch trees representing each victim and their family. Green twig dogwood surrounds the groves and meadows, edging the winter meadow in white and green, which are the school colors of Sandy Hook Elementary.

project will grow and change over time. The memorial takes action by offering spaces for the community that respond to seasonality and use. In the winter, the snow-filled meadows edged with birch trees and green-twig dogwood represents Sandy Hook Elementary's colors. During these winter anniversary events, the memorial is exposed, views are expanded, and spaces become interconnected. In the summer, the memorial is more intimate; lush with foliage, the spaces are quiet and shadowy in contrast to the sunny meadows. As Newtown develops its resilience, so too does the Memorial. Growing and changing, this memorial landscape expands and contracts, offers refuge and community, builds existing networks and provides new paths—the very definition of resilience.

Karen Lewis is an associate professor of Architecture at The Ohio State University whose design examines the intersection of graphic and infrastructural systems. Professor Lewis is the author of *Graphic Design for Architects* (Routledge). She holds a Bachelor of Arts degree in Architecture from Wellesley College and a Master of Architecture degree from the Harvard Graduate School of Design.

Notes
1   Jill Baron, "Resilience: Community Health Assessment," *OneNewtown*, (August 26, 2013), www.onenewtown.com.
2   Ibid.
3   Shannon Hicks, "Llodra Calls For A 'Period of Rest,'" *The Newtown Bee* (Newtown, CT), July 2, 2013.

CREATING A NATION'S MEMORY

Jin Young Song

The city and architecture are embodiments of our present culture as well as cultural memory. John Ruskin specifically refers to civil and domestic architecture's critical capacity to achieve perfection through becoming memorial.[1] Understanding memorial practice as the building of objects or spaces for the purpose of preserving particular human events or identities, it is crucial that this preservation finds a truthful representation. Often, new memorials to past events purposely misrepresent history to enact a future shaped by contemporary responses to the memorial. In this context, the memorial is positioned as a device to manipulate perception either toward action or inaction (amnesia). In extreme examples, this device operates as propaganda or a redemptive tool deployed by authority. The divided Koreas have exemplified the problematic and often subversive function of memorials. *Slanted Memorial* is a proposal to both governments as well as the United Nations, to build housing on the site of the Demilitarized Zone (DMZ) in Korea for families separated by the Korean War (1950–53). It is intended to serve as a memorial to provoke action towards reconciliation, beyond mere symbolic stimulation and sensational expression.

The Korean War was responsible for more than two million deaths and resulted in millions of separated families.[2] Following the signing of the Armistice of 1953, both sides agreed to establish a buffer zone, the Demilitarized Zone (DMZ).[3] During the last sixty years, each Korea has developed its own mechanisms for remembering the past. Today, the war has still not officially ended, and more than seventy thousand families from South Korea remain separated from their families in North Korea.[4]

In North Korea, monuments and memorials are considered sacred objects that actively engage with everyday life. For instance, memorial park attracts everything from dance parties to newly married couples who are worshipping and offering their vows. Simultaneously, memorialization can easily turn into an act of propaganda when the artifact is imbued with strong biases. For instance, the former leader of the nation and his destiny have been immortalized on the main street, under which everyone must reify his will in their daily commute. Conversely, in South Korea, memorials have been used as redemptive tools. Gigantic,

A. Monument to the founding of the Worker's Party, Pyungyang, North Korea. Illustration shows a dance party celebrating Kim Jong-il's fiftieth year in the central committee of the Worker's Party.

B. Monument to the Immortality of Kim Il Sung, Pyungyang. It is believed that there are 3,200 immortality monuments in North Korea.

C. Reunification Monument, Pyungyag

D. Grand Monument on Mansu Hill, Pyungyang: According to North Korea's Rodong Newspaper, 26,000 people per day visit this memorial park to vow allegiance to their past leader.

E. Monuments in South Korea memorializing the countries of United Nations command.

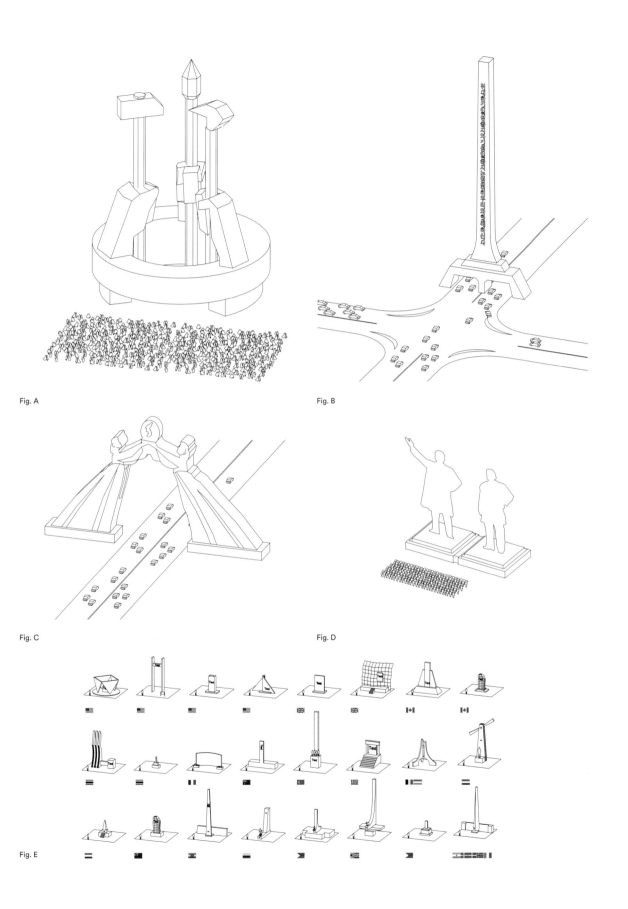

Fig. A

Fig. B

Fig. C

Fig. D

Fig. E

singular, and heroic, the South Korean War Memorial Museum, located in the heart of Seoul, seeks to compensate for this loss. The majority of other monuments, located at otherwise nondescript highway rest areas, provoke an intentional amnesia from past events while also being disconnected from everyday life. These contradictory uses of memorials incite the question of how to measure the legitimacy of either regime's memory. Further, what is at stake in continuing to permit North and South Korea to shape their own futures based on two diverging histories?[5] Lastly, what role can art and architecture offer in highlighting the tensions, biases, and divergent readings within this national conflict?

To answer these questions, *Slanted Memorial* first presents a direct reference—irrefutable evidence. What we overlay onto the artifact requires legitimacy to construct our current collective memory, just as the explorations of overlay in the work of artist Shimon Attie's *The Writing on the Wall*.[6] In the case of the *Slanted Memorial*, this manifests in the selection of site and its inhabitants. The DMZ can be considered a memento produced from the politics of war—the no-man's land protected and isolated from people for more than half a century. Separated families are a very real keepsake that the war bequeathed to both North and South Korea; and thus they serve as living and irrefutable evidence for the "original, uncorrupted form" of the memorial.[7] The separated families are proposed to be the first residents on the land of the DMZ—now free of ideology, propaganda, and amnesia. The site, located on a railway line severed by the DMZ, is also a direct reference to the past and a symbol of the reunion between the North and South.[8] Secondly, by confirming memorials as mnemonic devices, the mechanism linking the object and the act of commemorating should be artistically defined. Remembering critically, intersects with sensation and perception, which are the key to

East and West elevations showing the building as a 'field-object'.

Partial model, showing the relationship between units within the thickened slab.

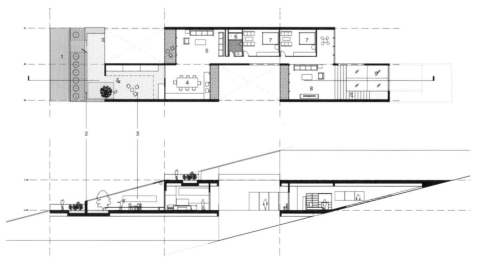

Unit plan and section showing the field of domestic space.

1 Public street & open terrace viewing west
2 Fence, the Korean traditional
3 Private Garden exterior
4 Dining Kitchen
5 Living Room
6 Bathroom
7 Bedroom
8 Second Living Room
9 Inclined window looking east river

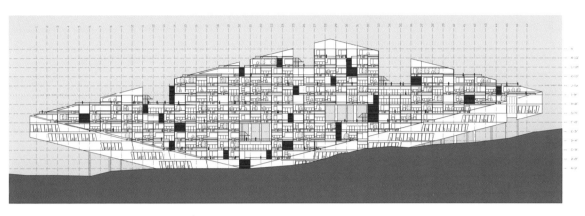

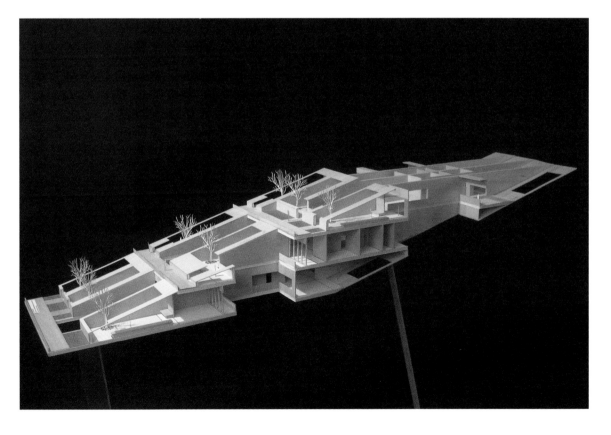

Site model showing the project's relationship to the surrounding topography.

this linkage—focusing on users' feelings and perceptions of the built object. The elevated and slanted ground plane symbolize the tragedy of separation.[9] The reunion—direct evidence of the memorial—is presented through the slanted façade, while the memorial space transpires under the clustered object of domestic space.

After sixty years of separation, it is believed that the act of witnessing the spatial reunion in the *Slanted Memorial* will incite Koreans to create a national collective memory for subtle but powerful action— action that talks between governments during the past half century were unable to achieve. In this way, the materiality of architecture operates as a cultural instigator for new forms of action.

Jin Young Song is an assistant professor at Department of Architecture, University at Buffalo and a founding principal of Dioinno Architecture PLLC, a Buffalo and Seoul based design firm.

Acknowledgements
This project is further developed from the author's Master in Architecture thesis project at Harvard University Graduate School of Design advised by Professor Jonathan Levi.

Notes
1   John Ruskin, *The seven lamps of architecture* (New York: Wiley, 1865). Ruskin explained, "Memory may truly be said to be the sixth Lamp of Architecture; for it is in becoming memorial or monumental that a true perfection is attained by civil and domestic buildings." (148)
2   Millett, Allan R. *Encyclopædia Britannica Online*, s. v. "Korean War," http://www.britannica.com/event/ Korean-War, See also: Statistics Korea (KOSTAT), 2005 Population and Housing Census, 3-BA. *Number of separated population in South Korea*, http://kosis.kr/
3   The Demilitarized Zone is a strip of land running across the Korean Peninsula that serves as a buffer zone between North and South Korea. It is 250 kilometers long and approximately four kilometers wide.
4   According to the Korean Red Cross, 129,264 people have applied to the meeting event over the last 25 years.

Due to the passage of time, currently only 71,480 applicants are alive and waiting to meet their families in North Korea. Read more at: Integrated Information System for Separated Families, Ministry of Unification, S. Korea, *Status of Separated Families*, https://reunion.unikorea.go.kr/
6   Pierre Nora, "Between memory and history: Les lieux de mémoire," *Representations* (1989): 7-24. Nora has viewed memory and history to be in fundamental opposition. Memory is sacred, plural, individual, and vulnerable to manipulation while history is the incomplete and a problematic reconstruction. The history of Korean War, separated families, and DMZ are incomplete but each regime is constructing their own memories, which are not contributing to reconciliation.
6   Shimon Attie, a visual artist, smartly explored the overlay in *The Writing on the Wall* by projecting photographs of Jews in the 1920s and 1930s back onto their original sites. Photographs and a physical site as direct references become a form of memorialization when they are artistically associated with each other. See: Shimon Attie, "The Writing on the Wall: Projections in Berlin's

Jewish Quarter, Shimon Attie, Photographs and Installations," *Heidelberg*, (Germany: Edition Braus, 1993).
7   Alois Riegl, "The modern cult of monuments: its character and its origin," *Oppositions* 25 (1982): 20-51. This term is borrowed from Alois Riegl. He views the memorial as a constructed cultural product to which meaning and significance are added. He states, "We are interested furthermore in the original, uncorrupted form of the work as it left the hand of its maker, and this is the state in which we prefer to see it, or to which we prefer to restore it in thoughts, words, or images." (23)
8   This proposed project would initiate the railway connection between North and South Korea. Reconnecting only two kilometers will complete the nine thousand kilometer route from Europe to the East Sea of the Korean peninsula.
9   Being slanted toward east, not North or South, creates generous outdoor terrace (Madang, the traditional outdoor space in Korean housing) on west side, while the living rooms face east capturing the morning sun light and the reflection of the water.

OFF THE WALL

Parker Sutton and Katherine Jenkins

"The distinction between the private and public realms, seen from the viewpoint of privacy rather than of the body politic, equals the distinction between things that should be shown and things that should be hidden."
—Hannah Arendt[1]

There is a boundary dispute along the walls of San Francisco—a contest between two acts of preservation. The first is an act of self-preservation, or Arendtian self-actualization: the graffiti signature, or "tag," is a declaration of the presence of the artist. The second act, known as "buffing," is one of masking, washing, and obscuring the first. This is building preservation. Neither act is frequently witnessed, but their resultant compositions—action and reaction—are a constant presence throughout much of the city. The attempt to maintain a graffiti-free cityscape is highly deliberate and comes at great public expense; San Francisco spends in excess of twenty million dollars annually on graffiti clean-up.[2] Reliefs of layered paint, mismatched colors, and strange collages of shapes that abstract the writing beneath, mark events in an ongoing exchange between the individual (the artist) and the collective (the city).

Though two dimensional, the accretion of marks on a facade has spatial and temporal implications; each layer of graffiti and its subsequent masking occurs at a distinct moment. The concealing marks that often intended to blend with the remaining façade rarely do so. The weathering effects of the sun in combination with San Francisco's marine climate are such that, even when the original paint color is re-deployed, the color of the façade no longer matches. Consequently, the act of buffing frequently heightens the contrast between old and new paint, "creating the condition for remembrance."[3] The cumulative effect of this process is the creation of a spatial register of civic tensions. Incidences of buffing are most abundant where issues of ownership, gentrification, and collateral political action are greatest: the Mission District, South of Market (SOMA), and Potrero Hill. In these neighborhoods, palimpsests of masked graffiti are visible on nearly every block. The Mission District has a particularly layered relationship with the painted facade, due to both a history of gang activity and a tradition of Chicano mural-making. Here, multi-storey murals expressing communitarian ideals stand adjacent to iterative tags. The coexistence of murals and graffiti may be more than coincidence: it is a common refrain among city planners that the ownership conveyed through murals deters deviant behavior.[4] When the anti-graffiti organization, Zero Graffiti International, held their inaugural conference in San Francisco in 2013, proceedings included a Mission mural tour.[5] Read across the whole of San Francisco, acts of concealment reveal how the city itself is quite literally fading.

Layers of paint on a warehouse located at Mississippi and 17th Street in the gentrifying Mission District, San Francisco.
PHOTO: COURTESY OF PARKER SUTTON AND KATHERINE JENKINS

I R. Slutzky

II R. Motherwell

III A. Reinhardt

IV P. Mondrian

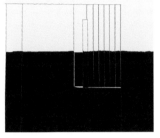

V L. Nevelson

VI C. Still

VII J. Albers

VIII H. Frankenthaler

Types

I Roller

II Ghost

III Patch

IV Sonic

V Beast

VI Quilt

VII Floodline

VIII Nimbus

Modes

Diagrams of graffiti and
its subsequent obfus-
cation: types and modes.

<—
Apartment building
located at Harrison
Street and 17th Street,
San Francisco, and
corresponding types
and modes: Roller,
Ghost, Patch, C. Still
PHOTO: COURTESY OF PARKER
SUTTON AND KATHERINE JENKINS

takes action

Action / Reaction × 7

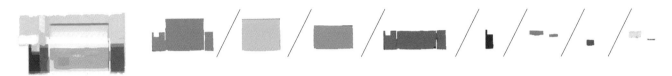

Action / Reaction × 8

Action / Reaction × 6

Shifts in scale mark changes in style and technique. A blockbuster tag features massive letters in a block-shaped style, often rendered with paint rollers on a wide surface. Pissing, another mode of graffiti, replaces the chemical agent in fire extinguishers with watery paint. This creates a high-pressure implement that sprays with the strength and accuracy that one expects from a device designed to coat entire rooms instantaneously. An apartment building at Harrison and 17th Street in the Mission District is home to a buffed tag painted in this style. Stretching three stories tall and covering eighty-five feet, its wavy lettering can still be read beneath the mask of red paint intended to hide it. Reading left to right, the tag is increasingly legible, suggesting that its sheer size either caused the buffer to grow fatigued or run out of paint. The resultant composition is rare for being both monumental and incidental, in a way that few things within a highly planned and regulated cityscape can be.

At times, the maintenance regime of tagging and buffing results in an array of textured patchworks that make striking, if accidental, compositions. Watery layers of mismatched paint swept over illicit marks evoke the color field school typified by Helen Frankenthaler. The impatient scrubbing of brushes over tags with no intention of blending conjures Robert Motherwell's high-contrast, inky abstraction. Precisely matched colors conceal all but the raised glossy spray paint beneath. This, with the subtlety of Ad Reinhardt.

There are Mondrians, Nevelsons, Stills, and Albers if you choose to look for them. Such compositions are unplanned, resulting from a property owner's desire to maintain a certain aesthetic virtue. Any attempt to discuss the aesthetics of graffiti is contextual and often contentious. By introducing classifications from contemporary art, we hope to suspend the ethical questions raised by tagging and buffing in an effort to parse their more objective aesthetic qualities.

Couched within a broader narrative of theoretical discourse, these compositions evoke mid-century connections between the architectural volume and the painted plane first elicited by Robert Slutzky and Colin Rowe in their seminal writings on transparency. Akin to phenomenal transparency, as they describe it, painted-over facades are charged with multiple perspectives, and a compressed time-scale, conjuring an activated field in the narrow space between the volume and plane. They differ in two critical regards: phenomenally transparent façade compositions articulate the views of multiple actors, rather than just one, and their creation is decidedly more public—both of which make these compositions inherently political.

Still, the façade's role as a repository for civic narrative and political speech is rarely identified or integrated into its design. The space of the facade, when embedded with speech, is almost uniformly appropriated for commercial use. This is not to overlook the notion of the architectural

Unpeeled facades: layers of paint that have accreted in response to graffiti on three building facades in San Francisco.

Garage door located at Mission Street and 19th Street, San Francisco, and corresponding types and modes: Patch, Floodline, R. Motherwell.
PHOTO: COURTESY OF PARKER SUTTON AND KATHERINE JENKINS

façade as a communicative, norm-setting device, in the urban environment.[6] The polarizing broken window theory holds that graffiti—or vandalism, in general—has a signaling effect that begets more vandalism and antisocial behavior.[7] Conversely, the theory holds that a well-kept public place discourages deviant behavior among its inhabitants. Looked at in this way, the "buffman," as he is known, is not erasing the presence of the writer so much as asserting his own. The reaction, then, becomes not only an aesthetic rebuke, but also a ritual act in the maintenance of social order. This "conflation" of the aesthetic values of space with the ethical ones—legitimate or not—raises the question of architecture's role in "constructing a good society."[8] It purports that the built environment is symbolic of such a society and is a means to that end. But is one aesthetic framework more virtuous, or ethical, than another? Aesthetic virtue is, after all, arbitrary.

And yet, the actions documented here affirm an enduring belief in the communicative power of the constructed environment. The debate over whether graffiti is art or vandalism clouds an equally valuable conversation about the ubiquitous but unseen compositions that occur at the intersection of graffiti's application and erasure. To reflect on these is to assess the evolving relationship between distinct actors within the community—the city, the property owner, the artist—and to consider the aesthetics of urban façades not only for their visual and material qualities, but also for their ephemeral, relational, and political ones.

Katherine Jenkins is a lecturer in the Department of Landscape Architecture at Cornell University and co-founder of the design-research collaborative Topo-logic.

Parker Sutton is an architect and co-founder of the design-research collaborative Topo-logic, based in San Francisco.

Notes
1   Hannah Arendt, *The Human Condition* (Chicago: University of Chicago Press, 1958), 72.
2   San Francisco Public Works, "Community One-Stop: Graffiti," www.sfdpw.org/index.aspx?page=1099
3   Hannah Arendt, *The Human Condition* (Chicago: University of Chicago Press, 1958), 18.
4   Project for Public Spaces, "Preventing Graffiti," Project for

Public Spaces, http://www.pps.org/reference/graffitiprevent/. Also see: San Francisco Arts Commission's "SF Street Smarts" initiative.
5   San Francisco Public Works, "Community One-Stop: Graffiti," *www. sfdpw.org/index.aspx?page=1099.*
6   George L. Kelling and James Q. Wilson, "Broken Windows: The Police and Neighborhood Safety," *The Atlantic*, March 1, 1982, http://

www.theatlantic.com/magazine/archive/1982/03/broken-windows/304465/.
7   Ibid.
8   Joan Ockman, "Ethics and Aesthetics After Modernism and Postmodernism," in *The Hand and the Soul: Aesthetics and Ethics in Architecture and Art*, ed. Sanda Illiescu, (Charlottesville and London: University of Virginia Press, 2009), 45.

OPEN MUSEUM FOR PEACE

Rafi Segal and David Salazar

The Kitgum Museum for Peace and War Archive was conceived as both a memorial to the victims of the civil conflicts in Uganda—a living archive to collect testimonies and stories of the war—as well as a museum space for cultural heritage and public events.

While the archive contains accounts of the crimes committed during the war, an exterior circular path and courtyard serve as an exhibition space for arts and crafts as well as a public educational meeting space. As such, by combining the archive, display of art, and a communal meeting space, the project addresses the three-fold understanding of peacebuilding as a process of individual and collective reconciliation, healing, and recovery. Reconciliation is achieved through the pursuit of justice by way of accountability for the atrocities of the conflict. Healing manifests as an individual and social process. Lastly, recovery transpires through the rebuilding of local traditions that acts of war have threatened to erase. Through its spatial organization, programming, and design, the project is positioned as a form of social-political action in response to these three stages of peacebuilding.

Archive and Public Space as a form of Action

Uganda is notorious for its long history of violence in the Great Lakes region and beyond. While memorials scattered across the country commemorate the World Wars and other violent moments in Uganda's past, the civil war and conflicts of Northern Uganda have not been adequately acknowledged through spatial representation nor included in an effective and transparent archival system. The official records and annals of the conflicts that do exist are kept out of sight in the basement of the National Agricultural Research Organization (NARO) in Entebbe. Other documents concerning Uganda's conflict-ridden history—primarily media reports, independent research projects, and accounts by international institutions—have often been distributed in a disorganized fashion, failing to reach the communities that they represent.

The Beyond Juba Project was established to generate support for a national reconciliation process in Uganda as part of a joint initiative between the Refugee Law Project, the Human Rights and Peace Centre, and the Faculty of Law at Makerere University. The project set out to

Site plan showing the project as the circular structure that connects the disparate buildings into a collective experience.

A. Existing condition highlighting the two-story archive building.

B. Museum path connects to the archive building and it's open structure allows passage through it.

C. Walls define the inner courtyard and outer open spaces.

Fig. A

Fig. B

Fig. C

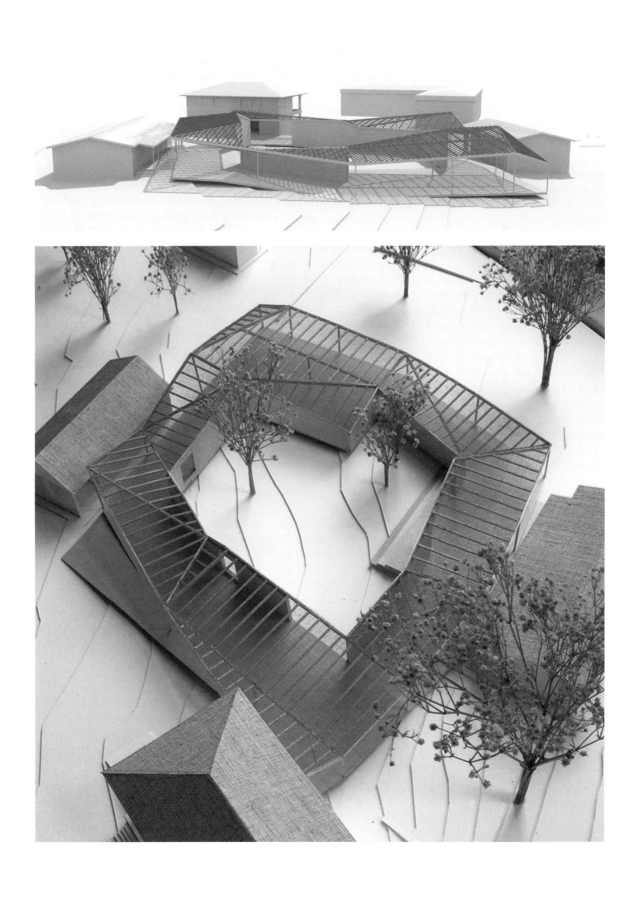

Elevation showing
how the project adapts
to the grade changes
on site.

Physical model
showing the project
in its surrounding
context, and how
the roof connects the
separate buildings
into a collective form.

demonstrate the extent to which conflicts and their legacies are a national problem and how appropriate transitional justice mechanisms can be developed to address their legacies. Yet, rather than solely formalizing a centralized model of national records and documentation, the project adapted a dispersed approach—understanding the importance of bringing spaces and programs to the communities in such a way that facilitates the collection of testimonies and the offering of support.

The town of Kitgum, located a four-hour drive north of Kampala, while perhaps lesser known, was in fact the epicenter of some of the most horrific massacres to have taken place by the Lord's Resistance Army (LRA) during the mid-1990s. The museum and archive site in Kitgum was selected to be in close proximity to the communities that suffered from many of the conflicts of the north. An existing two-story building initially built by the United States Agency for International Development (USAID) had been donated to the Refugee Law Project, which sought to utilize it for the museum and archive. The existing building was too small to house the program, too closed-off for the project's transparency, and too banal to symbolically represent the project's values. This prompted a proposal for a larger area of intervention, which changed the focus from the building to the new adjacent public space. The project thus acts as a local public space for the communities of Kitgum and a prototypical node within a distributed network of similar communal spaces across the country. The design challenge was to create a site-specific structure which related to its particular conditions, while at the same time develop an approach that could be implemented elsewhere. Appropriated from the typology of the circular path, what resulted was an open museum structure; a semi-open exhibition space shaped for movement and repose.

Open Museum, Living Archive

The unique museum and archive in Kitgum serves a dual purpose— as a memorial commemorating the victims of the conflicts and as a communal space to aid in the recovery process of those who survived the conflicts. The museum component of the project takes the form of a circular path and acts as the primary organizational element by connecting to the existing surrounding buildings and engaging the adjacent outdoor spaces. Disparate structures, that before seemed randomly scattered, are collectively united through this canopy. Architecturally, the circular path was conceived as a covered open space. Its outer perimeter remains open, allowing one to enter the museum through several points, while preserving the ability to move openly across the site. In relation to the exhibition, the path expands at places to create larger spaces or rooms, in which activities could take place without interfering in the continuous movement along the path and through it. The path serves as a curatorial device that connects fragments of stories and events without imposing a single narrative. An exposed concrete foundation defines this space and marks out the path itself. Alternating walls of wooden slats, framed in steel, serve as an open framework for the museum's display. The pitched-roof, also clad in wood slats, slopes gently towards the interior courtyard to promote human-scaled occupation. Through its scale, play of light, and open perimeter, yet enclosed volume, the project creates a place for reflection and contemplation. The openness allows for individual freedom of movement, interaction, and ultimately, framing and interpretation of past events. Visitors will create different narratives as they are given the freedom to move along the path and encounter the material in a variety of ways.

Contrary to the common conception of the museum exhibition as a closed, separate, and independent experience, this partially open structure creates an exhibition space that is dependent on, and integrated with, its surroundings. The project fully participates in the realities on site—both the elements of nature and the human activities and movements between the buildings—to the point that the exhibition pathway and the existing public paths on site become one. Thus, the site becomes the museum, and the museum becomes the site. The exhibition space is not merely intended for the display of images and artifacts, but more broadly programmed to embrace and celebrate the practice of local arts, crafts, dance, rituals, and other traditional communal activities. Creating a designated structure for these activities enables healing and recovery to be undertaken socially, as a collective process, with other surviving members of the community. Public space here is approached as a positive element, shaped and programmed for the immediate needs of the surrounding communities. Set within the dispersed low-density environment of Kitgum, the project physically and symbolically brings things together to form a larger whole out of individual structures.

Among the existing structures that the museum path connects, stands the two-story archive. Anchoring the exhibition path, this building's interior was completely renovated and re-appropriated to include spaces in which personal stories and testimonies of the conflict are recorded, documented, and published. In addition, the archive building also acts as a repository of materials and stories for the curation of exhibitions and organization of public events along the circular path and within the courtyard. The constant dialogue and exchange of materials between the archive and exhibition path promotes public awareness by bringing into appearance evidence and testimonies from the conflict. Given that the conflict in Northern Uganda is ongoing, the archive will be uniquely positioned to document and record events as they unfold. This diversed and continuously evolving archive will therefore also serve as an important resource for both historiographical studies and research seeking to link testimonies collected with forensic materials.

This two-faceted approach—exhibition and archiving—creates an educational edifice that puts forth a complex narrative of Uganda's war history, with a particular focus on the conflict in Northern Uganda.

The project aims to ensure that the experiences of those who suffered from the conflict are not forgotten, while at the same time provide a space for the continuous education of the public and, in particular, the younger generation. Far more than a site for preserving and symbolizing memories of a past conflict, the memorial in this case works in service of justice and reconciliation. This museum-memorial, through both its program and architecture, re-engages and re-imagines a public space as an act of establishing and supporting a physical site for collective purposes. Aiding both individuals and communities to move past their violent history, the outcome is a literal and symbolic foundation for peace-building.

Rafi Segal is an architect and associate professor of Architecture and Urbanism at MIT. His practice engages in design and research on both the architectural and urban scale and most recently included the winning proposal for the National Library of Israel in Jerusalem. Rafi Segal holds a PhD from Princeton University and an M.Sc and B.Arch from Technion—Israel Institute of Technology.

David Salazar leads DTSalazar Inc., a multi-disciplinary owner's representation, development and design practice in New York, San Francisco and Los Angeles. His work spans a broad base of categories ranging from unique residential and restaurant ventures, to socially-oriented work in Africa and the United States. Salazar completed architectural training at UC Berkeley and London's Architectural Association and holds Master degrees from Harvard University and Columbia University.

Design
Rafi Segal, David Salazar
Project Team: Andrew Amarra (Project Architect on site), Sara Segal, Landry Smith, Edgar Muhairwe, Olivia Ahn, Gabriel Bollag, Ian Kaplan, Jeremy Jacinth, Jeremiah Joseph, Harry Murzyn, Louis Rosario.

Client
The Beyond Juba Project, part of the Refugee Law Project of the Human Rights and Peace Centre and the Faculty of Law, Makerere University, Kampala, Uganda. Chris Donlan (Director); Moses Chrispus OKELLO (Project Coordinator, Senior Research Advisor); Andrew Simbo (Program Manager)

Donor
United States Agency for International Development (USAID), Northern Uganda Transitional Initiative (NUTI); Amanda Willlet (Chief of Party).

Implementation Team
Casals & Associates, Inc.; Richard Barkle Aaron Sheldon, Catherine Lumeh, Caroline Exile Apio, Caroline Joan Oyella (Project Leaders); Jolly Joe Komakech, Akena Walter, Andrew Kinyera, Boniface Ogwal, Walter Akena, Oyat Frederick, Fredrick Komakech, Patrick Loum (Project Team)

Contractor
WILBO Peyot Family Enterprises; IT: RAPS

For more information
The Beyond Juba Project,
www.beyondjuba.org;
The Refugee Law Project,
www.refugeelawproject.org

ELASTIC COMMEMORATION

Guy Königstein

Matters of Past and
Present, Adaptable,
Constructed,
Participative and
Playful Matters, 2013.

Memory = Action

We seem to remember and forget on a daily basis, in an almost unconscious automatic way. But as we remember and forget, as we commemorate and repress past and present narratives, we construct, cultivate, and preserve both our personal and collective identities. Objects of commemoration are an inseparable part of both the urban and rural landscape. While personal gravestones support individual memory, monumental memorials such as fountains, victory gates, and obelisks, among others, have been installed for centuries in public spaces to honor exceptional events or glorify remarkable people. Such memorials contribute to the construction of collective feelings of identification or antagonism, as they sanctify and eternalize the narratives for which sake they were created.

This objectification and eternalization of historical narratives became a political device that has discouraged participatory discourse. Commemoration in the public realm is often used by authorities or institutions not only in order to mention, respect, or cherish the past and its protagonists, but also in order to declare power or sovereignty over the present. Furthermore, by presenting a chosen narrative as singular and genuine, it excludes any alternative interpretations of past events from the collective memory; hence, the memories of the defeated, the weak, or the minority, are obscured and marginalized. In most cases only one past is shaped or cast into a static object.

The conventional design of memorials and their surroundings prevents an active participation in the past and its commemoration. It protects the chosen narrative with obstacles and borders it with fences so that it remains inaccessible. The solid and rigid character of the memorial, let alone its monumentality, leaves only one option: to consume it passively as it is. The common materials of memorials—concrete, iron, bronze, or marble—are resistible to harsh weather conditions and vandalism and thus emphasize their timelessness. Any external attempt to express an individual opinion and exert influence on them is immediately seen as destructive and offensive, or subversive and immoral. The transformation or destruction of memorials is reserved exclusively for designated authorities or, as often experienced during conflicts and invasions, for

PAST AND PRESENT
ADAPTABLE MATTERS

FOUNDATION FOR ELASTIC COMMEMORATION

PAST AND PRESENT
CONSTRUCTED MATTERS

FOUNDATION FOR ELASTIC COMMEMORATION

PAST AND PRESENT
PARTICIPATIVE MATTERS

FOUNDATION FOR ELASTIC COMMEMORATION

PAST AND PRESENT
PLAYFUL MATTERS

FOUNDATION FOR ELASTIC COMMEMORATION

emerging powers. Therefore, choosing what should be remembered or forgotten is a crucial action that bears far-reaching political, social, and cultural consequences.

Design = Activation

Quite exceptional in the memory landscape are less rigid memorials that follow the concept of "elastic" commemoration. This approach holds promise for political empowerment, activation, and public participation. Adjustable, or flexible, memorials are objects of commemoration that Wdo not adhere to one solid truth or to one singular version of history. Since they employ flexible materials or consist of interactive elements, they can be easily adjusted as needed or desired. They invite the public to interact, manipulate, or even offer more cynical uses. By way of example, you may encounter a holocaust or war memorial in which visitors could add or subtract from the number of victims, and by that dedicate the memorial to an alternative group. Similarly, an equestrian statue that no longer holds its horseman but instead invites the public to climb up and propose their individual political gesture empowers the present. A more subtle and abstract "elasticity" could be found in commemorative objects that embody more than one narrative, or are of a multi-vocal character. Like a victory column that oscillates between the pride of the triumphant and the loss and catastrophe of the defeated, they present the two sides of the same coin and allow different interpretations of the same historical event.

With elastic commemoration, design has the capacity to activate. It enables, or even demands from, the public to intervene and actively participate in the production of memories and remembrance—to take a stand, express an opinion and make a difference in the way the collective project develops. Elastic objects of commemoration reject the common ambition for consensus. Instead, they welcome disagreement, and by giving room for different voices and personal interpretations of historical and contemporary events, they encourage active participation and support the construction of alternative pasts towards alternative futures.

The following photographs were taken during the exhibition *Thou Shalt Forget* in Ramat-Gan Museum of Israeli Art in August 2014. Three commemorative installations transformed the exhibition space into a space of remembrance and forgetfulness. Further, they challenged the way Israelis deal with their commemoration habits, rituals, and construction of national collective memory.

Hebrew Horseman refers to a rather modest bronze horseman sculpture that was constructed during the British Mandate of Palestine on a hill adjacent to the Jezreel Valley. Commemorating a known figure from the Zionist movement, the memorial became a symbol of the New Hebrew—the brave guard and settler. By "removing" the known Zionist from the back of his horse, the alternative memorial invites the public to update the seventy years old settler-narrative, and produce new possibilities for relation to landscape and local past.

1948 merges two languages, two opposing narratives, two sides of a conflict, as it commemorates the events of this year: the Israeli victory and declaration of its independence, and the Palestinian catastrophe and loss of its homeland. It is an ambiguous structure that can be read dually—in state of construction or destruction, emphasizing the temporality and conditionality of historiography.

In their Memory is dedicated to the countless victims of every war, bloody conflict, massacre, or holocaust. It draws upon the recurring mention of their (often round) number and the cynical political appropriation of their memory. In this "remembrance device" the public can adjust the number of victims one by one—for life and death—and directly engage with the meanings the consequences of the memory work.

Guy Königstein was born in Israel and currently lives and works in Amsterdam. Confused in a world abundant of conflicts, paradoxes, and their constantly competing representations, Königstein re-acts and inter-acts aesthetically with his environment. Indecisive whether from the naïve belief in the ability to change the course of things, or rather from a somehow egoistic, (self-)therapeutic ambition, he simply keeps on.

EDITORIAL BOARD

Pier Vittorio Aureli is an architect and educator. His work focuses on the relationship between architectural form, political theory, and urban history. Together with Martino Tattara, he is the co-founder of Dogma. Since the beginning, Dogma has developed a specific interest in large-scale interventions and in urban research by participating in international competitions and by working with municipalities and other public parties. Aureli teaches at the Architectural Association where he is Diploma Unit Master and lecturer in the History & Theory Program. He has taught at the Berlage Institute in Rotterdam where he is still PhD Supervisor and Coordinator of the "City as a Project" PhD Program, Columbia University in New York, TU Delft, Accademia di Architettura in Mendrisio, Switzerland, Barcelona Institute of Architecture. Aureli is the author of several books including *The Project of Autonomy: Politics and Architecture Within and Against Capitalism* (2008), and *The Possibility of an Absolute Architecture* (2011).

Neeraj Bhatia is a licensed architect and urban designer from Toronto, Canada. His work resides at the intersection of politics, infrastructure, and urbanism. He is an Associate Professor at the California College of the Arts where he also co-directs the urbanism research lab, The Urban Works Agency. Prior to CCA, Bhatia held teaching positions at Cornell University, Rice University, and the University of Toronto. Neeraj is founder of The Open Workshop, a transcalar design-research office examining the negotiation between architecture and its territorial environment. He is co-editor of books *The Petropolis of Tomorrow* (Actar, 2013), *Bracket [Goes Soft]* (Actar, 2013), *Arium: Weather + Architecture* (Hatje Cantz, 2010), and co-author of *Pamphlet Architecture 30: Coupling—Strategies for Infrastructural Opportunism* (Princeton Architectural Press, 2010)

Vishaan Chakrabarti is the Founder of Practice for Architecture and Urbanism (PAU). Simultaneously, Vishaan is an Associate Professor of Practice at Columbia University's Graduate School of Architecture, Planning & Preservation (GSAPP), where he teaches architectural design studios and seminars on urbanism. His highly acclaimed book, *A Country of Cities: A Manifesto for an Urban America* (Metropolis Books, 2013), argues that a more urban United States would result in a more prosperous, sustainable, joyous, and socially mobile nation. Vishaan has been a guest on The Charlie Rose show, MSNBC's The Cycle, NY1, NPR, WNYC, and has been profiled in The New York Times and The Financial Times.

Adam Greenfield is a London-based writer and urbanist. His most recent book is *Radical Technologies: The Design of Everyday Life* (Verso, 2017).

Belinda Tato is co-founder and co-director of the firm ecosistema urbano established in 2000 in Madrid. She has led workshops, lectured, and taught at the most prestigious institutions worldwide. Since 2010 she has been faculty at Harvard University's Graduate School of Design in Cambridge and Columbia University Graduate School of Architecture, Planning and Preservation in New York.

Yoshiharu Tsukamoto (塚本由晴) is Principal of Atelier Bow-Wow based in Tokyo. He is also Professor in the Graduate School of Architecture & Building Engineering at Tokyo Institute of Technology. Yoshiharu Tsukamoto established Atelier Bow-Wow with wife Momoyo Kajima in 1992. The firm creates domestic and cultural architecture and researches the urban conditions of micro and ad hoc architecture. Atelier Bow-Wow has created over 50 residential houses, public buildings, public space and numerous installations, in addition to a substantial body of urban design studies and theoretical essays. Tsukamoto is an author of several books including, *Bow-Wow from Post Bubble City* (2006), *Contemporary House Studies* (2004), *Pet Architecture Guide Book* (2001), and *Made in Tokyo* (2001).

Mason White is an Associate Professor at University of Toronto, and a founding partner at Lateral Office. His research and design work are invested in questions about architecture's social role and impact. He has written about and led design-research on architecture's entanglement in environmental politics, energy publics, colonization, and infrastructure. The work of Lateral Office has received numerous national and international awards, including National Urban Design Award from RAIC (2016), Progressive Architecture Award (2013), Holcim Foundation for Sustainable Construction Gold Award (2011), and Emerging Voices from the Architectural League of New York (2011). His work has been featured in the Seoul Biennale of Architecture and Urbanism (2017), Chicago Architecture Biennale (2015), and the Venice Biennale in Architecture (2014), where Lateral Office received special mention from the international jury for the project "Arctic Adaptations." Mason is a co-editor of *Third Coast Atlas: Prelude to a Plan* (Actar, 2017) and co-author of *Many Norths: Spatial Practice in a Polar Territory* (Actar, 2017).

Editors
Neeraj Bhatia
Maya Przybylski

Editorial board
Andrés Jaque
Mitch McEwen
Markus Miessen
Ana Miljacki
Anna Puigjaner
Jeremy Till

Sharing is one of the humanity's most basic traits; we intrinsically recognize the benefits of pooling resources within a community in order take advantage of varied abilities and access in order to fulfill needs. Sharing is the key driver behind civilization's move towards collective living – first in small settlements and eventually in megalopoleis. The impact of sharing goes beyond simply satisfying the necessities for survival and extends itself into the social and cultural dimensions of our communities. In constructing an *urban commons*, composed of collectively managed and shared resources, we shape our physical, social, and cultural environments to achieve some degree of *shareabilty*—whether of goods, services, or experiences.

These historic and evolved cultural roots ensure that sharing is inevitably part of our daily lives. Yet, its central role in how we organize and manage our cities is increasingly threatened. Specifically, the resources previously contained within the commons are slipping into privatized forms of management. Commodifying elements of the public realm, such as energy, space, water, transportation and education, among others, has fragmented the commons and led to major, now too familiar, issues of injustice and inequality. Within a context of increased emphasis on the individual and privatization of the commons, sharing holds much promise for re-evaluating our economic, political, and social relations to equitably distribute resources and services at the scale of both the individual and the collective.

The prevalence of the *sharing economy* in cultural discourse has reconfirmed many of the benefits of collectivity by readdressing how we think about time, space, and excess. Yet, its deep connection with commerce prevents us from focusing on a holistic sharing practice that goes beyond economic transactions to include socio-political activities. Further, there has been little critical reflection on what Rebecca Solnit has termed the 'Sharecropping Economy' to understand how the commons is transforming with the convergence of physical and virtual space. Bracket 5 will examine the growing potential for sharing today—from innovative technologies to gritty resourcefulness.

We recognize that sharing is not easy — it requires compromise, negotiation, inconvenience, and patience. Can the challenges of sharing be designed for? How have recent design projects found innovative ways to share space, time, or resources? What types of spaces and conditions can foster contemporary models of sharing? Can architecture serve as a mediator for more effective sharing? What are the appropriate scales to share? How can sharing engage issues of equity and politics? Bracket 5 suggests that sharing needs to be re-learned today. We ask how can the design of our environments encourage new approaches to sharing that question our social, economic, and governmental practices.

The fifth volume of *Bracket* invites design work and papers that offer contemporary models as well as historic readings of the roles, mechanisms, and outcomes of sharing. Positional papers should be projective and speculative or revelatory, if historical. Suggested subthemes include:

Sharing Objects
Sharing Services
Sharing Histories
Sharing Resources
Sharing Time
Sharing Labor
Sharing Space
Sharing Technologies
Sharing Power

Please visit www.brkt.org for further information and schedule.

Bracket is an almanac of architecture, environment, and digital culture founded by InfraNet Lab and Archinect.

Published by
Applied Research and Design Publishing,
an imprint of ORO Editions.

Publisher
Gordon Goff

www.appliedresearchanddesign.com
info@appliedresearchanddesign.com

Copyright © 2019 Bracket

Editors
Neeraj Bhatia
Mason White

Editorial board
Pier Vittorio Aureli
Neeraj Bhatia
Vishaan Chakrabarti
Adam Greenfield
Belinda Tato
Yoshiharu Tsukamoto
Mason White

Collaborators
InfraNet Lab
www.infranetlab.org
Archinect
www.archinect.com

Designer
Haller Brun, Amsterdam
www.hallerbrun.eu

Project manager
Jake Anderson

Color Separations and Printing
ORO Group Ltd.

Sponsors
Graham Foundation for Advanced
Studies in the Fine Arts
www.grahamfoundation.org
John H. Daniels Faculty of Architecture,
Landscape, and Design
www.daniels.utoronto.ca

10 9 8 7 6 5 4 3 2 1 First Edition
ISBN: 978-1-943532-91-9

Printed in China

Acknowledgements
We would like to acknowledge the
contributions, energy, dialogue and sup-
port of the following people and institutions in the sphere of Archinect and
InfraNet Lab: David Gissen, Paul Petrunia,
Maya Przybylski, Lola Sheppard, Charles
Waldheim, California College of the Arts,
University of Toronto, and University
of Waterloo. At the Graham Foundation,
we would like to thank Sarah Herda,
Carolyn Kelly, and James Pike. At the
Daniels Faculty we would like to thank
Richard Sommer. At AR+D we would like
to thank Gordon Goff and Jake Anderson
for supporting the vision of the Bracket
project. At Haller Brun, we would like
to thank Sonja Haller and Pascal Brun for
their vision and patience in giving a new
identity to Bracket.

AR+D Publishing makes a continuous
effort to minimize the overall carbon
footprint of its publications. As part of this
goal, AR+D, in association with Global
ReLeaf, arranges to plant trees to replace
those used in the manufacturing of
the paper produced for its books. Global
ReLeaf is an international campaign
run by American Forests, one of the world's
oldest nonprofit conservation organizations.
Global ReLeaf is American Forests'
education and action program that helps
individuals, organizations, agencies,
and corporations improve the local and
global environment by planting and caring
for trees.